TRAINING *for* Organizations

BRIDGET N. O'CONNOR, PH.D.
NEW YORK UNIVERSITY
NEW YORK, NEW YORK

MICHAEL BRONNER, PH.D.
NEW YORK UNIVERSITY
NEW YORK, NEW YORK

CHESTER DELANEY
DELANEY LEARNING SERVICES, INC.
HOBOKEN, NEW JERSEY

CONSULTING EDITOR
ANGELA MCDONALD
BUSINESS DEVELOPMENT MANAGER
YORK GRAPHIC SERVICES, INC.

SOUTH-WESTERN
THOMSON LEARNING™

Australia • Canada • Mexico • Singapore • Spain • United Kingdom • United States

SOUTH-WESTERN
THOMSON LEARNING™

Training for Organizations

By Dr. Bridget O'Connor, Dr. Michael Bronner, and Chester Delaney

Executive Editor:
Karen Schmohe

Project Manager:
Dr. Inell Bolls

Consulting Editor:
Angela McDonald

Editor:
Carol Spencer

Marketing Manager:
Chris McNamee

Marketing Coordinator:
Cira Brown

Production Manager:
Jane Congdon

Manufacturing Manager:
Carol Chase

Art and Design Coordinator:
Michelle Kunkler, Darren Wright

Cover Illustration:
Timothy Cook

Cover and Internal Design:
Tim Creech

Compositor:
Electro-Publishing

Printer:
Edwards Brothers, Inc.

ISBN: 0-538-72461-7

Printed in the United States of America
3 4 5 6 7 8 9 0 05 04 03

For more information, contact
South-Western Educational Publishing
5101 Madison Road
Cincinnati, OH 45227-1490.
Or, visit our Internet site at
www.swep.com.

For permission to use material from this text or product, contact us by
Phone: 1-800-730-2214,
Fax: 1-800-730-2215, or
www.thomsonrights.com.

Combining experience in both the corporate and academic setting, this unique text will guide you to the front of the constantly changing training arena. Emphasizing new strategies, technologies, assessment, and evaluation processes, **Training for Organizations** *(0-538-72461-7)* is the leader in providing training solutions for all your needs.

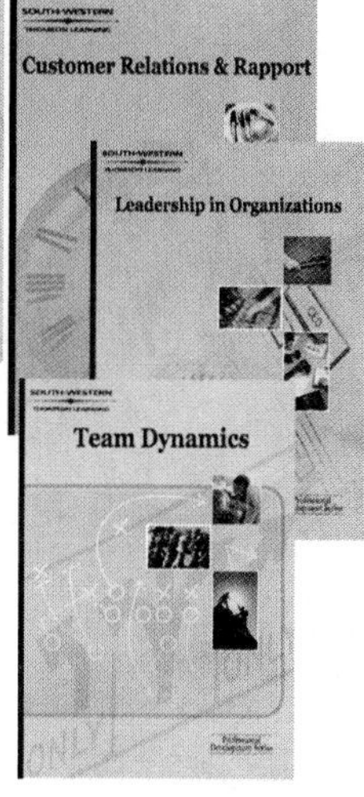

SEARCH for these additional training and professional resources from South-Western. Continue down the path of higher achievement with these leading texts for skill building and career planning.

Professional Development Series

Keeping pace with today's competitive marketplace is a challenge. The *Professional Development Series* is a perfect resource for learning the non-technical strategies and tactics needed to compete in today's business world.

Business Etiquette & Protocol	*0-538-72463-3*
Customer Relations &Rapport	*0-538-72527-3*
Leadership in Organizations	*0-538-72484-6*
Career Planning & Networking	*0-538-72474-9*
Team Dynamics	*0-538-72485-4*

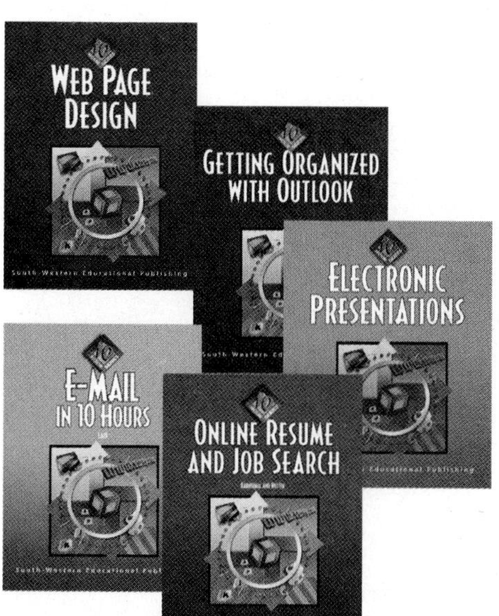

The 10-Hour Series

This series allows users to become proficient in a variety of skills in only a short amount of time with little or no instructional intervention.

Web Page Design	*0-538-72380-7*
Getting Organized with Outlook	*0-538-72384-X*
Electronic Presentations	*0-538-69848-9*
E-mail in 10 Hours	*0-538-69457-2*
Online Resume and Job Search	*0-538-69224-3*

Join us on the Internet at www.swep.com

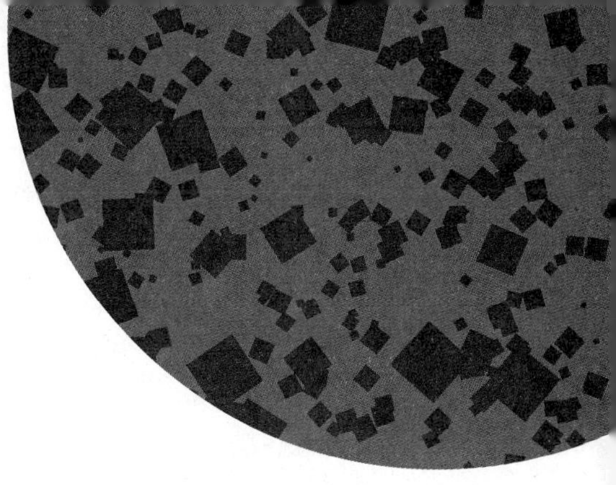

Table of Contents

PART 4 TRAINING DELIVERY

PART 5 ADDITIONAL PROFESSIONAL COMPETENCIES

PREFACE

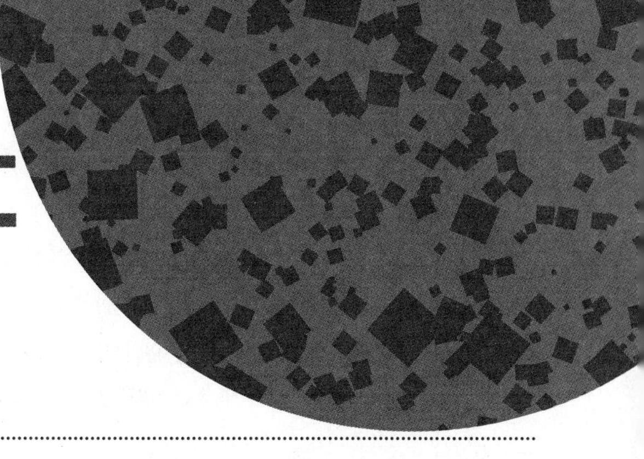

INTRODUCTION TO THE BOOK

This second edition of *Training for Organizations* underscores the notion that training is a crucial function in any organization. As a training professional, your job is to support your organization, and as such, you need to understand the needs of your particular industry, business, and personnel. You are a team player and a change agent. You are an adult educator as well as a savvy business person. You are a writer, teacher, coach, mentor, and administrator. You are versed in the role of technology in instruction and in administration. You are keenly aware of trends in your community, your organization, and in society at large that affect the workplace. In short, you are an active, integral, and vital part of your organization.

As a training professional you are increasingly involved in the personnel process: hiring, retaining, and rewarding. You offer training to job applicants as part of an employee selection process. You provide training for new hires and long-timers at all levels of the organizational strata. You provide counseling and educational programs that help personnel grow in their careers. You support staff and management development activities, including self-directed learning and mentoring programs. If organizational downsizing occurs, you develop job search strategies for those that leave and stress management programs for those who stay. As organizations adapt to new work processes, as organizational structures become flatter and less hierarchical, your role as a problem-solver and facilitator becomes more vital to the organization's success. Also, as promotional opportunities expand and contract, you are involved in designing new reward structures that acknowledge individuals at all levels for what they know rather than who they manage.

Your many roles include needs assessor, instructional designer, instructor, evaluator, and project manager. Your job demands, thus, are complex and varied. You apply theoretical foundations—problem solving strategies, adult learning theory, group behavior, and planned change—in developing sound training/learning practices. You are continually questioning, testing, and evaluating what you have come to know as sound workplace learning practices.

This second edition of *Training for Organizations* includes topics not typically covered in a train-the-trainer workshop or book. These topics include treating training as an innovation and techniques to ensure training success *before* implementation. The text emphasizes the practical as well as the theoretical in discussing needs assessment and evaluation strategies. It stresses the art and science of writing a training proposal. It discusses the promises and limitations of technology on the delivery of learning experiences as well as on the administration of training departments. In short, *Training for Organizations* offers you an understanding of the many roles you will play in your training career and provide concrete experiences that can transfer not only to your first job or to your current job but also to help you move up your future career ladder. New to this edition is *Voices from the Field* interviews with six successful training professionals, whose experience and expertise may inspire you as you find new directions within your career as a professional trainer.

Overview of the Book

Training for Organizations is divided into six parts and twelve chapters. The parts and chapters are presented in a logical order, but each part can stand on its own. This means that you can start at your key point of interest and move toward topics and chapters as your interests expand.

Part 1, "The Training Function," sets the stage for the entire book. In the prologue to Part 1, we describe the need for organizational training against a backdrop of social trends and issues. We begin the first chapter by discussing the concepts of the learning organization and Knowledge Management from the training professional's perspective. Then, we describe how the mission of a training department influences its structure and the services it provides, as well as the competencies required of the training professional. Training itself is a continuum of activities, not only classroom instruction. With this in mind, the chapter concludes with an overview of the *training cycle*. The training cycle can help you understand the training process—how assessment, design, implementation, and evaluation tasks are separate and distinct yet interrelated and interdependent. This training cycle serves as a framework for managing training projects as well as understanding this book.

Part 2, "Needs Assessment and Evaluation," consists of three chapters. The first chapter in this Part emphasizes that training is done to address organizational needs and new opportunities. The best training solutions are based on a careful needs assessment that takes into account the organizational environment as well as the needs and abilities of individuals. The next chapter stresses that evaluation should be considered up-front in designing training programs, rather than as an afterthought or "it's nice to have, but hard to do, so we don't do it" philosophy. Tying the outcomes of the needs assessment with strategies to determine if those outcomes actually occurred is the focus of the chapter on evaluation. The concluding chapter in Part 2 provides the practical how-to for these vital training roles. Research techniques related to designing and using selected methods—observations, interviews, questionnaires, and simple experiments are discussed.

Part 3 is "Instructional Design." In the first chapter of this Part, the best of what we know about learning is reviewed: adult learning theory, cognitive science concepts, and motivation theory. The next chapter shows how program design flows from needs assessment outcomes and is based on established theory and sound educational practices.

Both chapters in Part 4, "Training Delivery," discuss training delivery strategies and how their effectiveness can be evaluated. First, training delivery methods, based upon live instruction are discussed. Methods are categorized by the nature of the group to be trained, and include "how to" deliver a lecture, use a case, conduct a role play, etc. The next chapter describes the many possibilities in "mediated instruction." Mediated describes a situation in which instruction is delivered by some form of media rather than a live instructor.

Part 5, "Additional Professional Competencies," consists of three chapters that are all about creating an environment where learning solutions can flourish. To ensure that learning plans are well communicated, an outline guide is provided for writing a training proposal, and suggestions for developing oral presentation skills are offered. Administrative tasks, while not glamorous, are also crucial to training department success. To this end, the chapter on administration includes a description of course registration and scheduling systems, checklists for facility administration, and even a special learning module on developing training department budgets. To better appreciate the role of learning in all organizations, the final chapter of Part 5 overviews theoretical foundations for planned, systematic change efforts and techniques for facilitating group processes. It is suggested that the training professional can play the role of a change agent by working with organizational stakeholders to ensure that new learning is assimilated into the organization.

Part 6, "Trends for the Future," gives you a glimpse into what's next for the training professional. In this Part, the trainer of the present is transformed into the trainer of the future. This future-based scenario is designed to move you to think creatively beyond what currently *is* to what *can* and *may* be.

Features of This Book

- *Learning Objectives.* Each chapter opens with learning objectives to help you focus on key points in the chapter.
- *Think it Through.* Each chapter closes with questions designed to reinforce key concepts and to provide a structure for critically thinking about what you have read.
- *Ideas in Action.* Each chapter includes suggestions for further research or practical activities that are intended to extend your thinking about training issues.
- *Voices from the Field.* Each part concludes with an interview of a professional trainer who offers insights and experiences related to the part's contents as well as perspectives on his or her training career.
- *Additional Readings.* Each chapter concludes with a short list of annotated recommended readings.
- *Resource Web sites.*
- *Appendices.* Appendices list recommended training resources such as popular journals and scholarly journals in the Field. Also included is a listing of professional organizations (and their Web addresses) as well as listservs that training professionals may find valuable.

Training for Organizations attempts to synthesize not only what we know about training and the management of the training function in organizations, but it is also an attempt to explain why some training practices succeed while others fail. Combined, we have a wide range and many years of experience as academics and practitioners. Our professional lives have been spent in teaching, researching, and consulting in the field of training. Our key purpose in writing this book is to share our enthusiasm about the future of this dynamic field and to attract the very best of our education and business professionals to rewarding and satisfying training careers.

The Authors

Bridget N. O'Connor is Associate Professor and Director of the Program in Business Education at New York University. Her research and writing activities have focused on the effective application of technologies to support a wide range of individual and group processes both in the workplace and in adult education programs. She is co-author of *End-user Information Systems: Implementing Individual and Work Group Technologies* (2nd Ed.) Prentice Hall, 2001. She is editor of the *Information Technology, Learning, and Performance Journal* (www.osra.org). She has served as president of the Organizational Systems Research Association (OSRA) and as chair of the Special Interest Group, Workplace Learning, of the American Educational Research Association (AERA). She is active in the New York Metropolitan Chapter of the American Society for Training and Development (ASTD), serving on its newsletter advisory committee. She serves on the board of trustees for American Skandia University. In 1997, she was named "Professor of the Year" for the NYU School of Education.

Michael Bronner is a Professor in the Program of Business Education at New York University. His research and writing activities center on effective teaching and learning. He is author or co-author of more than 60 publications, articles, and yearbook chapters. He is a frequent contributor to numerous journals and speaks out on issues related to business education research, training, and professional matters. He is a former president of the New York Academy of Public Education and has been president of the Organizational Systems Research Associations (OSRA). He has also served two terms as the National Research Coordinator for the National Association for Business Teacher Education (NABTE) and two terms on the Eastern Region Board of the International Society for Business Education (ISBE) as well as numerous other positions with local, regional, and national professional organizations. In 1990, he was named "Professor of the Year" for the NYU School of Education.

Chet Delaney, an adjunct associate professor at NYU, is an independent consultant and writer with experience in both corporate and academic settings who lives and works in metropolitan New York City. He worked for 24 years in New York's financial district, 8 years at the Federal Reserve Bank, and 16 years with Chase Manhattan. He served as a programmer, systems analyst, and programming manager, and as a trainer and training manager in both information technology and management development settings. He was the Human Resource generalist for Chase's Corporate Systems Department, and the manager of the division that provided HR services for the bank's decentralized computer population. He twice won the Glass Apple, a performance award within the Systems Function at Chase. He is an adjunct associate professor at NYU. He has published numerous articles and book contributions. He wrote a regular column in *Data Training Magazine* from 1983-93. He wrote the *ITG Trainers Forum*, a bi-monthly essay/letter published by The Interpersonal Technology Group, and is a contributing editor of *Inside Technology Training*. He continues to write for trade journals and general magazines. One of his essays won a bronze medal for *Notre Dame Magazine*, and another was included in "Best of HRD" by *Training and Development Magazine*. He is a frequent speaker to professional and community groups on technology, HR, and educational issues.

PART 1
The Training Function

PROLOGUE TO PART 1

Companies in the United States spend more money annually on training than all the public school systems in the country. No better commentary on the importance of organizational training exists than this $100+ billion investment by American employers in informal and formal training. However, this investment may not be enough as the skills of workers must be continually upgraded. No organization today can afford to ignore the learning needs of its employees.

Moreover, in the recent past, organizational training tended to focus on managers, technicians, and professionals, not the rank-and-file-workers who make up 75 percent of American workers. These workers are increasingly challenged as their basic job skills are simply not sufficient to maintain jobs that require continually changing skill sets. This problem is so acute that a special report sponsored by the American Society for Training and Development has inspired federal legislation that would require all companies to invest at least 1 percent of their total payroll in training. Others suggest increasing this to a levy of 1.5 percent coupled with elected employee councils that would work with managers to determine the nature of their own training programs. In short, training professionals are being forced to reassess their organizational role as one that responds to changing workforce demographics, changes in the global workplace, and changing job demands.

Because unemployment rates are high, companies are often unable to find and keep qualified workers. Companies, therefore, are working harder to hold on to their existing workforce and to increase their productivity. Recruitment and retention strategies based on the availability of training programs that provide mutual satisfaction for the organization *and* the individual are critical.

Organizations are also becoming less hierarchical—as business processes are redesigned to make better use of technical and human resources, the organizational chart is flattening. This means there are fewer mid-level managers within a more fluid organization. The trainer's role in these efforts is multifold. Training professionals find themselves developing programs ranging from the very difficult task of changing the culture of the organization to teaching team development strategies to working on ways of rewarding individuals for what they know, rather than for who they manage.

Furthermore, the promise of technology in addressing the need for higher productivity and quality goes unfulfilled when the workforce cannot adapt to changing work procedures. The minimum skills once adequate to survive in the workplace for workers of all ages and levels are changing at a dizzying pace. Globalization is changing the very nature of work and its demands on the worker, and the concept of lifelong employment within one firm is no longer applicable. Experts predict that the average employee will change careers—not jobs—from five to seven times in his or her lifetime. Changing careers implies learning to do new things; moreover, it implies taking charge of your own learning needs, of becoming a self-directed learner.

As accountability for training program outcomes is increasingly the responsibility of training professionals, trainers are developing partnerships with line managers. Line managers are the individuals who are ultimately responsible for ensuring that work gets done and have the go/no-go say with regard to training program development. The term *partner* implies mutual goals as well as reliance and trust. Likewise, trainers are working closely with target training audiences themselves to ensure that training programs result in skills that are transferable back to the workplace. Accountability mandates communication and good communication invariably results in training programs that are relevant and deemed important by organizational decision-makers and the training population.

Thus, the ability to learn and *relearn*, is as important as the specific skills any job training program can develop. Trainers who use only passive teaching techniques may find themselves out of a job. Trainers are increasingly accountable for not only classroom instruction, but also for the transfer of learning from the classroom to the workplace. Training, therefore, is a *business process*, not a one-time exercise. Yet despite the perceived need for a well-trained workforce, trainers must sometimes sell the concept of training to line managers who have not traditionally viewed training as a vital corporate resource.

Organizations are increasingly responding to and addressing these demands. Motorola, Inc., for example, is one of many organizations that has redefined its clientele to include not only its own employees, but its suppliers, customers, and even the local community. Motorola reports that for every $1 it spends on training, it gets $30 in productivity gains within three years. Operating costs have been reduced by $3.3 billion by training workers to simplify processes and to reduce waste. Corning, Inc., mandates that all employees spend 5 percent of their time at work on training. Some of this training is in-house at Corning, and outside training is offered at a local community college. At least once a year, Federal Express requires that all couriers and customer service agents use a Web-based program that tests their current job knowledge. The exam results are used to identify areas where workers need help and to prescribe remedial action. These three examples illustrate how organizations find training solutions to address business problems.

Therefore, the responsibilities and opportunities are immense and dynamic for those who choose careers in the training field. While Chapter 1 is not intended to directly address these important societal trends, it will address how these issues impact training decisions and practices. The needs of the organization always mirror those of the larger society within which it exists. Training professionals who can understand big picture issues and who are well-versed in organizational theory, sound business practices, and the promises and limitations of technology are those most able to lead a training organization.

With a backdrop of these shifting demographics and changing workplace patterns, it is important to understand why training departments are structured the way they are. To this end, Chapter 1, "The Training Organization," describes the training organization, its range of philosophies, mission, roles, responsibilities, and structuring models. Chapter 1 also gives an overview of the *training cycle*, the training process model that provides a basis for project management and serves as the framework for this book.

CHAPTER 1

The Training Organization

- Provide the rationale for tying an organization's training/learning services to organizational goals.
- List examples of strategic, informational, and operational training.
- Discuss how the philosophy and mission of a training department impacts the way it is organized and the way learning services are provided.
- Identify the advantages and disadvantages of the faculty model, the client model, the matrix model, and the corporate university model as a means for structuring the training organization.
- Explain the usefulness of the training cycle for training project management.

PUTTING TRAINING CAREERS IN PERSPECTIVE

In *The Third Wave*, Alvin Toffler divided history into three major eras, or waves. The first wave, from 8000 B.C. to 1750 A.D., was termed the agricultural revolution, and was based on farming as the world's primary occupation. In the second wave, from 1750 to 1955, the rise of industrial civilization and the industrial revolution, manufacturing became the main occupation and the developed world was engaged in or moving toward mass production.[1] The third wave, which began in the mid-1950s, is sometimes referred to as the information age, or the information revolution, and is based on the delivery of services. Important to note from Toffler's schema is that all human society was profoundly transformed with each wave, and that the transition to the next wave was never easy.

Toffler's perspective is useful to the training professional of today and tomorrow. Sometimes in determining training goals, the training professional relies on methods and approaches appropriate for times long past. Overall, the goal is to prepare today's diversified workforce with its evolving job demands and its changing skills and knowledge. Sometimes that translates into training workers to adapt to *existing* jobs; but more important, the goal is to enable workers to adapt to *changing* work environments and demands. Toffler's categories help training professionals understand that the magnitude of these dramatic changes affect all aspects of our society, including our organizational lives. Two concepts that can help address the changing nature of a training professional's world are the learning organization and knowledge management. A discussion of these concepts follows.

The Learning Organization

A learning organization responds to the demands of both the organization and the individual learner. In the learning organization, the organization itself learns not only from its past errors, but also from its past successes. In the learning organization, the rewards for individual success are high and the risks of failure are low, thus encouraging people to try something new. In the learning organization, individuals are empowered to do their jobs well and creatively. "Organizations learn only through individuals who learn," said MIT Professor Peter Senge, who calls this empowerment "personal mastery." Individuals with this freedom are more committed to their jobs, take more initiative, and have a broader sense of responsibility in their work.[2]

In a learning organization, business managers and training professionals work together for a common purpose. In a learning organization, training professionals and managers share accountability for training programs. The training professional is more than just the deliverer of training programs. The training professional is a full business partner and organizational change agent, relying on a wide repertoire of skills including problem-solving, facilitating, mentoring, and counseling.

In a learning organization, individual workers have an increasingly self-directed responsibility to both learn and share what they know. William Bridges says that jobs as we know them are disappearing, being replaced by projects.[3] Bridges used Microsoft software designers to illustrate his point: Designers have no regular hours and no one keeps track of their hours, just their output. New employees are given a buddy/mentor to help them learn. Projects are usually team-based, and team members learn together and share what they know, a concept known as a *community of practice*. In a community of practice, individuals are responsible for their own learning and sharing what they know with others.

The implications, then, for training specialists is that they will play an increasingly important role in responding to and anticipating both organizational and individual demands, particularly in identifying the skills an organization and its workers need and helping learners choose and use a wide range of appropriate learning options. This trend is clear from changing job titles. Training professionals hold job titles such as performance consultant, learning specialist, knowledge engineer, and relationship manager. Just as broad are changes in the names of their departments:[4]

- Training Excellence
- Skills, Strategy, and Vitality
- Human Resources Capacity and Business Planning
- Personal and Professional Development
- Human Resources Effectiveness and Education
- [Name of Company] University

Knowledge Management

The learning organization can be played out through a concept known as Knowledge Management (KM). While many different definitions exist for the concept, KM is basically a concerted effort to codify an organization's collective experience and wisdom—including the tacit know-how that exists in people's heads—and to make it accessible and useful to everyone in the enterprise.[5]

Knowledge Management systems are not about technology but rather are enabled by technology. They are about learning, particularly learning over time and across boundaries. They are about ways to capture experience from a wide range of people within the organization–from all *possible* people. KM is about ways to capture the accumulated wisdom of employees, the benefits of their experience, and the lessons to be learned from their mistakes. It is also (and here is technology's crucial role) about storing all this knowledge in secure, reliable ways that provide easy, context-useful access to it.

Just the title of Jan Duffy's 1999 book speaks volumes: *Harvesting Experience: Reaping the Benefits of Knowledge* (Prairie Village, KS: ARMA). It is instructive–and powerfully ironic—that Duffy uses imagery from the agricultural age to describe one of the critical needs of the information economy. The knowledge of which Duffy and others speak is, of course, not knowledge for its own sake. It is knowledge for a purpose, knowledge in the service of learning and performance. KM reinforces the key notion that learning is not limited to the classroom.

It is more than evident that learning takes on a strategic role when an organization's employees' knowledge appears on its corporate reports as an asset called *intellectual capital.* It is clear that capturing knowledge, and ensuring that knowledge is shared, are high priorities in such organizations. To this end, the role of Chief Learning Officer (CLO) or Chief Knowledge Officer (CKO) is emerging. The CLO or CKO is a high-level executive equal in rank with the Chief Financial Officer (CFO) or Chief Operating Officer (COO) all of whom report directly to the Chief Executive Officer (CEO).

Chapter Overview

To support learning in knowledge-based organizations, training professionals need a mix of know-how. Moreover, as savvy business professionals and adult educators, they must know the strengths and limitations of training department organizational models and the myriad of options for supporting learning and thus organizational goals.

This emphasis on learning, knowledge, and change means that training efforts are increasingly tied to seeing that problems and opportunities are addressed in new ways. The first section of this chapter presents this challenge to training professionals to take a more active role in the organization, tying training department goals to organizational goals. The next section helps put these organizational challenges into focus by providing perspectives on how the structure of a training department supports organizational aims and mirrors the training department's philosophy and mission. Best practices evolve when there is a match between organizational goals, the philosophy and mission of the training department, and the career development needs of the individual. This chapter also includes a listing and discussion of current and emerging roles for the training professional. Part of the discussion provides a perspective on the many interrelated yet distinct roles training professionals may be asked to play within their careers. The training cycle, a problem-solving model for training project management as well as the organization of this book, concludes this chapter. The training cycle depicts the four stages of training program development while emphasizing their interrelationships.

INTEGRATING TRAINING GOALS WITH ORGANIZATIONAL GOALS

In many large organizations, a human resource department is charged with a set of staff functions such as hiring (and firing), salary administration, benefits administration, union relations, and possibly the training function. In other instances, the training department is distinct from the human resources department. However organized, decisions that affect the existing or needed labor pool impact the entire organization, and the training professional plays a crucial role in ensuring that the organization has the workforce that it needs.

Training resources, like all resources, are limited. The challenge is to use them wisely and to provide evidence of their value to the organization. While it is difficult to measure learning and its organizational impact, the premise is made that training programs that contribute to organizational goals can be linked to tangible outcomes of some sort. Tangible outcomes could include an increase in sales, reduced turnover, or higher production levels.

To make these links between organizational goals and training efforts, it is useful to consider training strategies as responding to one of three identified organizational thrusts: strategic, informational, and operational. While many training efforts transcend these categories, categorization can help describe the impact of training efforts and thus establish the link from organizational goals to training activities.

Strategic Training

Strategic training means that training plans take into account long-term organizational goals and objectives. Examples of these goals might include the development of new or better products; operating with fewer people; or expanding to a global market. Strategic training efforts are typically initiated by top management—the Chief Executive Officer or the Chief Learning Officer.

Developing a workforce with *core competencies* is strategic. Core competencies are the knowledge, skills, abilities, and attitudes the organization has deemed critical to long-term success, such as creative thinking and problem-solving; leadership and visioning; and self-development. The development of core competencies not only contributes to organizational goals, but also adds to personal mastery. Such core competencies become the foundation for specific job skills.[6]

For example, assume that a large U.S. corporation is in the midst of expanding its business to include distributors in Mexico. In its global central office, workers must be relatively fluent in Spanish and should be knowledgeable about Mexico's history and culture. A training program to teach these language skills and cognitive skills would be considered strategic as individuals' success in such a training program would be paramount to the organization's being successful in this new global environment.

Providing training programs for partners, suppliers, and customers may also be considered strategic. For example, Motorola, Anheuser-Busch, and Harley-Davidson not only invest between 3 and 5 percent of their payroll on training; they extend their training through their entire customer and supply chains.[7] Such efforts (see Featured Case) address the very nature of an organization and are easily labeled *strategic* and thus appropriately linked to organizational goals.

FEATURED CASE

Training Harley-Davidson's large network of dealers (900 in the United States and Europe) has become more important than ever now that Harley-Davidson has greatly expanded its merchandising and product line beyond motorcycles to include such items as clothing and collectibles. This immediately created a learning gap that Harley-Davidson University was responsible for closing. Harley-Davidson University, through its use of technology and a heightened awareness of the importance of connecting to dealers, has developed an integrated curriculum that offers hard business literacy skills such as financial analysis, inventory control, and smart buying practices, as well as skills in customer service and negotiation. What's more, Harley-Davidson University also developed a toolkit for dealers to create their own Web sites. Dealer Web sites are designed to link to the main Harley-Davidson Web site, which in turn provides links to the dealers' sites. This interlinking of electronic marketing serves as a metaphor for Harley-Davidson's concerted effort to include dealers in the training process.

Harley-Davidson is also expanding its Intranet to become a communications link between the company and its dealers, providing information on warranties, product updates, etc. For Harley-Davidson University, dealers are not peripheral elements of the whole training process, but crucial links whose education needs have to be addressed continually and through a variety of different approaches in order to maintain a fully integrated dealer-manufacturer partnership.

Source: *Meister, Jeanne C. (1998) Corporate Universities: Lessons in Building a World-Class Work Force. New York: McGraw Hill. Cited with permission.*

INFORMATIONAL TRAINING

Informational training is training based on the need to give the workforce information about the organization. The training department's role in informational training is very important, and includes, but is well beyond, programs that describe the organization's benefits packages to new employees. The Training Department is usually also responsible for a broad orientation program for new hires. The goal of such programs is to develop corporate citizenship and create a contextual reference for employees.[8] Developing *corporate citizenship* means developing training efforts that result in the employee knowing the organization's history, culture, traditions, and values. Creating a contextual reference means ensuring that employees understand big-picture issues related to the firm's products and services and its relationship to its competitors, suppliers, and customers. Thus, informational training efforts provide information that will empower the employee to be a contributing player in an organization whose mission, goals, and operating policies are understood.

Informational training efforts are usually not directly applicable to the trainee's specific job or task, but rather enhance the trainee's overall awareness and understanding of the firm, its culture, and its product line. A workforce that knows and understands its organization and whose managers attempt to communicate the rationale for directions and policies is a workforce that is more likely to be able to contribute to a learning organization. Informational training efforts can be directly linked to the organizational goals that improve employee retention rates or raise employee job satisfaction. Thus, information training efforts are *ongoing* in nature—not one-shot events—to maintain open lines of communication.

Operational Training

Operational training efforts are those that relate to the day-to-day operations of an organization and are directly related to an employee's job. Successful operational training programs call for line managers and training professionals to work together at all stages of program development. Examples of operational training abound, as this category of training includes new work methods and procedures, skills needed to use new technologies, or new skills required to upgrade to a new task/job. Every organization offers operational training of one type or another. Because this type of training is so vital to the ongoing day-to-day activities of an organization, linking operational training efforts to organizational goals is usually a simple and direct task.

Increasingly, operational training is seen as being built upon strategic and informational training efforts, rather than the other way around. This does not mean that operational training is less important than developing core competencies. Nothing is more important than ensuring that the work of the firm can be done. This building block view means that training departments and managers are finding that they also need to develop their employees' core competencies as well as their contextual framework. Increasingly, many job tasks cannot be done well unless the worker already has a baseline of strategic and informational knowledge and skills.

To restate, it is not so critical to categorize each and every training program as strategic, informational, or operational, since in reality much overlap exists. The value of these categories is to help put training efforts into perspective and to help describe how a specific training effort addresses the overall goals of the organization. Using the descriptive terms of strategic, informational, or operational can help make a clearer link from organizational goals to training practices.

ORGANIZING THE TRAINING FUNCTION

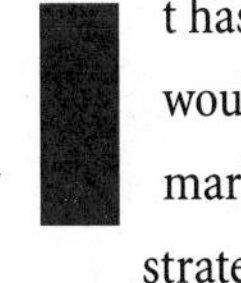

It has been said that a training professional must be both a priest and a prophet. The former would provide good counsel to the individual employee; the latter would be able to predict market, technological, and organizational developments. As a counselor and a business strategist, the training professional works from inside the organization to ensure that the organization has a well-trained and motivated workforce. To do this, it is important to have articulated a training philosophy and mission on which to build an operating structure for the training organization.

A Training Philosophy and Mission

A *philosophy* is a system of values. A *mission* is an activity that is to be carried out. A corporate philosophy for the training department originates at the executive level. Training departments are typically based on one or more of the following philosophies:[9]

1. To prepare employees to develop specific skills necessary to perform effectively in their current job assignments.
2. To build skills and impart knowledge that will make employees more effective in a variety of possible job roles.
3. To prepare employees to take on broader or more demanding job assignments in the future.
4. To help employees recognize and realize their full potential as human beings.

These philosophies are ordered from the most concrete to the most abstract. Under the first philosophy, *to prepare employees to develop specific skills necessary to perform effectively in their current job assignments*, training resources would be directed at operational training activities that impact worker behavior. Results would be measurable and would affect the organization's outcomes and profits.

A training department takes on an *informational and strategic* role when its philosophy is akin to numbers two and three above: *To build skills and impart knowledge that will make employees more effective in a variety of possible job roles*; and *to prepare employees to take on broader or more demanding job assignments in the future.* Ideally, training efforts within these roles are rewarding to both the organization and the employee. The most successful programs match what the organization needs with what employees want to learn.

An organization primarily espousing solely the fourth philosophy, *to help employees recognize and realize their full potential as human beings*, would have a mission similar to the nation's educational system. No training department should base itself on employee education to the exclusion of operational, informational, and strategic training. However, strategic training programs have added value to employees, as those skills contribute to personal mastery and are transferable to any number of different jobs.

Given these philosophical definitions, this book will consider a training department's role to be concerned with a variety of strategic, information, and/or operational learning outcomes. Moreover, assisting employees to achieve their potential is indeed a desirable outcome, and one that is increasingly important to keeping a skilled, knowledgeable workforce.

A training department's *mission statement* is a much more concrete version of its philosophy. The mission statement offers an explanation as to why a training department is organized in a certain way, what the staff does, and how services are delivered. Note that these specific activities set the stage for what the training department actually *does*. The mission statement typically falls under one or more of the following descriptions:

1. To establish a basic curriculum of programs and courses that management can access to ensure that employees can do their jobs.
2. To anticipate changing conditions (internal and external) and provide programs to help employees cope with these changes.
3. To provide expertise in analyzing performance problems and devise appropriate solutions.
4. To provide programs that will improve productivity.
5. To respond to requests from individual managers/supervisors for employee training and development.[9]

American Skandia Life Assurance Corporation is a financial services organization. Its training organization is American Skandia University that includes a College for Financial Professionals. Figure 1-1 shows mission statements for both entities. Note the strong connection to business goals, its workforce, its customers, and its community.

Figure 1-1
American Skandia Life Assurance Corporation Training Mission Statements

American Skandia University

Our mission is to support American Skandia as an industry leader by building on the tradition of valuing intellectual resources and offering training and development solutions that enable outstanding individuals to drive the success of the company.

To serve as a strategic business partner.

To model our corporate values as we touch the lives of our employees, our customers, and our community.

College for Financial Professionals

The purpose of the college is to provide a forum for American Skandia to serve as a strategic business partner with each financial professional by

- presenting top financial industry experts
- meeting senior management and service teams
- providing skills training for both personal and professional development, and
- offering technology insights as we build a stronger foundation upon which to achieve our mutual success.

Courtesy of American Skandia Life Assurance Corporation

Models of Training Department Organization

Organization charts are graphic illustrations of who reports to whom in an organization and the scope of their respective duties. Organizational charts in most large organizations are not static in nature; they are dynamic—constantly changing. As organizations evolve into learning organizations, the organizational chart in some companies changes daily. Sometimes titles change; sometimes duties are shuffled among key players. Sometimes new people are hired; sometimes organizations are forced to downsize (a more positive term is *rightsize*). Sometimes organizational charts change to assign an individual more responsibility for a given project.

Training departments share the shifting, dynamic nature of today's organizations. A training department may be organized to do some or all of the following: needs assessments, program/course development, identification of internal and external consultants and learning materials, training delivery, and program evaluation. The training department structure itself can be considered either "mostly" a *faculty* (product) model or "mostly" a *client* (customer) model.

Sometimes, too, the product and customer models converge to form a *matrix* model. Some large organizations are also adding a *corporate university* approach to addressing their mission and organizing their learning resources. In reading descriptions of each of the following models, consider the philosophy and mission that a training department demonstrates when it uses a particular model.

Faculty Model of Training Department Organization

As Figure 1-2 shows, the faculty model of structuring the training department is much like that of a college. A training manager operates much like a dean, with a staff of experts, often referred to as consultants, who develop, update, and deliver instruction. Informational and operational training programs are kept current and repeated on a scheduled basis for a wide range of audiences, or custom-designed to meet the needs of a specific group on a particular subject. Examples include ongoing new employee orientation programs, and workshops in SEC regulations, business communications, or presentation skills. Upgrading sales techniques or improving telephone behaviors are yet other examples. With the faculty model, subject matter experts, who are employees of the organization, are responsible for updating and delivering instruction.

A training department that is organized on the faculty model offers some real benefits. One advantage is the careful coverage of the topics they teach. Also, laying out training plans is considerably simplified: What will be taught and when it will be offered are defined primarily by the training staff capabilities and availability. This arrangement makes planning and control easy. Moreover, the faculty model—at least in the ideal—is an efficient use of staff, drawing precisely on the strengths of the instructors and ignoring their weaknesses.[10]

However, the faculty model has its limitations. By its very nature and organization, its use can result in ignoring content areas in which the trainers lack expertise. This means that a department of instructors may teach only part of the skills needed in the organization and may even teach skills the organization does not need at all. Another danger is that a department of teachers tends to focus evaluation on instruction, not on whether specified skills were obtained or were useful on the job. In other words, the faculty model can put too much emphasis on what the faculty can do and not enough on what the organization or individual needs.

Client Model of Training Department Organization

With a customer, or *client,* approach to structure, as shown in Figure 1-3, a given training professional might have responsibility for an entire department or component of an organization. In this illustration, the trainer, who may be called an internal consultant, would work with line business managers and staff to identify the skill/competency needs of a particular target

FIGURE 1-2
FACULTY MODEL OF TRAINING DEPARTMENT ORGANIZATION

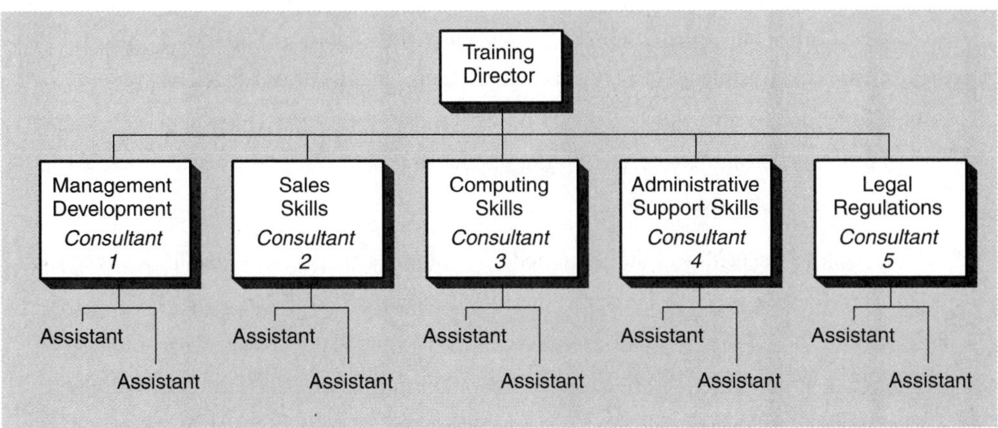

FIGURE 1-3
CLIENT MODEL OF TRAINING DEPARTMENT ORGANIZATION

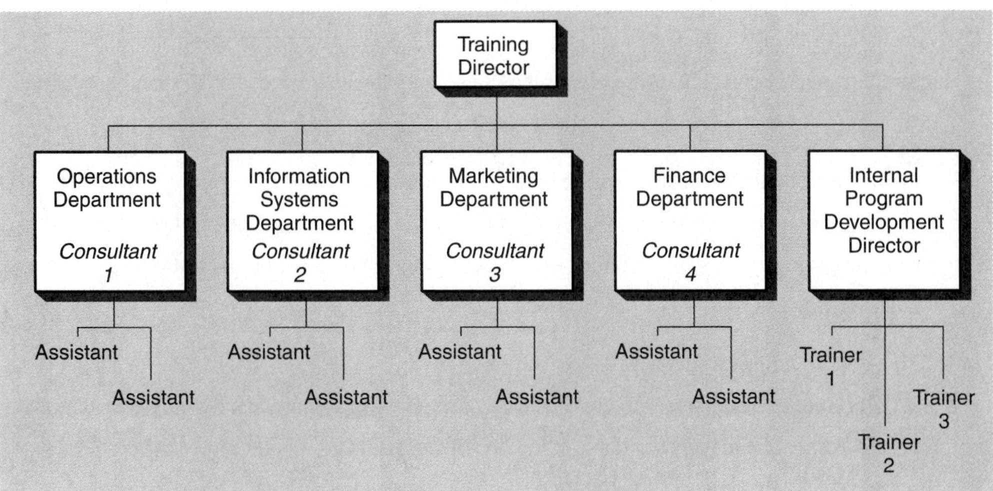

population and ensure appropriate training programs. In this model, the internal consultant can obtain training solutions (e.g., training programs) from outside training vendors (outsource) or from an internal training program development group. The emphasis in this model is on ensuring that the learning needs of a given functional department or group of individuals are addressed, with the internal training consultant serving as a broker or consultant in meeting these needs.

A client model of organization results in built-in responsiveness to changing business needs. In this highly flexible model, needs assessment (discussed in the next chapter) can focus on business needs rather than training staff capability, since the consultant does not necessarily have a personal investment in a particular subject being taught. The design and delivery of training can more easily focus on learners' needs and their learning styles without overt or covert influence by instructor preferences. This is a significant benefit given adult learners need for individualized, self-motivated learning.

A compelling picture of the client model for training emerges from *Running Training Like A Business* by David van Adelsberg and Edward A. Trolley (San Francisco: Berrett-Koehler Publishers, Inc., 1999). The authors are executives at The Forum Corporation, a major training vendor. In their book, they describe their collaboration with the DuPont Corporation in which Forum provides for the learning needs of DuPont employees. The inspiration was to seamlessly incorporate an outside vendor's resources into a customer's training efforts. The outside vendor, in effect, *became* the customer's training department. Out of this experience, the authors produced this book that discusses the need to put training on a business footing. They also discuss various "insourcing" models, as well as transformations of training departments limited to internal resources only. The net result of all of these approaches is a focus on ensuring that a training department supports the business agendas of the organization it serves.

A training department operating in the client model is always in motion, always shifting, and always compensating for new emphases and directions. Planning is not always easy in such an environment, but training resources are always tightly coupled with organizational and individual learning goals.

Matrix Model of Training Department Organization

Training professionals who are considered part of the training staff in a *matrix* structure report to both a line manager and a training department director. In other words, the training professional has the duties of a faculty expert *and* a client representative. This situation is depicted in Figure 1-4, which shows the consultant as a subject matter expert (SME) within a centralized training department, and at the same time is responsible for coordinating needs assessment, development, delivery, and evaluation activities for a given population.

Proponents of the matrix structure explain that it helps ensure that training efforts match the needs of the line department, and thus most closely links with organizational goals. In addition, training resources can be shared and duplication of efforts can be minimized. This structure also allows for the career development of a training professional, who has the opportunity to continue to learn in a particular content area. However, critics of this structure explain that in a

FIGURE 1-4
MATRIX MODEL OF TRAINING DEPARTMENT ORGANIZATION

Training Director

Assignment	Consultant 1	Consultant 2	Consultant 3	N
Client Population	Financial Controller's Department	Marketing Department	Operations Department	etc.
Subject Matter Expertise	Desktop Technology, including CBT	Team Building and Self-Managed Work Groups	Executive Education	etc.
Special Projects	Selection of new PC-based training administration system	Development of video for new-hire orientation program	Selection of 360-degree feed-back instrument for use in perfor-mance reviews	etc.

matrix organization, the professional has two sets of supervisors—the line manager *and* the training department director. Such a situation can lead to conflict and confusion. Nonetheless, if carefully managed, the matrix organization can be a very effective way to balance the needs of a line department with the skills of a training faculty.

Corporate University

Taking these models one step further is the *corporate university*. These internal "universities" provide a organizational base for a wide array of strategic and informational services and programs that meet the needs of the individual employee, the organization, its business partners, and the community at large. What differentiates this model from the faculty, client, and matrix models is the description of who clients are, as well as who is involved in the needs assessment.

Figure 1-5 depicts the core workplace curriculum for a financial services firm under a corporate university model. Note that the foundation of the model is corporate citizenship. Next, the contextual framework identifies target audiences, trends, and best practices. Core workplace competencies constitute the next level, and they include learning to learn, global business literacy, and creative thinking. The schools of learning in Figure 1-5 are geared toward a financial services firm, and they include topics related to that company. The Z-shared hybrid skills "encompass deep expertise in one discipline along with enough breadth to see connections in other disciplines".[11]

FIGURE 1- 5
CORE WORKPLACE CURRICULUM FOR A FINANCIAL SERVICES FIRM

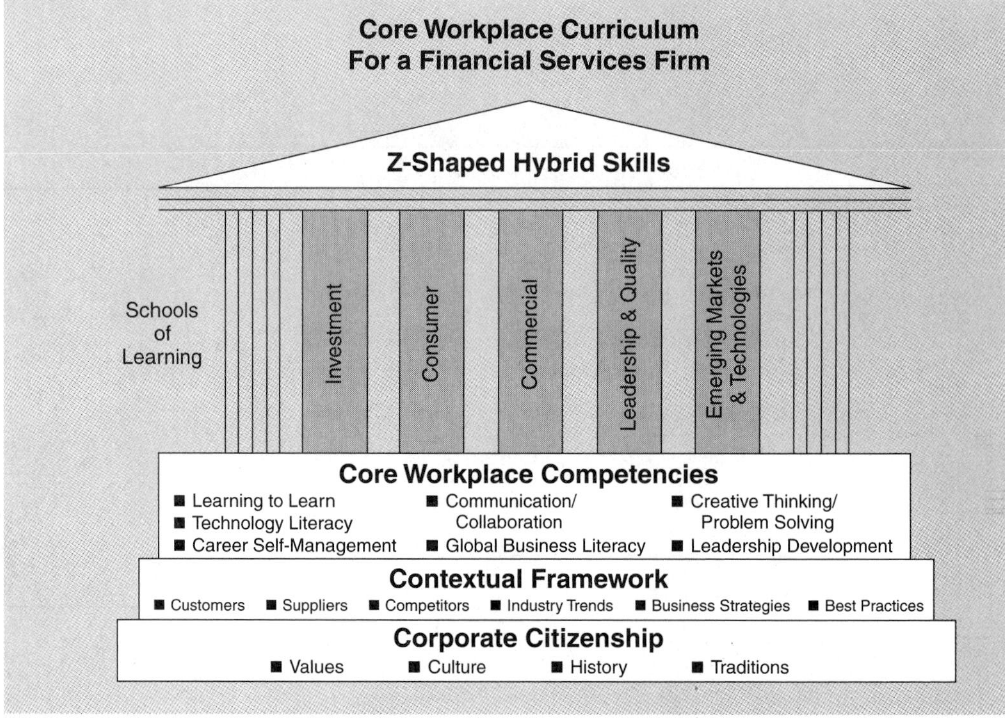

©1997 Corporate University Xchange, Inc.

The corporate university model has similarities to how traditional universities are structured as most also include a governing structure, including a board of trustees. Again, what also distinguishes the corporate university model from more traditional training organization models is its target audiences—employees, suppliers, customers, and even learners from the community—who take core courses together.

To support learners from the community, corporate university planners can work with educators at their local community colleges to develop core competencies. Community colleges are often targeted for such partnerships since one of their missions is to respond to the needs of local businesses. Such collaboration is a win-win situation for everyone involved. For starters, it ensures that the community college is developing competencies that are relevant in the workplace. Moreover, individuals who complete these community college core courses have a credential that is favorably considered should they apply for a job at the partnering organization. In addition, many organizations and colleges have developed plans that allow those who have successfully completed the *organization's* training program to transfer these credits to a local community college.

Whirlpool Corporation, for example, has such learning alliances with Indiana University, University of Michigan, and INSEAD in France.[12]

The corporate university model appears to be emerging as a very effective way to organize the training function in large organizations. Borrowing the strengths of traditional university structures, it offers economy in those tasks that are consistent across the corporation, such as registration and tracking individual learners (keeping transcripts). By providing one-stop-shopping for ways to address core competencies, the corporate university model offers economies of scale and more choices. Additionally, as the World Wide Web becomes a prevalent mode of communications, the model supports strategic, information, and operational learning by functioning as a portal to any number of live and mediated learning options. Moreover, in partnering with organizations throughout its supply chain—suppliers, distributors, customers, and the community in general—it provides a way of serving not only its own business needs, but also those of society at large.

To recap, keep in mind that a training department's organizational structure is often a merger and/or combination of the best of these four approaches. The value of these descriptions is that they allow the training professional to translate the relationship between a training department's philosophy and mission into a useful organization structure. A training department's structure facilitates its being able to provide an array of strategic, informational, and operational training programs.

The following section moves from these global, organizational issues faced by training professionals to a discussion of the skill set needed by individual training professionals. To provide an array of training activities, training departments rely on a variety of individuals who have a wide mix of competencies. Competent training professionals are the means through which a training department offers its services, enabling the department and the organization to achieve its goals and objectives.

IDENTIFYING CURRENT AND EMERGING ROLES FOR THE TRAINING PROFESSIONAL

Within a training career, an individual typically has many *jobs*. A given individual, for example, may have held jobs of "instructor" and "instructional designer" before being promoted to "department manager." Within each job, this individual played various *roles*. Roles are job functions. To perform specific roles, the training professional uses special skills, or *competencies*. Thus, a trainer builds a career by building a foundation of competencies that allows a variety of roles to be performed in a number of different but related jobs. In this discussion, we use the term *job* to describe how a training professional uses his or her competencies in a given workplace. We suggest "job" could be replaced with "project." In many situations, the project is more the organizer of roles than *the job*.

The American Association for Training and Development (ASTD), as part of a long-term, ongoing study of training and development practices, identified and defined key areas that are considered important for individuals to master if they are to perform roles within training. An initial list of 32 competencies was developed in 1983, and an additional 2 competencies were added in a revised study. These updated, redefined competencies are depicted in Figure 1-6. The 13 competencies marked with asterisks are those that were found to be critical for the majority of training careers.[13]

FIGURE 1-6
CORE COMPETENCIES REQUIRED OF TRAINERS

*1. **Adult Learning Understanding**: knowing how adults acquire and use knowledge, skills, attitudes; understanding individual differences in learning.

2. **Career Development Theories and Techniques:** knowing the techniques and methods used in career development; understanding their appropriate uses.

*3. **Competency Identification Skill:** identifying the knowledge and skill requirements of jobs, tasks, and roles.

4. **Computer Competence:** understanding and/or using computer applications.

5. **Electronic Systems Skills:** having knowledge of functions, features, and potential applications of electronic systems for the delivery and management of HRD.

6. **Facilities Skill:** planning and coordinating logistics in an efficient and cost-effective manner.

*7. **Objectives Preparation Skill:** preparing clear statements that describe desired outputs.

8. **Performance Observation Skill:** tracking and describing behaviors and their effects.

9. **Subject Matter Understanding:** knowing the content of a given function or discipline being addressed.

10. **Training and Development Theories and Techniques Understanding**: knowing the theories and methods used in training; understanding their appropriate use.

11. **Research Skill:** selecting, developing, and using methods such as statistical and data collection techniques for formal inquiry.

FIGURE 1-6
CORE COMPETENCIES REQUIRED OF TRAINERS (CONT.)

*12. **Business Understanding:** knowing how the functions of a business work and related to each other; knowing the economic impact of business decisions.

13. **Cost-Benefit Analysis Skill:** assessing alternatives in terms of their financial, psychological, and strategic advantages and disadvantages.

14. **Delegation Skill:** assigning task responsibility and authority to others.

15. **Industry Understanding:** knowing the key concepts and variables such as critical issues, economic vulnerabilities, measurements, distribution channels, inputs, outputs, and information sources that define an industry or sector.

*16. **Organization Behavior Understanding:** seeing organizations as dynamic, political, economic, and social systems that have multiple goals; using this larger perspective as a framework for understanding and influencing events and change.

17. **Organization Development Theories and Techniques Understanding:** knowing the techniques and methods used in organization development; understanding their appropriate use.

18. **Organization Understanding:** knowing the strategy, structure, power networks, financial position, and systems of a specific organization.

19. **Project Management Skill:** planning, organizing, and monitoring work.

20. **Records Management Skill:** storing data in an easily retrievable format.

21. **Coaching Skill**: helping individuals recognize and understand personal needs, values, problems, alternatives, and goals.

*22. **Feedback Skill:** communicating information, opinions, observations, and conclusions so that they are understood and can be acted upon.

23. **Group Process Skill:** influencing groups so that tasks, relationships, and individual needs are addressed.

24. **Negotiation Skill:** securing win-win agreements while successfully representing a special interest in a decision.

*25. **Presentation Skill:** presenting information orally so that an intended purpose is achieved.

*26. **Questioning Skill:** gathering information from stimulating insight in individuals and groups through the use of interviews, questionnaires, and other probing methods.

Figure 1-6
Core Competencies Required of Trainers (cont.)

*27 **Relationship Building Skill:** establishing relationships and networks across a broad range of people and groups.

*28. **Writing Skill:** preparing written material that follows generally accepted rules of style and form, is appropriate for the audience, is creative, and accomplishes its intended purpose.

29. **Data Reduction Skill:** scanning, synthesizing, and drawing conclusions from data.

*30. **Information Search Skill:** gathering information from printed and other recorded sources; identifying and using information specialists and reference services and aids.

*31. **Intellectual Versatility:** recognizing, exploring, and using a broad range of ideas and practices; thinking logically and creatively without undue influence from personal biases.

32. **Model Building Skill:** conceptualizing and developing theoretical and practical frameworks that describe complex ideas in understandable, usable ways.

*33. **Observing Skill:** recognizing objectively what is happening in or across situations.

34. **Self-Knowledge:** knowing one's personal values, needs, interests, style, and competencies, and their effects on others.

35. **Visioning Skill:** projecting trends and visualizing possible and probable futures and their implications.

***Core Competency**

Source: Patricia A. McLagan, *Models for HRD Practice: The Models,* ASTD, Alexandria, VA, 1989, pp. 43-45.

ASTD clustered these 35 competencies into five key, critical training roles. Each role has at least 75 percent of the 13 core competencies in common. To illustrate the relationship among competencies and roles, each of the five roles is followed by a list of competencies from Figure 1-6 that support the roles. The roles and competencies listed here are not meant to be comprehensive, only illustrative.

- Analysis/Assessment Roles: Researcher, Needs Analyst, Evaluator
  - Competency Identification Skill
  - Computer Competence
  - Industry Understanding
  - Data Reduction Skill
  - Research Skill
- Development Roles: Program Designer, Materials Developer, Evaluator
  - Adult Learning Understanding
  - Feedback Skill

Writing Skill
Electronic Systems Skills
Objectives Preparation Skills

- Strategic Roles: Manager, Marketer, Organization Change Agent, Individual Career Counselor
    - Career Development Theories and Techniques
    - Computer Competence
    - Training and Development Theories and Techniques Understanding
    - Business Understanding
    - Delegation Skills
    - Organization Understanding
- Instructor/Facilitator Role
    - Adult Learning Understanding
    - Electronic Systems Skills
    - Coaching Skill
    - Feedback Skill
    - Group Process Skill
- Administrator Role
    - Computer Competence
    - Facilities Skill
    - Cost-Benefit Analysis Skill
    - Project Management Skills
    - Records Management Skills

Again, within a career, a training professional typically holds several jobs, each requiring numerous roles that rely on specific competencies. Each job includes roles that may require a different mix of competencies or skills at different ability levels. For example, a training instructor needs a high level of presentation skills. A training manager who also uses presentation skills may take them one step further to include evaluation of others' presentation skills.

Keep in mind, too, that typically no one joins an organization as "training director" without first having field experience in a wide variety of training-related jobs. In building a career, a training professional becomes expert in any number of competencies; it is the mix of these competencies that determines the job and the inherent roles the individual plays in that position. Core competencies are at the hub of Figure 1-7. Note that it is the combination of competencies that defines roles. Roles in combination define jobs. Jobs in combination make up a training career. Thus, each training professional's career "wheel" is very specific as to how core competencies are built upon.

FIGURE 1-7
THE RELATIONSHIP AMONG COMPETENCIES, ROLES, AND JOBS WITHIN A CAREER

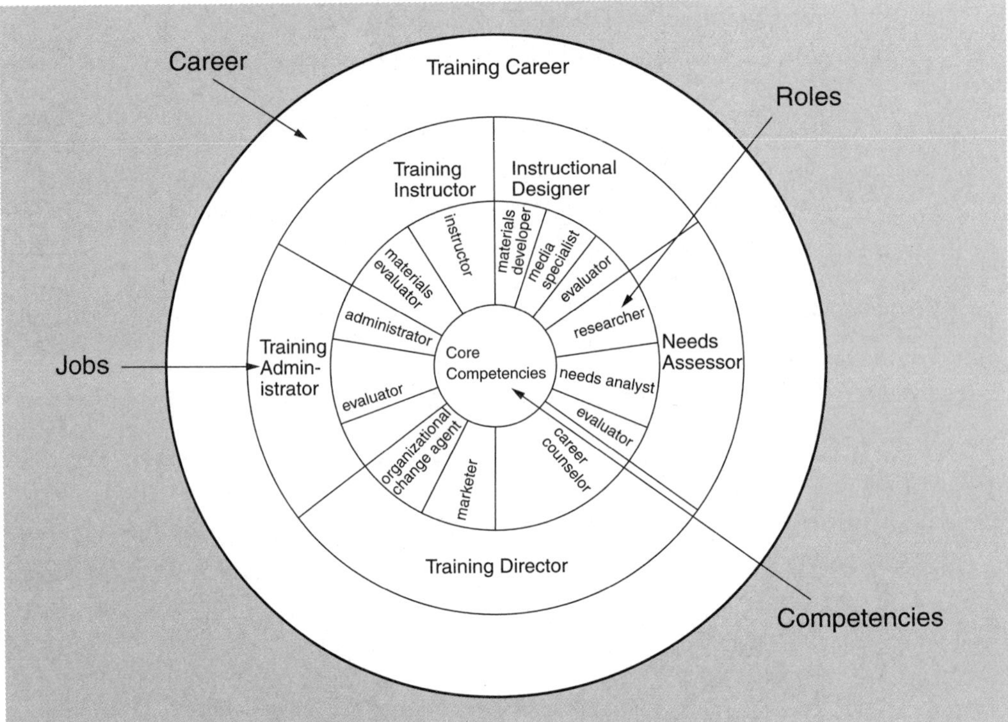

So far in this chapter, structures for organizing a training function have been overviewed along with the skill mix the training professional needs to perform various jobs within a given structure. Now, it is important also to understand what the training department or function actually does, putting individuals' competencies, roles, and jobs into a larger perspective of training processes. The *training cycle*, a conceptual project management strategy, is applicable to strategic, informational, and operational training efforts. It can be used within any model of training department organization. As discussed in the next section, what differs in the use of the training cycle is who is responsible for each stage and how activities at each stage relate to activities in other stages. As a project management strategy, the training cycle can help determine that:

- the *right* people are trained
- for the *right* things
- in the *right* way
- at the *right* time and
- in the *right* priority order.

UNDERSTANDING THE TRAINING CYCLE

Experts in the field of training and development have used a number of models that depict the training program development process in order to develop steps for designing learning experiences. The Instructional System Model (Irwin Goldstein); the Instructional System Development (ISD) methodology (the military); and Instructional Systems Design (also ISD) are examples. These approaches to training program development rely on observable inputs and outputs and are thus based on a systems orientation. Systems theory also says that everything is connected to everything else, and a change in one area impacts others. The theory is useful here as trainers attempt to design learning experiences to achieve maximum internal operating efficiency for each component of the system. However, the use of these models often assumes that a decision to develop training to solve a performance problem has been made and training has been determined to be the best solution.

The training cycle views training program development as one of problem solving, yet is also flexible enough to take advantage of organizational learning. The training cycle is similar to traditional systems models, emphasizing not only stakeholders solving problems, but the process itself is continually examined and refined. In other words, *planned change* and *action research* are key underlying components of the model (see Chapter 11).

Kurt Lewin, a noted social psychologist, described planned change as a three-part process: unfreezing (reducing negative forces toward the change); moving (making the changes happen); and refreezing (reaching a new status quo). Applying Lewin's thinking, learners are more likely to modify their own behavior and managers are more likely to support learning efforts when they are themselves involved in the process. This participation can occur in problem assessment, the design and implementation of the problem intervention (in this case, training), as well as its evaluation.

Continuous evaluation and stakeholder participation are the foundations of *action research.* Action research is a basis for solving problems in many different situations and is useful in conceptualizing organizational learning. Action research has at its base the assessment of a problem, the development of an intervention to solve the problem, the implementation of that intervention, and evaluation of the needs assessment, design, and delivery processes. A key element is that all stakeholders—whoever has something to win or lose by the success or failure of the intervention—are directly involved in this process. Action research has a goal of solving problems and the organization is the learning laboratory. Participants in the process learn what worked—and what did not work—in solving the problem in a particular environment, and profit from their experiences. Because of the strong, cyclical role of evaluation, action research supports the concept of a learning organization and the notion that training is not a one-shot event.

Planned change and action research are the bases for the *training cycle*, depicted in Figure 1-8A and 1-8B. Note that the assessment, design, implementation, and evaluation stages are distinct yet fluid. Feedback is continual (See 1-8B). The outputs of one stage become the inputs for the next stage. The process is cyclical, as the evaluation stage of one project can become the assessment stage of the next project. Ideally, training program development would include all stages. In reality, however, not all training programs are so neatly structured. Many training projects are effectively done quickly. The more strategic and larger the project, the more useful it is for planners to follow this more structured planning method.

FIGURE 1-8A
THE TRAINING CYCLE: AN ACTION RESEARCH MODEL

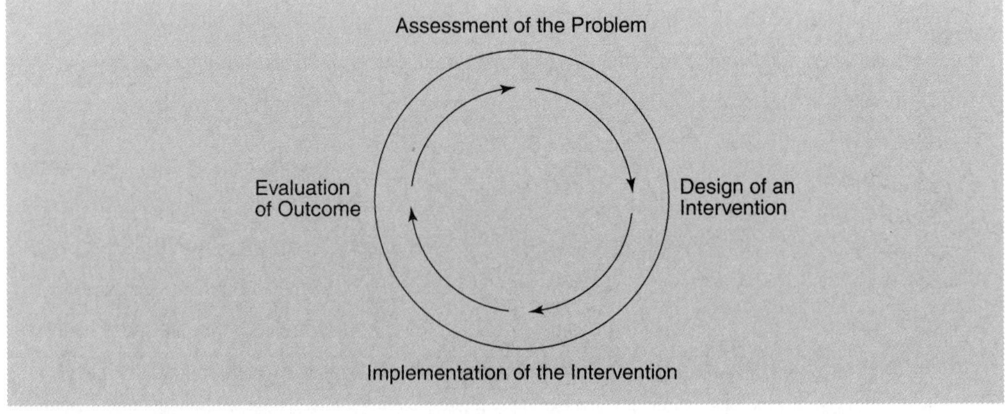

FIGURE 1-8B
THE TRAINING CYCLE: THE INTERRELATIONSHIP OF STAGES

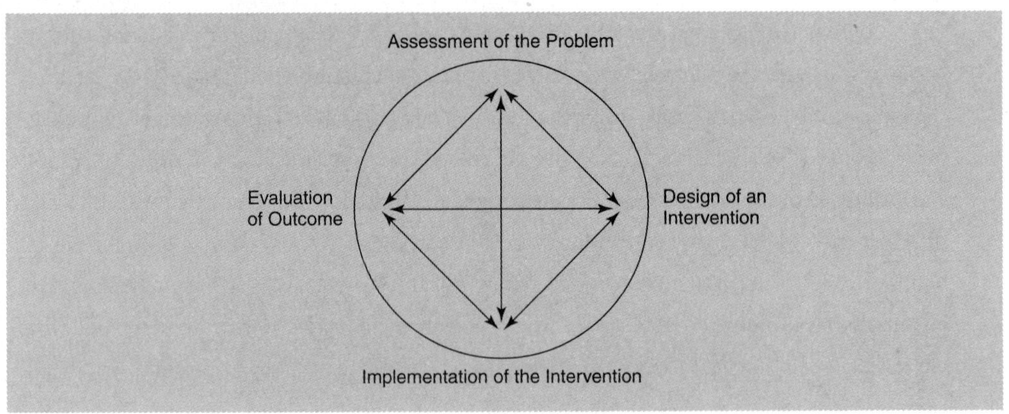

Each element in the training cycle encompasses a distinct and complete process. The circle in Figure 1-8A shows each element of this cycle. The first such process is defined as the *assessment* stage (or phase). Assessment is the investigation of the current "state" or scope of the perceived problem. Activities related to the assessment stage include organizational analysis, job analysis, task analysis, and person analysis. The second stage is *design*. Design can be defined as the creation of an intervention (in this case, a training effort), targeted at addressing the problem identified in the needs assessment. Examples of activities at this stage may include curriculum development, course design, Web-based Training (WBT) development, or the creation of learning aids or materials. The third stage, *implementation*, is the actual delivery of the intervention—the training initiative—which was designed in the second stage. The fourth stage is *evaluation*. Evaluation measures the degree to which the intervention had an impact on the problem.

Activities at the evaluation stage include not only the assessment of instructional delivery, but also materials evaluation, course and sequence evaluation, instructional evaluation, organizational impact, and of course, learning outcomes evaluation. To this end, Figure 1-8B depicts the relationship of each stage of the training cycle to each other. Note that each stage relies on *each and every* stage that precedes it. Feedback at each stage means that outcomes are continually being evaluated. Using the training cycle, evaluation criteria come about as the result of a valid needs assessment effort. Likewise, successful delivery of a training intervention assumes that not only the needs assessment was valid but also that the design phase was effectively carried out, and that the right population of trainees was being reached at the right time. The continual interplay between each of these four elements, while cyclical in presentation, is interactive in nature. This cycle supports the notion that a trainer is actually a change agent, as will be discussed in Chapter 11. Moreover, because stakeholders are involved in all phases, the cycle supports adult learning theory, discussed in Chapter 5, which says that individuals want a say in decisions that impact their lives.

Future chapters of this text will explain and expand upon each phase of the training cycle, offering theoretical foundations for practice and practices based on theoretical foundations. Two underlying premises will be repeated: training efforts must support the organizational mission, goals, and strategies, and training efforts must be both efficient and effective. Anyone considering the training field as a career should have an appreciation and a skill base for each of the specific stages of the training cycle. It follows that the more competencies that a training professional has, the more roles he or she can play—and be able to lead the enterprise toward becoming a third wave learning organization.

SUMMARY

n learning organizations, training has taken on a new importance. The globalization of the economy, demographic trends, and new technologies have changed the way work is done. These trends have forced organizations to rethink their roles and responsibilities to maintain a skilled, knowledgeable workforce. Knowledge Management systems, designed to collect, store, codify, and distribute what an organization knows to individuals at the time they need to know, is an organizing force for learning options that supports the idea that training is about individuals learning, and is not limited to classroom environments.

This chapter described strategic training, informational training, and operational training. Strategic training is related to the organization's long-term plans. Informational training addresses workers' overall awareness of the organization and/or its products. Operational training efforts apply directly to the day-to-day operations of the organization. Training efforts in all categories should be based on a well-planned needs assessment, and training outcomes should be identified in advance and used to evaluate training success.

A training philosophy is a set of values upon which a training department builds its mission and its structure. The philosophy may be operational (prepare individuals to perform their current jobs) and/or strategic and informational (prepare individuals to perform a variety of possible roles or take on more demanding assignments). Sometimes, by the very nature of the training programs, training can be considered educational (prepare individuals to realize their full potential as human beings). Models for organizing the training department were described: faculty, client, matrix, and corporate university. Under a faculty model, training professionals operate as subject matter experts and offer a range of ongoing courses and workshops. Under a client model, training professionals have responsibility for ensuring that training and development needs for an entire target population of an organization are addressed. The matrix model combines the faculty and client models, with the training professional working as a subject matter expert within a centralized training department and, at the same time, responsible for coordinating the needs assessment, development, and evaluation activities for a given population. The corporate university model goes a step further, providing a structure that allows a wide range of strategic and informational training programs to trainees who are not typically training department clients—customers, suppliers, partners, and the community. The corporate university model is also a useful way to offer continuing education services to employees at all levels. Because this model supports strategic training so well, the mix of individuals who are involved in the program planning efforts are often diverse.

Within a training career, a training professional uses a wide range of competencies to perform specific roles within jobs. The American Society for Training and Development sponsored a study that resulted in a detailed list of 35 of these competencies, which range from understanding how adults learn to computer competency to visioning skills. Clustered competencies are roles, and clustered roles are jobs. A mix of jobs constitutes a career.

The chapter concluded with an overview of the four-part training cycle—assessment, design, implementation, and evaluation. The training cycle is a means of understanding processes required to establish effective, efficient training programs. Cyclical in nature, with highly interdependent steps, its methodology encourages cooperation from all organizational stakeholders. Understanding the relationships among tasks related to assessment, design, implementation, and evaluation is important for project planning and organizational learning. The training cycle, based on principles of action research, has the dual goal of systematically solving the problem and at the same time learning from the entire problem-solving process.

THINK IT THROUGH

1. Why are trends in the world at large important to organizations? Identify two such trends and offer examples of ways that training departments have begun to address them.
2. What differentiates strategic training from informational training and operational training? Why is such a distinction important?
3. How might a training director's personal philosophy conflict with the philosophy of the training department?
4. As a training professional, would you prefer to work in a training department that was organized on a faculty, client, or matrix model? What are the advantages and disadvantages of each?
5. "Corporate University" is just a new name for a training department. Agree or disagree?
6. Describe each of the four stages of the training cycle: assessment, design, implementation, and evaluation. Why is it termed a "cycle"? Discuss why efforts at each stage are so dependent upon outcomes of other stages.

IDEAS IN ACTION

1. Begin a file from your local newspaper for news items and editorials related to the need to "train America's workforce," and the need for corporate training and education to maintain our competitive edge. Highlight important concepts and points and share selected copies of your readings with your classmates.
2. As a group project, brainstorm the wide range of roles that an individual could play in the following jobs: instructor, instructional designer, training manager. Which jobs appeal to you? Expand the list offered in this chapter. Which competencies do you already possess? Which do you need to develop?
3. Draw your own training career wheel that includes a vision of your future in the training field. When completing this exercise, you may find it useful to build on your answers to Question 2.

ADDITIONAL RESOURCES

RECOMMENDED READINGS

Duffy, Jan. *Harvesting Experience: Reaping the Benefits of Knowledge.* Prairie Village, KS: ARMA, 1999, 296 pp.

A solid, readable introduction to a blossoming field. The book is a nice mixture of philosophical thought and pragmatic reality. One of its best features is its insistence throughout that Knowledge Management is ultimately in support of business performance and goals. It ends with an attempt to forecast developments in the field over the next few years.

Goldstein, Irwin L. and Associates. *Training and Development in Organizations.* San Francisco: Jossey-Bass, 1989, 525 pp.

Sponsored by the Society for Industrial and Organizational Psychology, this collection of readings offer strategies for training, including retraining mid-career and older workers.

McColgan, Ellen A. "How Fidelity invests in service professionals." *Harvard Business Review,* 75(1), 1997, pp. 127-143.

McColgan reports on an interview with the CEO of Fidelity Retirement Services, who introduced Service Delivery University at Fidelity.

Meister, Jeanne C. *Corporate Universities: Lessons in Building a World-Class Work Force.* New York: McGraw-Hill 1998, 297 pp.

Meister provides a behind-the-scenes look at how 50 corporations are using the corporate university model to manage their investment in education.

Nilson, Carolyn. *Training & Development Yearbook 2000.* Paramus, NJ: Prentice Hall, 2000.

An annual summary of the year in training: new developments and classic themes. The yearbook devotes sections to training management, needs analysis, design, delivery, and evaluation, and sets out to capture the best of publications and web sites in the field, providing abstracts of some articles, reprints of others, and reviews of a variety of resources. It concludes with "The Trainer's Almanac," a directory of resources for those charged with facilitating learning–organizations, conferences, etc.

van Adelsberg, David and Edward A. Trolley. *Running Training Like a Business: Delivering Unmistakable Value.* San Francisco: Berrett-Koehler, 1999, 218 pp.

Another short, packed gem. This book discusses how to manage training so that it serves the agenda of the business that is paying for it. And *only* that agenda. The authors, both executives of the Forum Corporation, tap their experience as learning alliance partners with DuPont. They go well beyond that to discuss other models of training-as-business.

WEB SITES

http://www.corpu.com

The portal for the myriad of services offered by Jeanne Meister's organization, Corporate Quality Xchange. Through the site, you can subscribe to a variety of free services, such as a listserv and Web letter. Additionally, you can purchase books and research reports and learn of upcoming seminars sponsored by the company.

http://www.trainingdirectorsforum.com

The Training Director's Forum, sponsored by *Training, Technology Training, and Knowledge Management*. Check out its News and Resources area, which at the time of this writing includes a white paper on Knowledge Management and online learning.

http://www.masie.com

The homepage of the Masie Center. You can subscribe to their interactive newsletter, as well as access a wide variety of resources related to technology and learning, including Knowledge Management.

http://learning.mit.edu/com/peo/psenge.html

The homepage of Peter M. Senge, who is MIT Senior Lecturer at the Massachusetts Institute of Technology. He is also Chairperson of the Society for Organizational Learning (SoL), a global community of corporations, researchers, and consultants dedicated to the "interdependent development of people and their institutions." The site provides links to research in the area of organizational learning as well as services SoL provides.

ENDNOTES

1. Toffler, Alvin. *The Third Wave*. New York: Bantam Books, 1980.
2. Senge, Peter. *The Fifth Discipline*. New York: Doubleday, 1994, 423 pp.
3. Bridges, William. *Job Shift*. Reading, MA: Addison-Wesley, 1994, 258 pp.
4. Allerton, Haidee. "Hot New Job Titles for Trainers and Others." *Training and Development 50*, 1996: pp.20-23.
5. Gordon, Jack. "Intellectual Capital and You." *Training* 36, No. 9 1999 pp. 30-38.
6. Meister, Jeanne C. *Corporate Universities: Lessons in Building a World-Class Work Force*. New York: McGraw-Hill, 1998, 297 pp.
7. Ibid.
8. Ibid.
9. Zemke, Ron. "In Search of a Training Philosophy." *Training Magazine* 1985 pp. 93-98.
10. Delaney, Chester. "Alternate Models for Structuring a Training Department." New York: Auerbach Publishers, 1984.
11. Meister, op. cit.
12. Ibid.
13. McLagan, Patricia A. and Suhadolnik, Debra. *Models for HRD Practice: The Research Report*, ASTD, Alexandria, VA, 1989.

VOICES *from the* FIELD

Richard Chang on The Training Function

Richard Y. Chang is the CEO of Richard Chang Associates, Inc., and a past Chairman of ASTD's Board of Directors. He has managed internal training departments, worked in and chaired his local ASTD Chapter, and has consulted with a wide variety of clients across a range of industries. He is a sought after and compelling speaker on the subject of optimizing business performance.

CHET DELANEY: Richard, thank you very much for taking the time for this interview. I'd like to begin with, of all things, your E-mail address. The domain name in your Internet address is "rca4results." This is abbreviated cyber-speak for "Richard Chang Associates for results," correct?

RICHARD CHANG: Right.

CHET DELANEY: Is it accurate to say that this sums up your thinking about training? That training is strictly "for results"—for business results?

RICHARD CHANG: It certainly sums up one aspect of my perspective on training. Training must focus on making sure that the outcomes of the learning and training process contribute to business results. It has to create *performance* results, not just training or learning results. Training cannot be just an activity. Its themes must always be around generating the results the organization desires, the business results it is paying for.

CHET DELANEY: How do you make sure this happens?

RICHARD CHANG: I'll give you two answers:

1. When you design a learning experience, my recommendation is that you begin the design by identifying the outcome that is wanted. You determine what the performance outcomes are that the business wants, and then you design the training to deliver precisely those outcomes.
2. You've got to use and track measures. You must—*up front*—determine how you will know that the targeted performance outcomes have in fact been achieved. You may also create measures that are sort of interim measures—measures that you use as you go through the training to tell whether or not you are heading in the right direction.

CHET DELANEY: I take it you agree on these outcomes and measures with your client in advance?

RICHARD CHANG: Yes, always define the end results first, the business impact, and the measures that tell you whether or not you've attained them. Define all this first, then design your training back to those outcomes.

CHET DELANEY: Sounds like classic project management…or classic Steven Covey: Begin with the end in mind.

RICHARD CHANG: Absolutely. This is not to say that beginning with the outcomes and measures is always easy. But it is important that this insight about what comes first be kept in mind. And this has got to be a *business* impact, not just the outcomes of the training experience—impact in terms of the larger business, impact sometimes even in the marketplace.

CHET DELANEY: It may be that it's more natural for you and your company, competing in the open market as you do, to pay attention to business results. I have seen a lot of internal training departments lose sight of this need.

RICHARD CHANG: Well, that's one reason internal training departments often don't last!

CHET DELANEY: Ouch!

RICHARD CHANG: This is one of the things an external partner can do for a training department—help it stay focused on what it's supposed to deliver as a partner for business results.

CHET DELANEY: Let's talk for a bit about the internal training department itself. I know you and your firm have worked with numerous such departments. Have you seen a particular approach to organizing a training department work especially well? Or badly?

RICHARD CHANG: There are lots of ways to organize a training department, of course.

I would hone in on a couple. An approach that I have seen to be successful is to create a department of what I would call "learning generalists." The department is made up of people who are multi-disciplinary—they can do front-end analysis, they can do instructional design, they can do classroom or other modes of delivery. They are internal consultants around performance improvement, and thus learning. They have an internal client base that they support and work with. A department that operates like this is not just responding to requests.

CHET DELANEY: Trainers who work like this are not just order takers.

RICHARD CHANG: Right. They are not just a support force, certainly not doormats. They help—and *are seen* to help—achieve desired business outcomes. They come to be viewed as partners in planning and implementation, from the tactical to the strategic level.

CHET DELANEY: How does a training department come to be seen this way?

RICHARD CHANG: You have to make sure you understand the business first. Then bring to the table a breadth of learning and performance improvement capabilities, a mix of approaches to fit a variety of situations. And third, have access to a strong network of resources—internal and external—that have been successful in improving performance and attaining business outcomes. This inevitably includes an emphasis on various technologies, but notice that I put understanding the business and the organization and its needs *first*. This, in turn, puts a premium on good diagnosis skills—ways of determining the most appropriate solutions for a range of requirements.

CHET DELANEY: You mentioned having a network of resources to draw on because you may not have all the tools to fill all the needs...

RICHARD CHANG: You *won't* have them. The demands on an internal training department are so wide-ranging and so volatile, you really must know how to partner with suppliers. You want to establish long-term supplier relationships, get them to be part of your team and learn your organization, your culture. They can then move much more fluidly, much more agilely. This is in contrast to thinking of suppliers simply as a commodity.

CHET DELANEY: Yes, some things are in fact a commodity, depending on topic or type of service. But there are times when you need a very tight and knowledgeable partnership.

RICHARD CHANG: Right. I also want to point out that this training department I described above—the department of internal performance consultants—I have seen them work very successfully as self-managed teams of multi-disciplined professionals working with specific business units to achieve goals. I've seen this work without traditional hierarchical management.

CHET DELANEY: OK, and in both cases the focus is on learning for performance improvement, rather than on running training programs.

RICHARD CHANG: Exactly.

CHET DELANEY: Any other way of organizing a training department that has caught your eye?

RICHARD CHANG: I've seen departments organized successfully according to the type of learning—the mode of delivery—that's being used. A group of people was focused on classroom type learning and all the aspects of that delivery approach. Another group was focused on technology-based, Internet-based, delivery of material. This latter team was not delivering just technical skills, but all sorts of needed content. The group specialty was in the use of technology to do the delivery and in the support necessary for people to learn this way.

CHET DELANEY: Can you offer some advice to training professionals in ways to make training an organizational investment, rather than just another overhead expense? And in ways to help them persuade others to see training this way also?

RICHARD CHANG: I think this goes back to the concept we talked about in your very first question. Trainers have to, first, define (with their business partners) what the desired business outcomes are. Second, they must then design training to deliver those outcomes, and, finally, create the measurement and tracking mechanisms to make sure they actually achieve what was intended. One of the interesting things about the process improvement training that we do for some of our clients is that the training actually has people working on real processes that the business needs and uses. So the training participants are actually contributing to the business during the learning process. They are not only learning along the way, they are contributing in concrete terms.

CHET DELANEY: Learning and contributing at the same time...

RICHARD CHANG: Yes. You can also sometimes define competency improvements that the business desires people to have, improvements to specified levels of proficiency in those competencies. Here you are legitimately concentrating on people's capabilities, but you are doing so in terms of competencies the business wants in its employee population.

CHET DELANEY: If I hear you correctly, you are saying that we can talk about—and train for—higher proficiency levels in targeted skills. We can focus on developing people, but that ultimately the measure of success must still be bottom-line business results.

RICHARD CHANG: One is a leading and the other a lagging indicator. That is, developing people's capabilities is not immediately a bottom-line business outcome, but will ultimately contribute to such an outcome. The trainer here must make sure that the right capabilities have been improved, and that they get applied on the job. So competency improvement—while a perfectly legitimate training result—is not always the answer, and is in itself not enough.

CHET DELANEY: In fact, it's a bit of a risk?

RICHARD CHANG: Yes. You have to make sure that you define the competencies carefully and line with business plans.

CHET DELANEY: Otherwise, to borrow another Covey analogy, you might climb a ladder only to find out it's leaning against the wrong wall.

RICHARD CHANG: Too true.

CHET DELANEY: I'd like to ask you to focus on the roles trainers play within organizations. What sorts of roles do you see trainers playing over the next few years? How do you see training roles changing? What skills are going to be critical to training success?

RICHARD CHANG: I think it is going to be necessary for trainers—performance improvement consultants, if you will—to be more proficient at looking at data concerning the future, at trends occurring in the marketplace. Trends that will really affect the organizations they work in. This is true whether the trainer is a general consultant, working across multiple industries, or whether the trainer has made a career out of a specific industry and has moved deeper and deeper into that industry. In either case—for cross-industry or in-depth impact—I think trainers will have to be more skilled at researching/sourcing data about the arenas within which they work. They will also have to be more adept at interpreting the impact of trends they surface, with particular attention, of course, to learning issues. Impact on individual learning, impact on organizational learning, impact on organizational cultures. So that's one big skill area that I think will be important for trainers—to be able to find, shape, analyze, and use information about the environments in which they work.

CHET DELANEY: Are you saying trainers will need to be more strategic, whatever their organizational setting?

RICHARD CHANG: Yes, this is going to be more important because of the way organizations and the operating environments are shifting. Another thing that is going to be critically important for trainers is—I hate to keep harping on this—that training can no longer be an activity. It simply has to be a contributor to the bottom line. It feels so trite to keep saying this, but…

CHET DELANEY: Believe me, we say it often enough in the rest of the book!

RICHARD CHANG: A third role that I think is emerging in organizations for trainers is to play a part in Knowledge Management…the building of knowledge bases…managing intellectual capital.

CHET DELANEY: Could you say some more about that, please?

RICHARD CHANG: Well, Knowledge Management in general means building a base of accessible and usable information that others in the organization can access for lessons learned, for insight as to how learning was applied. The knowledge base will include information such as what actually occurred in a situation, what changes should be made, what customer perceptions and preferences are, etc. The Internet and Intranets, of course, add whole new dimensions of accessibility and ease of maintenance to gathering and managing this kind of knowledge. In this context, training professionals should position themselves to play a pivotal part in helping all this learning and learning material come about. In this context, training and performance interventions should be experienced less and less as one-off events—as a sort of Niagara Falls that you experience and then it's over. Learning is going to become part of the organization's way of working and doing business. Trainers have a natural fit with this trend.

CHET DELANEY: Anything else about specific skills for training professionals?

RICHARD CHANG: I've already mentioned research skills, accessing and interpreting it. These imply a significant demand for good data analysis capabilities. You clearly must also have the traditional performance intervention skills—facilitation, coaching, teaching, making presentation—the Training 101 kinds of skills.

CHET DELANEY: And people skills?

RICHARD CHANG: Right. You have to have the interpersonal skills, the "schmoozing factor," if you will. There's something else, something that I make a very high priority for the trainer. And that is (I've mentioned this earlier too) a focus on business and organizational knowledge. I give this a high priority because I see so many people in the training field focus on just training aspects and not nearly enough on the business side of things.

CHET DELANEY: So many people focused on teaching and not on learning.

RICHARD CHANG: Right. Or not on performance.

CHET DELANEY: Let me shift gears here and ask you a rather large question. Can you tell me a war story about a successful training effort you have seen or been part of? What was it, what did it accomplish, what was the key to its success?

RICHARD CHANG: Well, let's see. There was one situation that began as a small, simple training effort and evolved over about five years into an entire corporate university. This training department began with three full-time employees, a staff professional and two support people. The initial effort was to take care of some start-up needs. Over time, this organization has transformed itself repeatedly. Now, some five years later, it includes roughly 60 people full time, with additional adjunct faculty drawn from line managers and executives. It has integrated all aspects of learning and performance support that had been completely decentralized. It has created a very systematic learning and performance environment, building toward solid Knowledge Management.

CHET DELANEY: What was the key to this success?

RICHARD CHANG: The key was gaining direct involvement and support from the CEO. Learning and performance came to be seen as one of the organization's critical strategic priorities. Training came to be seen as the way to continually transform the capability of the organization. It came to be seen as a valued partner rather than a necessary evil.

CHET DELANEY: What did the training people do to make all this happen?

RICHARD CHANG: They began to track results and measurable impacts, contributions to the bottom line. And they did this across multiple skill areas, including some (e.g., running meetings) that looked like anything but high-level strategy but which helped the organization become more nimble, more future-oriented. Another important thing they did was make sure all of this tracking and measuring and impacting was reported. That it not only took place but was *seen* to take place. They not only contributed to the bottom line, they *showed* the contribution factors. So training came to be seen as a contributor to the business strategy and to the transformation of the organization.

CHET DELANEY: What about professional growth and networking for trainers? Are there groups outside the training field proper that people should consider connecting with? ASTD and ISPI are sort of givens, obviously. Are there other professional associations outside the training field? (ASTD: American Society for Training and Development. ISPI: International Society for Performance and Instruction.)

RICHARD CHANG: Well, I would offer a few possibilities:

1. One is ASQ—the American Society for Quality. They deal with hard-line quality and performance improvement, certainly issues that impact the kinds of things trainers get involved with.

2. There is also an organization called APICS, the American Production and Inventory Control Society. They offer good educational experiences. They are heavily focused on the operational side of business, especially in manufacturing environments. They are a good organization to network with because of their focus on performance in the area of operational management.
3. SHRM—the Society for Human Resource Planning—gives you a broader view of the whole HR responsibility, including training.
4. The Chamber of Commerce and other similar business organizations, to get a better feel for the business issues that are going on. Perhaps also a business association that is particular to the industry within which you work. The idea here is to keep a business focus in your own learning and networking.

CHET DELANEY: How about some recommendations on reading, on publications? Again, outside the field of training proper (*Training Magazine* and *Training and Development* are givens.)

RICHARD CHANG: There are a few I would suggest people consider:

1. *The Harvard Business Review* or a similar business publication. The possibilities are numerous—*Fortune, Forbes, Business Week, Inc. Magazine, The Wall Street Journal.* These are all vehicles that get the trainer to think outside the training box, as we should.
2. *Fast Company*—a really good, quick look at what's going on inside industry, especially the newer side of business.
3. *Across the Board*, a publication of the Conference Board—loads of good information, well presented, and free if you qualify for a subscription.
4. Publications that represent the industry within which you work—again, a business focus to ground your training work.

RICHARD CHANG: There's something I'd like to go back to....

CHET DELANEY: By all means.

RICHARD CHANG: This comes under the topic of skills important for the future in training—I think trainers are going to have to learn to deal with a variety of organizational infrastructures, from virtual companies to traditional hierarchies to dot.coms. Especially the last. The learning and performance side of a dot.com start-up is very different from a traditional organization. The learning and performance practitioner should expect to face all sorts of organizational shapes as they morph their way into the future.

CHET DELANEY: OK, what if you could talk to people who are in school now, preparing to become trainers. What would you say to them?

RICHARD CHANG: Well, I'd say:

1. First, you have to discover if your heart is really in this field for a career. I think it is becoming much more of a career field, less a transient type of role. So look in your heart and see if you have the passion for learning and performance...not just for yourself, but for helping others learn and perform. Unless your heart is in it, you could be seriously challenged in this field, because there are a lot of obstacles that you run into. You are also often not going to be in the limelight. You'll be more of an enabler rather than the doer. You can expect others to get the credit for bringing in the fish you enabled them to learn how to catch!
2. Second, get some ground-floor, real-world experience inside an organization before trying to be an external consultant. Get yourself a job inside an organization first, learn the tough lessons you can only learn there. I worked for four different organizations as an internal practitioner before going off on my own. I would recommend this kind of career route.

CHET DELANEY: Richard, you've given our readers here a lot to chew on. Thank you so very much for sharing your experience and expertise.

RICHARD CHANG: You're more than welcome.

PART 2
Needs Assessment and Evaluation

PROLOGUE TO PART 2

As discussed in Part 1, the very *raison d'être* of a training department is to ensure that the right people learn the right things in the right way at the right time and in the right priority order. The task essential to achieving this goal is to ascertain what must be learned, by whom, and what the business priorities of that learning are in terms of both topics and people. This task is referred to variously as needs analysis, needs identification, or needs assessment and is Step 1—at least conceptually if not chronologically—in the classic training cycle (See Figure 1-8). This book will use the term *needs assessment* to refer to this stage of the cycle. Evaluation is conceptually the fourth stage of the training cycle. However, because training is a cycle and not a one-shot event, evaluation data serve as input for the next investigation cycle. Therefore, in Part 2, we present an overview of needs assessment (Chapter 2) and evaluation (Chapter 3), and describe the tools you need to do both through a discussion of research techniques (Chapter 4).

The fundamental concept of needs assessment applies to a wide variety of situations. Marketing and sales departments are constantly attempting to discover what their customers' needs are. Doctors want to discover their patients' medical needs, beginning with symptoms and moving to causes. An entertainment conglomerate is always in search of consumer interests and needs and wants, so they can respond with profitable products. A *training* needs assessment follows the same line of thinking as all these others, but with its own particular focus. The goal of training needs assessment is to discover the learning needs of its customers so that those learning needs can be met.

Evaluation, the fourth component of the training cycle outlined in Figure 1-8, has particular relevance to needs assessment. Evaluation plays a part in the entire training cycle, but it is particularly important to the identification of learning needs. One major aspect of evaluation is to determine whether or not planned learning occurred. If it did not, or was only partially attained, or perhaps generated new needs, this information should be fed back into the training cycle as needs assessment data.

Conflicts can arise concerning the learning interests of employees. It is possible for the needs assessment process to uncover learning interests of a particular employee that the organization does not support. For example, the subject matter may not fit with either the organization's business plans or with management's view of the employee's job needs, skills, or potential. That is, an employee may consider it necessary or desirable to learn *X* or may simply express an interest in doing so because that is where he or she would like to move in terms of career. Management, on the other hand, may not agree, and thus may not support this learning interest. Management may not think that learning *X* will help achieve the individual's or the organization's performance goals. The employee's manager may judge that the employee's demonstrated performance record does not support his or her career interests, and thus having the employee learn *X* is not a good allocation of training resources.

In a large company, there may be many job options to satisfy the career aspirations and learning interests of virtually all employees. In smaller organizations, this may not be the case, and even in larger organizations a match is not always realistically possible. When such a difference exists, it frequently surfaces as part of the needs assessment process, and it is important that trainers be clear about the philosophy of the organization on how such differences are to be handled. One point of view says that any such conflict should be resolved in favor of the company's interests, and not that of the individual. The thinking here is that an organization's management must decide how its training resources are to be invested, and thus will ultimately determine not only what needs to be learned by employees, but also which employees should learn which subject matter, and when the learning should take place. A second point of view argues that the organization will, in the long run (and perhaps even in the short run), benefit if its members all strive to identify and maximize their own personal potential in terms of work. Thus, the employee's interests would prevail. The truly important thing for the trainer conducting the needs assessment is to be clear on how this potential conflict is to be resolved.

With these preliminary points made, we can now turn our attention to a more detailed look at Chapter 2, "Training Needs Assessment;" Chapter 3, "Evaluating Organizational Training;" and Chapter 4, "Research Techniques."

CHAPTER 2
Training Needs Assessment

- Identify the interrelated goals of a needs assessment effort.
- Summarize the value of systematic approaches to needs assessment.
- Apply the needs assessment template.
- Explain the value of the needs assessment bull's-eye in targeting the right individuals for needs assessment data.
- Determine the appropriate needs assessment techniques for a given situation.
- Explain why needs assessment is an ongoing activity, not a one-shot event.

LEARNING FOR PERFORMANCE

The basic definition of needs assessment is simple and straightforward (doing it may not be easy, but the definition is simple):

Training needs assessment is the process of identifying what employees need to learn

- in order for them to successfully perform their jobs;
- in order for them to grow their careers;
- in order for the organization to carry out its plans and achieve its performance goals.

The focus on *learning* in this definition is crucial. Training, like all other aspects of an organization, is concerned ultimately with performance, both the individual employee's job performance and the organization's performance as a whole. The particular focus that training brings to the performance issue is a focus on *learning*, either to enable or to enhance performance. The Training Department seeks to answer the questions: What do people need to learn in order to perform? What do people need to learn for the organization to perform? Where and how can learning support performance? Once these questions are answered, the training task is to help learning occur with maximum efficiency and effectiveness.

In any organization, there is a constant influx of *the new*. Employees are asked to take on new tasks. There are new job responsibilities to be met, new areas of business the organization has decided to get into, or perhaps a whole new business in which to engage. New tools and new processes are continually being introduced into the workplace. In all these cases, people need to acquire new knowledge or master new skills. That is to say, they have a need to *learn* in order to perform and in order for the organization to perform. A training needs assessment seeks to identify these learning requirements.

Organizations also have a recurring need to overcome *performance deficiencies* of one kind or another. Such deficiencies are caused by many factors, only sometimes by a lack of knowledge or a lack of skill. It is only a lack of knowledge or skill that can be addressed by *learning*. One of the key tasks for needs assessment is not only to identify performance deficiencies, but also to identify those that can be remedied by learning. Training professionals must be careful not to leap too quickly to training as solutions for all problems. Training solutions can be successful and should be applied if, and *only* if, training is the best remedy. This is not a question of being noble, nor is it merely as a matter of professional discipline on the trainer's part. It is an exercise in self-interest. Training applied as a solution to the wrong problem or to a non-training issue is an exercise in futility and a waste of valuable resources.

The definition of training needs assessment stated above also reminds us that organizational training is all about *employee learning*. Training needs assessment does not focus on instruction or on programs or on what the training department has to offer. It focuses instead on *learning needed*, on the knowledge, skills, and abilities (KSAs) employees need to learn for the sake of performance. This focus on learning may lead to a wide variety of methods for helping learning occur. It does not automatically lead to a classic classroom training program. When the focus remains on learning, the trainer will always search for the most efficient and effective way to make that learning happen, whether that means in a classroom or otherwise. Training needs assessment is not about setting up training programs. It is about finding the right response to opportunities and problems caused by employees' performance gaps.

The following discussion deals with issues related to each component of the definition of training needs assessment: learning for the job, for a career, and for the organization.

Learning for the Job

The purposes of learning listed in the opening paragraph of this chapter are in the order in which they are usually encountered. By far the most usual and frequent reason why learning is needed is so that employees can successfully perform their jobs, carrying out the tasks and meeting the responsibilities assigned to them. This covers an enormous range of possibilities, varying from project to project and job to job. A manager, for example, must learn different things than those required by a receptionist. Computer programmers have learning requirements vastly different from salespeople, who differ dramatically in their learning needs from the maintenance staff or the cafeteria workers or the auditors. Each member of an organization, from top to bottom, has the need to learn or relearn how to do his or her job.

This may mean learning how to do the job in the first place. Basic, entry-level training for all kinds of work is a staple of organizational life. Once the basics are acquired, additional learning needs will surface sooner or later. After a while, some part of these basics may need refreshing. More typically, as the individual gains experience and becomes more proficient, the need arises to learn more complex skills within the same job stream. An MBA fresh off the campus may be able to perform solid business analysis at a fundamental level, but may require additional training to deal with the complexities of a merger, corporate expansion, or issues of international taxation. People in management jobs face the need to learn new skills as their slice of the organization's resources change—grow larger or different—or as the organization's objectives and priorities shift with the tides of business, technology, demographics, or other factors that shape the world in which the organization lives. Certainly a major trend on the current organizational and business scene is the continuing push to reengineer. Business process redesign means that an organization undertakes to do its business in fundamentally different ways. The ripples from a reengineering thrust bring about changes in the workplace that continually require the relearning, new learning, and even unlearning of skills that were previously acquired.

In almost any job, there are core competencies that an incumbent must master. Core competencies are often defined as including organizational culture as well as problem-solving, computing, and interpersonal communications. To hold the title of administrative assistant or controller or systems analyst or supervisor implies the ability to carry out a skill set specific to the title, a skill set that someone new to the job may need to learn. Furthermore, given the basic core competencies, every job also makes other demands that are situational in nature. Such demands vary from company to company. Management philosophy, company goals and constraints, the company's vision of itself and its future, its equipment—a host of factors—make the application of a core set of skills very different from one company to another. Even though an individual may be experienced in a core set of competencies, a new circumstance may require learning on the job holder's part, learning that a needs assessment must surface.

Even within the same organization, core competencies for a job may remain the same, but vary in their application from department to department or from unit to unit inside a single department. Once again, the learning need is real and no less a job-related skill than the original core set. It is training needs assessment's responsibility to capture these learning requirements.

Learning for Careers

Beyond the learning necessary for individual jobs, there is the whole issue of career. Most organizations and managers think beyond the immediate present to recognize employees' needs for professional growth within their careers. It is almost always in an organization's best interests to support such career interests, and most do. Career-growth interests, of course, generate a great deal of learning requirements and are usually an exciting area for a training needs assessment to address.

There is also the issue of growth *across* careers. Learning needs often arise from an employee's desire to move into a career different from his/her present one, or to move to a substantially different aspect of the existing career track. Perhaps the most common example of this is the desire of an employee to move into management, which typically takes the form of a productive, successful worker being offered or seeking the opportunity to become a supervisor in the department or profession where that success has taken place. Such a move builds upon the technical job mastery the worker has achieved through experience, but it also necessitates mastery of a whole new set of skills. Moving into a management position makes it necessary to acquire the managerial skills of planning, delegating, staffing, work monitoring and evaluating, and the like. To this skill set must be added the interpersonal side of supervision, responsibilities such as performance appraisals, corrective discipline, coaching, and counseling.

The shift to a management position is perhaps the most common method that an employee uses to jump to an entirely new career, and in most organizations a whole range of careers exist to which people may aspire. Organizations are often supportive of such career moves. Given the organization's need for employees with management skills, the situation may be win-win all around. Recall the *caveat* in the prologue to this section of this text, however. The last thing a training department wants to do is help an employee acquire skills for which there is no existing demand within the organization.

Learning for the Organization

Learning for the organization is the goal that all training departments must keep in focus. Organizations make enormous investments in both people and the tools they use to do their work. Training programs with well-documented needs assessment data that can be explicitly tied to organizational goals are in the best position to have an organizational impact. Training is a business function, and its activities must align with organizational goals.

Needs assessment data provide baseline information regarding the current level of knowledge, skills, and abilities employees have. Evaluation data (discussed in Chapter 3) can provide evidence of the outcome of a training effort. Thus, the trainer can make a business case for training/learning initiatives. This business case is often referred to as return-on-investment (ROI), and techniques for computing ROI are offered in Chapter 9. A well-designed and executed needs assessment helps ensure that training dollars are spent on the right projects, and ensures that they align with organizational goals.

THE NEEDS ASSESSMENT PROCESS

Needs assessment means searching out and discovering who in the organization needs to learn what and with what priority. This can easily get confused with another process, that of distributing a list of available courses and asking managers whom they wish to send to which programs and when. To provide the information needed to plan and allocate resources ranging from instructors to material to classrooms to travel plans, and arrange learners' schedules is an important task, an administrative necessity. However, providing a list of courses is *not* the same as conducting a needs assessment. It is too limited to really address critical learning needs, which may extend beyond any existing courses or programs on hand.

However, when such an administrative task has been completed, the Training Department will have collected extremely valuable information. It will have a good handle on which of its programs people plan to attend. It will know which of its offerings should be either canceled or marketed more aggressively. It will know what it needs to plan for in the way of resources. It will even know that some people in the organization need to learn what its programs offer. But what it will *not* really know is the full picture, the full spectrum, of the organization's learning needs. Moreover, if it is not careful, the Training Department's marketing of its scheduled programs can circumvent the needs assessment process. For example, it can limit people's thinking to what the Training Department has planned to offer. These plans will almost certainly not cover all the learning that is needed. These plans merely reflect what has already been scheduled and needs to be administered. Thus, the Training Department must be vigilant to see that the identification of learning needs is not restricted to the programs it has already set up to offer.

BEGINNING WITH THE JOB

As we have already discussed in the earlier sections of this chapter, the process of needs assessment starts with identifying the learning needs generated by the jobs people do. This focus includes assessing the current job with all its changing demands, as well as any new assignments within the same job track. The process further includes attention to promotions and career goals that build upon the current job. All of these considerations seek to identify what the organization needs its employees to do so that both the people and the organization can operate successfully in the immediate present and with a reasonable eye on the future. In the simplest of terms, the focus of needs assessment is always the job, the job, the job: enabling a person to do this job here and now, or a future job that meets the organization's needs and the individual's career goals.

Beginning with the job is not a limitation, however. It is, rather, a way to ground firmly in organizational reality both what individuals need to learn here and now, and what they need to learn in order to grow and progress throughout careers that makes both personal and organizational sense. Thus, even though the process begins with a job, it does not remain there. It moves on to career. Moreover, as discussed later in this chapter in the sections entitled "Systematic Approaches to Needs Assessment" and "Targeting the Learner Population," the real starting point of needs assessment is the learner. Beginning with the learners in their jobs and building from there systematically provides a way to look at the entire organization's learning needs or any segment of it, since learners and jobs can be clustered into job families or departments or even the total organization.

Convincing the Customer

One of the difficulties trainers face is that their customers often do not understand the value of a needs assessment. Busy managers and professionals will often assume they know what the problems are and just as often will have preconceived notions of the solutions as well. This all too frequently takes the form of making assumptions about what training is needed, or even *that* training is needed. Trainers often succumb to these assumptions themselves, all too eager to prove themselves to their clients, and ready to jump into training activities and programs after the initial phone call from a potential client. Even worse, they are often ready to leap to *teaching* as a solution. Trainers must restrain their eagerness for the tried and traditional and they must also be prepared to educate their clients on the necessity— including justifying the costs— of needs assessment as an essential first step.

One suggestion toward convincing managers of the value of a needs assessment is to point out that the wrong solution almost always leaves things in worse shape than no solution at all. For example, doctors begin with assessment in order to get at root causes of illnesses rather than relying on mere symptoms. Yet another good argument can be drawn from the client's own experience. Most business professionals, whether focused on internal or external customers, are careful not to sell the wrong solutions and know the risks of doing so. Most of them do a needs assessment with their own customers to make sure they understand the real issue before recommending a course of action. A client pushing prematurely for a training response to a problem can usually be convinced to spend the time and the money for a needs assessment by invoking his or her own business practice or track record. It is very important to persuade them to do so.

Summing up the Definition

To sum up: The concept of needs assessment is a process that provides answers to a specific set of questions, answers that both the organization's management and its training professionals need to know. It responds to questions like:

- Who needs to learn what?
- Why do they need to learn it?
- At what depth?
- What is the priority of the learning in question?
  - Priorities in terms of learners
  - Priorities in terms of topics
  - Priorities in terms of time (deadlines for when the learning must be accomplished by each group of learners)

The assessment of learning need is thus a set of answers to the right questions asked systematically of the right people. What are these right questions? And what is a systematic approach to asking them and capturing the answers? And who are the right people to ask?

SYSTEMATIC APPROACHES TO NEEDS ASSESSMENT

The questions that need to be asked of people in an organization to identify learning needs must begin with business plans and projects and ideas about strategic direction. Out of discussions about these issues fall gaps in what people know or know how to do. Needs assessment does *not* begin with questions about required courses or training. It certainly does not begin with a list of classroom programs that the training department has available to offer. The focus must be on the organization's needs: its plans and problems and issues, and the learning requirements that follow from them. To *keep* the focus of needs assessment firmly on learning needs, it is best to be systematic about it. A systematic approach puts discipline in the process, and ensures both focus and follow-through. We will examine two such systematic approaches here. One, a traditional systems view, proceeds by examining person, task, and organization—and the interactions among these variables—to identify various forms of learning needed. The second is a learner-centered approach, which features a generic template as guidance for touching on all the right issues. The template is a pragmatic tool for putting the learners at the center of the process and keeping them there.

A Systems Approach

A traditional, and quite productive, way to undertake training needs assessment is to use a *systems approach.* Training systems lie within and are directly affected by the larger system that involves organizational policies, traditional work modes, and a variety of individual skills. The systems approach to needs assessment is concerned with three key variables and the interaction among them; a change in any of these variables affects the other two. The three variables, discussed in this section, are:

- the organization
- the task—the knowledge and skills needed for a specific job
- the individual who is to do the work

Organizational Analysis

Organizational analysis provides a viable framework for considering work and the people who do it: Organizational analysis provides background, setting, and context for all the other considerations in needs assessment. One goal of organizational analysis, for example, is to ensure that training is done for the right topics, topics that both fit and foster the organization's various agendas. Another goal is to ensure that learning outcomes can be transferred back to the workplace. That is to say, its goal is to make sure that what people learn in training actually suits the real workplace and its values. Indeed, *organizational culture* is a major preoccupation of organizational analysis, and it is beyond question that training outcomes must fit within the culture or be achieved in vain. Increasingly, many organizations today are working hard to understand their own specific cultures as a necessary backdrop to training activities. Beyond that, given the new economic realities of the turbulent, global marketplace, organizations are in many cases striving to *change* their cultures to support new ways of working and doing business. Organizational culture is addressed in the needs assessment process by ensuring that key *stakeholders* (trainees, management, reporting staff, HR professionals, customers) provide meaningful input to the needs assessment process.

Task Analysis

Task analysis is the dissection of a task into the knowledge, skills, and abilities needed to accomplish it, together with a description of these components in behavioral terms. As will be discussed in Chapter 5, the behavioral vocabulary includes very specific terms that provide the means to identify and measure the competencies needed to carry out a task. Human Resource professionals find such job descriptions to be very useful, particularly as standard job titles can be misleading or incomplete. "Administrative Assistant" is an example of a job title that can describe a wide variety of responsibilities and positions. Detailed, behavioral job descriptions can be used for hiring purposes, to help assess whether a particular candidate is capable of doing the work described. Job descriptions are also useful for performance evaluations, supporting judgements about the accomplishment—or lack thereof—of the work so carefully described. And of course, the details of behaviorally written job descriptions provide concrete means of identifying gaps in task skills and thus learning needs, and establish standards for evaluation purposes.

Person Analysis

Organizational and task analysis paint a picture of the organizational setting within which work is done. What is missing is a picture of the individual doing the work, the employee to be trained and the gaps in this person's knowledge and skills. *Person analysis* adds this missing dimension. It provides an understanding of the characteristics of the individuals within the target training population. Getting a solid picture of these characteristics is not always easy, since training is often provided for new hires or an entire new job. It is nevertheless invaluable information with which to shape the training provided. Moreover, it is often noted that the basic job skills of entering workers today are very different from those of earlier generations. Thus, knowing the target population, knowing its experiences, aptitudes, and attitudes adds important information to the training task.

A Learner-Centered Approach

Another approach to needs assessment puts the learners in the center of the process and keeps them there, while systematically reviewing the other relevant organizational issues to create a full picture of what people need to learn. The process begins by looking at people in their jobs and asking questions about job responsibilities and tasks. The questions then move on to issues that are broader in nature— less tactical and more general— and of greater interest to a managerial and strategic mindset than to the perspective of simple task accomplishment, with the learner remaining at the heart of the questions. The template depicted in Figure 2-1 captures precisely this flow of issues.

The learner-centered approach is the form of needs assessment espoused by this book. Not that there is anything wrong with the conventional systems approach. Keeping the learner central to the process is the single most important aspect of needs assessment. The template offered here is a tool for surfacing the right issues in identifying learning requirements, while keeping the learner firmly in mind. Comments on the template will be followed by a discussion of centering needs assessment on a large population, with a method for gathering the population's learning needs from multiple sources.

FIGURE 2-1
NEEDS ASSESSMENT TEMPLATE: THE FLOW OF TOPICS

TOPICS	INTEREST/NEED	
	Individual	Manager
1. Assigned Job Responsibilities	X	X
2. Planned Projects	X	X
3. Career Aspirations	X	
4. Organizational Plans		X
5. Technical Forecasts	X	X
6. Business Forecasts		X
7. Departmental Skills Mix		X
8. Dialog		X
9. Strategy		X

A NEEDS ASSESSMENT TEMPLATE

The first task of a needs assessment is to ask the right questions of the right people. The first column in Figure 2-1 lists a representative set of topics around which questions can be developed that can help you, the training professional, probe and explore learning needs with members of the organization. The second column provides a calibration of the likelihood of each member of the organization's interest in, or need for knowing about, the topics in the first column. Whether or not interest or need exists depends upon the person to be consulted and the position that person holds. As the template shows, not all the topics are appropriate for every member of an organization. The point is not to exclude anyone, but to be realistic. The X's in the second column reflect the topics that are likely to be of interest to individuals, and the third column shows topics that are classically of interest to managers. The template is intended to help you ask the right questions of the right person in the process of needs assessment.

Figure 2-1 is a *template*, not a straitjacket. It should be tailored as needed. The list of topics will change, depending on the organization being studied or the timing of the assessment. The list might be shortened, expanded, or changed. The X's in the second and third columns might also undergo modification, depending on the organization and its people. The template is a road map and provides a way to identify an organization's learning needs in systematic fashion. The example provided here is an illustration that can be applied as appropriate to a real-life situation.

Using the Template

To explain how to apply the template, each of its rows will be briefly discussed. The discussion will offer sample questions, probes, and ideas that training professionals can use in exploring the topics with real clients. Out of such explorations, job responsibilities, professional goals, business plans, and learning needs emerge. This explanation of the template is meant to suggest how to use it and to lay the groundwork for tailoring it to other situations.

1. Assigned job responsibilities. Every member of the organization, from the president to the lowest level, can usefully address this topic. All employees can talk about their responsibilities and identify what they need to learn in order to meet their responsibilities satisfactorily. Job responsibilities are a topic for everyone.
2. Planned projects. The question here has to do with special assignments taken on as part of or in addition to regular job duties. Work on specific projects, alone or as part of a team, can easily generate the need to learn tools, procedures, interpersonal skills, or a new facet of the business. Again, project plans are usually issues that concern everyone in an organization.
3. Career aspirations. The focus here is not the present but the future. What do individual employees want to do next? Or what would the organization like them to take on next, in either the near- or long-term future? What sorts of knowledge or skills might provide the proper positioning for a career move that is of interest and in line with what the organization needs and supports? This is a question that at first glance would seem to pertain to everyone at all times, but this may not be the case. The reality is that a career focus is not always appropriate, certainly not at every moment, not in every discussion of learning need. The X in the second column next to item 3, Career Aspirations, reflects the belief that attention to career issues should be driven primarily by individual employees, when they are ready for it.
4. Organizational plans. What sort of learning will be required by the plans the organization has put in place for the near future? The organization here might mean anything ranging from a small unit to a large department to the entire enterprise. A department may be planning to install a new processing system or a new standard with regard to its technology, or it may be planning to undertake a downsizing to meet budgetary structures. The enterprise as a whole may be planning similar moves or the entrance into a new business or a re-prioritizing of its existing ones. The point is that business plans should be clearly reviewed as a source of learning needs. As the sample template indicates, primary attention here is from management. Individual contributors should also take business plans into consideration in identifying what it is they need to learn, to the extent they have access to the plans. However, it is a classic management responsibility to make sure that employees are equipped with the information, skills, and knowledge that the organization's plans will require.
5. Technical forecasts. Technical specialties are always changing. Neither administrative assistants nor salespeople nor computer technicians nor human resource personnel nor machinists nor mechanics nor cooks—no professionals—work today the same way their counterparts did a decade ago. Or five years ago. Or even three years ago. Attention needs to be paid to this constant change, an equally constant source of learning need. Professionals must listen carefully to what experts are saying about where their fields are

going, and learn accordingly. This is an issue shared by the workers themselves as well as their managers.

6. Business forecasts. Business, too, is constantly changing. We live in what some have called a "whitewater world," a world of foaming business rapids and demographic rocks and fast-flowing technology streams, with quiet, placid pools few and far between. Once again, the management of an organization must keep an eye on where the best research thinks their business in particular, or the industry in general, is going. Once again, the goal is to make sure the organization's people are ready to handle what looks to be coming down the road. Learning needs based upon business forecasts tend to be a management concern more than an individual one.
7. Departmental skills mix. All managers want the people in areas of responsibility—a small unit, a large department, the organization as a whole—to be *cross-trained.* The idea is to enable people to back each other up, fill in for each other, keep things flowing smoothly when a team member leaves for any reason, and test out new tools and techniques before the old are discarded. Learning needs based upon a departmental skills mix is almost always a perspective on learning need provided by management.
8. Dialog. Within every organization there are boundaries—boundaries between departments and professions and geographical sites and even between floors. It is, or should be, a major management concern that these boundaries help the end goals of the organization, not hinder them, particularly in these days of flatter organizational structures. This often argues for communication across these boundaries, for dialog between and among the various communities of professionals inside the organization, *for learning about each other*. People in one organizational *silo* (a self-contained vertical unit) need to learn about the work of people in another. Systems analysts typically need to learn the language of business. Field personnel should learn how to communicate with managers in the central office. Product developers must do some cross-talk with sales. Again, these kinds of insights are almost exclusively concerns that will surface in discussions with managers and are often a rich source of learning need.
9. Strategy. Organizations are always thinking about where they want to be tomorrow, how they want to be positioned in their marketplace for the future. Over and above short-term business plans, thinking goes on concerning the longer, more strategic haul. Definitely a management issue and by most definitions not a front-burner one, this is a topic that deserves serious discussion at senior levels. While attention to long-term strategy may not identify near-term learning requirements, it can provide insight into what the organization must learn in order to survive and prevail for the long term.

Further Points about the Template

As you move down the list of topics in our sample Needs Assessment Template, the issues move from employee concerns to management concerns. There is some crossover around the middle of the list: Both individuals and their managers often share an interest in learning needs about business plans and forecasts concerning the future of the business and its professions. In much the same way, the list also goes from a focus on the tactical to the strategic; from the burning urgency of the task at hand to a longer-term perspective; from the immediate and urgent to the less obvious but more important. Accordingly, as you move down the topic list, the topics become more appropriate for the more senior levels of the organization.

The template is most emphatically not a mere order-taking form. As we have said, not all its topics are appropriate for all employees, but some issues may apply to people or situations that the learners themselves do not see. Most people, for example, tend to get caught up in the tactical, in the immediate job issues, in what they have to learn to do their assigned job or complete their project responsibilities. As we have seen, that is definitely the place to start. But needs assessment must go beyond that starting point. There are some issues that belong on an individual's learning agenda even if that individual does not initially recognize it. Here is where you add value by bringing ideas to the discussion rather than just being responsive. A new hire may quite appropriately not give any thought to technical trends, but a senior incumbent ought to be considering them and learning from/about them. It is up to you to raise such issues when the learner ought to be taking them into account but has not yet done so. It is the trainer's job to make sure all the right issues from the right people are covered in needs assessment.

Remember that the Needs Assessment Template is exactly that, a template. It is not intended to be a form that can be used in many different training situations. It is, rather, a guide as to the kinds of topics and issues to explore with the right people in order to identify key learning needs. Once a customized template has been created for your organization, it can be used as a chart for gathering and plotting information. Thus, in addition to systematically guiding the questions being asked concerning learning needs, the Needs Assessment Template can also serve as a tool for systematically gathering, pooling, and prioritizing the answers to the questions.

Needs assessment means getting the right population of learners to discuss the right set of issues in terms of their need to learn about them, and capturing the results of their discussions systematically. The next section of this chapter deals with how to focus on the right population, and what forms such a discussion might take.

TARGETING THE LEARNER POPULATION

The Needs Assessment Template provides guidance concerning the kinds of questions and issues to be explored with the target population of learners. This section will focus on the area where the need for learning really resides: on the learners themselves.

The goal of needs assessment is to find out what the members of the organization need to learn given their jobs, assignments, and careers, all against the backdrop of the organization's plans and directions. Except in the most unusual cases, it is virtually impossible to deal with the learning needs of the entire organization at once. The training professional must inevitably focus on a single group of employees at a time. The set of employees in question could be a project team. It might be a department in general. It might be a group of like professionals from all across the organization with presumably similar learning needs; for example, the programmers from every department. In a very small organization, it is possible that the target audience might be the entire membership as a whole.

Setting up the Bull's-Eye

As Figure 2-2 shows, whatever the population of employees is, the initial step is to place them in the bull's-eye of an imaginary target, making them the central focus of your needs assessment effort for the moment. The next step is to discuss with the targeted employees the topics listed in your Needs Assessment Template. Begin by asking them directly what they think they need to learn about particular topics on your template. Work these employees down the topic list as appropriate. Remember, not all topics on the template are suitable for all employees. Remember, too, that the trainer is expected to be proactive as well as responsive. Not only should you accurately capture the information about what the targeted group has to say, you should also add your own thinking to theirs. You should challenge the assumptions your target learners are making about what they need to learn. You should bring up issues they ought to consider but may have left out. It is important that you capture the learning needs that derive from these discussions in a systematic way (see earlier discussion about using the Needs Assessment Template itself for data capture).

Figure 2-2
The Needs Assessment Bulls-Eye

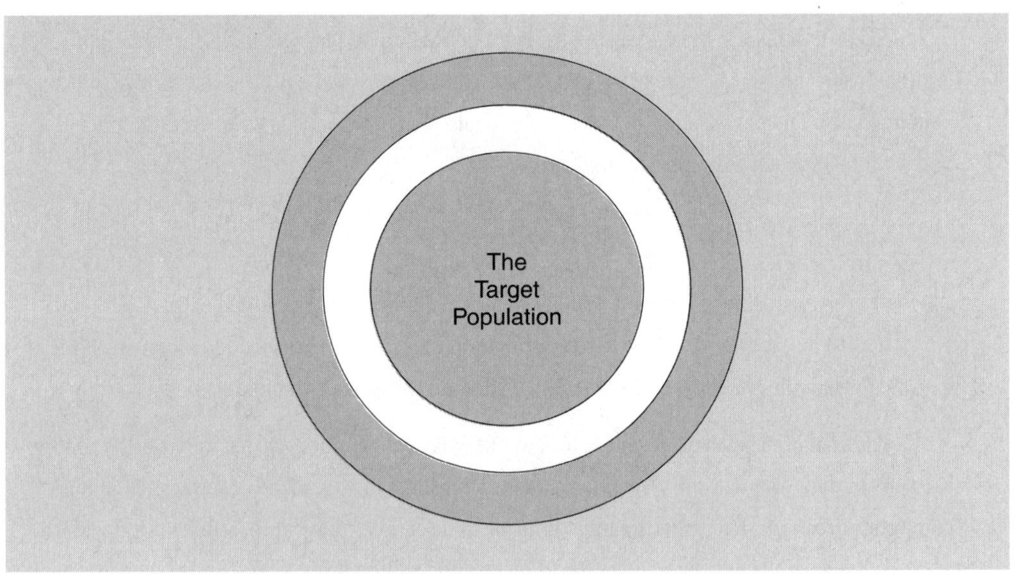

An Example of Targeting Learner Populations

Let us imagine that in the course of performing the needs assessment for your organization, working your way through the entire enterprise, department by department, you reach Recruiting. The manager of the Recruiting Department is delighted to have your help. She and her recruiters have a good track record in terms of timeliness and cost control, but she is concerned that her people are getting burned out and growing a bit brusque and abrasive with their customers, the hiring managers. You remind her that you do not want to sell anybody a false bill of goods. You can help only with problems for which training is a solution and burnout would, on the face of it, seem not to be a problem that training can solve. On the other hand, gaps in customer service skills usually are. So the two of you agree you will undertake a full-scale needs assessment to identify all the things the people in her department need to learn. (You recommend she get in touch with her HR Manager to discuss the burnout issue and develop some possible countermeasures. You also offer to help if you can be of service.)

The Recruiting Department has a membership of 23: sixteen recruiters, in teams of four, each with a senior recruiter serving as team leader; four AA's (Administrative Assistants), one in support of each recruiting team; the manager and her secretary; and a front-desk receptionist, who manages the waiting room and is also in charge of the department's resume bank and its high-volume copier. You make each component of the department the target of needs assessment in turn (See Figure 2-3).

Figure 2-3
The Recruiting Department: Taking Turns in the Bull's-Eye

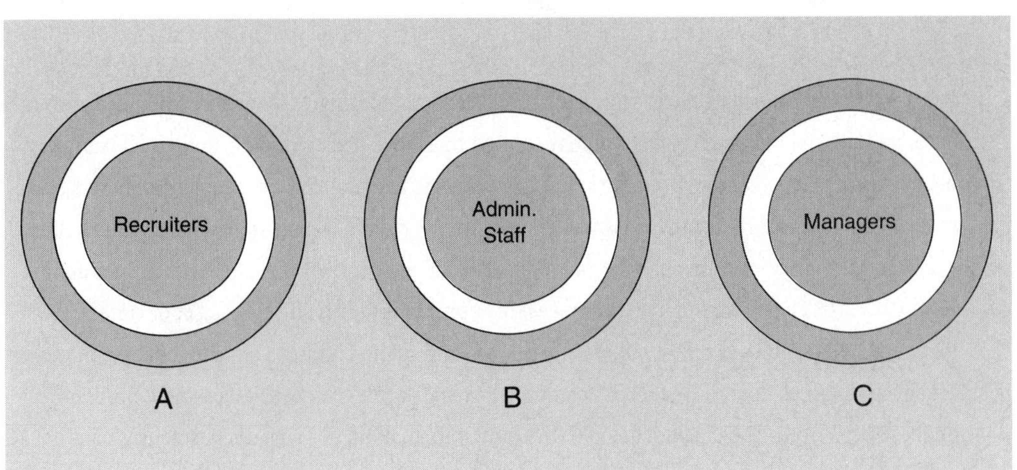

You begin the needs assessment discussions with the 16 recruiters (See Figure 2-3, A). You lead them through the Needs Assessment Template you have developed, covering the range of topics appropriate for your organization (Refer to Figure 2-1 as a sample). You hold these discussions in several different ways, fitting yourself into each recruiter's hectic schedule. You use phone interviews to accommodate several recruiters who are traveling. You also do several written questionnaires, a couple of personal interviews, and a focus group for six recruiters over a brown-bag lunch. In all these cases, you talk the recruiters through the topics on your Needs Assessment Template, getting their ideas about what they need to learn about each topic appropriate for them.

Next, you invite the administrative staff—manager's secretary and the four AA's—to a group discussion one afternoon (See Figure 2-3, B). Your thinking—and the manager concurs—is that these five make up a cohesive cluster of employees concerned with administrative support within the entire department. The discussion of their learning needs focuses heavily on the top half of your template's topic list. Business trends and strategic issues frankly do not seem to have much interest for or bearing on them. They are, however, keen to discuss some of the technical trends in administrative work, especially new desktop technology, the new computer system that the Computer Services Department is rumored to be implementing soon.

Finally, in a face-to-face interview, you put the manager herself into the needs assessment bull's-eye (See Figure 2-3, C). Your discussion with her ranges across the entire department, indeed across the organization as a whole. She focuses sometimes on her own need for learning and sometimes on things she wants to make sure her staff masters. She covers most of the items on your template's list, though you have to remind her of the potential impact of the new computer system being introduced into the organization.

Rings around the Bull's-Eye

With regard to all three of your Recruiting Department targets—the recruiters, the administrative staff, the manager—once you have gotten their own direct input as to their learning needs, the next step is to seek similar input from others. These others are people who have a stake in how and how well recruiting is done. They are the Recruiting Department's stakeholders, its customers. They include anyone who can offer a useful perspective on what the target population needs to learn. The picture of a target makes this point graphically: It shows a set of concentric rings around the bull's-eye itself. These rings surrounding the bull's-eye represent people in the organization other than the target population. They are people the needs assessment process ought to hear from. They include people who have information, perhaps unconsciously, concerning the learning needs of the population in the bull's-eye.

Figure 2-3 shows the three target populations from our Recruiting Department example, each one in the bull's-eye in its turn. The idea now is to expand the data gathering. We place into the rings around each bull's-eye those groups of people in the organization who have something useful to say about the learning needs of the target population. Who fills up these concentric rings will, of course, vary in real life from situation to situation. Figure 2-4 shows the result of filling in the rings for our imaginary Recruiting Department. An explanation of the rings follows the figure.

FIGURE 2-4
RINGS AROUND THE BULL'S-EYE

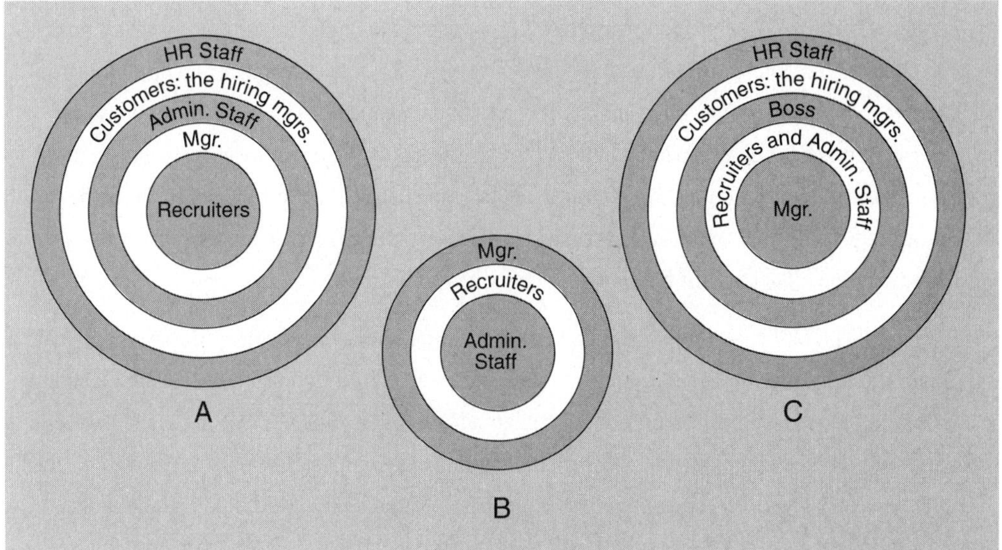

The concentric rings around the target populations are the following:

- With the recruiters in the bull's-eye (See Figure 2-4, A), the target contains four concentric rings representing four sets of people who have good input concerning the recruiters' learning needs: their department manager (the target population's boss is *always* one of the concentric rings), the administrative support staff, the recruiters' customers (the hiring managers—the target's customers are also always included wherever possible), and lastly the Human Resource professionals who provide HR services to the Recruiting Department.
- When the administrative staff is placed in the bull's-eye (See Figure 2-4, B), there are two concentric rings: the recruiters whom the AA's support and the department manager. (The recruiters are part customer and part immediate supervisor to the administrative staff.)
- With the manager in the bull's-eye (See Figure 2-4, C), there are again four concentric rings in the target: the manager's staff, both recruiters and AA's; the manager's own boss; the Recruiting Department's customers (the hiring managers); and the department's HR support professionals.

The concentric rings in the Needs Assessment Target can be any group of people with insight into the learning needs of the population in the bull's-eye. External customers and suppliers are also interesting sources of data about the target population's learning needs, and are increasingly part of needs assessment efforts. This is especially powerful for employees with jobs in sales, customer inquiry, field service, and the like. The point is to search out a picture of the target's learning needs from several sources. You want to be certain to get more than just their own self-portrait. And talking to those surrounding the target provides exactly that: Each ring around the bull's-eye will provide a different perspective on the target's learning requirements. Care must be exercised when involving a supervisor's subordinates in needs assessment, to make sure the exercise does not simply turn into a gripe session or something worse. The basic process remains: taking interested parties through your Needs Assessment Template and discussing the issues and questions the template raises concerning the population in the bull's-eye. This provides a rich, multi-dimensioned picture of what that target population needs to learn. Involving these *stakeholders* in the identification of the target's learning needs is powerfully beneficial to the target itself and to the organization as a whole. It is also a fundamental premise of Action Research, the model for this book's approach to the training cycle.

The picture of learning needs that emerges from this learner-centered process is one that can be presented to the organization's management at any level appropriate, validated with them, and then used to plan training and development for the target audience in a comprehensive way. Training decisions are thus made with an informed eye not only for *whom* but also on *what*, and the necessary priorities concerning both. Note that needs assessment information about one target population—the Recruiting Department in our example—can be pooled with the same kind of data concerning other populations. The result can be a mosaic of learning needed by larger and larger segments of the organization, all the way up to the entire enterprise. Thus, the approach described here has the major advantage of providing all levels of management with the information to make business-driven decisions concerning what the members of the organization need to learn and when they need to learn it. This, of course, is precisely what needs assessment is all about.

Gathering Needs Assessment Data

Finally, how do all the discussions mentioned above take place? The term *discussion* is used here in the broadest possible sense. Trainers in an organization need not always talk one-on-one with every member of the target population and then with all those in the concentric rings around it. Such an idea is unrealistic. One-on-one interviews are certainly a fruitful device for gathering data, but not the only one. The discussions of the issues and questions raised by the

Needs Assessment Template can also be done by questionnaire (paper, fax, E-mail, or Intranet-based), by telephone survey, by group interview, or by discussion or focus groups. Further data can be drawn from employee sources such as exit interviews, climate surveys, and end-of-course evaluations. Literature searches and the opinions of acknowledged experts can also play a part. The ways to collect information concerning learning needs can, in short, be as varied and efficient as the demands of time allow and the creativity of the trainer makes possible. See Chapter 4 for a discussion of choosing appropriate data-gathering methods and creating and using data collection instruments.

In the case of a training department with multiple members, the training manager often assigns key populations within the organization to specific training professionals. The purpose of such an assignment is to identify that population's learning needs on an ongoing basis, discussing learning needs with its members in a continuing, systematic way, using the structured guidance of a Needs Assessment Template and discussing learning needs as elaborated earlier. This models the way in which a sales manager assigns sales representatives to specific customers within the overall sales territory. The approach gives the training professional a rich and satisfying job. It also puts a useful emphasis on the point that gathering and pooling customer data is actually the engine that drives all the training department's activity. The customer is truly king. The approach, finally, serves notice that training needs assessment is not an event but an activity, an ongoing process used to identify learning needs over the inevitable shifts and changes of time and circumstance.

It is sometimes the case, of course, that a training department within an organization is asked not to take a broad-brush look at learning needs but rather at the needs that arise from a specific topic: a new product the organization plans to market, a new project a particular group is going to take on, a new set of tools they are going to be required to use, or perhaps a particular problem that has surfaced within the organization. Given such a fixed charter, the conceptual point remains the same. Needs assessment remains the identification of what the defined group needs to learn about a given. As before, the target group should be led through discussions of the issues and questions appropriate to the stipulated topic (a more narrowly focused Needs Assessment Template). Once again, the learning needs emerge from these discussions. And once again, the group's self-portrait of learning needs should be validated and expanded by similar discussions with other interested parties within the organization.

SUMMARY

eeds assessment is the first step in the training cycle, first conceptually if not always chronologically. This chapter began by providing a definition of needs assessment: identifying what the members of an organization need to learn in order for the enterprise to achieve its goals. The organization's goals, of course, include having individual employees do their jobs and grow in their careers. The process provides for attention to trends and directions for the future that are important to the organization and to the people within it.

One way to conceptualize the needs assessment process is through a systems approach. Using a systems approach, the analyst considers three distinct, yet interrelated variables in determining learning needs: the individual (person), the task, and the organization. While each of these variables is investigated separately, a systems orientation helps make the relationship among them clear—a change in one variable inevitably affects the other two variables.

The authors of this text suggest a learner-centered approach to needs assessment. To this end, we suggest that the process begin with identifying the right questions to ask of the right persons. The Needs Assessment Template was offered to guide this thinking. The user of the template identifies categories of topics that impact the learning needs of individuals and determines who in the organization has an interest in the topic or needs to learn about it. Then, the task is to target learners, putting them in the middle of the needs assessment bull's-eye as the primary target. Then, the task is to identify who else has input on these individuals' learning needs and then put them in the bull's-eye's concentric circles, questioning them on issues brought out through the Needs Assessment Template.

Ideally, needs assessment is an ongoing activity rather than an event, and the key to its successful accomplishment is to ask the right questions of those who can offer useful judgements concerning learning needed. The phrase, "ask the right questions," must be very broadly understood to include not only literally asking questions face to face, but also to explore issues by means of such tools as focus groups and surveys. The most important point of all is that if needs assessment is properly done, it will establish a solid foundation for all the other steps in the training cycle. Its absence puts the entire cycle (and the training department) at great risk.

THINK IT THROUGH

1. Training needs assessment is much more a matter of asking the right questions than of getting the right answers. Why is this so? What does it mean?
2. Why is it important for training needs assessment to be an ongoing process rather than an annual event? What are the implications of this?
3. One of the key outcomes of training needs assessment is a sense of the priorities regarding what must be learned and by whom.
   a. What are some of the factors likely to be important in determining priorities as to *what* should be learned by members of an organization?
   b. How about *who* should do the learning? What issues or criteria might set the priorities here?
   c. In either case, who should set the priorities with regard to learning?
4. What are some of the ways to gather needs assessment data? Have you had any experience with any of them? Which do you think would be particularly effective? Why?
5. Consider the distribution of a list of courses offered (or a catalog) and asking people to register for programs—why is this not really a needs assessment? What need does this process speak to? Whose needs are met by the process?
6. An academic institution does not undertake needs assessment as described here. Why not? What are the differences between schools and training departments within their respective organizations?

IDEAS IN ACTION

1. Using the key term "training needs analysis," search the Web for at least three consulting organizations that provide needs analysis services. Compare the information offered on each site as to the organization's general philosophy on assessment, as well as documentation of their past successes. Do any sites include links to other sources of useful information on this topic?
2. Interview a working trainer and find out how needs assessment is conducted in his or her organization.
3. Do a search of management and business literature (such as *Forbes, Fortune, Harvard Business Review, the Wall Street Journal, Journal of the AMA)* to see what business managers want from training or what they find lacking in it. Then do a search of training literature (such as *Training and Development, Training, HRM Magazine*) on the same issues. Compare the two findings. What do the findings suggest concerning needs assessment?

4. Search business literature for articles on companies that increase their training budgets in difficult economic circumstances. What do the articles tell you? What do they tell you specifically about needs assessment?
5. Prepare a one-minute "elevator speech," explaining to a potential training client why it is absolutely imperative to do a needs assessment before any training is designed or implemented.
6. Scenario Analysis:

   You have just been hired as director of training for a small cosmetics firm. Since reorganization took place in the late 1990s, the number of employees has dropped by half, and 70 percent of the remaining sales staff, who sell cosmetics at high-end department stores, have never had formal sales training. Moreover, nearly half of projected sales are expected to be made through the organization's new e-commerce division. Your department is small, consisting of you and a junior-level staffer. You have been charged with creating a new training thrust for the sales organization, both for the existing sales staff and for those working in the e-commerce division.

   Activity: With this information as a basis, create the topics that would appear in the Needs Assessment Template. Then, targeting first the department store sales staff and then the e-commerce sales staff, create the series of bull's-eyes that would depict your overall strategy for whom to include in the needs assessment.

ADDITIONAL RESOURCES

RECOMMENDED READINGS

Gupta, Kavita. *A Practical Guide to Needs Assessment.* San Francisco: Jossey-Bass, 1998, 224 pp.

This how-to handbook provides guidelines for implementing training needs assessment. Includes a 3.5" disk that includes forms, worksheets, and a glossary.

McClelland, Sam. "A Systems Approach to Needs Assessment." *Training and Development,* August 1992, pp. 51-53.

McClelland provides a solid focus on needs assessment from a systems-thinking perspective. This is short, punchy reading.

Zemke, Ron. "How To Do a Needs Assessment When You Think You Don't Have Time." *Training,* 35(3), 1998, pp. 38-44.

Zemke offers perspectives on ways to assess learning needs when time and resources are at a premium. One approach offered is to use already existing data—data that were gathered for a different purpose but may relate to the performance problem identified.

Zemke, Ron, and Thomas Kramlinger. *Figuring Things Out.* Reading, MA: Addison-Wesley, 1982 (1986 ed.).

In sharp, satiric, even funny language, this book makes the case for insisting (a) that needs assessment is an essential step in the training cycle, its absence a show-stopper, and (b) on training as a solution *only* for gaps in knowledge or skill, *only* for situations where learning can be the fix. Vintage Ron Zemke (a professional secret: Anything Zemke writes should be on the trainer's "must read" list.)

WEB SITES

http://www.camalott.com/~living/needs.htm

This site provides a listing of sources for ideas in developing assessment plans.

http://www.ispi.org

This site is the homepage of the International Society for Performance Improvement. The site includes links to the society's publications and services, including its two publications, *Performance Improvement Journal* and *Performance Improvement Quarterly.*

CHAPTER

Evaluating Organizational Training

- Discuss varying views of the need to evaluate training programs.
- Explain perspectives on evaluation's role in the training cycle.
- Identify domains of training criteria.
- Access sources of support and expertise for training evaluation.
- Describe a variety of evaluation strategies and the trade-offs among them.
- Develop and apply guidelines for using evaluation data.

EVALUATION AS A BASIS FOR SOUND DECISIONS

Late every year, *Training Magazine* publishes its annual "Industry Report." The report for 1999 appeared in the October issue[1] and was, as usual, packed with a wealth of information—numbers, charts, graphs, statistics, anecdotes. At the core of all that information is a rather startling number: US businesses spent *$62.5 billion* on training in 1999. And that total, the report hastens to add, is based strictly on formal training and on data from companies with 100 or more employees. It does not include all the informal on-the-job training (OJT) that goes on all over the business world, nor does it include the money spent by the thousands and thousands of businesses that don't meet that "over 100" threshold—all the mom-and-pop businesses, all the virtual companies, all the dot.coms and e-businesses popping up and deliberately staying small.

That number alone, apart from any other consideration, makes the evaluation of training a topic that deserves careful, disciplined attention. As one trainer put it many years ago, the rationale for spending time and money on the evaluation of training is simple: It may be more expensive not to evaluate it![2]

To *evaluate* means to assess or to judge. In this chapter, *evaluation* is defined as a systematic process to assess the effectiveness and efficiency of training efforts. Evaluation means putting to use data that describe training outcomes or results. Its goal is not to label a training effort as good or bad. Its goal is to provide feedback useful for a variety of business-related objectives. Organizations need to know if they are doing the right things right. Evaluation data provide evidence that can be used to correct costly errors or to support an exemplary process. Evaluation data allow an organization to learn from its experiences.

These data help decision-makers judge how well training solutions addressed the identified gaps in knowledge, skills, and attitudes, which were derived from individual, departmental, and organizational needs and goals. Evaluation data are used to determine if training affected success on the job, if one training program was more effective than another, and even if the organizational culture supports new ways of doing work. In short, evaluation data tell you what you need to know about your training program or activity.

Thus, the evaluation process includes much more than determining if trainees learned particular skills from a specific training program or if a particular instructor was well-prepared for a class. While these are important considerations, of course, a wide range of evaluation data are needed by various training stakeholders as they make decisions related to all stages of the training cycle.

Despite the known value of evaluation, training professionals can easily rationalize why evaluation cannot be done:

Time. *"We're on a schedule here. Who has time to do evaluations? We no more finish one project than we're starting another."*

Expense. *"We're on a budget here, and working with a limited staff. Where will the additional people and physical resources come from if we are to evaluate everything we do?"*

Expertise. *"We're instructors, not psychologists. I'm really not trained in evaluation. Evaluation is the purview of Ph.D.s in psychology, not me."*

History. *"We've always been successful with our training programs. Everyone tells us they enjoy the courses and learn from the instructors and materials we develop. There are no problems. That's evaluation enough!"*

W. Edwards Deming captured the essence of why evaluation is so important in training through the acronym PDCA: *Plan*, *Do*, *Check*, *Act*. Training *plans* abound. Trainers love to *do*, or train. However, at each step of the training cycle, it is important to *check*, to make sure the planned process is occurring correctly and the right kind of output is produced for the next phase of the cycle. No plan is perfect; error and variability inevitably occurs, requiring the need to *act* to correct it. Human nature is indeed human, and things human invariably need to be monitored for midcourse corrections. (There are those who say that the *A* in PDCA really stands for "Adjust," an idea that is certainly the fruit of experience.) The ultimate "why" for evaluation is that it brings the training department and its parent organization back to the reason for the department's very existence: Did training, in fact, help the right people learn what the organization needs them to learn in order to achieve its goals?

So there are many answers to the "why evaluate" question. A key objective of this chapter is to offer perspectives on the "when," "what," "who," "where," and "how" of evaluation, while incorporating the "why." First, the role of evaluation is discussed in terms of the training cycle. Then we move to identifying relevant, valid *criteria*. Criteria are measures of success. Criteria must be identified before any training effort is planned and delivered. After all, if you do not determine what is important—what constitutes success—before training efforts are implemented, how can you objectively determine if your efforts were successful? Relevant criteria are those that are important to someone who needs information on which to base decisions. We conclude with guidelines for ensuring that the training evaluation process is done in the right way for the right reasons. The next chapter, "Research Techniques: Methods for Training Needs Assessment and Evaluation," offers perspectives on *doing* an effective evaluation.

Evaluation's Role in the Training Cycle

Chapter 2, "Training Needs Assessment," focused on identifying the knowledge, skills, and abilities (KSAs)[3] needed for a targeted person, task, job, or career. In the training cycle (See Figure 1-8), the evaluation stage is adjacent to, and tightly linked with, the needs assessment stage. Evaluation strategies are planned once KSAs have been identified. Throughout the training cycle, evaluation data provide feedback as to the efficiency or effectiveness of a program's design, its supporting materials, and its delivery. In addition, because the training cycle is a cycle, evaluation results often serve as input to needs assessment.

In other words, evaluation is not merely an event that takes place once a training program has been run. It is, rather, a process that occurs in each phase of the training cycle:

- Evaluation in the *assessment* stage asks: Were the right objectives developed? Were organizational goals addressed? Were the right individuals identified? Was the right content identified?
- Evaluation in the *design* stage asks: Were quality learning materials and technologies developed? Were they consistent with adult learning principles? Were training programs designed to support the learning needs of the targeted group?

- Evaluation in the *implementation* stage asks: Was quality instruction offered at the right time and in the right priority order? Did trainees learn what the program was designed to deliver? Did they perceive that the training was worthwhile? Were they able to use what they learned back on their job? Were organizational goals addressed in a timely and effective manner?
- Evaluation of the *training cycle* itself asks: Are we doing enough training? Are we spending enough resources (or too much) on training? Is our training reaching the right populations? Is it moving the business agenda in the right direction? Is it contributing to the achievement of business strategies? Do our clients in the organization view training as accessible and worthwhile?

With regard to when evaluation takes place, keep in mind that evaluative data captured after training has been completed should be fed back into the needs assessment phase, bringing the training cycle full circle. It may well be that evaluation uncovers learning needs not fully addressed by the training just completed, or not addressed at all. Evaluation may offer fruitful avenues to explore for future needs assessments, and it is important to capture and use this information in a timely manner.

Criterion Development

Criteria are measures of success, or yardsticks, that can be used to evaluate outcomes. In buying a car, for example, the savvy consumer first identifies what he or she needs from a car. Let's say that you live in Alaska, with lots of snow and vast distances between major cities. In your needs analysis, you determine that your car must get good gas mileage and must have good traction in snow and ice. You have managed to save $20,000, and you really feel you cannot go into debt. Which of these cars do you buy?

- A Lincoln Towncar. Equipped with: power steering, power seats, a computer with a map facility, cassette/compact disk player, AM/FM stereo radio, dual airbags, and dual car seats for children in the back seat. Estimated MPG: 17 town, 21 road. $40,000.
- A Honda CRV. Equipped with: power steering, cassette player, AM/FM stereo radio, dual airbags, four-wheel drive, rack and pinion steering. Estimated MPG: 30 town, 37 road. $19,000.
- A Jeep Cherokee. Equipped with: four-wheel drive, cassette player, AM/FM radio, driver side airbag. Estimated MPG: 20 town; 27 road. $25,000.

Given the data available here, the obvious choice is the Honda. The Lincoln has many wonderful features and outstanding luxury. The Jeep is much closer to your identified criteria, but it costs more than you want to pay, and its MPG is much lower than the Honda. Neither the Lincoln nor the Jeep meets your established criteria. If you opt for one of these vehicles, you will have a car. However, you will not have the right car for you, and you'll realize this when making car payments, traversing difficult terrain, or buying gasoline.

Like the consumer buying a car, the training professional makes many choices in determining what to evaluate. The car-buying analogy illustrates why adherence to preplanned criteria is important. If you opt for the Lincoln, that means you changed your mind as to what your criteria are after the fact and your original needs assessment data are useless. Criteria developed early in the training cycle serve to keep the training professional on track, ensuring that what is evaluated matches intended outcomes.

Let us assume that outcomes from your needs assessment suggest that supervisors need to manage their time better. To address this issue, your training program design might include a combination of workshops, audio cassettes, printed materials, and a lecture series. If you have determined that the sole evaluation measure for this training effort is for supervisors to demonstrate improved time management skills, yet you evaluate the effectiveness of the training program by asking the trainees how much they enjoyed the time management lectures or the materials used, you have gathered interesting, but useless data. You really do not know if the training program met your original criterion. To evaluate training properly, the training professional needs to work from appropriate criteria that ensure that the right people are trained in the right way for the right things. Without these yardsticks to determine what is "right," training results cannot be accurately measured.

Relevant criteria are fundamentally derived from the knowledge, skills, and abilities (KSAs) identified in the needs assessment stage and documented there. Robinson and Robinson put it simply: "Write down the purposes of an assessment before you begin collecting information. Know why you are collecting the information and what decisions you plan to make from it."[4]

Furthermore, to be of value, data must be used. Another way to conceptualize what should be evaluated is to identify *who* in an organization is interested in knowing if or how well training outcomes met the identified criteria. Interested stakeholders include the training department managers, the training professionals, the trainees themselves, the line managers, and executives who make decisions about organizational goals and support/approve the training budget. Once your evaluation audience has been identified, the next step is to get its commitment to the criteria. Such up-front work ensures that your audience not only understands the goals of your training effort, but also buys into those goals.

The following discussion links the needs assessment to the development of training criteria. Criteria measures are grouped into clusters, called domains, and each domain includes brief descriptions of appropriate evaluation strategies, as well as how these evaluation data are used by decision-makers involved.

DOMAINS OF EVALUATION CRITERIA

D*omains* are categories of similar ideas or thoughts. Domains are also precisely defined content areas. To categorize what needs to be evaluated in training, Kirkpatrick identified four classic domains of evaluation: reaction, learning, job behavior, and organizational results.[5] With the notion of a learning organization in mind, we add a fifth dimension—the training process itself (See Figure 3-1).

FIGURE 3-1
FIVE DOMAINS OF TRAINING PROGRAM EVALUATION CRITERIA

1. Reaction
2. Learning
3. Job Behavior
4. Organizational Results
5. Training Process

THE REACTION DOMAIN

Reaction refers to the trainee's perception of the worth of a training activity. Trainees themselves are in a unique position to determine if their training experiences were worthwhile. This means much more than determining if training was an enjoyable experience. Reaction should also attempt to obtain learners' views as to the viability of the content, the learning materials used, the scheduling of the course, the instructor's performance, and even their own performance.

Program participants might, at first glance, seem to be only the recipients of training attention and evaluation efforts rather than key stakeholders. This is far too limited a perspective. Adult learners should be viewed as resources to the training process as well as its targets. Potential training participants, given the right information, can self-screen themselves for programs—deciding what they need or do not need—thus assisting in the evaluative process of making sure the right people get trained. They can also provide reviews of both training design and delivery *if* they are asked the right types of questions about training in which they have taken part. Data from reaction sheets can also serve as a training department marketing tool, as the ultimate consumers describe and rate their training experiences.

One way to judge classroom performance of instructors is to observe them, using a detailed observation guide, such as the one offered in Figure 3-2. An observation guide can ensure that raters focus in on established criteria. A trained observer can then document a trainer's performance. Recommendations when conducting observations are to use more than one rater and observe as many times as possible.

FIGURE 3-2
INSTRUCTOR OBSERVATION GUIDE

Instructor Observation Guide

Instructor ______________________ Date ____________
Course ______________________ Time ____________
Rater ______________________

Item	Comments
1. Preparation	
2. Knowledge of Subject	
3. Participant Involvement	
4. Use of Audiovisual Aids	
5. Correlation with Leader's Guide	
6. Transitions between Topics	
7. Naturalness or Ease with the Class	
8. Additional Comments	

The end-of-program participant questionnaire is far and away the most common method used to evaluate training programs. Such questionnaires are often dismissed as "happiness sheets" or "smile sheets," and they certainly can be constructed to be self-serving on the part of the instructor or the training department. On the other hand, these questionnaires can be designed to engage participants in determining whether the up-front learning objectives were well and fully addressed and whether these objectives were, in fact, achieved. They can, in short, enlist adult learners in the assessment of their own learning experience: Was it an experience that (a) lived up to its advance billing, and (b) helped or hindered participant learning?

Perhaps the most important thing to remember about end-of-program evaluations is this: whether or not reaction data are collected, trainees *will* evaluate their training experiences. The training department should exploit the inevitable: make sure the right evaluation questions get asked, collect the answers, and put them to use.

Figure 3-3 is an example of a tailored program reaction questionnaire. Often it is not possible to tailor an evaluation form for each training activity; generic, not program-specific, evaluation forms are often used.

FIGURE 3-3
PROGRAM REACTION QUESTIONNAIRE

Program ______________________________ Date ________________

Name (Optional) ________________________ Sector/Function ________________

1. Please rate each of the following items to indicate your reaction to the session. If ranking is less than average, please comment on the back of the form.

Item	Poor	Adequate	Average	Good	Excellent
Objective 1 (list)					
Objective 2 (list)					
Objective 3 (list)					
Applicability to your job, responsibilities, and needs					
Enough examples and chances to practice so you can apply your new skills back at work					
Opportunity for discussion with other participants					
Length of the program relative to its objectives					

2. Which part of the program was of most value to you? Why?

____

____

____

(Continued)

3. Which part of the program was of least value to you? Why?

____

____

____

4a. Please use the following scale to comment on each instructor's ability to lead the program where:

1 = Needs improvement 2 = Adequate 3 = Good 4 = Excellent

Item	Instructor 1 (name)	Instructor 2 (name)
A. Organization/preparation of subject matter	1 2 3 4	1 2 3 4
B. Presentation of subject matter	1 2 3 4	1 2 3 4
C. Clarity of instructions	1 2 3 4	1 2 3 4
D. Ability to control time	1 2 3 4	1 2 3 4
E. Ability to link content to your business	1 2 3 4	1 2 3 4
F. Ability to stimulate productive discussions	1 2 3 4	1 2 3 4
G. Ability to create a productive learning environment	1 2 3 4	1 2 3 4

4b. Please comment on the instructors' abilities to lead the program.

____

____

____

5. How would you rate your overall reaction to the program? 1 2 3 4
6. How would you rate your level of skill or knowledge
   a. before the program? 1 2 3 4
   b. after the program? 1 2 3 4
7. Other comments:

____

____

____

The Learning Domain

The second of Kirkpatrick's domains, *learning,* refers to criteria that determine whether or not learning took place. Was the training program an effective tool? Did trainees actually acquire the KSAs that the program was designed to deliver? The question here is one of *program efficiency:* Did the training experience (whatever its shape) deliver what it was supposed to? Did trainees learn what was intended for them to learn? Did their learning take place *because of* the training experiences, or *despite* them?

Participant reactions, as discussed earlier, are one measure of learning. Tests are another classic way to find out if learning has occurred. Paper-and-pencil exams, familiar from school days, are but one form of test. Tests such as these are arguably less suitable for adult learners in an organizational setting than in academic settings, and—whatever the setting—often measure test-taking skills rather than content mastery. However, tests do provide quantifiable data that may indicate changes over a given period of time. Figure 3-4 is an example of a group test on banking principles. Several of the questions refer to items in the course content.

FIGURE 3-4
COURSE EXAM

Team ______________________________ Score _________

Principles of Banking Course Exam

Exam Philosophy

A good exam helps you realize just how much you've learned and, if it is really good, will add to your knowledge by giving you the opportunity to put new concepts to work on relevant problems. Good exams concentrate on your reasoning abilities. They provide an opportunity for you to structure the problem and support your answer accordingly. Good exams do not have a single, unique answer, but stress the complexity involved in addressing realistic problems. Bad exams, in our view, just ask you to repeat specific facts and focus on tripping you up over relatively minor details. We've done our best to make this a "good exam." You'll do your best on it by keeping in mind that we're trying to evaluate your managerial reasoning skills. *Please be sure to make your reasoning process part of the answer to each question.*

In the managerial world, very few problems are solved by individuals working alone. Indeed, the ability to arrive at a team solution is one of the keys to success in a management career. In keeping with this, there is just one exam for the entire team and all team members will receive the same grade.

Weights for each question are indicated to help the team allocate its resources efficiently. The maximum score is 100 points. You may wish to divide up the responsibility for different questions among team members. This is an open book, as well as an open mind, exercise. Please use the space provided to write your answer.

Please write clearly and concisely. Remember, the course instructor is an experienced teacher and can readily differentiate between material relevant to the question and unrelated "fill."

Questions

1. Using the Executive Information Report* and the material in your handbook, currently what appears to be your:
   a. two greatest competitive advantages?
      1.(5)

      2.(5)

(Continued)

b. two worst competitive disadvantages?
   1.(5)

   2.(5)

2. Using the End of Simulation Analysis,* analyze how well structured your balance sheet is for the future economic outlook.

   a.(10) Briefly outline your economic forecast for the next two years.

   b.(10) List advantages of your current balance sheet structure.

   c.(10) Identify any changes you would make and why you would make these changes.

3. What role on your team exercised the most leadership and by what means did the person(s) in this role lead the team's behavior?

   a.(5) Role:

   b.(5) Leadership Style*:

   c.(5) How effective was your overall team behavior?

   d.(10) Knowing what you now know about the bank simulation and the composition of your team, what would you recommend to a similar team beginning the simulation to improve their overall performance?

4. Assume that you're now three years in the future, and the bank you've examined is being considered by your current bank as a possible acquisition. Assume that the acquisition would be structured as a tender offer at 120% of the bank's current stock price.
   a.(5) Would you recommend proceeding with the tender offer?

   b.(20) Cite reasons to support your recommendation.

*Note: This term refers to course content

Having people demonstrate acquired skills via role-play or actually doing what the training is teaching them to do—e.g., give a speech or a performance appraisal, keyboard a document at required speed and error rate, or write a program to spec in VisualBasic—is another sort of test. This approach has the advantage of simulating the use of the learning on the job. The simulation also avoids the baggage associated with paper tests (memories of bad experiences with school exams, cultural bias, and the like).

The Job Behavior Domain

The third of Kirkpatrick's domains, *job behavior*, refers to the degree to which the KSAs learned were transferred back to the job. Were trainees able to apply their learning outcomes in the workplace? Were those trained able to take the knowledge, skills, and abilities they learned in the training program back to their jobs and actually use them there?

Line managers play an invaluable role here. They, after all, make–or should make—the go/no-go decisions about training. They are ultimately the ones who say what subjects the organization needs its people to learn, what the timing of that learning should be, what training participants should be included, and in what priority order both the people and the topics are to be ranked. Note that all of these are issues on the evaluative side of planning training. While the training professional should take the lead in making sure all these issues are addressed, it is the organization's management that must ultimately make the decisions.

Line managers play yet another role in evaluation, at the other end of the training process. They provide uniquely valuable insights as to whether or not the completed training has had an impact on the work of the people they sent to training in the first place.

One of many ways to evaluate the impact of training on the job is to survey participants (and their managers) once the program is over and people have had sufficient time to put acquired skills and knowledge to use in their work. This usually takes from one to three months. Such survey data are inevitably anecdotal in flavor, but they can provide useful input to the evaluation of both the training design and the delivery of instruction. These data also send the useful message that the training department is paying attention to the impact of its programs and whether the organization is getting what it is paying for. Figure 3-5 is an example of a survey designed to solicit program evaluation from the trainees' manager based on job behavior. This survey could easily be adapted to target employees rather than their managers.

If you do survey trainees' managers, it is important to manage this process carefully. You want to make sure that a manager who has sent several people to training is not inundated with survey forms. You will also want to let trainees know about the management survey so they do not feel blindsided by the process.

FIGURE 3-5
SURVEY OF TRAINING'S IMPACT ON JOB BEHAVIOR

Evaluation Form: Writing Skills Workshop

Note: The information you offer on this form will allow us to determine (1) that workshop content matched your employees' needs; (2) that your employees have been able to apply what they learned back to their jobs; and (3) a plan for the future.

Name:

Functional Title:

Mailing Address:

Telephone: Fax: E-mail:

List of Employees Who Attended the Workshop

Name Telephone

(provided by the training department)

1. As a result of participating in the writing skills workshop, have you noted any changes in any of your employees' work? Please cite specific examples.

____
____
____

2. Are there additional aspects of business writing that should have been included in the workshop, but were not? Please be as specific as possible.

____
____
____

3. Are there any additional data that would help us assist you in working with your employees (e.g., changes in your job, major reorganization; change in business strategy; change in direct reports)?

____
____
____

4. Additional Comments:

____
____
____
____

The Organizational Results Domain

Kirkpatrick's *organizational results* domain refers to determining if training efforts paralleled either the short- or long-term goals of the organization. Has the training helped employees do their work or do it better, manage/grow their careers, understand the company's culture and business goals, and the like? Has the training helped position the company in its market? Has it helped the company achieve its strategic objectives? In short, has the training done whatever the organization funded the training to accomplish?

Top management typically is interested in having data that indicate that training objectives were linked to organizational objectives. They are not usually as interested in the outcomes of a particular training program as they are in the bigger picture that depicts the training department as a viable, contributing player in corporate strategies.

Organizational results—the ultimate reason for having training in the first place—are very difficult to measure, chiefly because they result from the intermix of a wide variety of variables. For example, if sales go up after training has occurred, this increase could be due to new product offerings, a seasonal fluctuation, or simply more advertising in the media. While training *may have* had an impact, it is very difficult to attribute the increases to the training effort.

On the other hand, it is possible to capture improvement data from the workplace that can legitimately be claimed as the result of training. Examples here might be a sustained drop in processing errors or increased production for an individual or a group of workers. The reality is that such improvements in the workplace cannot easily be tracked, much less can they be attributed solely to training. Many other factors usually play a part in workplace results. Nonetheless, if such data can be captured and tracked, so much the better. Note that if this approach to evaluation is to be pursued, it is absolutely *essential* that it be *planned* and *agreed to* up front, as part of the training design.

In a later chapter, specifics will be offered as to putting a dollar value on training costs and benefits, but it is important to consider the value of such calculations at this point. Cost/benefit figures allow comparisons between different kinds of training programs, helping the training professional to determine if a structured training program was more appropriate than say, on-the-job training. Even given that a training activity met all its objectives, if the bottom line is that production figures were not affected, or if the trainees are frequently moved from job to job without the opportunity to use the skills they learned in training, the training activity may not have been worth the money invested in it.

The Training Process Domain

Training process criteria extend Kirkpatrick's domain list. They are measures of what occurred during the assessment, development, and implementation of training. They form an assessment or audit of the training department as a whole.

Thus, the trainer will want to evaluate training programs in terms of questions such as the following: Does one kind of activity seem to foster learning more than another? What segment of the program worked best (worst) for this audience? Were any of the design objectives left unmet? Were any objectives given too much time and attention? Were any stakeholders missed in the needs assessment? Were any organizational needs in this topic area omitted?

These questions gather critical information about the training department's programs. After all, if a training program does not focus its participants on the right learning objectives, and help them learn these objectives faster, easier, cheaper, and more efficiently than otherwise, then why bother with a training program at all?

Evaluating *programs*, however, is not enough. The astute training manager will also evaluate the effectiveness of his/her *department* within the organization. The training department should, from time to time, evaluate whether or not it is:

- paying attention to the right issues
- playing its proper role as a staff resource to the management of its organization
- ensuring that its programs are on target, properly accessible, and viewed as cost-effective and helpful

A workplace survey is a good way to answer these questions. One-on-one interviews are another effective approach. Interviews with trainees, their supervisors, organizational decision-makers, and even training personnel could also be used to provide a rich source of qualitative data to be used to evaluate the training department. Interview data from key individuals who have content matter expertise, knowledge of the trainee group, or instructional design can describe training results. Questions such as the following all lend themselves well to the interview format: Were the right trainees selected? Were the right topics trained for? Was the training program itself designed for the needs of the adult learner?

In addition, one-on-many interviews, or focus groups, can provide qualitative data that can be immediately verified by others in the group. The same type of questions posed earlier can result in rich data when the interviewees have an opportunity to discuss their impressions with each other as well as with the training evaluator.

For the sake of objectivity, the training department should not conduct its own audit. An appropriate sister department within the organization—another training group, the company auditors, the communications/public relations people—can perform a quality audit of the training department's work and reputation. An outside resource such as faculty or students in a college academic program in Human Resource Management or Business Education, a consulting firm, or even a training department in another company could be a source of services. The outcome of such an audit is a healthy, deliberately independent evaluative look at the training department itself, most especially its achievement (or lack thereof) of its own mission of right people learning the right things at the right time, all in terms of organizational need.

Figure 3-6 shows a list of key stakeholders and their uses of evaluation results. It briefly summarizes, by criterion domains, what it is that training evaluation audiences need to know about training efforts, along with examples of evaluation strategies. The methods listed are discussed in detail in the next chapter.

FIGURE 3-6
KEY STAKEHOLDERS AND THEIR USES OF EVALUATION RESULTS

	Stakeholders			
Criterion Domain and Methods	**Training Professionals**	**Training**	**Line Managers**	**Organization Decision-Makers**
Reaction Participant Questionnaires Observations	Ensure programs deliver planned outcomes. Ensure delivery skills of trainers.	Compare their reactions with others in the group.	Interested only if there are problems.	Interested only if there are problems.
Learning Tests Simulations Observations	Establish that course objectives were achieved.	Serve as feedback that personal achievement resulted.	Establish that employees learned new skills, tasks, or abilities.	Establish a connection between organizational goals and training efforts.
Job Behavior Participant Surveys Management Surveys	Confirm that the right KSAs were identified.	Establish that new KSAs are appropriate for the targeted job.	Establish that learning was transferrable back to the job.	Confirm the connection between organizational goals and the transferability of training efforts.
Organization Results Department Audit Interviews Focus Groups	Provide evidence of the value of training efforts to the organization's bottom line.	Establish that the learning effort was valued by superiors.	Basis for deciding whether or not to send other employees for training.	Basis for determining the viability of the training function in the organization.
The Training Process Surveys Audits Focus Groups	Assess and modify needs assessment, design, and delivery stages.	Ensure participation in setting goals and identifying appropriate training solutions.	Ensure participation.	Ensure a connection between organizational goals and training efforts; probably not interested unless problems arose.

GUIDELINES FOR USING EVALUATION DATA

The *contingency approach* to evaluation strategies is "you do what is best under the circumstances." In other words, evaluation strategies are implemented based on the time, money, and people resources available, and often how useful the evaluation data are perceived to be. Ideally, training efforts are evaluated from many angles, with valid, reliable measures, and from many different approaches or strategies. In reality, the training professional plans evaluation strategies that take workplace constraints and opportunities into consideration. Based on the previous discussion, guidelines for planning training evaluation include the following:

- Make evaluation part of the training proposal.
- Ensure that stakeholders agree on criteria and understand their role in the process.
- Perform as many different evaluation strategies as feasible.

Remember that evaluation is feedback. Evaluation data do not have value unless they are used. Back at the proposal stage, you identified needed evaluation data and how you proposed to collect those data. You worked with key stakeholders to determine what business decisions would be based on the data. You decided if data would be quantitative (numbers) or qualitative (words) or a combination of both. Therefore, when it comes to using data, be sure to go back to your initial questions and answer them.

Guidelines for using evaluation data are to analyze as much evaluation data (qualitative as well as quantitative) for decision-makers as possible; provide reports (feedback), sharing credit for results; and hone your evaluation skills. Following is a discussion of each of these points.

Quantitative and Qualitative Data

Quantitative data are numbers; *qualitative data* are words. Data that are analyzed result in information. Evaluation data come from sources including questionnaires, tests, observation guides, interview guides, and organizational records. You make sense of data by analyzing them in a manner that will provide useful information to those who need answers to key evaluation questions. Assessment areas may have included the classroom delivery skills of the instructor, the post-training job behaviors of training participants, end-of-course cognitive learning outcomes, and the like. Making sense of numeric data relies on the use of statistics. Making sense of word data relies on coding schemes and summaries. While quantitative data are often described as the most objective and, therefore, the most useful (test scores and questionnaire data), qualitative data may be equally useful or serve to further explain or confirm the quantitative data. Qualitative data can provide a richness of information that mere numbers cannot provide.

Evaluation Reports—Examples

Reading this book will not make you an expert in evaluation; rather, its usefulness is to help ensure that you understand the role of evaluation in the training cycle and learn more about this essential process. Assume that you, the training director, have data that assess a newly developed leadership development seminar. You are sitting at your desk, looking at stacks of end-of-course employee reaction questionnaires. Two months after the course, you interviewed a sample of trainees and their managers to determine what use they had made of the courses since then. A computer printout detailing end-of-course achievement tests is rolling onto the floor. Another printout of scores from a leadership style inventory given to the trainees is on the windowsill. A videotape of the instructor delivering a unit of study is serving as a paperweight. What do you do?

Report to the Training Department

The training department needs to know if employees found the courses worthwhile and if the courses resulted in employees learning and applying key concepts. Data for this analysis come from the reaction questionnaires, the end-of-course test, and the interview data.

To create useful information, reaction data could be organized by offering the averages of scores on the quantitative end-of-course reaction forms and citing comments from the interviews as to the perceived long-term effectiveness of the course. A listing of raw achievement test scores—separated into averages, means, and modes—would provide a numeric or statistical description of the learning outcomes.

Report to Employees

The employees themselves want to know how their individual leadership style scores compared with both the test's norms and with their colleagues' scores. They are also interested in knowing how well they did on the objective test, which measured how well they understood the course materials.

You design a report for individual employees made up of two key parts. One part offers the individual's leadership style score and compares it to the group's and the test's norms. The second part is an overview in which statistical sense could be made of test averages, standard deviations, and percentile rankings. This allows comparisons of a broader nature to be made by each person.

Report to Instructors

Instructors want to know if their presentation styles were effective and if the materials used were helpful. Analysis of the videotape might require an observation guide or a simple checklist. Findings could be summarized in narrative or by providing scores for individual observation items. While you decide that the quantitative scores should be included in a printed report, you opt for oral, private feedback to the instructor. In addition, you give the instructor a copy of the videotape along with your instructor-observation checklist.

Report to Line Manager

Managers want to know if employees considered training a worthwhile experience, what they actually learned from the experience, and whether they were able to apply it back on the job. To this end, you summarize data from reaction forms, compile interview data, and perform statistical analysis of the actual test scores. Whether the manager has access to individual scores by employee name or if the scores are tabulated anonymously is a question that must be addressed at the proposal stage.

Line managers were ideally key players in the needs assessment and program design stages of the training program. In addition to thank-you notes, you give them credit for their involvement in the introductory part of your report. As managers often give the go/no-go decisions about training efforts, including their roles in the training report not only gives the manager a sense of ownership, but also makes the trainer more than just a deliverer of training programs. It highlights how training contributed to the achievement of organizational goals. Such joint accountability supports the trainer's role in becoming a key player in the overall organization.

Report to the Organization

Evaluation data are also a useful public relations tool for the training department. At the completion of a particularly successful and high-visibility training effort, consider putting an article in the company newspaper or on a company video broadcast. You can use evaluation data as part of employee briefings. You can take data to staff meetings where you report on the success of the program. Such public relations use of evaluation data serves to further the interests of the training department.

Honing Skills Needed for Evaluation

Ideally, the training professional takes the lead in evaluation efforts. It is a training department responsibility to make sure that evaluation appropriate to each phase of the training cycle is done properly. Training professionals coordinate the services and interests of others who have a role to play as well.

Depending on what is to be evaluated, the training professional relies on the expertise of others from inside or outside the organization. In evaluating subject matter content, the trainer typically turns to the literature and other people. This may involve literature searches, including trade journals in the field of training and the subject matter in question. Content evaluation also usually involves people—professionals who can provide knowledgeable input to the topic(s) at hand. These professionals may work within the trainer's own organization, or they may come from outside it. The need for these kinds of professional contacts is the best argument for networking and participation in benchmark studies where available.

Courses in qualitative and quantitative analysis provide the necessary skills to develop, understand, and report data. Because data are only as useful as the data collection instruments are valid and reliable, the more the trainer knows about designing evaluation instruments, the better. Trainers often rely on measurement experts to actually design evaluation instruments. Depending upon the complexity of the skill, the intended audience of the evaluation report, or time factors related to ensuring that a valid, reliable instrument measures training outcomes, those trained in psychology and testing can be invaluable resources. The next chapter provides an overview of methods related to designing and using evaluation tools.

SUMMARY

This chapter provided the "when," "what," "who," "where," "how," and "why" of training evaluation. Given the need to operate effectively and efficiently, training professionals must be able to determine that they are doing the right things right and be able to *document* training outcomes.

As part of the training cycle, evaluation is tightly coupled to the needs assessment stage. Outcomes of the needs assessment—knowledge, skills, and abilities—provide the basis for identifying training goals and, therefore, criteria to be used to determine if training efforts reached those goals. Two useful approaches were combined to offer a perspective on what needs to be evaluated: the grouping of criteria into domains and identifying who needs evaluation data.

Five domains of training criteria were identified. Reaction refers to the trainee's perception of the training experience and its value. Learning refers to determining that content mastery occurred. Job behavior refers to whether or not the content learned was transferred back to the workplace. Organizational results describe how training efforts were linked to short- or long-term organizational goals. The training process domain includes assessment of what occurred during the entire training cycle and an audit of the training department itself.

Training evaluation audiences—training professionals, trainees, line managers, and organizational decision-makers—were described in terms of what evaluation data they would find useful. Each of these groups has distinct and different needs and interests related to evaluation. For example, training professionals want data documenting appropriate content and effective training delivery. Organizational decision-makers want to ensure that training efforts match organizational goals.

The training evaluation planner often relies on content matter specialists and experts in measurement in determining and developing appropriate evaluation measures. Tests, observations, interviews, participant questionnaires, secondary data, and workplace surveys are all commonly used evaluation instruments. The appropriate mix of these approaches depends on time, people and money resources, and how useful evaluation data are perceived to be.

Because data have no value unless they are used, this chapter concluded by offering guidelines for using them. Understanding the nature of both quantitative and qualitative data, as well as methods of analysis, is extremely important in using evaluation outcomes properly. Training audiences and decision-makers must have data analyzed in a useful report format. Moreover, when report recipients participate in the needs assessment, design, or delivery of training programs, the acknowledgement of their contributions should be made clear. Shared accountability profits both the report audience and the training department.

THINK IT THROUGH

1. What rationales do training professionals offer for not evaluating training efforts? Are these rationales ever valid? Why? When?
2. Assume that a needs assessment phase concluded by identifying a group of employees who needed to learn project management skills. How would you, the training professional, go about identifying relevant evaluation criteria?
3. "The only criteria that really mean anything are criteria related to employee learning." Do you agree or disagree? Why?
4. Following is a list of criteria related to a sales presentation skills training program. Identify a different evaluation strategy appropriate for each item. In which evaluation domain does the strategy fall?
   - **a.** ability to provide an overview of the company's products in five minutes
   - **b.** trainees' perception of the value of the learning materials
   - **c.** the program content was transferred back to the job
   - **d.** the program content addressed the identified problem
   - **e.** the relationship of the program to improved sales figures
5. Brainstorm evaluation strategies appropriate for determining the effectiveness of a program designed to make managers more sensitive to a culturally diverse workforce. Is answering this question more difficult to answer than the previous question? If so, why?

IDEAS IN ACTION

1. Interview a training professional with regard to how his or her organization contends with the need for evaluation. Share the trainer's comments with your classmates. Were practices consistent with those outlined in this text? Why or why not? What patterns (small vs. large organizations, service organizations vs. manufacturing organizations, and the like) do you see when comparing your data with your classmates' data?
2. Review recent journals related to training and development, such as *Training, Training and Development*, and *Human Resource Management*, to identify what authors in the field say about issues related to effective training evaluation. Summarize your findings in a brief annotated bibliography.
3. In small groups, construct a reaction domain evaluation instrument for the effectiveness of this class. Compare your group's instruments with others in your class. How are they similar or different?

ADDITIONAL RESOURCES

RECOMMENDED READINGS

Brown, Stephan M., and Constance J. Seidner. *Evaluating Corporate Training: Models and Issues.* Norwell, MA: Kluwer, 1998, 400 pp.

The authors' purpose is to provide training professionals in business and industry, and students of HRD, with an overview of current models and issues in educational evaluation.

Mager, Robert F. *Measuring Instructional Intent.* Belmont, CA: Fearon Pitman, 1973.

This small book provides a disciplined and humorous discussion of developing measurable training objectives. Mager's perspective is strictly skills and programs, a classic in the field.

Nilson, Carolyn *Training and Development Yearbook 2000 and Training and Development Yearbook 1999.* Paramus, NJ: Prentice Hall.

This annual publication always includes useful information on evaluation, usually in its Section 5. The two years cited here pay particular attention to the concept of ROI and to evaluation in the evolving dot.com world.

Parry, Scott B. *Evaluating the Impact of Training.* Alexandria VA: ASTD, 1997, 216 pp.

Parry offers a reference book of tools and techniques for conducting training evaluations.

Robinson, Dana Gaines, and James C. *Training for Impact: How to Link Training to Business Needs and Measure the Results.* San Francisco, CA: Jossey-Bass, 1989, 308 pp.

This text provides a detailed, step-by-step approach to evaluation that links training efforts to organizational goals.

WEB SITES

http://www.hronline.com/forums/training/training.html

This is the entry to searching the archives of TREDV-L, a very useful listserv through Penn State University. Read what practitioners and scholars are discussing on any number of topics, including training evaluation.

http://www.workforceonline.com/archive

The archives of *Workforce Magazine*. You can use their research center to search using keywords to find current articles on human resource topics, including training evaluation.

ENDNOTES

1. *Training Magazine*, October 1999. Minneapolis, MN: Lakewood Publications. See especially pp. 38-39, 46, 64, 74.
2. Lotto, Jill Casner, and Associates. *Successful Training Strategies*, San Francisco: Jossey-Bass, 1988, p. 35.
3. The terminology "knowledge, skills, and abilities (KSAs)" is traditional. Measures of attitude exist, however, and in the world of training they are translated into behaviors.
4. Robinson, Dana Gaines, and James C. *Training for Impact: How to Link Training to Business Needs and Measure the Results.* San Francisco: Jossey-Bass, 1989.
5. Kirkpatrick, D. L. "Techniques for Evaluating Training Programs," *Journal of the American Society of Training Directors*. Vol. 13, 1959, pp. 3-9.

CHAPTER

Research Techniques

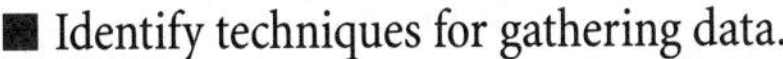

- Identify techniques for gathering data.
- Describe methods for conducting observations.
- Demonstrate methods for conducting interviews.
- Choose appropriate methods for conducting surveys.
- Explain instrument development and validation.
- Describe techniques of test construction.
- Plan approaches to creating experimental research designs.
- Construct suggestions for using research results.

ACQUIRING VALID DATA

A wise consumer comparison shops for goods and services by evaluating quality, price, location, and service. Likewise, trainers seek the most effective methods for conducting needs analysis and for the evaluation of the training delivered. This means determining how to obtain useful information upon which to make decisions about training program design and evaluation.

Once you have selected the best method to acquire the information needed, how will you go about putting this method into practice? What is involved in designing an action-oriented (as contrasted with a formal) research study? To begin, ask yourself the following questions: What data do I need? Where are the sources of these data? How do I go about collecting them? How will I analyze what I've collected? And finally, once this has been done, what does it all mean?

The term *data* refers to bits and pieces of detail from which information is derived; therefore, information is data that have been compiled in a useful way. Thus, data and information are *not* synonymous, but complementary. *Decisions* are made from *conclusions*, which are obtained from *information*, and information comes from *data*. This chapter will describe methods and tools used in the collection of *accurate, valid, and, reliable* data and explain how these data combine to provide information that is of maximum use to all stakeholders—the training department, instructors, line managers, the trainees themselves, and organizational decision-makers.

Needs assessment and evaluation are tightly linked stages within the training cycle. In fact, the evaluation of one project can become the needs assessment component of the next project. Moreover, as discussed in Chapter 3, evaluation is an ongoing activity that takes place at all points in the cycle. The training team continuously works to ensure that the right people learn the right things in the right way.

The essence of research begins with the definition of a problem to be addressed. This step is followed by identifying what is already known about the issue. This, in turn, is often followed by some educated guesses, called *hypotheses*—the relationships between two or more variables—that might be involved in solving this problem. All research tends to follow basically the same pattern:

1. Identifying the issue to be studied
2. Determining what is already known about the problem
3. Making assumptions about the problem (which leads to educated guesses about the relationships which may exist between the variables)
4. Identifying appropriate methods to collect needed data
5. Choosing or developing instruments that will result in the collection of valid data
6. Collecting the data
7. Distilling the results of this collection (What does it all mean?)
8. Formulating conclusions and recommendations that address or resolve the original problem

Earlier chapters covered items 1 through 4 above. This chapter begins at item 5 and will describe a variety of assessment and evaluation methods to acquire useful data, as well as how to use these methods effectively. While many assessment and evaluation techniques exist, this chapter will focus on those most frequently used in organizational training environments—observations, interviews, surveys, tests, and experiments.

OBSERVATIONS

Of all the data-collecting methods available, the most basic, and potentially the most useful, method is *observation*. Assessment by observation may be as simple as sitting down with a spreadsheet user and identifying instances where advanced features of this program could be used. On the other hand, it may be as complex as trying to identify the myriad of tasks a worker performs in a normal day. How simple or complex the observation process is depends on the questions to be answered and the value of the information gathered. To use the observation method, you first determine the type of activities to be observed, decide how to record observations, and create an instrument that will systematically guide data collection and subsequent analysis.

TYPES OF OBSERVATION VARIABLES

There are three basic types of variables in observation research: descriptive, inferential, and evaluative. *Descriptive* variables are measured by using checklists to describe situations or events. Descriptive variables, such as "resources used" and "voice and appearance," are relatively straightforward and, if recorded accurately, are relatively *valid*. Valid means that the observer's instruments, and the data thus obtained, truly measure what they are supposed to measure, not something else. Subsequently, when other raters use the same checklist and describe the same variables in the same way, the observation results are considered *reliable*. Reliability refers to consistent, comparable data. Data that are valid and reliable are two basic requirements for the observation method and for all other research methods used.

Descriptive variables, as this phrase suggests, describe a situation or event, and do not generally require major interpretations or projections on the part of the researcher. Inferential variables, however, do. *Inferential variables* take descriptive variables a step further. Inferential variables are developed by the researcher by drawing on past experiences to make sense out of what is currently being observed—what can be inferred from the data collected. Some activities contain so many interrelated actions and behaviors that inferences are difficult, if not impossible, to make. For example, when evaluating instructor performance, the observer may be called upon to interpret facial expressions and body language to see if the instructor is encouraging or discouraging participation. Recording an instructor's defensive posture, such as standing with arms folded, is a descriptive measure. The recording becomes inferential when the observer infers from this behavior that the instructor is uncomfortable or somewhat unprepared. It is likewise inferential to interpret vocal mannerisms or tones to imply encouragement or disapproval. Valid and reliable inferences may be difficult for a single observer to make; therefore, it is usual to have multiple observers and/or observations, depending on the complexity and importance of the situation.

*Evaluative variable*s are the most complex of all observations, as in addition to requiring an inferential reaction, the observer also evaluates performance and makes an informed judgment about what is seen. Measuring the quality of responses to questions, for example, requires more skill than saying simply that a number of learner-instructor interchanges occurred. Therefore, a single observation by one observer in a single setting cannot, on balance, provide an evaluator with adequate, reliable, and/or valid data upon which to judge the instructor's behavior.

Many firms that rely on customer contact use a type of observation called a "mystery shopper" in order to identify training interventions needed to enhance performance skills. This is an individual who observes, notes, and evaluates the nature and the quality of the contacts between a supplier and a customer. Mystery shoppers may be found as travelers on airlines, as customers in bank queues, as information seekers in brokerage houses, as diners in restaurants, and as retail shoppers in department stores. In short, they are found anywhere customer contact occurs and where skill improvements may be needed. This process involves the use of an observational checklist; however, due to the covert nature of this contact, the checklist is usually designed to record an event rather than the number or frequency of activities that have taken place. The next section describes strategies for recording these observational data.

RECORDING OBSERVATION DATA

Observational data may take many forms, and recording these data in a useable format is important. Decisions are made on information derived from many *data points,* or observations; therefore, the recording method is critical if sense is to be made of what is collected. At least four different types of observational recording exist: (1) elapsed-time recording, (2) frequency recording, (3) interval recording, and (4) continuous recording.

Elapsed-Time Recording

Elapsed-time recording relates back to the scientific management approach of the early 20th century and the work of Frederick Taylor. Taylor, often called the "father of scientific management," was an engineer who maintained that an expert, not the manager or the employee, could find the one best way to do a job or perform a task. Scientific management was based on the premise that every task could be observed and broken down into its smallest component parts. An expert could then determine how best to complete the task and how long it should take. Workers could then be trained to accomplish the task in the best way. Taylor is credited with being the first to use elapsed-time recording where the observer, complete with stopwatch and checklist, records the amount of time it takes someone to complete a specific activity or task. Today, the computer may be used to substitute for the paper and stopwatch checklist, but the concept of elapsed-time recording is still used.

Elapsed-time recording yields quantitative data that are relatively descriptive and relatively reliable. For this reason, this method is often used for certain types of repetitive tasks that lend themselves to measurement observation. Workers tracked via elapsed-time recording include order-takers for home shopping networks, stock and bond inquiry clerks, and airline and hotel reservation clerks. However, a number of extraneous variables often account for wide variations in these data. The time of day, the day of the week, and even the month or season could result in a wide variety and range of data. For example, the home shopping network order-takers are likely to be much busier in December, due to the holidays, than they are in August, when many people are on vacation. Other complicating variables include the personality of the caller or the degree to which detailed information is required, on either the part of the employee or from the caller. Yet another variable might concern the type of equipment involved—PBX, touch-tone, dial, headset, and the like. Downtime, 800 numbers, and "please hold" announcements all could influence these observations and thus impact the data noted on the observer's checklist.

Frequency Recording

Frequency recording is determining the number of times that the telephone user or the target individual performs a specific activity. Most frequency observations are best done under conditions of short duration with relative stability or consistency in the activity observed. More complex behaviors can be observed; however, they will take more time and effort. The more expert or experienced you are in the activities being recorded, the easier behaviors are to identify and, thus, record. For example, a former telephone operator may have a sense of the type of call being answered; a former teacher, a sense of the nature of a classroom observation; and a former production supervisor, a sense of the assembly line activity performed. The more complex the behavior is, the more important it is that an experienced, knowledgeable observer does the observation.

While these illustrations all show an observer tallying certain types of data, there are also instances where individuals can track their own activities. For example, how many calls come in to the help line throughout a three-week computer-mediated training course? How many times are customer service representatives unable to answer customer questions? Data about these kinds of questions can easily be captured on time and document logs maintained by the workers themselves and provide valid, reliable, *self-evaluation* data.

Interval Recording

Interval recording usually takes the form of observing target individual(s) at specific time intervals. Using interval recording, a recorder would observe a target at specific periods of time, say five minutes out of each hour over a one-, two-, or three-day period. If consistency is noted—that is, if the same actions occur within the observed period over a block of time—the observer might be able to conclude that those behaviors are typical. The difficulty of interval recording, however, is that peaks of high volume and valleys of low activity may not happen during the observation period. Activities observed, may thus skew the categorized data in one direction, or activity flurries may not be observed and recorded at all. On the other hand, interval observations make effective use of time when the observer has to record the behavior of multiple individuals.

Continuous Recording

Continuous recording involves noting all the activities or behaviors of the target(s) throughout an entire observation period. For example, if you wish to determine what tasks an employee engages in during a normal day, you would, of course, have to observe him or her throughout the entire day and record every task performed. This is usually done during the exploratory or opening phase of a research project to determine patterns or significant clusters of actions, which can result in the development of categories useful for developing future observation guides.

Using the Observation Method

The observation form itself largely determines not only *what* is observed, but also *how* it is observed. As such, the form is critical to the observational process and must be carefully designed *and* validated to make sure that the data you collect are both accurate and valid. Many samples and styles of observation forms are available from commercial sources; however, the best form is one that you design for your specific purpose.

The Observation Form

Figure 4-1 is an illustration of a *partial* observation checklist used to observe a new training instructor. To create an observation form, first decide what you wish to observe. Second, determine how you want to observe it (in person, covert, videotape). Third, list the questions or items you need to record, referring to your first step. Fourth, pilot-test the form with an actual observation to see if it actually does what you want it to do. Finally, revise the form accordingly. These steps, of course, have many subparts; however, the essence is to design a form that can be used to gather the needed data most effectively and efficiently.

One way to reduce the problems related to observer interpretations and to cut down labor costs is to consider audiotaping or videotaping behaviors. Audiotapes and videotapes provide a running commentary of the observed phenomenon to which you can return time and time again for clarification. Videotaping provides additional value because you can film the precise activity desired during the observation. When conducting any type of observational study using recording devices, you must be responsive to the ethics of observational data collection. Permission from those being observed must be acquired. Remember that if your presence influences or impacts the observed in any way, your data may be contaminated and, thus, of little real value.

Computer-Assisted Observation

Computer-assisted observation is an increasingly used method for data collection. For example, a computer program, sometimes called a "cookie," can easily track the number and type of features people use in doing on-line data searches. Such data can be incorporated into training designs to ensure that the most frequently used commands are taught to new employees and to enhance the program. Computers might also record data showing that some employees are using only a small set of the features that they *could* be using and thus, could benefit from additional training classes or the development of a users group.

Keep in mind, however, that these computer-based observations/data collection procedures must be openly announced and fully explained lest they be interpreted as "big brother" employer keeping tabs on employees. How you approach this issue is critical to the success of all of your data-gathering activities. Being able to "opt out" of such tracking procedures at the outset has received a great deal of publicity in recent consumer contact situations, as individual privacy issues are involved. When such acceptance and approvals are acquired, the computer can be an invaluable aid in collecting, tabulating, and even (later) analyzing data.

FIGURE 4-1
INSTRUCTOR OBSERVATION CHECKLIST (PARTIAL)

Instructor Observation Checklist (partial)

Name of Instructor ______________________ Date of Observation ____________

Class Observed ______________________ Course/Module ID ____________

Number of Participants ______________________

1. Instructional aids used (number and type) ____________
2. Interactive questioning involved (number and type) ____________
3. Medial summaries used for each topic (number and type) ____________
4. Mannerisms noted (positive) ____________
5. Mannerisms noted (negative) ____________
6. Others . . .

INTERVIEWS

nterviews are meetings between an information gatherer and an information giver. Interviews can be conducted face to face, via the telephone, or in a group (focus groups). The key to success in using this method is identifying the right people to interview, knowing what information is needed, and designing a good interview guide. Observation data can provide a

framework for developing interview guides, ensuring that the right questions are asked of the right people.

Types of Interviews

Interviews can be open or structured. Open interviews are exploratory and are used when only a small number of interviewees are needed; almost all of the resultant data are qualitative. Structured interviews are primarily based on questions that require yes/no, categorical, and other specific answers. Whether interviews are open or structured, the interviewer should use an interview guide that ensures that the right questions are asked and allows data to be interpreted easily. A guide also serves as a means of ensuring data that can be compared among respondents. Conducting interviews takes skill and practice; however, the steps and sequence of interview research involve similar procedures used in the observation method. Following are guidelines for using the interview method, coupled with an illustration of applying this method to address a perceived problem.

Using the Interview Method

Step 1. *Define the purpose or problem to be studied.* The first step in any investigation is to identify the problem to be studied. It must be assumed that the problem *can* be answered through the interview process. Data from previous assessments and evaluations should also be reviewed to ensure that the organization has not already answered the question or addressed the issue.

Step 2. *Select the sample to be interviewed.* Select the individuals to be interviewed carefully to provide a range of responses. Avoid tapping those willing (or eager) to participate, as they may not be the most appropriate subjects. Avoid this trap: "Why not interview Harry? He is between projects this afternoon and has nothing pressing to do." Another bit of advice is to include as many stakeholders as possible. As discussed in Chapter 1, participation in the assessment stage is highly correlated with success in the implementation stage.

Step 3. *Design the interview guide by determining the major points, questions, and sequence of the interview topic.* An interview guide should be neither too long nor too short. Its purpose will determine if it is to be open-ended or structured. One way to develop an interview guide is to brainstorm questions to which you'll need answers, and then structure or cluster these questions into a logical order. Remember, the guide should focus on the objectives and outcomes desired. Figure 4-2 illustrates a partial sample interview guide to assess current and future sales training needs.

Figure 4-2
Sample Interview Guide (partial)

Interview Guide (partial)

Name and Position of Subject ______________________ Date ____________
(attach business card if possible)

Location of Interview ______________________ Telephone ____________

Subject of Interview ______________________________________

Topics and/or Questions

1. How large is your Sales Department? Is it growing, shrinking, or steady state?
2. What has been your experience with the training conducted for members of your staff? (positive/negative/neutral/unknown—and to what degree)
3. In what cases has training been effective? How did you measure this effectiveness?
4. In what cases has training been ineffective? How did you measure this?
5. What products does your staff find the easiest to sell?
6. What products are the most difficult to sell?
7. Where do you see the gaps in your staff's effectiveness that the training department might be able to fill?
8. Others…

Step 4. *Pretest your interview guide by conducting pilot interviews with similar individuals to determine the validity, accuracy, reliability, and shortcomings of the interview.* Developing a good interview guide takes time and practice and often many revisions. Pretest your interview guide by asking people who reflect your target group to help you test the interview guide and procedures. In such a tryout, you can determine if questions are worded in a way that will result in useful data, as well as practice or test your skills as an interviewer. You can also see if your note-taking ability is adequate or if you need to audio- or videotape the interview. The tryout interview also serves as a way to determine how much time an interview will take, as well as the difficulties in asking questions or keeping the subject on track. How do you get beyond what the interviewee is saying to capture what is being *meant* rather than what is being *said*? Most important, can the questions you really need to have answered actually *be* answered?

Step 5. *From the pilot data, develop and refine a coding or tabulating method which will allow you to arrange and categorize responses.* The tryout session also provides you with data that can be used to form your coding and analysis structure. Since interviews frequently result in lengthy transcripts (qualitative data), what type of coding will you use—key words, phrases, images, themes? Should quantitative data also come out of the interview, how will you compile or tabulate these data so they are useful? Many interviewers find coding to be the most difficult step in the interviewing process. Coding responses to a 30-minute interview may take longer than the interview itself. At the problem development stage, you decided on *what* data you needed—key themes or issues, important processes, and the like. Coding may be done by looking for key phrases which occurred throughout the interview. Coding may also be done by listing the specific issues you wish to identify through the interview.

One of the most effective methods of interview coding involves listing your desired outcomes—your interview goals—as column headings across the top of a large sheet of paper. Figure 4-3 is an example of such a coding matrix. For each item down the left-hand side of the page, identify the specific question(s) you intend to ask that you hope will meet these goals or objectives. In this illustration, the first column identifies the products sold; the second column identifies the training required; and the third column identifies the learning strategies to be considered. As you review your notes or listen to your tape recording, fill in the blanks accordingly. You may have to read between the lines from time to time; however, after a few tryout sessions, you will become more comfortable with this process. Data reduction skills such as these are developed over long periods of trial-and-error experience, so do not be discouraged if your first efforts do not produce the hoped-for results. Time and experience will hone these skills to where you will become proficient in the process. Figure 4-3 illustrates three topics from the sample Interview Guide shown in Figure 4-2.

Figure 4-3
Interview Coding Matrix

Questions	Types of Products	Training Needed	Learning Strategies
1. What new products will your department have to sell in the next two years?			
2. What training will be required for your sales staff in the next two years?			
3. How many *new* sales staff members will need orientation training in the next two years?			

Step 6. *Collect data by conducting interviews as scheduled.* When scheduling an interview, it is important to make sure that the concept of timeliness is maintained. Since many interviews attempt to get at time-sensitive issues that your training efforts must address, request and hold interviews as soon as possible following the approval to conduct them. Since interviews generally are best held on the interviewee's home turf, you may have to make arrangements for tape recording or videotaping ahead of time.

Plan to conduct interviews at a time when the least number of interruptions occur; however, be prepared for interruptions nevertheless. Be alert to possible sidetracks on the part of your subject and keep the focus on the topics established. Try to differentiate between facts and opinions and avoid inserting your own ideas into the interview process. Finally, make sure you ask your subject for any final comments. It is at the end of the interview when rapport has been established, that the interviewee may provide the most valuable data. Also, remember to thank your subject for the interview, gather up your materials, and depart on good terms. Since it is likely that you will need additional information or clarification of some of the discussion content later, leaving on good terms is crucial to your success in the interview.

Step 7. *Analyze and interpret the results of your interview.* Following the interview, assemble your materials and begin to analyze the details as soon as possible. A good deal of interpretative data may be contained in the interview activity—impressions, body language, setting, and tone—all of which will fade with the passing of time. Transcribe notes or tapes as quickly as possible and search for themes and answers to questions. If you have questions concerning gaps or interpretations from the interview, contact your subject for clarification as soon as possible. Do not wait until a complete series of interviews has been completed before transcribing and coding data.

When you have completed your transcript, summarize your findings and conclusions and make recommendations based on the interview(s). Ask yourself what can you learn from the results? What training programs need to be developed? If your investigation was part of an evaluation of the training department's effectiveness, which programs might need to be created, revised, or deleted? Make recommendations for the next steps in the process.

Despite the complex issues involved with interviewing, it is one of the best ways to gather valuable information needed to focus on a problem. Many researchers use a selective interview process both before gathering survey data to ensure that they are asking the right questions on the questionnaire and after gathering survey data to add meaning and depth to the responses received from the questionnaire. The use of surveys and questionnaire design skills are discussed next.

SURVEYS

When data are needed from a large number of people, when they are geographically dispersed, or when time and expense do not permit observations, a personal questionnaire is the data-collection instrument of choice. As in observation and interview research strategies, you begin by defining your objectives. This section will cover some of the essential elements in the survey method: designing and validating questionnaires, selecting the people who can give you the data you need, and developing follow-up strategies to acquire missing data or to contact nonrespondents.

TYPES OF SURVEYS

Surveys are very helpful in acquiring a great deal of data from a large group, because statistical techniques can be used to ensure that only a small sample needs to be selected to represent the larger group. You need to design and validate a questionnaire or locate one that has previously been used and validated. As previously mentioned, surveys are usually distributed through office mail. They can be E-mailed or they can be distributed through in-person contacts, such as corporate meetings, or at the end of a training class. You can correlate data acquired through the survey method with demographic variables, such as age, gender, department, years of service, etc., to better understand the respondent.

USING THE SURVEY METHOD

Step 1. *Identify needed data.* What data are needed? By focusing on identified objectives, you will be better able to construct a questionnaire that addresses these specific issues. These objectives can be generated through needs assessments, observations, and interviews.

Step 2. *Determine who has the answers to your questions.* Unless you have access to everyone to whom your research results will apply, you will have to select a sample group from a larger *population.* Population is the term used for the entire group that you want to target—your department, your site, or your entire organization. When you send out a questionnaire to gather data, respondents must reflect the views of the larger population. If you are targeting a small department, for example, you want to send a questionnaire to everyone. If, however, the size of your group is large—your entire organization, for example—you will need to identify a *sample.* A sample is a subset of the population that reflects all of the characteristics of the larger population. For example, if your population is the entire organization, you cannot send a questionnaire to people in one department and then assume that the responding department can speak for everyone else. Not all departments operate in the same manner and individual needs and reactions may not be similar. Drawing a sample that reflects the larger population, however, is easily done through *randomization.*

Randomization means selecting individuals on a pure chance basis. This means you need to take steps to ensure that everyone in your population has an equal chance of being selected. Randomization helps ensure that the individuals who are asked to respond to your questionnaire reflect the characteristics of individuals throughout the entire organization. Techniques for randomization include picking names from a hat, using a table of random numbers, or using a computer program to generate a random list.

Step 3. *Design the questionnaire.* Once you find out what you need to know and who has the answers, you then turn to the development of the questionnaire instrument itself. One of the first major cautions in questionnaire design is to avoid reinventing the wheel. This means that before you put pen to paper—or fingers to computer keyboard—you should check your company files and the research literature to see if a data-gathering instrument or questionnaire already exists that will do the job you want.

When measuring broad constructs, such as organizational culture or group behavior, it is useful to check references for instruments already in print: Two such references may prove helpful: *Tests* and *Test Critiques* (1994), and the *Thirteenth Mental Measurements Yearbook* (1998) are good examples. These reference books describe hundreds of test instruments, their development, background, previous use, reviewers' comments, and validity and reliability figures.

The advantage of finding an existing instrument, of course, is manyfold. You will have a validated instrument that you know does what it is supposed to do, is already in print, and is available at a lower cost than would be possible if created from scratch. The disadvantage is that what you find may not mesh *exactly* with your objectives; it may be too long for your practical use and it may be too complex for your population or sample under investigation. On balance, however, by checking out these reference guides, you will at least know what *does* and what *does not* exist—and that alone may support your next task of questionnaire development.

If no instrument does what you need it to do, you will need to draft a questionnaire yourself. For the sake of illustration, assume that your objective is to determine the attitudes toward training's effectiveness within your organization. What questions will you need to ask? For example, what do former and current participants think about their training experiences? Can they translate their learning into greater job-related efficiencies or effectiveness? Did their training experiences result in higher productivity? higher wages? greater responsibilities? Did they have a good experience and would they return for more training if the opportunity arose? Did they have a favorable attitude toward training and the training department or staff? Did participants at various levels hold similar attitudes—positive, negative, or neutral—towards training?

Once you have drafted a number of these basic questions, what other information will you need or find helpful? This "other" information may include demographic questions relative to time on the job, age, gender, or title. This information will provide you with relationships concerning your sample's responses to their attitudes toward training's effectiveness and these demographic variables. You may, for example, find that younger employees have higher positive attitudes toward training and that among these employees, women are especially enthusiastic. You may also find that job titles may correlate highly with the assessment of training. Such data will be used to make a judgment concerning your training's effectiveness.

Step 4. *Submit the draft to a jury for review.* After a draft of your questionnaire has been completed, your next step is to make sure that you have not missed any critical issues or forgotten to ask essential questions. This is why you should submit your draft to a small panel of experts. This panel can number as few as three or as many as nine, as odd numbers are better to avoid ties in their evaluations. This panel, of course, should have some expertise in the objectives of your questionnaire and be able to provide an evaluation of the contents of your draft. They will, no doubt, add questions, delete others, and make suggestions concerning the wording and sequencing of items. The panel can also provide input as to the nature of the questionnaire responses: Will you use a separate response sheet? What type of response will you anticipate? Are your responses a yes-no type or spread across a Likert-type scale from 1-5; and if the latter, what descriptors or codes will you give to each number? These questions, and more, should be addressed by your panel of experts. Remember to keep your ego in check—you *want* critical responses from this panel. You may have to return to your panel with a second draft in order to refine your questionnaire further. A consensus of your panel is generally the agreement necessary to proceed.

Step 5. *Field-test, then distribute the questionnaire.* Once you have the panel's responses and have incorporated them—to whatever degree you feel appropriate—your next step is to pilot or field-test the revised instrument. This means that you will select a small group, similar to your sample, and administer the questionnaire as a test measure. This is done to identify any problems with the content, distribution, and the return of the instrument, the nature and type of responses given, questions relative to ambiguous or vague questions, and the like. This process will also enable you to get an idea of responses you should anticipate with the actual survey. The pilot or field test will provide you with the last step in validating your questionnaire before you distribute it to your sample.

All questionnaires should include a cover letter that explains the nature and importance of the survey. In the letter, you should also explain why the individual was targeted to receive the

FIGURE 4-4
QUESTIONNAIRE TEMPLATE

Categorical-type question

1. How many people do you supervise? ____________

or

2. How many people do you directly supervise? (circle one)
   a) none; b) 1–6; c) 7–20; d) 21–50; e) more than 50

or

3. How many people do you directly supervise? (place answer in block to the right)
   a) none; b) 1–6; c) 7–20; d) 21–50; e) more than 50 ____________

Likert-type question

Rate yourself in each of the following categories by circling the number that best describes your self-assessment.

1 = I do this *very* well—no help needed
2 = I do this OK most of the time
3 = I do this about average
4 = I could use a little help here
5 = I could use a *lot* of help here

4. Orienting new employees 1 2 3 4 5

or

Rate yourself in each of the following categories by placing a check mark on the line in the position that best describes your self-assessment.

(same categories as above)

5. Orienting new employees 1 2 3 4 5

(As you can see in the first example above, by asking for a certain number to be circled, you get one specific response. In the second example, by asking for a check mark on the line that best indicates the respondent's self-assessment, you may have to make judgment calls when such reponses fall between numbers—which they will. Both illustrations have advantages and disadvantages.)

END OF QUESTIONNAIRE: (This is where you provide space for any open-ended final comments, thank the respondent for his or her help, and say where and how the questionnaire should be returned. You should also provide your name and telephone number to provide for any respondent questions. Finally, make sure you include, in bold type, your requested response date. It is almost always a good idea to offer a summary of the results as a response benefit in order to get the results back and in a timely manner.)

survey, give deadlines for responding, and name who to contact for answers to any questions about the survey itself. You may need to conduct one or more follow-up mailings or make individual contacts to get respondents to reply. It is a good idea to plan for this ahead of time by coding survey forms to allow for follow-up efforts. Numbers or codes printed on each questionnaire allow you to track those who have responded as well as identify follow-ups for those who have not yet responded. These codes also allow for confidentiality of the respondent, since no names need appear on the questionnaire and only you have the key; however, it also allows you to check off the name of the respondent when the survey has been returned to avoid unnecessary remailings. A sample code might be 1023 where the 1 is the department and 23 represents the individual contacted. A code of 1023X would indicate that the survey form was a follow-up to a person who was a nonrespondent earlier. Confidentiality of responses should be explained in your cover letter in order to enhance your response rate. While mail surveys used in marketing often result in a very low response rate (1–10 percent), you should strive for at least a 50 percent response rate to be able to generalize your findings to your entire population. Salant and Dillman (1994) offer a number of suggestions to enhance response rates.

Step 6. *Analyze and interpret the data.* Once you have exhausted the ways for convincing your sample to reply and the final batch of questionnaires are now piled high on your desk, your next step is to compile your data. You can use descriptive statistics to show the responses to each of your questions, such as the average response (*mean*), the midpoint response (*median*), and the most frequent response (*mode*) to describe your respondents. These three terms reflect the clustering of responses and together provide a picture of the group as a whole. Another descriptive statistic is the *standard deviation*, which is a number that indicates the distance away from the average each response falls. Standard deviations are expressed in terms of plus or minus numbers, usually up to 3. Large deviations, such as ±2 or higher, might suggest areas for further examination, as they show where a lack of agreement occurs. Small deviations, such as 0 to ±1, tend to suggest a homogenous sample with most of the scores clustering about the average or mean score. This, too, may be worth further examination since important "outliers" may exist but may not be shown.

The next logical step may be for you to look at how certain responses relate to other responses—for example, do gender, age, or job title differences show up on certain responses, or do they correlate highly with other responses? This information is important if you are to design a training program to meet the needs of different populations who may have very different interests, learning styles, or objectives. This step requires you to enter the data obtained into a statistical software package, such as SPSS, and ask your computer to perform one or more of these relatively simple statistical tasks. Once you have performed as many calculations as you feel are necessary, it is time to go back and answer your original questions. Some researchers suggest using a cut-off point to indicate statistically significant findings; however, in a training environment, one looks for meaningfulness or importance rather than relying solely on statistical results.

In addition to statistical techniques, which may be applied using pencil, paper, and hand-held calculators, there are a number of statistical packages for the computer that make acquiring and interpreting statistics easy. To use these software packages, you identify the type of statistic needed (t-test, analysis of variance, correlation), enter your data or scores from the data-gathering instrument, and with a mouse-click, the software program calculates the statistics.

TESTING

A test measures how well an individual does a specific task or what they know about given content. In addition, it may also measure how well an individual takes tests, too. Trainers use tests for both assessment and evaluation. When you use a test, just like other measures, you must take care to ensure that the test to be used is both valid and reliable. In other words, does the test measure what you want it to? And is it fair? Care must also be taken in preparing the test for use, administering it, and scoring the results. The purpose of this section is to briefly overview written test considerations.

TYPES OF TESTS

There are a wide variety of test types: standardized tests, such as the traditional IQ, SAT, GMAT, and GRE tests; achievement tests to measure the accomplishment of a learning objective; and performance tests used to assess how well a task is or has been done. Remember, too, that tests involving adults may also include open-book and self-checking measures of achievement or progress.

Tests are used for many purposes. The training professional must first know how the results are going to be used. Prior to a training effort, tests may be used to determine the knowledge level of a target audience (placement); during a training activity, a test may be used to evaluate learning progress (formative) or to identify learning problems (diagnostic); and at the end of training, a test can be used to determine the total learning that occurred (summative). Once you have made this important decision—how the test will be used—you can begin the process of test development and use.

CREATING AND USING TESTS

Step 1. *Record test items.* The test developer begins with the list of objectives, the expected outcomes of a training experience, and an outline of course content. The test developer often makes up a table of specifications—a chart that works as a test blueprint—to make sure important details are included. Figure 4-5 is an example of this, showing content coverage for a course in principles of banking. Choices are also made at this time as to what types of questions to use: true/false, matching, multiple choice, or essay. The first three of these are termed objective-type questions; essay responses are called subjective-type questions.

Figure 4-5
Table of Specifications (Partial)

BEHAVIOR	Financial Statement Design	Framework for Financial Analysis	Types of Ratios	Totals
1. Describe the format and contents of basic financial statements	2 items	1 item		3
2. Determine the earning power of a company using established techniques	1 item	3 items	3 items	7
N (continue)...				40
Total Items	10	20	20	50

Step 2. *Review and edit test items.* The table of specifications helps ensure that major topical areas are covered and that test items are developed to measure each of the objectives. The reviewer of a test has a dual purpose: to ensure that the test is valid—that is, it measures what it is supposed to measure—and to ensure that the test questions are clear and unambiguous.

Step 3. *Arrange the items in the test and prepare directions for the test.* Test item arrangement may impact the results of the test. By placing objective, true-false questions first, followed by multiple-choice questions, the test-taker is moved from the simple to the more complex response. Likewise, moving from easier questions to more difficult questions is also a positive test motivation factor. Essay, short-answer questions, and problems should be left to the end on a multiple-section test; however, participants should be directed to allocate their test-taking time with this in mind. Finally, it is a good idea to weight the test items according to their difficulty and importance. A true-false question, for example, should not receive the same weight as a short-answer essay question or a problem.

Step 4. *Administer and score the test.* Test administration should be as carefully done as is the development of the test. Make sure that your participants are comfortable and settled in prior to distributing the test. Ensure that, insofar as possible, pressures as to the outcomes of the test are reduced or removed. Provide all of the necessary materials prior to the distribution of the test so that everyone begins at the same point and with the same resources. Likewise, provide all directions and answer any questions before the test begins and then remain available for questions during the test. The attitude of the test administrator has a great deal to do with the results of the test. A confident, comfortable, and relaxed environment will provide the most reliable and valid data as a result of the test experience. Figure 3-4 was an example of a test on banking principles. Note that this test was a *group* test, measuring a group's understanding of concepts. Such a test is a teaching or reinforcing device and may be used for diagnostic purposes (how well they are doing), rather than for a summative evaluation (how well they have done).

When scoring a test, take the time to review the responses to each question. This is called conducting an error analysis. If a substantial number of participants miss the same question, it is likely that the topic was not covered during the discussion, it was too difficult to answer correctly, or it was worded incorrectly. It is also possible that your answer key may be inaccurate, as well. In such cases, you may want to discard the question and not count either right or wrong responses. In any event, use the test results to measure what has been learned as well as a teaching device for the next session or course. Keep the primary purpose of the test in mind—placement, performance, formative, diagnostic, or summative as this defines how you will use the test results.

EXPERIMENTS

Kelsey Owens and Everett Cortez, trainers with XYZ company, are considering two methods of training and want to know which of the two will provide better results. Owens has used the direct, instructor-oriented hands-on approach before and feels intuitively that it is effective; however, Cortez says that he has found good results with mediated self-paced independent study. The problem they face is that while both types of training have proven effective, not much hard data exist to provide comparisons of the relative effectiveness in their organization. Instructor-directed training is expensive; however, Owens knows that the personal touch can be very important to achieving desired learning outcomes. Cortez, on the other hand, reports that since the trainee is already motivated to learn, independent self-paced study is better, as trainees can learn at their workplaces on their own time. Independent self-paced training also reduces the expense of traditional classroom instruction.

Other issues at play in making this decision include the costs and time allocations. Materials involved in live training are cheaper to develop, but more expensive to deliver; relatively easy to revise, and cheaper to change. Mediated materials, on the other hand, are more expensive to develop, cheaper to deliver, and much harder to maintain and change. The primary issue, however, is trainee learning and as such, what may be more expensive in cost may also be more effective in the long run of employee learning.

Owens and Cortez may agree that an experiment might be the best way to collect data that would be useful in solving their dilemma. *Experimental designs* are research experiments that look at outcomes after a certain *treatment* (in this case, a specific training program) has been presented or interjected into a setting. An experiment would compare the results of an intervention on a selected group, or cluster, of individuals. For example, since Owens and Cortez want to determine the learning effects of each of the instructional methods, an experiment sounds reasonable. They want to determine the impact of offering training via mediated independent study as compared or contrasted with traditional group instruction. For example, what would be the impact on the learners' performance evaluations? What would be the lasting effect of any treatment, even if short-term gains were observed? What differences do such variables as gender, age, experience, job title, or previous training have on achievement or productivity? These questions all can be considered through the conduct and analysis of results of experimental designs.

However, because of the number of variables that must be controlled in any experiment, the training professional probably does not use a true experimental design to assess differences between treatments in the workplace. It is difficult, if not impossible, to control every facet or variable between two or more groups involved in an experiment. Location, lighting, interruptions, resources, time, and other conditions simply may not conform to learner differences or preferences, nor to the rigid controls necessary for a true experiment to take place. However, this is not to say that one cannot conduct an experiment in the workplace; the contrary is true as long as one takes into account how these uncontrolled variables may affect the results. For example, if you want to determine the effect of classroom versus video training in your office site prior to institutionalizing either program, an experimental design can be a useful tool.

Using Experimental Designs

This section briefly describes five of the most common experimental designs: post-test only design; pre-test, post-test design; two group pre-test, post-test design; four-group designs, and time series. The difference among the designs is the effort involved in controlling for extraneous variables. In other words, the more controlled the experiment is, the more you can say that outcomes were a result of the treatment (in this case, the specific training effort). Keep in mind that each of these designs is also considered a *quasi-experimental* design due to the inability to precisely control extraneous variables, such as individual backgrounds and abilities, experience, and prior knowledge that may impact the results. Designs are generally illustrated using the terms observation (O), and treatment (X). Thus, an illustration O_1 X O_2 would mean an initial observation or pre-test (O_1), a treatment or intervention (X), and a second or follow-up observation or post-test (O_2).

Post-Test Only Design

The most common experimental design is a post-test only design, shown on the next page. It is used whenever a pre-test is not possible or feasible.

$$X\ O_1$$

An example of a post-test only design would be where participants take a test or complete a reaction sheet at the conclusion of a training experience. The learning or reaction to the instruction can be measured; however, there is no way to determine if this learning resulted from the instruction or from some other interaction. For example, how much did respondents know about the subject prior to the training? Post-test only designs cannot provide answers to this question.

Pre-Test, Post-Test Design

The pre-test, post-test design shown below, however, can compensate somewhat for the post-test only design weakness, as it provides for a pre-test observation—for example, to measure what was known *before* the training experience.

$$O_1\ X\ O_2$$

Following the training program, a post-test observation—for example, the same or a similar measure used prior to the instruction—can determine if a change in understanding or perception has occurred and to what degree that change has occurred—either more or less favorable—as compared with the earlier test results. Obviously, a wide variety of influences, such as time to use the skills on the job or previous learning experiences, may impact the results of *either* of these tests or observations, and these influences may cause an erroneous interpretation of the results. In experimental research, a general rule is that the more control you have over the variables, the more you can trust your results.

The disadvantage of the single group pre-test, post-test design is that you cannot tell if the results were due to the intervention and not some other reason—such as maturity (or aging) of the subjects, or some other uncontrolled element. One of the more common contaminants is the presence of the pre-test itself, which may serve to sensitize the subjects to the post-test, thus artificially inflating the results. One way to compensate for this is with the two-group design.

Two-Group Pre-Test, Post-Test Design

One way to compensate for the possibility that the pre-test provided clues that influenced the post-test, is to involve two separate groups, both using a pre-test and post-test. Using the opening example, only one group would receive the traditional instruction, and the second group would receive the self-paced program. This design, of course, demands that both groups must be as *comparable* as possible in terms of job title, age, prior knowledge, etc. The two-group pre-test, post-test design is shown on the next page.

$$O_1\ X_a\ O_2$$

$$O_1\ X_b\ O_2$$

The first group is termed the "control" group—that is, the treatment (X_a). This group is exposed to the traditional training program. The second group (X_b) is termed the "experimental" group—in this case, the group exposed to self-paced instruction. Care is taken to ensure that the groups are comparable and receive the same pre-test. Individuals in both groups also receive the same post-test. If both groups are comparable to begin with, any differences in outcomes—understanding, attitudes, or whatever—should be due to the treatment. Of course, if there is *no* difference in the results, it would mean that both training programs are equally successful, and that either could be used with equal effectiveness.

When we look at differences in learning outcomes with this design, we may see differences in numeric measures, but are these differences significant? Statistical measures can be used to determine if these differences are, indeed, significant or too small and/or due to chance. It is also very important to keep in mind that what may be statistically significant may *not* be meaningful. That is, you may find statistical significance between test scores of the two groups, but these differences are not sufficiently meaningful to warrant any substantial conclusions or changes in your operating procedures. An example of this might be that if you find a 5 percent positive difference in attitudes about self-paced study, but only a 2 percent positive difference in these same attitudes from the traditional group, is this difference large enough to make a major decision on continuing the traditional classes? Likewise, is this difference sufficient to make a decision *not* to offer the traditional classes? Probably not. Of course, this is an oversimplified illustration; however, it is important to point out that what may be meaningful may not be statistically significant, and what may be statistically significant may not be meaningful, given the context of the experiment.

Four-Group Designs

The final formal experiment to be discussed here is the four-group design, commonly called the "Solomon Four" design because it uses four separate but comparable groups and is intended to compensate for most potential contaminants—maturation and pre-test bias or sensitivity. The four-group design is shown below.

$$O_1\ X_a\ O_2$$

$$O_1\ X_b\ O_2$$

$$X_a\ O_2$$

$$X_b\ O_2$$

This design has been simplified to show only the experimental training programs variable (X_a)—the self-paced study—and assumes that the other two groups (X_b)—receive the traditional treatment. As you can see, the effect of this design is to compensate for any pre-test bias as well as for different training treatments. Should scores be higher for the first and third groups, there is added assurance that the self-paced treatment *was* effective and scores were not contaminated by pre-test sensitivity since group three was not exposed to any pre-test. If the scores for groups two and four, on the other hand, are higher, you can feel comfortable that the traditional treatment was more effective and also not impacted by any pre-test bias.

The four-group design is much more difficult to use, since four separate but comparable groups must be assembled and all other potential contaminants are held equal. In addition, if statistical treatments are to be incorporated, there must be sufficient numbers of individuals within each group, which adds significantly to the difficulty of this design. On the other hand, the results from this powerful design are substantial and for this reason, should numbers exist and be available, this design has much to encourage its use. In the training environment, the more important the training program is to the organization's goals, the more care should be taken to ensure that it's the *right* training.

Time Series

The time series design is merely a variation of the previously mentioned experimental designs. All of the foregoing illustrations may incorporate the time series element to identify long-range effects.

In experimental research projects, you find that your experimental training program works or does not work. If it works, you report it, make recommendations concerning it, and then move on to another research activity. Because training needs change so rapidly, only rarely can you look at the long-range effects of your program. However, findings can be impacted by the trainee knowing that he/she is involved in a research project, the uniqueness of the environment, and/or the attention paid to the activity itself. The trainee, being aware of these issues, may unconsciously react differently, thus causing the results to differ. What, then, is the long-range or long-term effect of your findings? There is a relatively simple way to determine long-term effects, if any, and this is through the use of a time series experimental design. A single-group pre- and post-test design involving a time series approach appears below.

$$O_1\ O_2\ O_3\ O_4\ X\ O_5\ O_6\ O_7\ O_8$$

As can be seen here, a number of observations (or pre-tests, if you will) are taken prior to the insertion of the treatment variable— in this case, self-paced study. In the observation immediately following the treatment (O_5), you can determine the *immediate* results of the training. However, unless you make additional observations, it will be impossible to know if the treatment results were, indeed, lasting. Two, four, and six months later, for example, did the self-paced group remember what they had learned? In addition, by making multiple observations prior to the program, you can determine the benchmark progress of the group. Sometimes increases in scores may be due largely to the group's natural maturation, and score increases following the intervention may occur for the same reason. Thus, the time series has much to recommend it. The negatives include the time needed to make such early and post-intervention observations, as well as the potential impact of each observation. Most researchers tend to agree, however, that on balance, the potential gains offset any negative factors.

Using Statistical Measures

A wide variety of statistical measures can be used to treat data acquired through the use of any of these research designs. This text will not address the statistics issue, leaving an extended discussion of this up to the many excellent statistics texts and software packages available. It is important, however, to refer again to the difference between statistical *significance* and *meaningfulness*. In the first case, one may find that differences occurring in a treatment group A, as compared or contrasted with differences in a treatment group B, may be statistically significant; that is, due to the treatment intervention rather than to just mere chance.

The results of statistical significance may also suggest a difference between groups; however, this difference may not be *meaningful* enough to justify the time or investment of other resources to achieve the same results. For example, if you were measuring the acquisition of spreadsheet knowledge between one group of trainees using mediated self-paced methods and another group using a more sophisticated (but more expensive) self-paced computer-aided method, and you found that a small but statistically significant difference existed, would it be worth the cost of adding the new technology needed to achieve these results in the future? A trainer must always keep in mind the differences between significance and meaningfulness when making recommendations concerning the results of training.

SUMMARY

This chapter has presented, in just a few pages, what research texts and courses cover over entire semesters or more. Research is a complex, yet essential, element in training, as it provides answers to questions upon which critical business decisions are made. Training is a key element to business success; however, because training resources are limited, as are all business resources, research provides a road map as to where these resources should be directed in order to obtain the biggest bang for the buck—the greatest return on investment. Therefore, research efforts—observations, interviews, surveys, tests, and experiments—are all used to answer these essential research questions.

Observational variables were described as either descriptive, inferential, or evaluative. Descriptive data provide relatively straightforward pictures of events, whereas inferential data require that the observer interpret behavior. Evaluative data require that the observer assess or judge the behavior. Developing a useful observational guide is all about creating a form that will help the observer record data in a useful format. This chapter reviewed four different types of recording observational data: elapsed-time recording (timing behavior); frequency recording (determining how many times an event takes place in a given time frame); interval recording (recording behavior for short periods and at numerous instances); and continuous recording (noting all the behaviors throughout a specified observation period). Once the type of data needed is determined and the target audience is selected, the researcher determines what behavior is to be examined, and how many observations of what type and duration will be needed. The resultant form is, ideally, examined by a panel of experts and then field-tested and, if necessary, revised further.

Interviews are meetings between an information gatherer and an information giver. Knowing what data are needed and who has it is the first step. To develop an interview guide that will ensure that valid, reliable data are gathered, the researcher develops either an open-ended or structured interview guide. Open-ended interview results are used when a small number of people are needed to explain processes, offer opinions, or forecast needs, and are largely qualitative. Structured interview guides usually result in more quantitative data. This chapter included tips on wording and sequencing questions in a manner that will result in the acquisition of useful data. Actually conducting interviews requires an interpersonal skill set combined with a good understanding of the problem at hand. Analyzing interview data may require the transcription of audiotapes or videotapes or coding of notes using some type of an interpretation matrix or software to make sense of the results.

Surveys are large-scale data collection efforts. Survey skills discussed in this chapter included selecting individuals as a sample for the project who are representative of the larger population to which the results may be generalized. Designing an effective questionnaire centers on creating a valid, reliable instrument. How questions are worded and sequenced has an impact on the usability of these resultant data. As with pointers offered for developing effective observation and interview guides, developing a questionnaire is an art and a science that can benefit from input from many individuals. It is important to have a number of experts critique a draft questionnaire, as well as have a small representative sample actually complete the instrument prior to its being sent to the larger sample. These latter steps can help ensure that valid questions are developed, resulting in usable data.

Tests are very useful instruments for collecting data concerning the effectiveness of participant learning. Tests are most effective when they are developed in conjunction with the course objectives established. In many cases, the test is developed along with the course so that all important facets are included in the test in the right sequence and with the appropriate weights and emphasis. Tests are not only useful to measure learning outcomes, but also should be used as instructional tools to modify content for future courses.

Experimental designs are used when the training professional wants to know how effective a given treatment (training effort) was. Experimental designs discussed in this chapter ranged from the very common post-test only design to the time series, which measures outcomes at various time frames. The main difference among these designs is the degree of control that helps ensure that outcomes are the result of the treatment and not the result of something else. Finally, keep in mind the differences between *significance* and *meaningfulness* when using statistical assessment tools. While it may be important to report significant findings of your research, it is even more important to ensure that these findings represent results that are meaningful to the organization and to its strategic goals.

THINK IT THROUGH

1. Describe the differences between the terms *reliability* and *validity*. What impact do they have on data-gathering activities such as observations, interviews, questionnaires, and tests?
2. List a variety of instances where using each of the following research methods would be appropriate:
   - **a.** Observation
   - **b.** Interview
   - **c.** Survey
   - **d.** Test
   - **e.** Experiment
3. For the same group of tools listed above, provide at least three strengths and three weaknesses for each research technique.

4. Evaluate, *within your own abilities and interests*, which of the five tools *you* would consider using in any given instance.
5. What advantages occur from the use of a pilot test of a research tool or instrument?
6. Compare the advantages and disadvantages of each of the experimental designs presented in this chapter.

IDEAS IN ACTION

1. In groups of two, draft a one-page questionnaire that might be used to describe your instructor's teaching style. When complete, act as a "jury" to evaluate other groups' questionnaires. Make specific recommendations to enhance both the validity and reliability of this instrument.
2. Design a simple experiment that would compare the achievement of your class as contrasted with the achievement of another similar class. Consider at least three important variables.

ADDITIONAL RESOURCES

RECOMMENDED READINGS

Babbie, E. *Survey Research Methods*, 2nd edition. Belmont, CA: Wadsworth, 1990, 395 pp.

A thorough and easy-to-read text concerning survey research methods and tools. Survey examples and specific recommendations for sampling and follow-up activities in survey research.

Campbell, D. T., and J. C. Stanley. *Experimental and Quasi-Experimental Designs for Research*. Chicago: Rand McNally, 1966, 84 pp.

Surviving nearly 20 printings, this little paperback is *the* reference to use when designing experimental or quasi-experimental studies, regardless of their environment. An outstanding reference and resource.

Czaja, R., and J. Blair. *Designing Surveys*. Thousand Oaks, CA: Sage, 1996, 269 pp.

An excellent little paperback text written by a sociologist and director of a survey research center that covers the basic territory of this type of research.

Dillman, D. *Mail and Internet Surveys: The Tailored Design Method*, 2nd edition. New York: Wiley, 2000, 464 pp.

The second edition of one of the most widely read and recommended texts in the field of survey research. By following Dillman's TDM recommendations, survey responses of all types can be greatly enhanced.

Freed, M. N., J. M. Ryan and R. K. Hess *Handbook of Statistical Procedures and Their Computer Applications to Education and the Behavioral Sciences.* New York: American Council on Education, Macmillan/Oryx, 1991, 397 pp.

Don't let the title of this text put you off as, while it *does* deal with statistics, it tells you what type of statistic you need for the type of research you are conducting and then provides the details about how to go about using it. A rich appendix provides the reader with advice *and* details of how each type of statistic might be approached for a number of personal computer software packages. A gem!

Gall, M.D., W. R. Borg, and J. P. Gall. *Educational Research: An Introduction*, 6th edition. New York: Longman, 1996, 788 pp.

A complete text that covers all aspects of research. A strong resource reference for any serious research library.

Impara, J. C., and B. S. Plake, eds. *The Thirteenth Mental Measurements Yearbook*, Lincoln, NE: The Buros Institute of Mental Measurements, 1998.

This is the primary reference and resource for tests and test information in the U.S. This reference is one of the 36 publications in the yearbook and test reference series.

Leedy, P. D. *Practical Research: Planning and Design*, 7th edition. Upper Saddle River, NJ: Merrill, 2001, 318 pp.

An easy-to-use, full-of-examples, paper-bound 8 1/2-by-11-inch "users guide" for novice researchers. If you're just starting out in research, this text is for you.

Murphy, L. L., J. C. Conoley, and J. C. Impara, eds. *Tests in Print*, Volumes I & II. Lincoln, NE: The Buros Institute of Mental Measurements, 1994.

Another excellent reference in the Buros series that describes a wide variety of test instruments, along with their reliability and validity assessments.

Nachmias, C. F., and D. Nachmias. *Research Methods in the Social Sciences*, 6th edition. New York: St. Martin's Press, 2000, 550 pp.

A good, thorough text designed primarily for empirical research methods. Somewhat statistical, but an excellent addition to your research library.

Salant, P., and D. Dillman. *How to Conduct Your Own Survey*. New York: Wiley, 1994, 232 pp.

Don Dillman, one of the gurus of survey research, teams up with Patricia Salant, from Washington State University, to produce a "nuts and bolts guide" to constructing your own high-quality professional survey.

Schloss, P. J., and M. A. Smith. *Conducting Research*. Upper Saddle River, NJ: Merrill, 1999, 236 pp.

A useful paperback 81/2-by-11-inch guide to research, emphasizing the management of research activities, as well as teaching discrete research skills.

WEB SITES

www.etsu.edu/educator/elpa/surveyed/

The American Educational Research Association's Special Interest Group (SIG) on Survey Research has an excellent survey research site.

Srmsnet@umdd.umd.edu

The American Statistics Association's Survey Research Methodology Section has a listserve, which is very informative.

surveys@usa.net

The Survey System is a software package available for questionnaire development, which includes interviews, questionnaires, data entry and analysis, and Web surveys.

from the FIELD

VOICES

Mary Paul on Training Needs Assessment and Evaluation

Mary Paul is responsible for rider education at Harley-Davidson Motor Company in Milwaukee, Wisconsin. Her exact title is Rider's Edge SM Product Development Manager. Harley-Davidson (HD) is well-known for its innovative training and development strategies, and Ms. Paul is on its cutting edge!

BRIDGET O'CONNOR: Mary, I always knew my ole University of Evansville roommate would go places … but on a Harley?! Wonderful. Thanks for agreeing to this interview.

MARY PAUL: Well, it's always good to hear from you. And it's fun to reflect on what one has done over the years.

BRIDGET O'CONNOR: Our readers are interested in what's happening in training at Harley-Davidson. Can you tell us about Harley-Davidson's overall training strategy? How is training organized? Where is your position within the overall organization?

MARY PAUL: Harley-Davidson Motor Company has several training departments. Employee Training is decentralized among all HD sites, but has both corporate and site responsibilities. Harley-Davidson University serves HD dealership employees. And Rider's Edge, The Harley-Davidson Academy of Motorcycling, serves both existing and potential customers. I work in Rider's Edge, and am responsible for development and implementation of programs for customers and for instructors of Rider's Edge programs.

BRIDGET O'CONNOR: So, you have a unique role in HD—*customer* training. How do you determine what needs to be taught? How do you evaluate your efforts?

MARY PAUL: We have done extensive research regarding the availability and accessibility of existing and potential motorcycle training venues. We also work closely with the Motorcycle Safety Foundation and State Motorcycle Safety Administrators to determine training needs across the country. We also use research from our own marketing department, plus marketing information from various general sources to determine possible training needs. We evaluate our efforts in several ways: course evaluations, dealer feedback, and data detailing the growth of the motorcycling sport.

BRIDGET O'CONNOR: What business benefits have you seen derived from your assessment and evaluation efforts?

MARY PAUL: The sport of motorcycling is an active and challenging sport. However, the sport can be intimidating without proper training. By making training more accessible to both new and existing riders, we can grow the sport in a number of ways, including motorcycle and accessories sales. Plus, we promote the enthusiasm of the sport.

BRIDGET O'CONNOR: It's clear that training is directly tied to business results at Harley-Davidson. What sorts of trouble have you seen people get themselves into in trying to collect needs assessment and evaluation data?

MARY PAUL: With the wealth of data available from the Motorcycling Safety Foundation, we have had little trouble regarding needs assessment. We also continue to do telephone surveys, surveys at Harley-Davidson/Buell Motorcycling events, public events such as the Women & Motorcycling Conference, focus groups, and inquiries from our Rider's Edge Web site (http://www. ridersedge.com). Since our first official courses began in March 2000, we don't have much evaluation data to work from as yet. However, response has been positive and we are achieving our initial goals of bringing more people into the sport of motorcycling.

BRIDGET O'CONNOR: What do you see as major trends concerning how needs assessment and evaluation are conducted?

MARY PAUL: We are fortunate to have a lot of data available on an ongoing basis. We have found people are very open about their questions and concerns regarding motorcycling. We collect and tabulate data from our program evaluations, but that is on a much smaller scale. We find our participants very open in responding to both our needs assessments as well as our evaluation requests.

BRIDGET O'CONNOR: So your client base is eager to tell you what they want to learn! What impact do you think information technologies will have on how you conduct needs assessment and evaluation?

MARY PAUL: Information technologies allow us to do extensive research on motorcycling statistics. We are able to obtain this data immediately, formulate hypotheses, and develop programs based on data we receive from various Web sites across the country.

BRIDGET O'CONNOR: How do you know when you have been successful?

MARY PAUL: Even though we have our standard course evaluations, we know we've been successful when participants are excited and enthused about the sport, Bridget. We call it the "Rider's Edge Experience." We want our participants to fully "experience" the great sport of motorcycling.

BRIDGET O'CONNOR: It's clear that you, too, are enthusiastic about your work! As you have had many successes in your needs assessment efforts, what books or other resources would you recommend concerning needs assessment/evaluation?

MARY PAUL: Mostly, I find the information available on ASTD's Web site helpful.

BRIDGET O'CONNOR: What advice do you have for individuals just starting out in a training career?

MARY PAUL: Even though I've spent close to 15 years in Training and Organizational Development, I often raise the question whether or not training is the solution. I have seen too many instances where corporations reach for training as the "fix all" approach, when the real solution rests in managerial responsibilities, including setting performance expectations, communication, and resource allocation. Training professionals need to look at the entire organizational structure and the systems that are in place before jumping on the training panacea bandwagon.

BRIDGET O'CONNOR: What roles do you see trainers playing over the next few years or so? How do you see the training role changing within organizations?

MARY PAUL: Even though trainers may "love" training development, design, and delivery, it is often not the solution to a problem. I see training taking on a more comprehensive role, including organizational effectiveness using a systems-thinking approach, and analyzing current systems and structures in place, questioning management's responsibilities, and holding management responsible for any training success.

BRIDGET O'CONNOR: What would you say are the most important tasks training professionals must do for their organizations? And what are the key skills trainers need to carry out these tasks?

MARY PAUL: Situation analysis, needs assessment, and continued coaching are key tasks. To do them well, a trainer could benefit from a background in organizational design and development. This would give trainers important skills in assessing the need for training.

BRIDGET O'CONNOR: What specific advice can you offer training professionals to help them make training an organizational investment rather than an overhead expense? And help them persuade others to see it as an investment rather than an expense.

MARY PAUL: Boy, that's a tough one. Haven't we all been trying to do that for years? Technical training is usually not at issue here. So-called "soft-skills" training, and team-based training can be extremely difficult to quantify directly, especially in the short term. Convince managers to start small with a training pilot. Then, watch over a couple or three months for some flow to the bottom line for that area. I have had some success in this area, with manufacturing teams. However, this is often impossible to do when management wants instant results and a corporate-wide rollout in a short period. At this point, there are so many variables in play. It's impossible to tell if the training activity was an organizational investment.

BRIDGET O'CONNOR: Mary, what is the most successful training effort you have ever seen in an organization? What did it accomplish? What was the key to its success?

MARY PAUL: We use a business fundamentals training tool from ROOT Learning, Inc. Six to ten people and a facilitator hold a two-hour discussion using a large colorful map, and scripted questions. We use six maps at Harley-Davidson, covering such topics as: market trends in the motorcycling industry, our business process, the financial process, the product cycle from design to shipment, our dealer network, and our brand and marketing strategy.

BRIDGET O'CONNOR: Now, the flip side to that question: What is the worst, most unproductive training effort you have ever seen? Why was it a disaster? What lessons can be learned from it?

MARY PAUL: Oh, I've had lots of these, and of course they are the greatest learning lessons one can have! The majority of unproductive training efforts I've experienced have to do with large corporate rollouts, where results were expected almost immediately after training. This "giant aspirin" approach to training usually frustrates all parties in the end—the management, the participants, and the training department. I've had this happen in two organizations with regard to team-based training. The training and organizational development departments wanted a pilot group to first experience the training, get feedback, fine-tune the training, and test the initial results. Leadership wanted the training to be given to all parties at once, sort of the "shotgun" approach, to get a quick fix. Unfortunately, launching training to 50-some teams at once was overwhelming for not only the teams and the training department, but also the leadership. Such important factors as job relevance, expected outcomes, adequate resources, and just "time" to incorporate the new skills were not properly anticipated. What happened? After about a year of foundering, the training department was asked by leadership to do an assessment, and start over small, with a pilot group. Go figure ....

BRIDGET O'CONNOR: You've mentioned the high value you place on resources associated with ASTD. How about outside the field of training? Are there groups trainers should join or network with? Are there publications trainers should read based on your experience?

MARY PAUL: The Human Resource Management Association is an excellent source for networking. I would also highly recommend the Myers-Briggs Type Indicator certification as a must for trainers, along with Kolb's Learning Styles Inventory.

BRIDGET O'CONNOR: Anything else? Anything you would like to say to college and graduate students preparing for a career in training? Anything for experienced, mid-career training professionals?

MARY PAUL: Patience is truly a virtue when it comes to training! Even though you may be right, and have the solution to a particular issue, that's no guarantee that the "powers that be" will see it. Many times over the years, I have come to the leadership table with the answer, only to be told "no." However, in time, divine order prevails, and the training solution is implemented at a later time. Sometimes you just have to wait for the organization to catch up with you.

BRIDGET O'CONNOR: Mary, thanks for sharing your experiences and expertise with us.

MARY PAUL: And thank you—I really enjoyed the interview!

PART 3
Instructional Design

PROLOGUE TO PART 3

What is known about the process of designing instruction? While a large body of literature exists and a good number of models have evolved, every instructional designer seems to take a different approach to this question. Many factors affect the process of design, including the content, the organizational climate, the background and personality of the training professional, and the urgency or perceived strategic value of the instruction. These and other variables interact, making the design activity a learning process in itself, and the instructional designer learns what works best through trial and error.

Instructional design represents the second stage of the training cycle, the stage where learning solutions to problems are developed. Design begins with the outcomes of the assessment stage. And just as the training professional was a team member in needs assessment, that same team-focus often continues in the design stage. Design requires input, feedback, and ideas from a wide range of stakeholders. Therefore, training designs are based on multiple perspectives and are an iterative process; designs are usually not one-person, one-shot responses to problems, although sometimes circumstances dictate exactly that. Instructional design is essentially all about shared learning and experimentation. From systems theory, we know that more than one solution exists for any given problem; the challenge to the designer is to convert identified needs into a learning solution that works for a given organization.

Chapter 5, "Learning Theory," provides a theoretical rationale for instructional design as well as delivery (Part 4 of this book). Chapter 5 is concerned with understanding the adult learner, what we know about teaching and learning, behavioral and cognitive science, and what motivates people to want to learn, thus providing a useful theoretical framework for the next chapter, "Training Program Design." Keeping in mind that no "one best way" exists, Chapter 5 helps us understand that we have choices to make when designing effective instruction.

Chapter 6, "Training Program Design," takes a very pragmatic, how-to approach. The design model offered in this chapter is an approach to translating identified knowledge, skills, and abilities into deliverable training solutions. Chapter 6 describes the design process itself and offers a step-by-step guide, the Training Design Funnel, to manage the process. Illustrations and charts are offered to help the design team translate identified needs into goals and break goals down into detailed learning objectives. A sample work sheet to support this process is offered. A theme throughout this chapter is that instructional design is a group effort. Because not all solutions have to begin from ground zero, and because a number of external vendors exist that can provide design services, this chapter concludes with an overview of how to evaluate off-the-shelf training solutions and materials, as well as how to work with external training vendors.

CHAPTER
Learning Theory

- Discuss the need for learning theory to guide the design and implementation of training programs.
- Compare and contrast instructor-centered (pedagogy) and student-centered (andragogy) approaches to instruction.
- Discuss the importance of learning style as a basis for instructional design.
- Explain how the behavioral model of learning has impacted organizational training.
- Discuss the role of learning objectives in the design of training programs.
- Summarize the assumptions of cognitive science as a basis for designing adult learning programs.
- Point out the role of motivation in adult learning by summarizing the work of Maslow, Herzberg, Rotter, Rogers, and McGregor.

FOUNDATIONS FOR ADULT LEARNING

Theories help us understand why something happened or predict what will occur under given circumstances. A trainer needs to understand *learning theory* as a guide for the design and implementation of effective instructional programs. Learning theory explains and predicts how individuals learn. It provides the framework for answering the question of how to structure learning materials so that the learner can grasp the concepts and/or skills being presented. However, there is no single theory that explains how or why different learners learn the same material in different ways.

Individual adults learn differently, depending upon their experience, aptitude, and attitude. Whether you learn best in a classroom environment, by reading a book, or through Web-based training, depends on a number of elements. These include, for example, your individual characteristics, the perceived value of the learning task to you, and how much experience—and perhaps success—you have had with the topic in the past. Thus, no single theory explains how or why different learners acquire the same material given different approaches.

One reason learning theory development is so incomplete and imprecise is that it is difficult to agree on a definition of learning. In the first half of the 20th century, learning was mainly defined as some type of behavior change, influenced largely by the environment. Differences of opinion, however, led to the following questions: If no change could be observed, did learning actually occur? If a change in behavior was observed, did this change result from learning? Does maturation—growing older—alone result in learning? One useful definition was put forth by Maples and Webster: "Learning can be thought of as a process by which behavior changes as a result of experiences."[1] In other words, learning is a process, not an output; a journey, not a destination.

The purpose of this chapter is to provide an overview of historical and current thinking about how adult learning occurs. The chapter begins with an overview of teaching and learning styles. Traditional learning theories that fall under the categories of behaviorism and cognitive science are then overviewed, with emphasis on their relationship to training program design. Because no training program will work unless the learner does, the chapter concludes with a review of some well-known motivation theories, including the work of Maslow, Herzberg, Rotter, Rogers, and McGregor.

ADULT TEACHING AND LEARNING STYLES

As students, we can all recall classrooms where the teacher determined the content, structure, sequence, presentation, and evaluation of instruction. As a matter of fact, most formal education relies on this model. However, for some students who are curious and internally motivated, striking out on their own can result in a richer and more successful learning experience than one directed by the teacher. Likewise, teaching styles depend on the instructor and can differ profoundly from individual to individual. An individual's teaching style will usually result in greater or lesser degrees of comfort with the many instructional tactics employed, such as lecture, role-play, small group activities, simulations, etc. When these two conditions—the learning orientation of the student and the teaching style of the instructor—are successfully integrated, effective learning can occur.

Early childhood learning focuses on a body of fundamental rules and content rules. This includes learning how to read, how to write, and how to compute (add, subtract, multiply, and divide). When these basic building blocks of learning are mastered, the student is then ready for higher-order learning; learning that requires making connections of analysis and evaluation.

When students have learned how to learn, they can take on more responsibility for their own education, and that includes self-directed learning. Education and effective training should target the merging of teaching style and learner orientation.

Adult Learning

Andragogy and pedagogy refer to the study of teaching and both are made of two Greek words. "Andra" comes from the Greek word *aner*, which means "man, adult." "Peda" comes from the Greek word *pais*, which means "child." Both terms use the second Greek word, *ago*, which means "leading." Those labels, however, tend to be somewhat misleading, as the terms more appropriately refer to teaching strategies than to the chronological age of the learner.

Pedagogy originated with early monks who recorded common characteristics among children who were learning basic skills. Much study has been done in child development, learning, and teaching. However, it was not until the middle of the 20th century that instructors realized their assumptions about how children learn did not fit the adults they were teaching. Andragogy, a term first used in 1833 by a teacher in Germany, then reintroduced by a German social scientist in the 1920s, and next adapted by adult educators in Europe in 1957, was first used in the United States by Malcolm S. Knowles in the 1960s.[2] Andragogy focuses on learner-directed instructional approaches; pedagogy, on teacher-directed learning experiences. Knowles emphasized that these two assumptions can and do coexist. The task to be learned and the individual's learning style, in combination, dictate whether a pedagogical, andragogical, or a combination of both approaches should be considered in the design and delivery of a training program.

For example, what would your preferred learning approach be for each of the following?

- to be oriented to a new job
- to understand union politics
- to improve your writing skills
- to understand the technical aspects of the Internet
- to use a new spreadsheet program

How you responded to these illustrations reflects a learning style that relates to both pedagogy and andragogy. How each question was answered reflects your own particular background and learning preference. While a young MBA may learn best about union politics through the lecture method (using elements of pedagogy), someone with more experience or a greater need to know may want to assist in a membership campaign or actually run for union office to acquire the perspective that is desired. Likewise, to improve your writing, you may need a refresher course in grammar; you may read Strunk and White's *Elements of Style;* or you may need an intensive, hands-on practical workshop. To learn to use the Internet, you may need classroom lectures, hands-on experiences, and/or coaching from an expert. To develop skills using a new spreadsheet program, you may learn through a hands-on directed workshop or through your self-directed study of a software manual.

The point of this discussion is that andragogy and pedagogy are approaches to guide learning, no matter what the age of the learner is. The assumptions and process elements used by Malcolm Knowles to contrast these two orientations about teaching/learning are illustrated in Figure 5-1. While one may argue the terminology within these two positions shown in this figure, they are presented from the andragogical point of view in order to illustrate these extreme differences.

FIGURE 5-1
PEDAGOGY/ANDRAGOGY ASSUMPTIONS

Assumptions About	Pedagogical	Andragogical
Concept of the learner	Dependent personality	Increasingly self-directed
Role of learner's experience	To be built on more than used as a resource	A rich resource for learning by self and others
Readiness to learn	Uniform by age-level and curriculum taught	Develops from life tasks and problems
Orientation to learning	Subject-centered	Task- or problem-centered
Motivation	By external rewards and punishments	By internal incentives
Process Elements	**Pedagogical**	**Andragogical**
Climate	Tense, low trust Formal, cold, aloof Authority-oriented Competitive, judgmental	Relaxed, trusting Mutually respectful Informal, warm Collaborative, supportive
Planning	Primarily by teacher	By learners and facilitator mutually
Diagnosis of needs	Primarily by teacher	By mutual assessment
Setting of objectives	Primarily by teacher	By mutual negotiation
Designing learning plans	Teachers' content plans Course syllabus Logical sequence	Learning contracts Learning projects Sequenced by readiness
Learning activities		Inquiry projects Independent study Experiential techniques
Evaluation	By teacher Norm-referenced (on a curve) With grades	By learner-collected evidence validated by peers, facilitators, experts Criterion-referenced

Figure 5-1 shows that learning concepts and the assumptions generated by pedagogical and andragogical points of view differ substantially. And the conditions that are manipulated—the process elements—likewise differ as to *who* controls them. Training efforts, therefore, will differ significantly, depending upon the approach taken by the training planner and the instructor. The following discussion defines six implications for developing effective training programs.

Learning Is Not Its Own Reward. Children learn for reasons quite different from adults. Adults are not motivated by gold stars or good report cards; they want a learning outcome that they can put to use in concrete, practical, and self-benefiting terms. Therefore, training designers should remember that adult students prefer practical, hands-on training sessions over general, theory-oriented classes. The best way to motivate individuals to learn a spreadsheet software package, for example, is to show them how they can apply it in their own environment.

Adult Learning Is Integrative. The adult learner brings a wide variety of knowledge and a vast array of experiences to the learning situation. Adults learn best when they are able to integrate new ideas with what they already know. If the information conflicts with what the learner knows or values, learning is more difficult. Such a conflict may be used as an attention-getter, or it may simply be explained. The point is that the conflict must be dealt with or it will generate resistance to learning.

Value Adjustment. Value judgments must be considered. Because training changes how work is processed, the adult learner must understand *why* the learning is useful and *why* he or she should master new skills. In this case, value adjustment means understanding why work that has been done a specific way in the past will not be performed the same way in the future. Trainees will accept change more readily when they know *why* the change is taking place.

Control. Adult learners want control over their learning experiences. Instructors should collaborate with trainees about the pace and the content of the training curriculum. Such an approach gives trainees opportunities to contribute to course content and to identify instructional methods that fit individual learning styles.

Practice Must Be Meaningful. Repetition for repetition's sake does not produce a substantial learning effect for adults. However, if repetition has meaningful results, learning will take place. This principle is borrowed from the work of E. L. Thorndike, an early leader in developing learning theory, who was opposed to meaningless drill. A related premise is that adults tend to be slower in some physical, psychomotor tasks than are children. Adults are also less willing to make mistakes, and they tend to compensate for this by being more exact. Thus, they make fewer trial-and-error ventures and, consequently, fewer errors. Rather than have trainees work on textbook drills, the trainer should have them practice on actual work-related tasks in the learning environment. A similar suggestion is that trainees should apply what has been learned in the classroom back at their desks as an immediate follow-up assignment. In the language of training, this is a *reinforcement* for a learning session just completed or *prework* for the next learning session to come.

Self-pacing. Because they tend to acquire psychomotor skills more slowly, which is a normal tendency that increases with age, adults should be given every opportunity to proceed at their own pace. In many instances, content can be designed to support self-paced learning. Some companies, such as Intel, Ford, Delta Airlines, and Hewlett-Packard, give their employees a laptop computer for their own use at work and to facilitate self-directed learning at home.

Learning Styles

The term *learning style* is often used to describe an individual's preferred approach to learning. There are many learning style models. One model suggests that there is a single orientation for any given individual. Another model claims that an individual generally uses several learning styles. And yet another model suggests that one can use a style selected from any number of possibilities. Finally, a fourth model contends that everyone has many different combinations of learning styles. Others, including David Kolb, who developed his Learning Style Inventory (KLSI) in 1981, integrates the last three of these models.

Kolb described experiential learning as a cyclical process that includes four states: (1) The learner has a concrete experience. (2) This experience is observed and reflected upon. (3) The experience is abstracted, conceptualized, and generalized. (4) The generalization is tested in new situations that lead to a new concrete experience. Because the elements of this process model of learning are polar opposites (i.e., concrete experience is the polar opposite of abstract conceptualization and active experimentation is the opposite of reflective observation), learners tend to develop more skill in one of the four quadrants (states). The KLSI measures individuals' preferences toward each state, and scoring results in a descriptor that shows how much one uses (or favors) one of four prominent learning styles.[3]

- Diverging: combines preferences for concrete experiences and reflection
- Assimilating: combines preferences for reflection and abstract conceptualization
- Converging: combines preferences for abstract conceptualization and active experimentation
- Accommodating: combines preferences for concrete conceptualization and active experimentation.

Try to identify your personal learning style in Figure 5-2.

Figure 5-2
Text adapted from Kolb's Learning Style Types

CONVERGER
The *converger* combines the learning steps of **Abstract Conceptualization** and **Active Experimentation**. Individuals with this learning style are best at finding practical uses for ideas and theories. If this is your preferred learning style, you have the ability to solve problems and make decisions based on finding solutions to questions or problems. You would rather deal with technical tasks and problems than with social and interpersonal issues. These learning skills are needed in specialist and technology careers.

DIVERGER
The *diverger* combines the learning steps of **Concrete Experience** and **Reflective Observation**. Individuals with this learning style are best at viewing concrete situations from many different points of view. Their approach to situations is to observe rather than take immediate action. If this is your learning style, you enjoy situations that call for generating a wide range of ideas, such as in a brainstorming session. You probably have broad cultural interests and like to gather information. This imaginative ability and sensitivity to feelings is needed to be effective in the arts, entertainment, and service careers.

ASSIMILATOR
The *assimilator* combines the learning steps of **Abstract Conceptualization** and **Reflective Observation**. Individuals with this learning style are best at understanding a wide range of information and putting it into concise logical form. If this is your learning style, you probably are more interested in abstract ideas and concepts and less focused on people. Generally, people with this learning style find it more important that a theory have a logical soundness than a practical value. This learning style is important to be effective in information and science careers.

ACCOMMODATOR
The *accommodator* combines the learning steps of **Concrete Experience** and **Active Experimentation**. Individuals with this learning style have the ability to learn primarily from hands-on experiences. If this is your style, you probably enjoy carrying out plans and involving yourself in new and challenging experiences. You may have a tendency to act on your instincts rather than on logical analysis. In solving problems, you may rely more heavily on people for information than on your own technical analysis. This learning style is important for effectiveness in action-oriented careers such as sales or marketing.

LEARNING THEORY AND INSTRUCTIONAL DESIGN

The predominant learning philosophy underlying the design of many of today's training programs comes from the behavioral tradition that dominated the psychology of learning until the 1960s.[4] Behavioral science defines learning as changes in behavior. Because this single definition of learning is questionable, other theories—particularly cognitive science—have evolved that provide more insight into how individuals learn the way they do. As individuals mature, their early learning style—developed as a result of experiences founded in childhood learning—may no longer be effective because of a wider variety of inputs and more diverse stimuli. Two primary learning approaches predominate in training and are discussed here: behavioral and cognitive.

A Behavioral Approach to Design

The *behavioral* model is grounded in the following basic assumptions:

(1) Observable behavior, rather than ideas or mental activity, must occur to confirm that learning has taken place; (2) The environment shapes the behavior of the learner, not the reverse; and, (3) How closely in time teaching and learning bond together and reinforcement occurs is critical.[5]

The best-known behaviorists include Edward L. Thorndike, Ivan Pavlov, and B. F. Skinner. In the 1880s, Thorndike's experimental work with animals and birds resulted in the stimulus-response (S-R) theory of learning. Thorndike said that connections between stimuli (sensory impressions) and responses (subsequent behavior) are strengthened or weakened, depending upon the consequences of the behavior. When given an appropriate stimulus, the learner responds positively—that is, accomplishes the task correctly. A response can be strengthened or changed, depending upon the particular stimulus applied.

The S-R theory says, in other words, that consistent, desirable behavior is formed by continually offering appropriate stimuli and rewarding the positive behavior that results. Stimuli must be appropriate *not only* to the respondent, but also to the task to be performed and to the environment, among other things. At its most basic level, S-R theory requires a number of conditions to be met *prior* to the anticipation that appropriate responses will be forthcoming. For example, if the conditions in the training environment are poor—lighting, equipment, facilities—the effectiveness of even good training will be compromised. Likewise, positive motivation for learning, which is established ahead of the training experience, may contribute above and beyond inadequate or weak conditions.

Thorndike proposed three "laws of learning" to explain his findings: the law of effect, the law of exercise, and the law of readiness.[6] The *law of effect* suggests that the learners will acquire and remember responses that led to aftereffects that were satisfying. The *law of exercise* says that the repetition of connections that are meaningful will result in substantial learning. The *law of readiness* says that the learner must be ready for this connection for learning to take place. If the learner is not ready, learning will be inhibited. Thus, learning that is satisfying, repetitive, and motivated results in maximum effectiveness.

Other researchers built upon and modified these premises, most notably Ivan Pavlov (1902) and his experiments with dogs in Russia, and B. F. Skinner's (1971) operant conditioning work with pigeons and mice. Operant conditioning can be summarized as: Reinforce what you want the individual to do again; ignore what you want the individual to stop doing.[7] The concept of reinforcement is critical to operant conditioning. If you accept the premise that the environment (stimulus) controls behavior, then modifying the environment means that positive behaviors can be encouraged and negative behaviors can be discouraged, and possibly even eliminated.

Applying the Behavioral Approach

The application of the behavioral approach to training has had traditional roots, stemming from Frederick Taylor's (1911) work at the turn of the 20th century. Taylor, called the "Father of Scientific Management," believed workers wanted to perform well, and his goal was to ensure that they were instructed in the one best way to accomplish a given task. Taylor attempted to quantify his workers' output by recording each motion made, every tool utilized, and the time needed to perform a specific task. Each worker's actions could then be examined and modified, and the worker then trained to do a specific job the one right way according to Taylor's observations. Many current education and training activities can be traced to this approach. The structured and systematic design of instruction, development of behavioral objectives, programmed and computer-aided instruction, competency-based education, and instructor accountability are all grounded in behavioral learning theory, as well as in business practicality.

A behavioral approach to designing a learning experience requires activities that sharpen associations between stimuli and behavior, create chains of alternative responses, and develop discriminations between responses of differing effectiveness. Such training programs, thus, would emphasize drill and practice. For many beginners and for routine tasks, behavioral approaches can result in rapid and effective learning by the trainee.

For example, when you get into your car, fasten your seat belt, and start the engine, your first action is probably to check the gauges to see if all is in order (stimulus). This review determines what your next step will be (association). If the gauges are all within normal ranges for your car, you probably then check for traffic, put the turn signal on, shift into the appropriate gear and drive away. A chain refers to the almost automatic steps that result from the first association and are generally taken without consciously thinking about them. Chains are typically developed by practice. Discrimination—the ability to make fine distinctions—would handle cases that are exceptions. If the engine gauges did not register normal readings, for example, you would probably not initiate the next steps in the driving process until remedies or explanations could be found.

Writing Learning Objectives

The training designer who uses a behavioral approach develops a learning program by first identifying expected outcomes. These *learning objectives* (also known as *course goals* or *behavioral objectives*) define what the trainee is expected to do as a result of the training. After all, how can people know what route to take or that they have reached their destination if they do not know where they want to be? The point is that the most effective training relates directly to expected job performance. Learning objectives, as discussed in earlier chapters, also provide the basis for evaluating the effectiveness of training efforts.

Recall that for the behaviorist, learning occurs when a demonstrated behavior change occurs. Therefore, built into the development of behavioral learning objectives, are precise details of observable behavior change or development. These changes are based on learning activities within one of three domains of learning—cognitive, affective, and psychomotor. The *cognitive* domain deals primarily with mental activities, such as thinking and problem-solving. The *affective* domain deals with attitudes and appreciations, such as ethics and feelings. The *psychomotor* domain focuses on physical actions, such as performing a specific task or activity.

Benjamin Bloom developed a hierarchical learning taxonomy that identified sequential learning stages or steps in the cognitive domain. As Figure 5-3 shows, the cognitive learning taxonomy ranges from recall at the lowest level to evaluation at the highest level.[8] Bloom's six steps or stages—knowledge, comprehension, application, analysis, synthesis, and evaluation—have been modified by others; however, it is Bloom's taxonomy to whom most of the behaviorists turn for the development of behavioral objectives. According to Bloom, learning is developed in stages, with each step built upon the preceding one. Thus, measurable training program outcomes can be developed by using one or more verbs appropriate to a specific level (See Figure 5-3).

FIGURE 5-3
BLOOM'S TAXONOMY

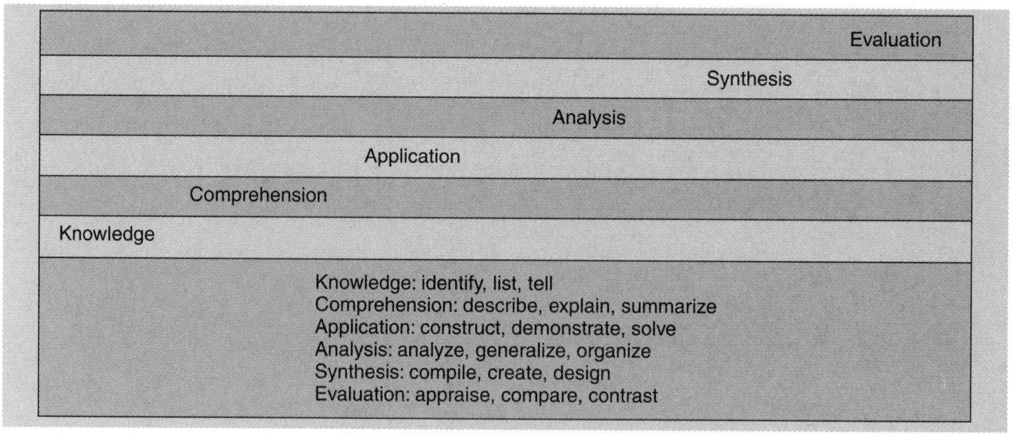

Evaluation
Synthesis
Analysis
Application
Comprehension
Knowledge
Knowledge: identify, list, tell Comprehension: describe, explain, summarize Application: construct, demonstrate, solve Analysis: analyze, generalize, organize Synthesis: compile, create, design Evaluation: appraise, compare, contrast

Robert Mager[9] has contributed greatly to the use of behavioral objectives in business training, setting forth these essential elements for the measurement of an objective within Bloom's taxonomy. These elements are the *conditions* under which the desired activity will occur, the *performance* to be completed, and the *criteria* established for acceptable performance. Each behavioral objective must contain all three elements. The learner may not move forward in the process until completion of the objective has been met according to a specific performance level or standard. Some training experts believe that the time frame for the completion of the task should also be identified. After all, if one can describe machine safety features but takes an hour to do so, the effectiveness of the performance objective is compromised. A sample behavioral objective for a knowledge-task may be expressed as:

> *Given* (the condition) a diagram of machine tool "X," the learner/trainee will be able to *describe* (the performance) all safety features *with 100 percent accuracy within one minute* (the criteria).

The behaviorist, therefore, sets out to define and measure learning (behavior) with some degree of precision. These measures can take into consideration a wide variety of conditions, including increasingly complex skill and knowledge levels. However, since each behavioral objective addresses only a small segment of a larger learning task, a combination of them is required as the task expands or becomes more complex. Because it is a hierarchy, Bloom's Taxonomy becomes a useful guide for training programs and curriculum design. Learning goes from the simple (knowledge) to the complex (evaluation). Once the terminal (or end) objective is identified, intermediate units or enabling objectives provide the structure and sequence of learning activities. These learning objectives are more meaningful when they reflect the business goals that the organization is attempting to reach.

Learning objectives are valuable to the trainer who must be able to document the fact that learning has occurred. Objectives are practical and concrete goals. The assumption is that if one can measure learning outcomes, the learning process is easier to manage. It is also important to note that learning objectives deal with more than simply task performances, but encompass acquired knowledge as well. These knowledge outcomes can also be measured by the use of performance-based learning objectives.

Despite their value, many trainers hesitate to write learning objectives because they find the task difficult and time-consuming. Several reasons have been identified for this reluctance:

- Writing is difficult for most people.
- Skill is involved in choosing the right terminology for performance verbs and identifying the proper amount of qualification and quantification criteria.

- Objectives are only as good as the standards for the task being taught, and if no standards exist, they must be developed or identified.
- Trainees often come to the learning experience with various levels of skill. Common goals are difficult to identify.

Learning objectives are the outcomes of needs assessment activities (Chapter 2). Whether one uses a behavioral approach or a cognitive science approach to the *design* of the learning activities, most training programs begin with *learning* objectives.

A Cognitive Science Approach to Design

As the task becomes less routine, traditional behaviorism becomes less useful as a basis for designing learning programs. Behaviorism defines learning as changes in behavior. Cognitive science, on the other hand, views learning as changes in mental structures—what goes on inside our heads. Learning in the cognitive sense is discussed in terms of building an internal infrastructure, or schema. Cognitive science-based learning programs often begin with learning objectives. However, rather than going from the simple to the complex on terms of program design, learning programs begin with the "big picture," which is then broken down into parts in a problem-solving mode.

Cognitivists say that since the individual interprets sensations and gives meaning to them and to their events, the mind is more than a simple system where stimuli arrive and responses leave. Learning involves the reorganization of experiences in order to make sense of environmental stimuli. Sometimes this sense comes through flashes of insight. A problem, according to cognitivists, can exist in only two states: solved and unsolved; there is no state of partial solution in between. A major difference between cognitivists and behaviorists, therefore, is where the control over the learning activity resides. For the cognitivist, the control lies with the individual learner. For the strict behavioralist, on the other hand, control lies with the environment or the instructor. Fundamentally, one must look at not only the symptoms of a problem to be solved or the learning to be accomplished, but also at its causes if any resolution is to be permanent.

Cognitive psychologist Jean Piaget (1952) suggested that learning occurred when individuals interacted with their environment in an ever-expanding number of experiences. From the cognitivist point of view, new research interests in information-processing theories, including memory and metacognition research, computer simulations, and artificial intelligence, have emerged. Researchers such as Bruner (1965), Gagné (1965), and Smith (1982) are among the cognitivist advocates.

Bruner's "learning through discovery" method requires three virtually simultaneous processes from the learner: (1) the acquisition of new, or the refinement of old, information;

(2) the transformation of this information to make it fit new task requirements; and (3) the evaluation phase—checking to ensure that resulting actions are appropriate and adequate to the task. Smith, moving forward with Gagné's earlier concept of learning how to learn, states that "Learning how to learn involves possessing, or acquiring, the knowledge and skill to learn effectively in whatever learning situation one encounters."[10] Smith's ideas of learning how to learn are a key feature of adult learning. Learning how to learn is a concept designed to move the learner from reliance on training to develop a specific task performance to creating in the learner an understanding of how learning one task can be transferred to another, more complex activity. Once these connections are made, the learner can build on individual competencies to create a better understanding and more effective knowledge of his/her larger system. In short, learning how to learn provides the employee with lifelong survival skills in the workplace and shifts the responsibility of learning from the environment to the individual learner.

The cognitivist's position focuses on the mental processes within the learner's control which impact and, therefore, influence learning. These conditions include the learner's needs (internal motivation), learning style (orientation), and the instructional events (training).

Applying Cognitive Science

Given the challenge of knowledge management and its emphasis on worker performance, AT&T calls its instructional designers "knowledge engineers." Cognitive science is concerned with the study of mental processes such as remembering and problem-solving.

Remembering. How can you explain what you remember and what you do not remember? Memory is often divided into three major processes: encoding, storage, and retrieval. Encoding is taking meaning from information. Storage is how much and how long we can remember. We can keep a great deal of information in long-term memory, but short-term memory is capable of holding only a few items for a few seconds. As a rule of thumb, we can remember seven things—plus or minus two—in our short-term memory (a telephone number is a good example). Retrieval is accessing information in long-term memory. Following are suggestions from cognitive scientists about how to facilitate remembering:

1. Organization facilitates recall.

   Memorize the following list:

   lake, ocean, bus, pond, truck, car, brook

How did you memorize these items? Without any given structure, people generally will organize items into similar groups (lake, ocean, pond, brook; bus, truck, car). Such an organization facilitates recall. While everyone agrees that organization helps recall, there's no agreement as to how an individual organizes, just that this organization does exist.

What the trainer can learn from this principle is the need for organization in training programs. Learning activities should go not only from the simple to the complex, but should also group like concepts together.

2. Complex processes operate on an "as needed" basis.

Knowing how to write a database program entails procedural knowledge (knowing how to do something) rather than factual knowledge (knowing a fact). While we might understand concepts that define a relational database (facts), being able to group those facts into rules (procedures) that would allow us to write the program is yet another issue. Over time, facts are transformed into production rules, and these mental production rules increase efficiency. The following is an example of production; note that the term *then* for one rule becomes the *if* of the next one.

> *If* your car does not start, *then* check to see if the shift lever is in either Neutral or in Park.
>
> *If* the shift lever is in the appropriate gear, *then* check to see if you have any battery power by turning on your lights.
>
> *If* your lights work, *then* you may have to check your starter motor.

What the trainer can learn from this principle is the desirability of developing procedures. Components of a task that can be made into procedures are logical groupings of instructional materials.

3. Schema can be formulated.

Schema are diagrams or outlines of something. Schema can be expressed by scripts or frames. A script is a scenario and is stored in a time sequence. A frame is information about a particular circumstance. Cognitive scientists believe learning takes place by building schema. For example, an insurance claims adjuster who gets a call from a policy holder who has had an accident, relies on his or her schema to handle the claim. Data are collected from the policyholder in a particular order to ensure that all information about the claim is complete. The adjuster continually modifies schema to fit particular circumstances. Another example is how a doctor treats a patient who complains about feeling poorly. By identifying the area of discomfort and by precise and focused questioning, the doctor is able to isolate and identify the problem. Once diagnosed, the problem becomes treatable and an appropriate remedy can be prescribed.

What the trainer learns from this principle is that by analyzing a learner's errors, incorrect knowledge structures can be identified and addressed. Moreover, knowledge is built by continually modifying schema and the relationships between separate and sometimes isolated elements. Schema provide the learner with a picture of inferencing capabilities.

Problem-solving. Problem-solving is composed of many processes, of which memory is a major player. Previous experience is the basis for means/end analysis. The problem-solver (the learner) tries to figure out how to solve or get to the heart of the problem. Problem-solving is at the crux of cognitive science and requires organizing facts, recalling rules, and applying schema.

What the trainer learns from this principle is first that the problem-solving skills of novices and experts differ markedly. We know that the learner progresses from a knowledge-based state to a rule-based state, then to a skill-based state. We may find that by organizing training around a problem-solving approach, learners will see relationships and develop schema to establish an understanding of how to accomplish tasks and jobs.

Comparing Behavioral and Cognitive Science Approaches

The behaviorist takes the position that the learner moves from a low-level, knowledge-based state through a rule-based state to a skill-based state. And by organizing training around this philosophy, outcomes can be determined through a series of measured and measurable accomplishments. The cognitivist, on the other hand, assumes an interrelationship between knowledge and skills to be learned rather than isolating these elements. The cognitivist takes the position that the problem-solving approach is more effective, as it brings into play relationships, which may help describe or redefine models within a system or schema of experience.

A comparison of behavioral and cognitive positions in the teaching of network troubleshooting was developed by Rob Foshay[11] and is shown in Figure 5-4. This comparison shows how these theories could be used in developing a course on network troubleshooting. While the two approaches begin similarly, the behaviorist concentrates on the individual parts of the network. The cognitive designer, however, spends equal time on concepts and the production systems that explain how the network operates.

Implications of Learning Theory for the Workplace

For effective training to take place, it is essential that one understands learning theory not merely as a set of buzz words and jargon, but how different theories can contribute to successful learning. The trainer's view—and attitude—toward learning and toward the individual learner has much to do with the success of training. The greater the fit between the trainer's attitude and teaching practices—based on a sound understanding of theory—and the learner's style, the more effective training is likely to be. Thus, content knowledge and appreciation of learning theories are essential to the success of the training endeavor.

To provide a guide to understanding how learning theories inform practice in the workplace, Knowles (1989) suggested that training activities must account for tasks that range from simple to complex, and account for trainee abilities that range from low to high. Cognitive science, on the other hand, would suggest beginning with a problem (the complex) and working backward, using problem-solving skills and past experiences as a means for learning.

For adults engaged in a training activity, certain assumptions must be made to include not only the intelligence of the learner, of course, but also a wide range of other variables that impact individual learning such as motivation, previous experience, environment, and resources available. The more these variables occur in a positive state—high motivation, successful prior experience with similar or like tasks, a positive work environment setting, and adequate available resources—the more effective training will be.

FIGURE 5-4
BEHAVIORAL AND COGNITIVE ANALYSIS AND DESIGN STRATEGY FOR TEACHING NETWORK TROUBLESHOOTING

Behavioral	Cognitive
Analysis Approach	
1. Identify the parts of the network.	1. Identify the parts of the network.
2. Identify the cues for network monitoring.	2. Identify rules governing how the parts interact.
3. Identify the network's most common failures.	3. Identify the failures which are common and represent all key parts of the network; for each, identify failure probability and time or resources required to test and to fix.
4. Develop procedural chains for each common fault, using a split-half strategy, including conditions, action, and feedback for each step.	4. Group the faults into categories. For each category, develop a general solution algorithm which takes into account the probability of the failure, the cost of the test, and the cost of the fix. Also derive general rules for developing specific solution algorithms for any problems within each category.
Design Strategy	
1. Teach the network part names.	1. Teach how the network works when it works normally.
2. Teach the cues to network malfunctions and which troubleshooting procedures go with each.	2. Teach a selection of categories of failures and how the network works with each failure category.
3. Teach each procedural chain separately, using realistic simulations, until it is mastered; then go on to the next one.	3. Within each category, teach the failure modes of components, the probability of each, and the cost of each test or replacement procedure for each failure. Have the learner design algorithms by applying the general solution algorithm and general rules to the knowledge of network structure and function. Use realistic simulations, but provide feedback on the quality of the algorithm, as well as success or failure in finding the fault.

In addition to the trainee's abilities, the complexity of the task to be learned is equally important. Generally, the simpler the task, the easier it will be to offer successful training. As the task becomes more complex, the more able the learner and the more precise the training must be in order to complete the task successfully. There is a caution here, which evolves from research that suggests that one can overtrain for task complexity, resulting in a *negative* learning curve. That is, the simpler the task, the fewer instructions that are needed; the more complex the task, the higher the level of instruction needs to be. When this process is reversed—when a great deal of instruction is given for a simple task—the trainee may resist performing at an optimum level. Likewise, for a very complex task, the less instruction provided, the more limited are the chances of success.

While not always the case the use of behaviorist theories to satisfy low-level tasks with low-ability learners, results in detailed directions provided to achieve very specific and observable outcomes. This correlation continues to be high between the use of cognitive theories and a balanced task/ability teaching environment, one that takes a middle-of-the-road approach to the tasks to be performed and the ability level of the learner. Finally, this correlation can be extended to encompass humanistic concepts for the most complex tasks, which involve the motivated individual in a self-directed learning activity. In short, the combination of the individual's abilities and the nature and complexity of the task to be performed tend to fit a particular learning theory—the better the fit, the better the results.

When there is a high correlation between task complexity and learner ability, the learner has the most potential for success. A mismatch between task complexity and learner ability has an equally high potential for missing its mark in effective training. It is the identification of these variables—task complexity, learner ability, and the trainers' use of effective methods based on appropriate theory—that results in the most effective training.

WORKPLACE MOTIVATION: A HUMANIST APPROACH TO IMPLEMENTATION

What drives the potential learner? Adult learning tells us that the need to know is the best motivation. However, what makes one individual more responsive to training than another has been the topic of investigation for years. We will review several of the motivation theories that impact performance learning as part of a humanist orientation.

While behaviorists consider observed changes in behavior to be based on environmental interaction, and the cognitivists think internal mental information processing activities are keys, a third approach considers learning from the perspective of human growth potential. This approach, termed *humanist*, suggests that individuals are able to control their own destiny. People are inherently good and free to act. Behavior is the consequence of human choice and individuals hold unlimited potential for growth and development. Therefore, humanists do not accept the view of either the behaviorial or of Freudian psychologists since these positions imply that behavior is determined by the environment or by the subconscious. From a humanist's perspective, learning theory involves an individual's perceptions that are centered in experience and a person's capacity for self-determination. This principle is basic to the concepts underlying self-directed learning, of which adult learning is a critical extension.

The effectiveness of workplace training is significantly impacted not only by the learning style of the individual, but also by the attitude toward training and development held by the organization and its managers. If, for example, a firm's attitude is one of authoritarian and directed leadership and the learning orientation of the trainee is self-directed, conflict will probably occur. Likewise, if the training program is designed for highly complex tasks and the trainee's orientation is completely behaviorist in nature, again, conflict is apt to occur. It is the agreement between the organizational environment and the trainee's orientation that will provide for optimum results. This can be illustrated through a brief review of the work of motivational theorists Maslow, Herzberg, Rotter, Rogers, and McGregor.

Maslow's Hierarchy of Needs

Abraham Maslow (1954) stated that real motivation is inner-directed and is not something externally imposed or produced. Intrinsic, or inner-directed, motives incite the individual to some kind of action. Moreover, as Figure 5-5 suggests, the lower, more basic level of human needs must be satisfied before the next level of human needs can be addressed. Until lower-level needs are fulfilled, the next level of needs do not serve to motivate. Also, once the need is satisfied, more of the same need does not serve to motivate further. Needs are situational in nature. They must fit the environment and timeliness of the experience.

If one assumes that learning comes from within, motivation to learn would not require stimulus-response activity or the environment to cause it. At the peak of Maslow's pyramid, self-actualization, one reaches the point where self-directed learning exists. For Maslow, learning is a form of self-actualization and, thus, contributes to psychological health.

Herzberg's Two-Factor Theory

Frederick Herzberg (1959) suggested that because Maslow's lower-level needs are provided for by society, individuals are, overall, relatively secure. Because these lower-order needs are secure and, thus, satisfied, a neutral job attitude or state of equilibrium exists. The contrary also occurs. If these lower needs are *not* satisfied, dissatisfaction occurs. Job satisfaction, thus, is

FIGURE 5-5
MASLOW'S HIERARCHY OF NEEDS

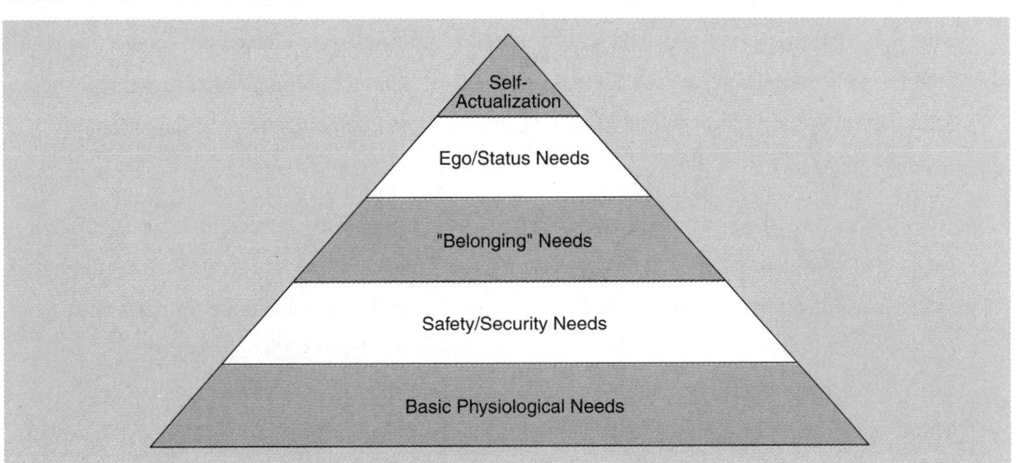

enhanced by having the worker's higher-order needs satisfied. However, if these higher-order needs are not satisfied, yet other positive factors are in place, job *dissatisfaction*, per se, may not be the result, leading to a "motivation-neutral" state. For example, work that is challenging tends to be satisfying. The reverse concept is also true. Jobs that are not challenging do not satisfy and, therefore, they do not attend to Maslow's higher-order needs.

Herzberg thus proposed a two-factor theory of job satisfaction. The first set of factors, called satisfiers, or *motivators*, are those things that make for stimulating and challenging work. The second set of factors, termed dissatisfiers, or *hygiene factors*, are those elements that contribute to the environment, rather than to the work itself. Motivators or satisfiers include such things as achievement, advancement, growth, recognition, responsibility, and interesting work. Hygiene factors or dissatisfiers include company policy and administration, interpersonal relations with others on the job, job security, salary, status, and supervision. While there is some overlap, motivators map to the upper levels of Maslow's hierarchy of needs, while hygiene factors fit into the lower portion of the pyramid.

Therefore, according to Herzberg's two-factor theory, by enhancing the motivators, one should improve a worker's motivation, and consequently, his or her productivity. Training programs that clients readily see as addressing their need for performing satisfying work will be more readily accepted than programs that do not appear to meet these needs.

ROTTER'S LOCUS OF CONTROL

Most learning involves some type of human interaction. These interactions, which involve behaviorist, cognitivist, and humanist elements, and especially personality, have been identified with Julian Rotter (1954). Rotter's work suggests that within a social context, one's personality impacts one's learning style and orientation. This has been stated as "expectancy and reinforcement." Expectancy is defined as the probability that a particular reinforcement *will* occur as the result of some specific behavior. "The way in which the person ... defines the situation will affect the values of both reinforcement and expectancy, thereby influencing the potential for any given behavior to occur."[12]

Rotter described personality types as being either inner- or-external directed. Internal or external *locus of control,* as Rotter termed it, suggests that some personality types respond to their internal or self-directed needs, while others are external and respond to outside or "powerful others." Such individual motivation—internal or external—has a significant impact on one's learning orientation and, thus, on the effectiveness of training styles and methods involved. Those who are internally motivated will tend to have personalities that are more self-directed and will be more comfortable with learning activities that are also self-directed in nature. Learners who are externally motivated may, by contrast, tend to be comfortable with a structured environment and with tasks that lend themselves to behavioralist approaches.

Rogers' Learner-Centered Approach

Carl Rogers (1983) applied the notion of client-centered therapy to education, which dovetails with Maslow's concept of self-actualization and self-directed learning.[13] Personalized learning of this type can lead to an individual's growth and development and fits also with Knowles' (1984) concept of andragogy. Rogers suggests that the following elements comprise a learning centered approach:

- Personal involvement of the learner
- Self-initiated activity coming from within the individual
- Pervasive, in that the activity affects behavior change
- Learner-evaluated and assessed
- Essence of learning takes on permanent meaning for the learner

Both Maslow and Rogers contend that if learning is to be worthwhile in a larger social context, the humanistic approach should be involved, as contrasted with either the behaviorist or cognitivist approach. As adult problem-solvers, adult learners differ substantially from children, as childhood educational experiences are generally grounded in the behavioral and cognitive theories.

McGregor's Theory X and Theory Y

In *The Human Side of Enterprise*, McGregor (1960) identified two separate and opposite concepts of human nature. These concepts McGregor termed *Theory X* and *Theory Y.* At one extreme, Theory X suggests that individuals inherently dislike work and will, if possible, avoid it. Because they dislike work, people must be forced in some way to perform in order to meet organizational objectives. These forces include a variety of pressures: coercion, control, or threat. Theory X contends that over a period of time, the average worker has been conditioned to accept and prefer to be directed. He or she wishes to avoid responsibility, has little ambition, and desires security most of all.

On the other hand, Theory Y suggests that work—the expenditure of physical and mental effort—is as natural as play or rest. And while that may be effective in some cases, external controls and threats are not the only methods of achieving organizational objectives. Individuals who are committed to bringing about organizational goals will exercise self-direction and self-control toward those ends without coercion and threats. The individual's commitment to organizational objectives are functions of the internal rewards associated with one's achievement and work satisfaction. Therefore, under proper conditions, Theory Y people learn not only to accept, but also to seek out responsibility. As such, these individuals have a high capacity for imagination, ingenuity, and creativity in solving organizational problems, not the opposite. Sadly, however, within much of modern industrial experience, management has been more concerned with controlling than expanding the intellectual potential of the average employee.

Implications of Motivational Theory for Training

Carl Rogers' thinking about *learners* provides an interesting parallel to the theories concerning those of *workers* provided by McGregor. McGregor's concerns dealt with assumptions by managers; Rogers', with assumptions by educators. Paralleling McGregor's concept of Theory X, but from within an educational context, Rogers suggested that much of educational practice assumes that students cannot be trusted to pursue their own learning. Teacher presentations of facts equal learning, and the aim of education is for the learner to accumulate pieces of factual knowledge. It also follows that truth is a known and teachable element, that creative citizens develop from passive learner, that evaluation equals education, and that education equals evaluation.

Rogers sharply criticized this Theory X approach to education and used McGregor's Theory Y assumptions to suggest that people have a natural potential for learning and that learning occurs when the subject matter is perceived to be relevant. A great deal of learning is acquired through one's own activity outside of a training classroom, and this is facilitated by participation in the learning process itself. Figure 5-6 illustrates these comparisons.

FIGURE 5-6
COMPARISON OF ASSUMPTIONS ABOUT HUMAN NATURE AND BEHAVIOR UNDERLYING THEORY X AND THEORY Y MANAGEMENT PHILOSOPHY

Theory X Assumptions about Human Nature (McGregor)	Assumptions Implicit in Current Education (Rogers)
The average human being inherently dislikes work and will avoid it if he can. Because of this characteristically human dislike of work, most people must be coerced, controlled, and threatened in the interest of organizational objectives. The average human being prefers to be directed, wishes to avoid responsibility, has relatively little ambition, and wants security above all.	The student cannot be trusted to pursue his own learning. Presentation equals learning. The aim of education is to accumulate brick upon brick of factual knowledge. The truth is known. Creative citizens develop from passive learners. Evaluation is education and education is evaluation.
Theory Y Assumptions about Human Nature	**Assumptions Relevant to Significant Experiential Learning**
The expenditure of physical and mental effort is as natural as play or rest. External control and threat of punishment are not the only means for bringing about effort toward organizational objectives. Man will exercise self-direction and self-control in the service of objectives to which he is committed. Commitment to objectives is a function of the rewards associated with their achievement. The average human being learns, under proper conditions, not only to accept but to seek responsibility. A high capacity for imagination, ingenuity, and creativity in solving organizational problems is widely, not narrowly, distributed in the population. Under the conditions of modern industrial life, the intellectual potential of the average human being is only partially utilized.	Human beings have a natural potentiality for learning. Significant learning takes place when the subject matter is perceived by the student as relevant to his own purposes. Much significant learning is acquired through doing. Learning is facilitated by students' responsible participation in the learning process. Self-initiated learning involving the whole person—feelings as well as intellect—is the most pervasive and lasting. Creativity in learning is best facilitated when self-criticism and self-evaluation are primary, and evaluation by others is of secondary importance. The most socially useful thing to learning in the modern world is the process of learning, a continuing openness to experience, an incorporation into oneself of the process of change.

SUMMARY

*ndragogy* and *pedagogy* refer to teaching styles used to expose individuals to new skills, knowledge, and attitudes. Each style differs in assumptions about the learner and about the instructor. An understanding of learning theories is critical to the success of training and

provides guidance in the assessment, development, implementation, and evaluation of the training activity. Individuals differ markedly in the ways they learn. These differences include individual learning styles that may be behavioral, cognitive, or humanistic—or some combination of all three.

"Learning how to learn" is essential for organizational success as we move further into the 21st century. And as new information makes previously acquired knowledge obsolete, it is critical that trainers be equipped with the skills, knowledge, and attitudes to cope with the pressures these demands will certainly bring. Knowing the trainee's learning style, understanding learning theories and the contexts within which each are most effective, and evaluating training results are all hallmarks of the effective trainer.

Learning theories generally fit within two basic models: behaviorist and cognitivist. The behaviorist model suggests that observable changes in behavior as a result of training or stimuli reinforces learning. For a behaviorist, learning occurs when a demonstrated behavior change occurs. The cognitivist suggests that perception, meaning, and insight are keys to learning and that learning how to learn occurs through discovery, flashes of insight, and motivational activities. When learning is viewed from a perspective of human growth potential and stresses the motivational development of the learner, an individual's needs, locus of control, and self-direction are the strengths of the humanist's point of view. Figure 5-7 summarizes these.

Figure 5-7
Learning Orientation Summary

Element	Behaviorist	Cognitivist	Humanist
Learning process view	Behavioral change	Internal mental process action	Personal potential fulfillment
Learning locus	External	Internal	Affective and cognitive
Education's purpose	Behavior change	Capacity to learn	Self-actualization and autonomous
Role of instructor	Sets environment	Structures content of learning	Facilitates whole-person development
Adult learning connection	Behavioral objectives, competency-based training, skill development training	Cognitive development, memory, and learning how to learn	Andragogy, mentoring, locus of control, and self-directed learning
Learning theorists	Thorndike, Pavlov, Skinner	Lewin, Piaget, Bruner, Gagné	Maslow, Rogers, Rotter

Finally, individuals respond in accordance with their perceptions and reactions to motivation. The individual may be driven by external factors such as direct leadership, coercion, and threats, which may prove effective for one who is externally motivated. However, to an inner-directed person, this same type of motivation may result in just the opposite reaction and thus, be counterproductive. Likewise, those who are inner-directed and respond well to encouragement and higher levels of responsibility would blossom in corporate environments of a sharing and caring nature. What serves to motivate one person is not necessarily the same thing that will motivate another. A sensitive and competent trainer, well-versed in motivation theories, must also be able to assess individual learning needs, as well as the learning style of the trainee. No one theory will fit every training experience due to the complexity of human nature, the content and the context of the tasks to be learned, and the environment within which training occurs and is to be applied. It is critical for the trainer to be aware of these theories and issues in order to make the most effective bridge between trainer and trainee. Learning, in its most effective context, may never be completely identified and isolated. We do know, however, that for effective learning to occur, the fit between the learner, the content of the material to be acquired, the environment, and the instructor or trainer must be as congruent as possible. Learning and motivation theories provide this guidance.

THINK IT THROUGH

1. How might the learning styles differ between a college student and a new employee of a major organization?
2. What are the primary characteristics of the following learning theories: behaviorist, cognitivist, and humanist? Of what value are they to the training professional?
3. What critical elements are required for the development of a learning objective in the cognitive, psychomotor, and affective domains? Write three objectives relative to a course on presentation skills.
4. What motivated you to take this course or read this book? Analyze your motivation using terms found in this chapter. Were, or are, you internally or externally motivated?
5. A Theory "W" manager has been described as a Theory X manager masquerading as a Theory Y manager. Can you offer examples of Theory "W" behavior in the workplace or at your school?
6. For the following situations, which pedagogical or andragogical elements would be most effective?

a. upgrading word processing software to a new version

b. sexual harassment seminar

c. report writing course

d. new EEOC guidelines seminar

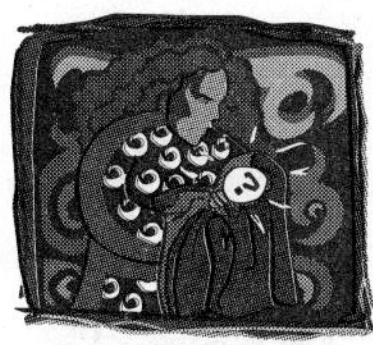

IDEAS IN ACTION

1. Using the Kolb Learning Style categories, attempt to identify your own learning style. Then compare it with what motivates you to learn. Are you in congruence or are there differences? If there are differences, what might account for them?
2. Contrast the results in the foregoing question with those of three or four of your colleagues. What differences, if any, did you observe?
3. Observe an introductory class in the natural or computer science area and note the professor's instructional style. Identify the instructional approach used and, if possible, find out why this style was selected by the professor. Compare this observation with one in a training environment and note the differences, if any.

ADDITIONAL RESOURCES

RECOMMENDED READINGS

Bloom, B. S. *Taxonomy of Educational Objectives. Book 1: Cognitive Domain.* New York: McKay, 1956, 196 pp.

A classic in the field of developing behavioral objectives, this little text provides a step-by-step approach that involves Bloom's taxonomy and the appropriate verbs to use in developing cognitive behavioral objectives for each of his six stages.

Clark, M. C., and R. S. Caffarella, eds. "An Update on Adult Learning Theory." *New Directions for Adult and Continuing Education*, Monograph No. 84, San Francisco: Jossey-Bass, Winter 1999, 106 pp.

A monograph containing 11 brief and thoughtful chapters concerning adult learning theory from a variety of authors.

Kemp, J. E. *Designing Instructional Systems.* Palo Alto, CA: Fearon, 1964, 164 pp.

A small text that provides a good introduction to developing instructional systems from a behavioral standpoint.

Knowles, M. S. *The Adult Learner: A Neglected Species*, 3rd edition. Houston, TX: Gulf, 1984, 292 pp.

A wonderful text on adult learning as seen through the eyes of "Mr. Adult Learning," himself. An excellent resource for any trainer.

Krathwohl, D. R., B. S. Bloom, and B. B. Masia. *Taxonomy of Educational Objectives. Book 2: Affective Domain.* New York: Longman, 1964, 196 pp.

The second in the taxonomy series focusing on the affective domain. A five-step taxonomy is provided, along with a series of appropriate verbs to apply.

Mager, R. F. *The New Mager Six-Pack.* Belmont, CA: Lake, 1984 – 1988. Six handbooks.

The authority on developing instructional and performance objectives. This package of six small books includes *Making Instruction Work, Preparing Instructional Objectives, Analyzing Performance Problems, Developing Attitude Toward Learning, Measuring Instructional Results*, and *Goal Analysis.*

Merriam, S. B., and R. S. Caffarella. *Learning in Adulthood*, 2nd edition. San Francisco: Jossey-Bass, 1999, 502 pp.

This book is an up-to-date overview and synthesis of what we know about adult learning, examining not only the learners, but also the context in which learning takes place.

WEB SITES

http://web.indstate.edu/ctl/styles/ls1.html

Indiana State's Center for Teaching and Learning's Web site provides links to models and articles about learning styles.

http://trgmcber.haygroup.com/learning/lsius.html

At the time of this writing, TRG Hay/McBer, publishers of the Kolb Learning Style Inventory, offer you the opportunity to take the Kolb Learning Style Inventory on-line for $10.

ENDNOTES

1. Maples, M. F., and J. M. Webster. "Thorndike's Connectionism." in G. M. Gazda and R. J. Corsini, eds., *Theories of Learning*. Itasca, IL: Peacock, 1980, p. 1.
2. Lee, Chris. "The Adult Learner: Neglected No More." *Training*. March 1998, p. 50.
3. Kolb, Daniel H. Leaning Style Industry. Boston: McBer and Company, 1981, p. 5.
4. Howell, W. C., and N. J. Cooke. "Training the Human Information Processor: A Review of Cognitive Models," in I. L. Goldstein and Associates, *Training and Development in Organizations*. San Francisco: Jossey-Bass, 1989, p. 123.
5. Grippin, P., and S. Peters. *Learning Theory and Learning Outcomes*. New York: University Press of America, 1984. In Merriam, S. B., and R. S. Caffarella, *Learning in Adulthood*. San Francisco: Jossey-Bass, 1991, p. 126.
6. Hergenhahn, B. R. *An Introduction to Theories of Learning*, 3rd edition. Englewood Cliffs, NJ: Prentice-Hall, p. 19.
7. Skinner, B. F. *Beyond Freedom and Dignity*. New York: Knopf, 1974.
8. Bloom, B. S. *A Theory of Educational Objectives: The Classification of Educational Goals*. New York: McKay, 1956.
9. Mager, Robert. *Preparing Instructional Objectives*. Palo Alto, CA: Fearon, 1962.
10. Smith, R. M. *Learning How to Learn: Applied Learning Theory for Adults*. Chicago: Follett, 1982, p. 1.
11. Foshay, Rob. Sharpen Up Your Schemata. *Data Training*. May 1991, p. 24.
12. Rotter, J. B. *Social Learning and Clinical Psychology*. Englewood Cliffs, NJ: Prentice-Hall, 1954, p. 40. In Merriam, S. B., and R. S. Caffarella. *Learning in Adulthood*, 2nd edition. San Francisco: Jossey-Bass, 1999, p. 2.
13. Rogers, C. *Freedom to Learn for the 80s*. Columbus: Merrill, 1983, p. 20.

CHAPTER 6 Training Program Design

- Define the design process.
- Describe and plan the "how" of training.
- Assess program development.
- Evaluate instructional designs.
- Create a Leader's Guide.

THE DESIGN PROCESS

The output of needs assessment, Step 1 of the training cycle (See Figure 1-8), is the input for the *training design* phase of this cycle. Needs assessment provides a picture of what members of the organization must learn, with a reasonably clear indication of the depth of coverage required. The process of training design begins with the assessment of these learning needs.

The first step in design is to group the learning needs together into logically connected clusters. Next decide which clusters will be linked together to form the *goals,* or *outcomes,* of a particular training program. Once established, the goals of the program are then, one by one, separated into *learning objectives*: the specific things which the participants must *know* or *be able to do* as a result of completing the program. One or more such learning objectives for each program goal are the results.

COGNITIVE AND BEHAVIORAL OUTCOMES

The difference between the terms *know* and *able to do* is an important distinction between *cognitive* and *behavioral* learning outcomes, respectively. In Chapter 1 of this text, these types of outcomes were referred to as *informational* and *operational* training. Whatever the terminology used, both types of learning outcomes reflect legitimate organizational needs. There are those who argue that training should concern itself exclusively with behavioral outcomes—with skills for *doing*, such as seen in the work of Robert Mager. This argument contends that knowing *things*—a cognitive outcome—is the result of education, not training, and that a training department cannot just provide knowledge, but must *always* and *only* deal with programs that deliver physical skills as outcomes—physical skills that are reflected in workplace job behaviors.

Whether or not one agrees with the theoretical validity of this position, the reality is that an organization often has a need for its people to know things, without necessarily requiring them to turn that knowledge into specific behaviors. Moreover, providing a way for people to obtain this knowledge is frequently seen as a training responsibility. *Awareness,* or *informational, programs,* with cognitive outcomes, are the result. Such programs can take many forms and serve many organizational purposes. An example is the organization's need for employees to understand—to *know*—its strategic direction. Another example is the need for managers to understand demographic, societal, or industry trends. Still another kind of awareness program, often critical to an organization's success, is a management overview of a particular product and its potential. The outcome of this last kind of program is precisely one of awareness, a conceptual grasp of the features and power of a product (e.g., a new line of artificially intelligent oil-drilling rigs) as distinct from the ability to *use* this awareness.

An organization may view informational programs as the responsibility of its communications department or, in the case of product knowledge, see these programs as the marketing department's responsibility. The fact is that many organizations consider informational programs as belonging to the training department. Thus, cognitive outcomes are often the target of training program design. The training professional should recognize that informational programs offer a great opportunity to contribute to the organization's operation and bottom line, a chance to add real value. Informational training programs can mobilize people's energies around a new organizational vision. They can galvanize motivation in the face of an industry challenge. They can ensure understanding of critical business decisions, and they can orient people to new organizational structures or institutional policies. Providing programs that deliver these kinds of information—all *cognitive* outcomes—makes a significant organizational contribution.

Furthermore, informational programs often provide a big-picture perspective that is ultimately more important than specific behavior. Informational programs may, in fact, provide an absolutely necessary context for behavior, a context without which the most perfectly sharpened skill is useless. In short, a training professional should expect to deal with both cognitive and behavioral learning outcomes, both informational and operational programs, in both education and training arenas.

A Training Example

Training design is an art as well as a science. As a science, it takes into account the purpose the organization wants the training to achieve, appropriate principles from learning theory, and pragmatic considerations, such as cost and organizational sponsorship. As an art, the instructional designer provides creative solutions for learning needs. We begin our discussion of this process by exploring an example. Suppose an organization's needs assessment indicates that its supervisory staff needs to learn the appropriate policies and procedures concerning performance management. When further reviewed, this generic organizational need results in specific elements the company wants supervisors to learn—the following three learning outcomes for a training program in performance management:

1. Supervisors must know the company policy on performance management (a cognitive learning outcome).
2. Supervisors must follow the company rules and procedures in managing employee performance specifically, the following (all behavioral outcomes):
   - **a.** set individual performance objectives and measures of success
   - **b.** monitor performance against objectives, using agreed-upon measures
   - **c.** coach ongoing performance to ensure alignment with objectives
   - **d.** communicate performance judgements to employees
3. Supervisors must know the legal limits concerning performance management: pitfalls to avoid, risky language, etc. (another cognitive outcome).

THE DESIGN TEAM

A training department team is assigned to design a program to address the identified learning needs. The team's first step is to seek a wide representation of the organization in this design effort. The team believes this is especially important for this particular training program because the outcomes will touch virtually everyone in the organization. Therefore, they want significant department involvement in the design effort; they do not want the program to be the creation of the training department alone. Thus, they enlarge the design team to include representation from all the major departments and hierarchical levels within the organization. They also make a point of including nonmanagement personnel who will be the recipients of the performance appraisal process. Finally, they seek out representation from the Human Resources and Legal Departments to ensure proper handling of employee relations and legal technicalities.

From Learning Goals to Program Modules

The expanded design team studies the findings of the needs assessment, which includes the three learning goals previously mentioned. They make a preliminary judgment that all three learning outcomes can be achieved in a training program that will be one to two days in length. They group the previously identified outcomes #1 and #3, policy and legalities respectively, into a single module that will cover the following:

AN AWARENESS MODULE

A. The organization's policy on performance management consists of four points:

1. All employees will receive a formal appraisal of performance at least once a year and will sign a summary of the appraisal discussion as proof that it took place (the actual appraisal itself may be oral or written, at the manager's discretion).
2. Managers will involve employees in setting performance goals and in defining measures of successful goal attainment.
3. A mutually accepted professional development plan—or a mutually signed explanation of why one is not appropriate—will be one result of every employee's appraisal.
4. Part of every manager's own performance plan will be how well he or she does performance appraisals for employees, as measured by signed summaries of appraisals filed for all the manager's staff members (see A,1), and by anonymous feedback from appraisal recipients as captured in regularly scheduled company-wide climate surveys.

B. The legalities of dealing with performance appraisal are:

1. Appraisals against objectives other than those mutually agreed upon are unfair and may put the organization at legal risk.
2. Discriminatory language or practices may not be used.

The design team determines that the program will open with a module that explains the details under points A and B above. This will be Module #1 and will serve as a conceptual introduction not only to the subject of performance management but to the program itself. This introduction will present both the policy aspects of performance appraisal and its legalities as an umbrella set of definitions under which the specific appraisal skills and practices will fit. The introduction will deliver the awareness of policy and legalities—the cognitive learning outcomes—which the organization considers necessary for its managers.

A Skills Module

The design team next turns its attention to the requirement that supervisors learn the actual procedures the company wants followed in managing employee performance, items (a) through (d) under program goal #2. The team spells out very specific behaviors necessary for item 2a, then item 2b, and so forth—the action steps a supervisor must actually take to carry out each of the tasks identified in the list. These actions are specified in the form of *terminal behaviors*—i.e., what the successful program participant (one who has successfully learned) will be able to *do* at the *termination* of the program.

Program goal #2 is "Supervisors must follow the company rules and procedures in managing employee performance." The design team develops more specific learning objectives for this program goal. These learning objectives are the items identified as 2a, 2b, 2c, and 2d in the list that follows. The team then defines these learning objectives still further—creating for each objective a statement of the detailed behaviors supervisors must be able to do if they are to carry out the organization's policy regarding performance management. These detailed behaviors are the terminal behaviors for this module of the training program and follow each learning objective below:

2a. set individual performance objectives and measures of success—

at the end of this program, a supervisor shall be able to

- identify specific performance goals for individual employees that result in the achievement of assigned job responsibilities
- identify measurable indicators of success for each goal identified
- include staff members in the definition of goals and measures
- establish checkpoints during the planned performance period to review performance objectives and redefine them as needed

2b. monitor performance against objectives, using agreed-upon measures—

at the end of this program, a supervisor shall be able to

- establish reporting mechanisms and/or project milestones to ensure performance is reviewed in a timely and realistic way
- review interim performance results to ensure they are on track to achieve planned objectives
- uses mutually agreed upon measures in reporting/reviewing

2c. coach ongoing performance to ensure alignment with objectives—

at the end of this program, a supervisor shall be able to

- exhibit helping, rather than fault-finding, behaviors in reviewing performance outcomes with employees
- assist staff members in finding ways around difficulties they may be encountering in achieving desired results, offering perspectives they may not have thought of or resources they may have overlooked
- assist staff members in setting/adjusting/sticking to priorities

2d. communicate performance judgements to employees—

at the end of this program, a supervisor shall be able to

- discuss performance in terms of results and job behaviors, rather than in personal terms such as motivation or attitude
- state clearly and directly to staff members, when the situation calls for it, that performance results were unacceptable and why, utilizing agreed-upon measures of success and remaining calm in the face of negative employee reactions

The Training Design Funnel

The design team in our example has now documented the "what" of its proposed training program. The careful listing of program modules, with learning objectives and terminal outcomes for each module, creates a complete, clear outline of what the proposed training will cover. This outline serves to document their plans, both for their own further work in developing the program and for review by other interested parties. (See the later discussion concerning reviews by various stakeholders.)

The design team has taken a set of generic learning requirements for supervisors and turned them into learning objectives for a training program—*terminal knowledge* (awareness gained by the end, or *terminus*, of the program) and *terminal behaviors* (skills acquired by program end). This design process is one of progressive narrowing, a narrowing that can be graphically represented as a training design funnel, as shown in Figure 6-1.

FIGURE 6-1
THE TRAINING DESIGN FUNNEL

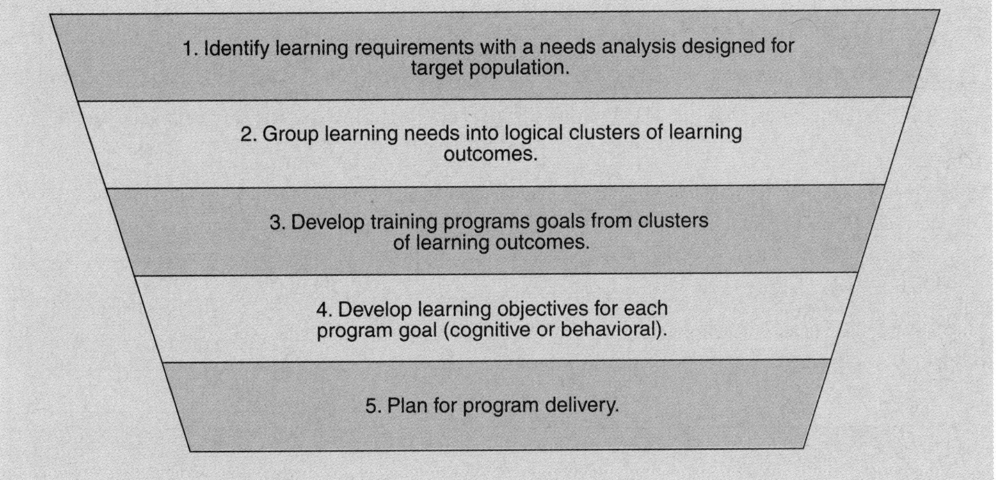

PLANNING THE "HOW"

The first four layers of the design funnel pictured in Figure 6-1 focus on the "what" of training: (1) determining what it is that program participants need to learn, (2) clustered into logical groupings, (3) translated into program goals, and (4) then stated as learning objectives that can be used by the design team to develop appropriate program activities and materials. Only when the design team has a clear picture of the "what" of the program, does the team shift its attention to the "how" phase, and begins to plan the ways in which the program will present material to its participants to enable them to achieve the planned program outcomes.

A cautionary word is in order here. Trainers often move too quickly into the fifth layer of the design funnel, the "how," which is the focus on planning program delivery. For many trainers, this is where the most excitement lies in the design process. This is perfectly understandable, since program delivery is where the instructor meets the learner, and is precisely the interaction point that most trainers like best. Moreover, program delivery is concrete, familiar work with tangible outcomes, which provide additional reasons for its appeal. It is important, however, to make sure that the "what" of training receives due attention in the design process so that the "how" will be the best solution.

The Design Work Sheet

Typically, at Step 5, a design team uses a work sheet something like the one in Figure 6-2. The purpose of the design work sheet is to plan in complete detail how to deliver instruction so that participants will learn what is needed for the successful attainment of a particular learning objective. The team creates a separate work sheet for each learning goal of the program, clustering work sheets into modules or program sections. Recall that in the program structure assumed here, each module of the program contains one or more program goals, and each program goal is broken down into one or more terminal learning objectives. It is at the level of these last items, the learning objectives, that the design work sheet serves to outline specific program activities.

Figure 6-2
The Training Design Work Sheet

Program Name:____________________ Work Sheet Date: __________
Module#: ____________________ Module Name: ____________________

Program Goal#________________: *(statement of goal, cognitive or behavioral)*

Learning Objective	Active	Timing	Materials Costs	Who
1	What will be done in the program to ensure participants acquire this piece of knowledge or this behavior — e.g., instructor lecture, showing and debriefing a video clip, group work, quiet time, role-play with group feedback, etc.	Length of time planned for this activity	Whatever materials may be necessary for this activity— a film, flip charts, handouts, game material, etc. Costs of developing the materials needed for this activity	The parts played by each actor in the program— the role of the instructor—the participants, guests, etc.
2				
3				
N				
TOTALS	Total time estimated for this module →	Hrs/mins	Total cost estimate: $	

The major focus of training design at this point is the activity column in the design work sheet. The work involved here is on the creative side of training responsibility. Here is where trainers bring their science and art to bear—devising ways for people to learn what they are supposed to learn, and learn it faster, easier, better, and with greater retention than if they were merely left to their own devices. This is where the techniques and tricks of the training trade are employed. Here is where the decisions are made to use live or mediated instruction or some other form of self-study, and whether to include prework. Here is where the instructional choices are made concerning the use of feedback instruments, Web-based training, video to deliver information, or for skill-practice feedback.

TRAINING DESIGN CHALLENGES

The challenge of training design is heightened here because unlike preparing course material for one's own use as a teacher, the design team is faced with the necessity of creating instructional material that will be used by others. This makes a necessity of thoroughness far beyond personal preparation. It requires spelling out every step and every nuance for each step. Experienced instructors can sum up a great deal in personal teaching notes with a single word or phrase, assuming correctly that one knows one's own mind. However, such an assumption is a luxury the design team does not enjoy. As it creates and describes activities for each learning objective, the team must always remember that others will be delivering the material. The designers themselves may teach the pilot offering of the program, and can thus leave the final fine-tuning until the pilot is completed. But the designers will eventually have to be exhaustively explicit about every single instructional step and incorporate these details in a *Leader's Guide*. The Leader's Guide will be described later in this chapter.

A major responsibility of the training professional is, of course, to see to it that the activities designed into a program follow good instructional design principles and adult learning theory. There must be variety in the activities, with more emphasis on interaction and group work than on readings or lecture. The design should draw on the experience and pre-existing knowledge of the learners. The program must accommodate individual differences, while at the same time clearly convey the messages that the organization wants people to hear and learn. The program must reflect awareness that adults are motivated to learn by pragmatic need on their part, rather than by the theoretical value of the material presented to them. The organization and its culture must always be the backdrop for the methods and activities that the program includes. Above all, designers must work with one eye always on the realization that the goal of the program is participant learning and nothing else. The goal is not elegance of materials nor cleverness of design, and it is certainly not ease or novelty in instruction. Finally, design for adult learning should go to any lengths to ensure/empower learning. At the same time, it should be prepared to stop when the required learning has taken place. A program's activities, its instruction, and its very design, are all totally in the service of participant learning. When the learning has taken place, the astute trainer gets out of the way, satisfied that the training task has been accomplished. Good training design keeps in mind that the program is a means to an end, not the end itself.

PROGRAM DEVELOPMENT ISSUES

M*odule* is a word used in this book to organize programs into manageable segments. Modules are rolled up and combined into units, and units are rolled up and combined into days; however, nothing is sacred about the terminology used here. A variety of words and outlining approaches can be and are used by trainers to compartmentalize their programs—unit, section, segment, component, module, etc. What *is* important is that the program, having been framed overall in terms of content, must now be segmented. This segmentation allows the design team, and ultimately the participants, to focus on deliverable/learnable pieces of the content, one piece at a time. The practice reflected in this book is to divide programs into *days*, days into *units*, units into *modules*, the last being the smallest, basic division of a program. Each module delivers one or several learning objectives—cognitive or behavioral. It is, of course, possible to omit the unit level of organizing material and just have a number of modules per day, in which case the modules would be numbered 1 through N for each day, or 1-N for the entire program. Whatever the decision as to levels of organization and terminology, one design work sheet per program goal builds the program from the bottom up.

It should also be noted that programs can be linked together to form a curriculum, a series of courses that lead as a whole to some larger, overall learning objective. Curricula are perhaps most often established for management development, where the organization has an interest not only in learning outcomes that can be delivered via individual programs, but also in a planned progression of programs spread over time. A management development curriculum, for example, is often a sequence of learning events that intersperses traditional classroom programs with developmental job rotations, university courses, etc. Other subject matter may also lend itself to being organized into curricula, depending upon the organization and its interests. A good example of a curricular approach is to be found in corporate universities (See Chapter 1), where specific corporations have developed curricula based on their belief in the benefits of an integrated, long-term response to organizational learning needs.

Stakeholders and Sponsorship

A program's design work sheets should be shared across the whole design team and with others as well. The work sheet is a perfect tool for obtaining reviews from colleagues on the design team. It is also a good tool for getting feedback from various stakeholders in the organization concerning what the program is aiming at and how it is going about achieving that objective. Very often, particularly in the development of mission-critical management training initiatives, a training design team will set up some sort of formal sponsorship. *Sponsorship* often takes the form of a board of reviewers who provide input into the program content and evaluation plan, critique its proposed processes and materials, help select participants for its offerings, and evaluate the program both at the pilot stage and thereafter. Sponsors also sometimes play a role in the actual delivery of the program, kicking it off with an opening talk, teaching one or more of its modules, or hosting a reception or dinner as part of the agenda. In general, sponsors help establish the program's validity for, and credibility with, its intended target population and are almost always a valuable resource that a design team should use.

The design team and other stakeholders must ultimately review and accept the program as a whole. An ideal vehicle for this review is a module-by-module outline of the program mapped into the time frame the design team recommends. That is, once all learning objectives have been covered and the work sheets are complete, each module is allocated a time slot in the program. The scheduling process is ongoing, so that the time required for the various learning activities can fit into the total time available for the program. The ideal, of course, would be to design the learning activities and let the time requirements be simply a function of the design. This ideal, however, is rarely available in the real world of training. There is almost always a requirement that the program take only X-amount of time, a constraint the design team must accommodate.

In any case, the design team produces an overall module-by-module outline of the program in the time allocated to it. Module work sheets should be attached as supporting detail, with break times included in the outline. The final result is the ultimate review and sign-off document, the full statement of what the program in question will deliver: what its topics are, what its participants will learn, what the instructional material will be, and how the delivery of that material will be accomplished. A program outline for a corporate new-hire orientation program is provided here as a sample in Figure 6-3.

Figure 6-3
The Program Outline

PROGRAM: New-Hire Orientation (one day, no units; module details attached)

			Minutes
start:	8:30 a.m. (coffee available 8:00)		
	MODULE 1:	Ice Breaker + self-introduction by new associates (Facilitator-led)	30
	MODULE 2:	"From Today to 2000 – The company Vision" (Guest Lecture – Management Committee Member)	30
		Group Exercise – Implications of Vision/Values (Facilitator-led, group reports/drawings)	60
out:	10:30		
		—— break ——	15
back:	10:45		
	MODULE 3:	"How We Make Our Money" (Guest Lecture – Business Development Group)	45
		Business Simulation – whole class exercise: tracing a customer purchase through the company	45
		"What We Look Like This Morning" Facilitator Lecturette on organization at the corporate level + major staff resources	30
out:	12:45	—— Lunch ——	75
back:	2:00		
	MODULE 4:	"Where We Came From" (Video, company history)	30
	MODULE 5:	"Where We Are & Where We're Going" Current Major Business Initiatives – teams of program participants interview visitors representing each initiative, prepare team presentation to whole class, visitors present for questions (activity includes break time)	120
	MODULE 6:	Company Jeopardy (Facilitator-led game as review of the day)	30
end:	5:00		

Program Costs

The work sheet shown in Figure 6-2 includes a cost estimate for developing materials for each activity. Development costs are totaled at the end of each work sheet, and such estimates are important because there is usually a dollar limit at work in the design process. While design should ideally dictate the program's budget, the reality is that the reverse usually occurs—budgetary limits are often set for the program. The total cost of developing the program is a major factor in its design, and there is more than one instance of a design being returned to the team for rework based upon budget unavailability or, more rarely, availability.

The design team must also give consideration to the cost of rolling the program out once it is designed. That is, the costs of developing a program are not limited to design factors such as the cost of making the master of a film or a workbook or a set of handouts. There are also implementation costs. These costs include the expense of making participant copies of master documents and the purchase of consumables the program requires. The consideration of implementation costs must be part of the design team's choices of materials and activities, and must be included in its estimates. Whether the design team begins with an up-front budgetary limit or is given a free hand to propose a program and its associated costs, the budget for development and rollout must be approved before the design team can proceed any further. A major cost consideration is whether the development work will be done by in-house or contract resources (See later section on internal vs. external development).

INSTRUCTIONAL MATERIALS

With the program reviews in, the original plans modified to the satisfaction of the design team and its reviewers/sponsors, and the budget approved, work can start on the development of materials for the learning activities planned for the program. This activity can start earlier, of course, and often does, but the bulk of materials development should wait until the team is certain of the final form of the program and the budget available.

The design work sheet in Figure 6-2 provides the planning guide for the materials needed for program activities. The next step is to actually create these learning materials, which can range from the simple to the complex, from the everyday to the unusual. Lectures, games, a vast array of group activities, individual work, simple reading, case studies—both paper and electronic versions—and computer-based materials are examples in an endless list of program activities that support learning. Delivery strategies are limited only by the imagination of the designers and the constraints of reality factors, such as cost and time. The only other proviso is the overarching principle that participant learning is the most important consideration of all.

Many good sources of off-the-shelf instructional materials exist. Two magazines, *Training and Development* (National ASTD Office) and *Training* (Lakewood Publications), are filled issue after issue with ideas for a wide variety of instructional material and approaches. In their articles, their regular features, and their advertisements, writers in both magazines offer suggestions, samples, experience (both successful and not), and sources of materials. In addition, two annual publications specialize in instructional materials: *The Training and Development Yearbook*, edited by Carolyn Nilson and published by Prentice Hall, and *Annual: Developing Human Resources*, edited by J. William Pfeiffer and published by The Pfeiffer Company, San Diego. Both of these latter publications stretch back for several years, and both are filled with actual games, exercises, and ideas to use, as well as articles discussing trends in the field and experiences with various kinds of materials.

Internal vs. External Development

It is possible for a training department to hire contract resources to help with its workload. The issue that usually comes first to mind when this possibility is brought up is cost. Consultant costs in the field will vary, depending upon locale, type of assignment, subject matter, level of the contractor's experience, length of the consulting relationship and frequency of its use, and any number of other factors as well. In New York City, at the time of this book's publication, training consultant costs typically began at approximately $850 per day for program delivery, somewhat less for simple design consulting.

Consulting help can also be purchased on the basis of a fixed price for a stipulated product, rather than on a daily rate. Again, based upon experience in New York City, for a consulting firm to completely develop a three-day management training program, from initial design through delivery of a pilot offering with all materials, including a full Leader's Guide, and with the program then belonging totally to the client, the cost would be in the neighborhood of $150,000 for a generic program, and $250,000 for a fully customized program. These are prices for a program based upon live classroom instruction. Other forms of instructional delivery result in different cost estimates. The generic estimate for creating a video or a movie is $2,500 per finished minute for a professional-level, commercial-quality training film. For computer-based or Web-based Training, the delivery of instruction via a computer, or through the World Wide Web, the usual rule of thumb is $20,000-$30,000 of development cost for an hour, with all the necessary support and ancillary materials included.

Computer-mediated training is increasingly being created and used for multimedia desktop workstations, which incorporates sound, moving graphics, and video into the instructional delivery. Cost estimates for state-of-the-art multimedia programs typically range around the $50,000 mark for each finished hour, again including all appropriate support materials.

Large as these numbers may appear, money is not the only—and perhaps not the most important—issue in decisions about using in-house or consulting resources to design a training program. Consider these others:

- *Desirability of the task.* Design is often the creative, exciting part of the training job. Some people even consider design as having a higher status than other training tasks. Thus, it might be wise to keep design in-house and if resource shortages surface, contract out some of the training department's delivery responsibilities instead of design activities.
- *Credibility.* This is a tricky issue. Both inside and outside resources can bring credibility to a program. The perspectives of an outside consultant can add stories about other organizations or situations, and can easily be considered more reality-based, less inbred, and more credible. While this perception of the outsider may be groundless, it is no less real for the trainees and can be used to good advantage when it helps people pay attention and learn. On the other hand, there are times when only an insider will do: A program on the organization's strategic direction would typically not best be taught by an outsider, no matter how gifted or experienced.
- *Skill.* It is entirely possible that the training department's own personnel may not have the experience or knowledge to handle the design task. Thus, it may be that consulting assistance is absolutely necessary. On the other hand, this is also a situation where a team approach, with insiders learning from outsiders, provides win-win possibilities.
- *Time.* It can easily happen that the need for a program to be available *soon* means that outside help becomes imperative. This is particularly true if the outside help already has a program on the shelf that largely, or even partially, fills the learning need being targeted.

EVALUATION IN INSTRUCTIONAL DESIGN

valuation was discussed in great detail in Chapter 3. However, for emphasis here, consider the following two points concerning evaluation in training design:

1. One kind of evaluation examines the learning outcomes of the program in design. Designers must take the time during the design process to ask themselves over and over, for each learning objective, "How will we know this particular learning outcome has been achieved?" Sometimes, design teams even add this question as another column on the design work sheet pictured in Figure 6-2.
2. The second kind of evaluation concerns the quality of the design itself. Training design includes the activities planned to deliver the learning objectives, the sequence, the instructional logic, the materials developed for use in the program, and the instructions for their use. These components of design must be evaluated repeatedly in the design process itself to make sure they serve the required learning objectives and to ensure they meet the criteria of good instruction in general, and adult learning principles in particular.

While the design team itself must constantly evaluate its own work as it proceeds through the design process, it is important that others assess the design outcomes on these dimensions, too. These individuals can be other training professionals, sponsors and clients of the training program(s) being developed, and particularly potential participants. The basic principle here is that it is important to involve the eyes of others in the evaluative process, eyes which see things through different perspectives.

A very productive way to involve key stakeholders in evaluating the design is the use of a materials test or one or more pilot offerings of the program. Both of these strategies involve getting what has been designed conceptually or in draft form into useable shape, then actually delivering it to an audience and then folding the resultant reactions back into the design process. Pilot offerings, in particular, are a powerful way for the design team to test its ideas in a simulation of the real world. And pilot offerings need not necessarily wait until the training program is 100 percent complete. Pieces of the program—a particular module or a specific exercise or a new feedback instrument—can be tested with sample participants all along the design path. Pilots are especially important if there are differing audiences to whom the program must be delivered; for example, participants at very different levels within the organization or people from different geographies or cultures.

The most important principle of training evaluation is this: It must be planned for up front. It cannot be left to last, treated as an afterthought, and left until the program activities have been identified and the materials have been developed. Chapter 3 dealt with methods of evaluation, and that material will obviously not be repeated here. What does bear repeating is the overriding goal of evaluation itself: Does the training program help its participants learn what the organization needs them to learn, and do they take what they have learned back to their work? These are the essential questions that the design team must answer for it to know if the planned learning objectives have been achieved. The answers to these questions may have a bearing on the instructional activities, methods, and materials the team develops in the body of its design work. Thus, evaluation activities cannot be left to the end of the project, but must be considered at every stage in the design process.

THE LEADER'S GUIDE

Leader's Guide is a generic term for a critical item in the design of a program where content will be delivered by live instruction (See Chapter 7). The Leader's Guide may go by other names: Trainer/Instructor/Facilitator Guide, Teaching Outline (as distinct from a content outline), Teaching Manual, even Lesson Plan. The name is not so important—we use the term

Leader's Guide here—but the item itself is crucial and involves a major design task. The Leader's Guide is the ultimate "how-to" training manual. It tells the instructor how to use the program's activities and materials to enable the participants to achieve the program's learning objectives. It is much more than a mere content outline, which is simply a list of the points to be covered in the program. A Leader's Guide provides detailed instructions on how to deliver the program content, what to say, how to say it, and how to make transitions from module to module. While the Leader's Guide is not a script, it *is* a statement of all the talking points the instructor is expected to make; it states what must be said, while allowing the instructor to put it in his or her own words.

Consistency of content and preparation assistance are the two goals underlying a Leader's Guide. There are even situations where an organization's need for consistency of message makes the Leader's Guide a means of control over delivery, where little or no deviation from the Guide is allowable. More frequently, the Guide gives an instructor a running start, eliminating the need to do program preparation from scratch since it provides the bulk of what needs to be said. Good examples of Leader's Guides are usually found for corporate programs, those an organization wants delivered the same all across its reach, or for training programs for which training vendor certifies instructors in its customer companies or on the open market.

A Leader's Guide should be the design team's final effort. It is often done in progressive stages of draft versions, each approximating the final product and fully completed only with the results of program pilot(s) considered. A practical way of getting the Leader's Guide written that has evolved in one training department involves the use of outside consulting resources. The department developed the practice of members of the design team teaching the pilot offerings of its programs and hiring a consultant to observe the pilot, armed with detailed program outlines and design work sheets, with the goal of documenting what the design team instructors did and said. The consultant then used these documented observations, plus the supplied materials, to produce a Leader's Guide.

With regard to external programs being purchased or designed by an outside consulting resource, both detailed content outlines and Leader's Guides are important items for a potential training purchaser to expect to receive. A sufficiently detailed content outline documents *what* a program will deliver, enabling the potential training purchaser to make reasonable judgements as to the program's fit with what is organizationally needed. A Leader's Guide will specify not only *what* will be delivered, but *how* the delivery will be achieved. This information will help the purchaser make reasonable judgements concerning the content, methods, and schedule of a program being considered for purchase.

Both program dimensions—*what* and *how*—are topics on which good judgement must be exercised, and the demand to see both is entirely reasonable. It will sometimes be resisted by a training vendor, especially the request for a Leader's Guide. Fears that intellectual property rights will be infringed upon are part of such resistance, but there are contractual ways to protect such rights, and nondisclosure agreements are a standard feature of research-to-purchase agreements. The resistance is also often grounded in the fact that a true Leader's Guide does not exist—content outlines are often proffered instead—and it is an enormously demanding task to produce one. Insisting on a Leader's Guide is reasonable, however, since one of the reasons a consultant instructor commands a larger daily fee than a simple consultant is that the instructor must spend preparation time getting ready to teach. A Leader's Guide is essentially the documentation of that preparation and ought to be available given the proper professional and legal safeguards.

When instruction is to be delivered by mediated instructional materials (See Chapter 8), guidelines to support trainer facilitation are also required. Implementing mediated learning solutions requires care in ensuring that the materials are indeed implemented, and feedback systems must be built into the total package.

SUMMARY

The process of designing a training program begins with the output of the needs assessment that details what it is that people in the organization need to learn. These learning requirements are grouped into logical clusters, which then become the planned outcomes of training programs to be created. Some outcomes call for learning cognitive skills, *knowing* content. Other outcomes call for learning behavioral skills, how to *do* something. Program design is typically done by a team of people, and the process of design is initially one of progressively narrowing the needed content down to specific learning goals that can be defined as terminal learning objectives and delivered in the modules of a program.

Module by module, the design team plans the activities that will enable program participants to achieve the learning objective(s) for that module. The modules are then aggregated to form the program as a whole. One of the key challenges for the design team is that it is creating learning and instructional material for use by others, not simply for themselves. An important design activity is to have the program plans reviewed by people outside the design team, key stakeholders who bring differing perspectives to the design work and help ensure its applicability across organizational boundaries.

Pilot offerings of the program also test the program's usefulness to learners, all the more so to the extent that pilot participants are a representative sample of the program's target audience. Program costs, for both design and rollout, make up an important issue with which the design team must deal. The question of internal vs. external program development involves cost, but the decision to use one or the other also involves such issues as credibility, time, skill, and task status.

Evaluation in the design phase of the training cycle focuses (a) on whether and how well the planned learning outcomes have been achieved and (b) on the extent to which the program materials reflect sound instructional practice and the principles of adult learning. The final product of the design effort for a program of live instruction is a Leader's Guide, a formidable but essential element of designing a program for delivery by people outside the design team.

THINK IT THROUGH

1. Why can the design process discussed in this chapter be characterized as one of progressive narrowing?
2. Read the short case study on page 172, The Imago 1024. Answer the following question with regard to the case. What training programs do you think the Eidekon Corporation will need to create in this case? Answer in terms of modules.
3. Explain the meaning of cognitive skills and behavioral skills. What are three key differences between them as training outcomes? Which type of skills do you think it is easier to train for? Why?
4. What are some of the advantages of having the design of training programs reviewed by people outside the design team? Who are some of the typical stakeholders in an organization concerning training programs?
5. What kinds of costs must a training design team consider? What are some of the key factors that go into these costs?

IDEAS IN ACTION

1. A blank copy of the design work sheet Figure 6-2 can be found at the end of this chapter. Use all the columns to:

   a. Plan program activities that will deliver the learning objectives for program goal #2.

   OR

   b. Plan the program activities for one of the training programs required in the Eidikon Corporation case study on the Imago 1024 on page 172 .

OR

c. Plan the activities for a real-life training program at your place of work.

2. Repeat Action 1a or 1b in teams of four to five classmates, all working together.
3. Prepare whatever notes you would need to give your classmates a four-minute lecture about any topic you choose—your favorite sport or time of year, the best vacation you've ever taken, the best/worst teacher you ever had in school, etc. Do not *give* the talk; just prepare it. Then create a Leader's Guide for the talk you have just prepared—whatever notes and materials you think someone else would need in order to present your exact same four-minute talk. Test your Leader's Guide: Pair up with a classmate, give your partner your Leader's Guide, and see if he or she can, in fact, give your talk from your Leader's Guide. Your partner's experience in using your materials should rule here. Report the results of this exercise to the class.
4. Contact a working trainer in an organization and explore that organization's use of Leader's Guides. Discuss how they are produced and how they are used; ask to see a sample.
5. Contact a training vendor that certifies instructors in its programs and explore the materials used for certification. Explore with the vendor how important it is for them to manage (control?) what instructors do in a classroom with their material. What kind of programs might call for the same kind of management/control of instruction inside a company?

MAKE A DECISION

The Eidekon Corporation manufactures and sells desktop copying equipment to the business marketplace and is about to bring a new model copier, the Imago 1024, to market. Eidekon's product development department notified internal training of the imminent release of the new copier, and the training people at once undertook a needs analysis among the company's sales representatives concerning the 1024. While the new model is not totally dissimilar to other models in the company line, there is a clear need on the part of the sales reps to learn the 1024 thoroughly. Consultation with sales management and the product development staff (two kinds of relevant subject matter experts here) has made it clear that the sales reps need detailed knowledge of the functions, features, and benefits of this new product. They must be able to (a) identify customer need for the 1024 and explain its features and benefits verbally as solutions to identified needs, (b) put together a presentation of the family of products into which the 1024 fits, an important contextual consideration for customers and an important step in differentiating it from other Eidekon models, and (c) demo the product completely and flawlessly. Finally, because Eidekon is a small company and has a tradition of its salespeople providing customers with after-sales support, the sales reps must also be able to install the 1024, educate customer personnel in its operation, trouble-shoot problems after installation, and make sure customers know how to acquire and deal with the consumable supplies the 1024 requires—toner, ink, paper, etc.

Needs analysis data have also surfaced learning needs on the part of the supervisory staff in the sales department, the managers of the sales reps. These managers need a functional overview of the 1024—not the detailed knowledge necessary to operate and trouble-shoot, but sufficient knowledge to allow them to discuss the copier intelligently with potential customers and guide/manage their sales reps in marketing it. See Figure 6-4.

FIGURE 6-4
THE TRAINING DESIGN WORK SHEET

Program Name: ______________________ Work Sheet Date: ____________

Module #: ______________ Module Name: ______________

Program Goal # ____________: *(statement of goal, cognitive or behavioral)*

Learning Objective	Active	Timing	Materials Costs	Who
1				
2				
3				
4				
5				
6				
N				
TOTALS	Total time estimated for this module --->	Hrs/mins	Total cost estimate: $	

ADDITIONAL RESOURCES

RECOMMENDED READINGS

Abella, Kay T. *Building Successful Training Programs: A Step-by-Step Guide*. Reading, MA: Addison-Wesley, 1986.

A short, yet comprehensive, guide to designing and implementing training programs. Above all, a practical, hands-on template to follow. Includes a useful glossary of training terms.

Eitington, Julius E. *The Winning Trainer*, 2nd Edition. Houston: Gulf Publishing Co., 1989, 496 pp.

A wide-ranging, easy-to-use collection of delivery techniques and materials for providing training experiences. This handbook provides a wide array of hands-on illustrations and handouts for instructional use.

Furjanic, Sheila W., and Laurie A. Trotman. *Turning Training Into Learning: How to Design and Deliver Programs That Get Results.* New York: American Management Association AMACOM, 2000, 308 pp.

A fresh, up-to-date, and easy-to-read handbook that focuses on learning as well as on instructional methods and practices. Chapter 2, "Designing Learner-Based Training," is especially helpful.

Romiszowski, A. J. *Designing Instructional Systems: Decision-Making in Course Planning and Curriculum Design*. New York: Nichols Publishing Co., 1981, 415 pp.

This classic book describes the major areas of decision-making that face the instructional designer. Romiszowksi describes the design process as a heuristic, dynamic problem-solving process.

Rowland, Gordon, Designing and Instructional Design. *Educational Technology Research and Development*, Vol 41., No. 1, 1993, pp. 79-91.

In this article, Gordon Rowland, a professor of corporate communication, discusses the problems inherent in describing the instructional design process. Of special interest to readers is his comparison of instructional design with other design efforts—such as music and architecture.

Silberman, Mel. *Active Training: A Handbook of Techniques, Design, Case Examples, and Tips.* San Diego: University Associates, 1990, 284 pp.

Case examples make this book a useful resource for instructional designers. Emphasis is on why trainers make specific design choices.

Smith, Patricia L., and Tillman J. Ragan. *Instructional Design*, 2nd edition. Upper Saddle

River, NJ: Prentice-Hall, Inc., 1999, 399 pp.

A rather sophisticated curriculum-oriented and driven handbook that covers instructional design and delivery concepts from K-12, post-secondary and higher education levels, and corporate training. A solid reference manual.

WEB SITES

http://www.astd.org

The homepage of the American Society for Training and Development. The site includes a detailed listing of member services, as well as links to their multitude of publications.

http://www.trainingsupersite.com/learningcenter/

The "super" homepage of Lakewood Publications and the services and products they provide.

from the FIELD VOICES

Patricia Coglianese on Instructional Design

Patricia Coglianese is a Senior Vice President and Director of Education at Chase Manhattan Bank in New York City. Her responsibilities include the oversight of the design of management leadership development programs at Chase, and after 17 years in the field, she has experienced the training spectrum from technical topics to managerial policies.

MICHAEL BRONNER: Pat, since your responsibilities include the design and development for all Chase's employees, including the highest level of management, where do you see this leading?

PATRICIA COGLIANESE: We see more technology-mediated instruction playing a role in the training process, changing the length of programs from formal two to four-day instructor-led training programs into much shorter events enhanced with the use of technology-based learning methods. Virtual classroom is definitely on our agenda. While the traditional classroom will not go out of style, we're using that environment for more skill application and group learning that may be followed or preceded by technology-mediated instruction. The magic is in the mix and we have to figure out what mix is appropriate to achieve the maximum learning in the shortest period of time.

MICHAEL BRONNER: Since Chase is such a large organization, to what degree do you see training activities being housed within the firm over the near term?

PATRICIA COGLIANESE: We already outsource delivery of 98 percent of all of our programs within the corporate group. Across the organization, however, it's more like 50 percent. We still do a lot of our own instruction across Chase using our own internal staff, but have learned to build strategic partnerships with other organizations and leverage them as an extension of us as an organization. We can't respond to all of the firm's needs because our head count simply can't handle it, so our approach has been to use our own internal resources where they can have the greatest impact. For example, it takes a lot of resources to do the design and development; however, if you have someone internally who understands the design process and can work with an outside consultant, then you're leveraging your resources most effectively.

MICHAEL BRONNER: You mentioned the impact of technology on instruction and learning. Can you tell us a bit more about how Chase sees this integration?

PATRICIA COGLIANESE: Well, we've used multimedia for years to enhance learning; however, the real explosion will center on Web-based instruction, both synchronous and asynchronous. We are a large organization, 80,000 employees located in 51 countries and across 39 states. We need to leverage technology to ensure that employees can learn where, when, and how they need to.

From a design perspective, we have to be very careful that we design appropriately—that we design in chunks and clusters of learning—because integrating learning across media is critical. Fortunately, we have a number of staff at Chase who have come out of a classroom design arena and are technology savvy. So, for example, when we design a learning experience, we use a team approach and are able to engage learning professionals throughout the organization, in different businesses and geographic locations, to assist in this process. This ensures that what we design and deliver will be relevant to all our populations, regardless of culture and location. We've found that technology has had a very strong impact on learning and we'll continue to use it where it is most effective.

MICHAEL BRONNER: You spoke of learning before. How do you know when learning has taken place in any of your training programs?

PATRICIA COGLIANESE: This is where the assessment process becomes very important. If you design not only the process, but also the evaluation of the outcomes, you can tell if and when it [learning] happens. We look at level 1 (reaction), 2 (learning), and 3 (job behavior), outcomes for the most part, unless our training design is to be a very high-impact, high-volume, and high-cost program; then we might look at level 4 (organizational results). For those programs, we usually contract for results up front so we can see what impact we expect, and then design measures to assess it.

MICHAEL BRONNER: What are some of the roles relative to learning that have to be considered?

PATRICIA COGLIANESE: The lines between training and other ways of learning are blurring. There is a shifting emphasis from training to learning, which is an entirely different way, philosophically, of looking at the issue. The message that needs to be sent is that it's all about learning! Training is usually not the only answer to a business problem . . . and it's not training *or*, it's training *and!* In some places at Chase, the *training* term is not even used—rather the term *learning*, as in the "learning professional" is used. There is also an increasing juxtaposition of training and coaching, and to the extent that trainers can build their coaching skills, all will benefit. Managers at all levels should be exposed to some formal coaching processes to develop the skills for providing a bridge between training and the application of learning on the job. It's important for us to understand how and why people learn so that mentoring, coaching, and training can be most effective. This is an important issue at Chase and it focuses on the identification of learning styles and preferences, as well as the work environment and culture.

MICHAEL BRONNER: The return on investment (ROI) is so critical in such a large organization. How does Chase view the training operation in this regard?

PATRICIA COGLIANESE: At Chase, I've not seen this as a significant issue. When you have credibility with your client, you've delivered quality based on a long series of small successes—you've had a positive history. What you're delivering is aligned with the business goals. If you do this correctly, you don't need to as stringently justify the budget investment. Chase executives see the value of our programs and pay for them. Of course, you always have to carefully articulate how your offerings align with the business needs.

MICHAEL BRONNER: What successful training examples have you seen at Chase?

PATRICIA COGLIANESE: I've seen a number of sales training initiatives that have had a high impact from a sales perspective and they were very measurable. New products, selling skills, consultative selling—where the salesperson does not sell the product, exactly, but consults with a client in order to determine the needs, and then provides the client with options that would fit that perceived need. Another example is when management sees a need and encourages training initiatives, such as training for diversity that goes well beyond affirmative action. These programs have been very successful since they involve individuals' personal and internal motivation. We've had many examples of successful training initiatives at Chase, focusing on all populations, from the executive team to our branch tellers.

A while back, on the other hand, a huge failure was the attempt to get our technology operations and business functions to work more closely together to achieve business objectives. We built what I thought was a good program, instructionally very sound with sponsorship from a senior executive. It failed terribly because, as I learned, the culture was just not ready for it! We had three silos—technology, operations, and business. They all were used to throwing the requirements "over the wall" to each other; however, where the organization wanted to go was toward more collaborative teams and they just weren't ready for it. The senior executive said "get 'em together in one room and make it happen." So we brought them together with the senior sponsorship, which we thought was sufficient—but we didn't get enough business sponsorship from the silos. Some of the participants forged strong relationships that they could take with them, and others built strong partnerships that just couldn't survive in the existing culture. So we redesigned the program, then redesigned the program again—and finally put it on the shelf and said, "Someday this may work. But not today!" Since that time, our culture has shifted significantly. I believe that this program, designed about five years ago, would have been quite successful if we had paid more attention to the cultural barriers.

MICHAEL BRONNER: For those beginning in the training field, what associations and publications can you suggest?

PATRICIA COGLIANESE: There are so many publications and associations. They are wonderful resources if you find the right article or information at the right time. But there's almost too much reading material out there now—you can't keep up with it. Then add the Web, and it's close to total information overload. Two specific publications that I read include *Training Magazine* and *Fast Company*. As far as professional organizations, I recommend ASTD and the local Metropolitan Chapter. I also recommend something called the Organizational Development Network (ODN) for information-sharing purposes. I think you need to select the organizations in which you'll participate, depending on where you are and what your current or future interests are. For example, ASTD is a wonderful organization, and it has certain affinity groups to get involved with. It's also a great association if you're just starting out, as it provides a wide breadth of information about a field and great opportunities for networking. Something like the Masie Center, where you can get better versed in learning technologies and the future of learning, is also useful. Jeanne Meister's group—the Corporate University Xchange—is also a good group to look at if you're managing a training function. Finally, outside the field—at Chase, of course—various banking associations related to the position and/or department would be appropriate in order to better understand our business. Other related organizations that might prove helpful include special interest groups (SIGs) from larger organizations such as AERA and the curriculum group,

ASCD. Chase supports individual memberships and encourages participation in such activities. As professionals in our discipline we need to stay abreast of what's happening in our industry as well as in our organizations.

MICHAEL BRONNER: Thanks, Pat, for providing your insights on training at Chase.

PART 4
Training Delivery

PROLOGUE TO PART 4

There are two fundamental approaches to the delivery of training: (1) *live instruction,* which means that the instruction is delivered by an instructor face-to-face with one or more students; and (2) *mediated instruction,* which means that the instruction is delivered through some medium other than a live instructor.

We are familiar with the live instruction from our own experience in school: twelve or more years of teachers, in front of the classrooms in which we sat, providing instruction in the material we were to learn. Live instruction is an ancient tradition. Aristotle employed it as he strolled with his students around the *stoa*[1] during the Golden Age of Athens. Indeed, it was used by the first person in human history who realized he or she knew something another needed to learn.

Mediated instruction is also very old, almost as old as live instruction: The live instructor is not present, but has left something behind from which the student is to learn. The oldest form of this "something left behind" was perhaps a clay tablet with cuneiform script, or maybe a carved tree. It may have been a cave wall with petroglyphs or a simple piece of bark or leather with pictures.

Mediated instruction means that there is some medium for carrying and delivering instruction from a teacher who is not present. The number and types of media have expanded dramatically over the centuries. Today, the absent teacher's instruction can be presented to the student(s) by means of video, through a computer's software, via the World Wide Web, by a simple information manual, or through a Walkman's audiocassette or compact disk. The varieties and possibilities of mediation are many and growing, limited only by the creativity and resources of instructional designers. Mediated instruction is sometimes referred to as *self-study* or *self-paced instruction*. It will be discussed in Chapter 8. Live instruction will be discussed in Chapter 7.

Each of the two fundamental approaches to instruction has advantages and disadvantages. The live instructor can adjust material and method on the fly, in real time, adapting to the needs in ways that no preprogrammed medium can possibly match. A live instructor can also be prepared to deliver instruction far more swiftly and less expensively than the time and costs associated with developing instruction on media. Mediated instruction, on the other hand, offers an absolute consistency of content that live teachers cannot equal, no matter how thoroughly they have been trained. Moreover, media can be shipped around the world much more easily and cheaply than human teachers can travel, especially given the power of the Internet. Neither of the fundamental approaches to instruction can be said to be better than the other in any absolute sense. There are, however, circumstances and requirements which seem to call for one or the other approach, as the examples in Figure P4-1 show.

Figure P4-1 shows that decisions concerning methods of instructional delivery are highly situational. The training professional must be aware of his/her personal preferences and beliefs, and be appropriately wary of them. One instructional designer may favor live instruction, while another may be biased toward a multimedia software approach. These personal preferences, however, cannot be allowed to become guiding principles. The overriding decision criterion in the area of choosing the best delivery method is participant learning. *Instruction, live or mediated, is all about learning.* If participant learning does not take place, the most elegantly designed, most sophisticated instruction in the world is simply useless. This learner-focused thinking must go into the design stages of training, as well as into its implementation. Design decisions about delivery options must ultimately be governed by the target audience—their learning styles, their needs, and their preferences. Cost, geographic spread, type of content, urgency of need, audience level, and other factors are all part of the decision affecting the "best" instructional approach. The ultimate determinant, however, is the answer to the question: *What will help the target population learn the most, the best, and the easiest?*

Trainers must above all be careful not to make delivery methods into screening devices. If an organization insists that all its training be done by method X, then only those who do well with that method will be successful learners. The organization, thus, will be screening out all others without even having made a conscious decision to do so. This is a classic case of unexamined assumptions driving outcomes, and it is often what takes place when design and delivery decisions are left solely to factors such as cost, at the expense of learner need and preference.

MATCHING GOALS TO INSTRUCTIONAL DELIVERY TECHNIQUES

Delivery is typically what trainers like to do best, and it is thus the component of the training cycle to which they tend to move to quickly. It is an important professional discipline for trainers to ensure that instruction is undertaken only when it is clear that the organizational need—the performance gap—is one that will respond to training. That is to say, the performance gap can be closed by learning, by the acquisition of new skills or knowledge.

FIGURE P4-1
A SAMPLING OF SITUATIONS AND APPROPRIATE APPROACHES TO DELIVERING INSTRUCTION

SITUATION/REQUIREMENT	APPROACH
Need to equip sales personnel with necessary product knowledge for the release of a major new product family two months from now.	Live instruction would appear to be the best choice. Experienced designers/instructors assigned full time can deliver the new program(s) in time. It is not possible to do justice to the information needed via a mediated approach in the time frame available. (The really important question here is: Why was the training need left until the last minute in the product development life cycle?)
FASB XLJ00 - New accounting regulations will require the controllers in each department in the organization to handle asset calculation and tracking in an involved new way. The new regulations go into effect in 11 months.	Complexity of topic prevents handling by means of a simple informational desk drop (as was done in support of the installation of new phone equipment last year). Ninety-three percent of the controllers are on the corporate Intranet, the requirement has almost a year of lead time, and this population has a track record of successful use of self-study approaches—the discipline is there. WBT (Web-based Training) software distributed through the Intranet will furnish satisfactory instruction in this case.
A continuing need to orient new hires to the culture of the organization, its vision of the future, its strategies, and its values, all with allowance for appropriate tailoring for businesses and geographic circumstance. Hire rate: 130 people per month, in seven different HR centers around the world.	The training job here is to design something that can be handed off for use in the seven HR centers as part of their new-hire intake process. The material may well include a videotape of the organization's president talking about the organization's culture and values. An advantage of this is that the tape can be dubbed in all the needed languages; the acculturation demands, however, preclude the *sole* use of videotape. Live instruction will be necessary, including the involvement of local senior management as guests. Materials will have to include a full-scale Leader's Guide for the host facilitator, written to the lowest level of detail, in all the right languages, and thoroughly tested before release.
Incoming clerical staff in the Indianapolis Operations Center consistently need work on basic skills: math, reading, keyboarding, word processing, and analytics.	Needed programs can be bought off the shelf, both self-study materials and live instruction. No need to reinvent these wheels. A mix of programs will allow the Indianapolis Center to provide employees with the approach that best suits their learning styles and preferences. Self-study modules may also serve as prework or reinforcement for live programs where this makes sense.
New middle managers need to learn the core job requirements of being the managers of managers, particularly with regard to (a) policy demands concerning performance management, and (b) the value and use of employee attitude surveys.	Some of the need here may be simply informational and can perhaps be met by simple lecture, live or mediated. Learning about performance coaching and appraisal, however, requires hands-on skill practice. Major portions of this learning requirement can be met only by live, interactive instruction, with people working in classroom groups where skills practice and peer/instructor feedback are possible.

Once this is clear, the move to designing and delivering instruction makes good organizational and professional sense.

Similarly, most trainers love to teach, and tend to jump to conclusions about live instruction being the delivery method of choice. This natural, preferential leap is to be respected for the power and motivation it supplies to the work of teaching. Once again, however, professional discipline requires that the trainer look long and hard at the organizational situation to determine the best form of instruction. That "best form of instruction" is the one that will enable the target audience to learn the required content, and do so as efficiently as possible.

While no absolutes exist here, the voice of experience says that most people tend to prefer the traditional classroom as a learning vehicle because it is the approach with which we are all most familiar. Most of us seem to respond better to the motivation, discipline, and structured momentum of a classroom full of peers with a live teacher and a clear agenda driven by that teacher. Most of us do not seem to learn as well if left completely to our own devices in a self-study situation. The point is that if *learning* is the purpose of training (as it is), then decisions about how to provide instruction are decisions about how to help people learn what they need to know. Instructional decisions cannot be left totally to trainer preference or to the cost of different types of instructional delivery. Such decisions must be driven by the understanding that instruction is not a goal, but a means, and is totally in the service of something else—namely, participant learning.

A GENUINELY NEW FORM OF DELIVERY?

As new types of self-instructional media have been introduced in the modern business world, they invariably have been surrounded by a repeat cluster of vendor promises. This new medium, the ads promise, will provide consistency of content delivery, enable learners to move at their own pace, obviate the need for live instructors, and above all lower costs. The ads trumpet that the new medium will *finally* break the ancient mold of training (meaning live teacher + student) and *finally* move your training into the 21st century. These same sorts of claims were made for training first broadcast by radio, then for programmed instruction, then for televised teaching, then videotapes, then CBT, then interactive video, then WBT. Indeed, the original laptops were, of all things, *slate.* It was a powerful educational innovation in the 18th century when educators gave class participants their own small, personal-sized slates so they could write, calculate, and draw right at their seats, along with the teacher at the classroom's large slate blackboard. And some of the same things that are said now about the educational possibilities of portable laptop computers were said then about those individual laptop slates!

Interactive Multimedia Systems, delivered via CD-ROM or through the Web, is currently the hot form of mediated instruction. This form of *computer-based training (CBT)* is increasingly popular because PCs are powerful enough to provide not only text *or* graphics *or* video, but they also can provide them all simultaneously and in an integrated way. Interactive Multimedia Systems can provide text, graphics, animation *and* full-motion video on PC screens all at once, in multiple windows, with sound capability (including voice input and output), along with expert systems software that can support both the presentation of content and learning activities. Moreover, as the speed and capacity of the Web expands, such learning resources can be accessed by anyone with a connection to the Internet.

Multimedia instruction offers potential beyond the other means of self-learning. As we shall see in Chapter 8, it is critical to surround mediated instruction with the support systems that make it an effective tool for learning. These include attractive up-to-date materials, learning exercises that motivate and coach the learner, questions that require the learner to reflect on what he or she has learned, and strategies to ensure follow-up from training professionals and managers. Such support mechanisms add substantially to the cost of self-instructional media and are generally necessary to be effective for learning. The power of multimedia appears to reduce the need for such support systems since it can build them right into the instructional software. This is a capability that other forms of mediated instruction tried for and often claimed, but were never really able to deliver.

Furthermore, the power and speed of today's networked workstations provide the capacity for a kind of *performance support* also not heretofore possible. Remember, *learning*, which is the goal of training, is itself a means to the goal of *performance.* The digital networks of today and tomorrow can offer just-in-time support, including on-line reference material at the worker's fingertips. This information can be kept current with relative ease because new policy or product information can be entered into a centrally maintained database, which all nodes on the network can access. These reference tools will actually *reduce* the need for learning. Think about how the alphabet reduced the need to memorize the tribe's stories and epics, because now they could be written down, read, and referenced when desired. The handheld calculator has made memorizing the times tables less a requirement than before. Similarly, multimedia workstations tapping into the information superhighway may make it less necessary to learn some of what has to be learned today. What will be critical will be to know how to access these reference tools that reduce the need to learn, just as library research skills were crucial for the paper-intensive knowledge worker of yesteryear.

Keep in mind, too, that learners learn from each other as well as from an instructor or learning media, and the Web can support interactions. In addition to E-mail, instructors and learners have a wide range of communications tools, including listservs, bulletin boards, discussion boards, and chat rooms. Comprehensive Web-based Training solutions bundle communications tools with multimedia instruction. In such cases, the Web serves as a distributor of instruction, as well as a means to enable a learning community to stay connected despite platform differences, time differences, or location differences.

THE CHALLENGE OF INSTRUCTION

Teaching others, whether done live or with mediated tools, has a certain inherent challenge that cannot be removed by any instructional stratagem, no matter how clever or leading edge. The essential task is to get information or skill from the head of someone who knows into the head of someone who needs to know. This process of information transfer must work its way through the filters on both sides of the person-to-person communication, and then must work back through those same filters to ensure that the message was received, and received as intended. This alone makes teaching a daunting task. In addition, the outcome of instruction—learning—means change in the learner, and change is never easy. Resistance to change can be lessened by good instructional design, by strong motivational techniques, and by the effective use of technology. Resistance, however, always exists around new ideas and innovations.

Most important, for instruction to be successful, the learning mind must choose to take in and absorb what the instructing mind has presented. This interaction, which defines instructional success, cannot be forced or made to happen, let alone made automatic or effortless or self-sustaining. Chapter 7, *Live Instruction*, and Chapter 8, *Mediated Instruction* describe strategies and proven approaches that trainers can use to help people learn. Choosing appropriate instructional methods is a very important part of training responsibility and a very important skill set for training professionals, but the trainer should have no expectation that method can eliminate instruction's dependence on learner preference and choice.

ENDNOTES

1. Stoa is the Greek word for "porches," the colonnades Aristotle and the other *peripatetic* (Greek for "walking around") philosophers used as their classrooms.

CHAPTER 7

Live Instruction

- Examine the impact of teachers who have "made a difference."
- Describe instructional techniques that work for large groups.
- Describe instructional techniques that work for small groups.
- Discuss ways in which a training department can support self-directed learning groups, coaching, and mentoring.
- Describe a variety of technologies that can support synchronous distance learning.
- Depict situations where distance learning is the method of choice.
- Use guidelines for developing instructional materials and aids.
- Summarize the issues in managing live instruction.

THE TEACHER IN A CLASSROOM

A teacher in a classroom with a group of students is what most of us tend to think about when we think of instruction. Teachers with students are a part of human history, a constant in our universal collective consciousness. From the *sensei* in snowbound Himalayan monasteries, to the *griots* of storytelling cultures, to the academies of ancient Greece and Rome, to the books and movies of our own time, the teacher who makes a difference in our lives is a stock character. The movie list includes Robert Donat in *Goodbye Mr. Chips*, Glen Ford in *Blackboard Jungle*, Sandy Duncan in *Up the Down Staircase*, Sidney Poitier in *To Sir With Love*, John Voigt in *The Water Is Wide*, and Robin Williams in *The Dead Poets' Society*. Even more importantly, this stock fictional character is a reality in many of our own individual lives. For many of us, there indeed has been a teacher who has made a difference. Memorable or forgettable, help or hindrance, a teacher is the chief means of instruction most of us encounter from kindergarten through graduate school, and live instruction is still the most frequently used form of instruction in the world of organizational training today.

This chapter describes a wide range of live instructional methods and how to use them. In the first two sections, methods are classified as to whether a class of program participants is dealt with as a whole, a large group, or is broken down into small teams. The third section examines distance learning options—the technologies and teaching techniques that support live instruction, but where instructor and learners are not physically in the same place. In addition, instructional materials and aids are described, and pointers for their effective use are offered. Of special interest in this section are directions for designing and using the Leader's Guide, which is a detailed teaching aid that helps to ensure consistency of content and delivery when the same program is taught by a number of different instructors. The chapter concludes with suggestions for managing live instruction.

WHOLE GROUP METHODS

n many occasions in a training program, an instructor works with the program participants as a whole. The methods for doing so involve, fundamentally, *lectures* and *discovery learning techniques.* For a given learning goal, these two strategies can be used individually or in concert.

The Lecture Method

Traditionally, the lecture has been the primary method of instruction, and is a part of almost every classroom situation. A lecture is an efficient way to present a great deal of information to large groups, and it leverages the expertise of the teacher so others can share in it. Like every teaching method, however, it fits some situations, not all.

Some educators argue that the lecture should be used very sparingly. "If You Must Lecture ..." is the title of Julius Eitington's chapter on the lecture method, and he is not enthusiastic about its use. "Problem laden," he calls it,[1] and he is not alone in this assessment. Lectures enable instructors to be in control and to feel that they have accomplished what they planned for that class. A lecture can be extremely effective if not overdone in terms of length. However, the lecture method remains primarily *instructor-centered*, not learner-centered. One certainty that has emerged from research and experience with adult learning is that long stretches of uninterrupted instructor talk, with nothing else going on, is usually a recipe for poor learning.

Lecture as the Method of Choice

Given these cautionary remarks, there are many situations where a lecture, delivered by a knowledgeable instructor, is clearly the delivery method of choice. A lecture is particularly useful when the learning goal is informational. Lectures are efficient ways to present information about a topic that learners need to hear, see, and have the opportunity to ask questions about. Many such situations exist, ranging from the announcement that the organization is opening a new branch office in Milan to describing the policy for the organization's new tuition reimbursement program.

Also appropriate for lectures are those points in a training program where something needs to be explained more fully. In a workshop on writing skills, for example, a short lecture on how to avoid overuse of the passive voice might be a good way to introduce exercises in active/passive sentence construction. Sometimes, a procedure to be followed in the next segment of the training program itself needs to be fully explained:

> Your group will be responsible for developing a list of activities that would be appropriate to solve the case. Keep in mind that teamwork is vital to your success here, so use the nominal group technique to ensure that everyone's ideas are included. To use the nominal group technique, you'll first ....

Such *lecturettes*, brief presentations which tend to run 5-15 minutes, provide information that other program activities process, reinforce, exemplify, and expand upon. While the program's design may call for most of the learning to take place through planned activities—e.g., a game or a role play—the importance of properly setting up the activity cannot be overestimated. The cleverest, best-designed exercise will stumble if its participants do not understand what they are to do. The lecturette that introduces and explains the activity is crucial to this understanding, and thus, even though short, is a critical instructional responsibility.

Using the Lecture Method Effectively

In developing a lecture, it is helpful to keep four major points in mind. The first point is to anticipate your audience and the relevance of the content to them, as well as their learning styles and motivation. At this stage, too, try to identify essential knowledge or skill outcomes that you can measure. The second point involves your preparation for the lecture. A structured outline of the major points you wish to cover, illustrations, and time segments may be critical. In preparing for your lecture, visual aids in the form of overhead transparencies or PowerPoint slides (see discussion later in this chapter) are recommended.

The third point is the execution, or delivery, of the lecture. An important aspect of lecturing is encouraging and handling questions from the audience. Questions should be anticipated and welcomed. A lecture should not be a situation in which the speaker is active and the audience is passive. Active participation from the listeners is a way of clarifying and expanding on points the speaker has made, as well as a way of enabling the audience to tap into its own knowledge and experiences. The smart lecturer handles questions well. Questions that are received gratefully can be an occasion for wider learning. Questions that are put down say that the speaker's point of view is the only one that counts. Questions—and the responses to them—early in a training program will set the tone for the rest of the instruction. That tone should be one of shared inquiry, curiosity, and a penalty-free opportunity to learn from mistakes. An instructor must always be aware that the way a question is handled is as important as the answer: The way in which a question is dealt is a message that will be heard and heeded by the questioner, as well as by all who are listening. Experienced lecturers suggest these practical techniques for handling audience questions:[2]

- Listen to the learner; be sure you understand the question.
- Maintain eye contact; wait a second or two before you respond to be sure that the participant has stopped speaking.
- Vary your reactions; you can:
  - rephrase the question in your own words,
  - ask for clarification, expansion, or examples,
  - expand on what the participant has said,
  - acknowledge the contribution, but ask for another view, or
  - nod or look interested, but remain silent.

Whatever its length or purpose, a lecture should engage its audience as much as possible. This means putting variety and vitality into the oral presentation, which can be done by the effective use of tone and volume, pitch and pace, and phrasing and repetition. Pausing frequently for questions, having participants write summaries, create lists, break for small group work, or stage a debate also helps to engage learners.

A lecturer in a classroom should also present information visually, as well as through words. Flip charts, overhead transparencies, and computer-generated presentations are common forms of visual aids, and are discussed later in this chapter. For the most part, such tools are readily available, inexpensive, straightforward, and capable of adding an important dimension to a verbal presentation. The lecturer's goal is to get the ideas into the learners' heads, rather than simply present prepared materials. This goal puts a premium on making the presentation attractive and memorable. It puts a further premium on considerations of length. A wise, seasoned speech teacher once put it this way:

> When you think about the length of your speech, plan to leave them hungry. You don't want them to stop listening before you stop talking. Above all, you want them wishing you hadn't stopped rather than wishing you would![3]

The final point involves follow-up evaluation of your lecture. A videotape of your performance may provide handsome dividends as you reflect on your presentation. In addition, peer reviews, participant reaction forms, and the like will also serve to enhance future lectures.

Discovery Methods

Another approach to dealing with a class of students as a whole is the *discovery method*. The name highlights the key to this instructional tactic. Its goal is to lead the participants to find things out for themselves, or self-*discover* the content they are to learn. Note that the concept of discovery is consistent with adult learning theory. Through the use of questions, cases, and other activities, the instructor draws on the knowledge and experience of the participants, relying on their judgement and involving them not merely as recipients of learning, but also as generators of it. Unfortunately, discovery methods have the disadvantage of taking longer to get to the point than does a straight lecture. Moreover, discovery works well only when the participants have reasonable levels of knowledge and experience to draw upon.

After a brief overview of three sample variations of discovery methods—the Socratic Method, the case study, and the informational treasure hunt—suggestions for their effective use are offered.

The Socratic Method

Socrates, a philosopher/teacher in ancient Greece, made a practice of presenting information to his students not by telling them what he wanted them to hear, but by asking them questions. The process drew from them collectively the points they were to learn, an approach that came to be called the *Socratic Method*. Note that this method is not simply open discussion, which certainly has a place, and an important one. Open, unstructured discussion inherently involves learner control of the direction of a discussion and may digress (legitimately) into topics the instructor did not predict or perhaps even want. The Socratic Method, on the other hand, is a tool an instructor consciously uses to lead learners to a particular answer through an established line of reasoning,[4] although the leading is accomplished through astute questioning.

The Case Study

The *case study*, common in professional schools and management training, is capable of providing a forum for a discussion of complex issues. The method involves having participants read a case, a story in which real-world elements and the learning points to be acquired are contained. The reading of the case, often augmented by an assignment to outline the case or prepare written answers to a set of preplanned questions, is processed by a class discussion. It is common for a class of experienced professionals to develop solutions far different from what the instructor expects or has heard before. Another reality about teaching adults is that the instructor usually joins in the learning!

Informational Treasure Hunts

Still another form of discovery method is an informational treasure hunt. Participants are asked to make decisions about a carefully chosen situation by first finding relevant information in, for example, the organization's personnel policy guide or code of ethics. Participants then discuss solutions and judgments based upon both their own experience and what they discovered in the policy guide or code. The chief design goal of this kind of exercise is to enable the learners to handle decision situations independently, yet remain aligned with organizational policy.

Using Discovery Methods Effectively

Discovery methods can be put to good use by the skilled trainer as a productive and engaging alternative or complement to a straight lecture. The instructor who uses the discovery method must prepare very thoroughly in advance by first developing good cases and questions. Some questions elicit the material of the case, to make sure the salient facts are understood by all. Other questions ask for conclusions, decisions, or recommendations. The questions, of course, cover the real learning points that the session is constructed to deliver. C. Roland Christensen, a professor emeritus at Harvard University and a proponent of the use of case studies, suggests that instructors develop a typology, or inventory, of questions to help lead class discussions. Figure 7-1 shows such a typology of questions adapted from his work, which may be useful in many situations.[5]

The discussion leader should obviously know the target audience well. Discovery sessions are typically driven by the instructor, who should ensure that all learners participate over time. The instructor must plan discussions partially around knowledge of particular individuals in a class—those who never volunteer, for example, or those who tend to dominate discussions. Choosing how to address the first question—to the class as a whole or to a specific person—should be planned ahead of time. It is the instructor's responsibility to find a graceful way to ensure that everyone is a part of the discussion.

SMALL GROUP METHODS

An important part of training work involves dividing a class of participants into teams of two to eight people for activities that bring about the desired learning of the program. Small group methods may be used to encourage conversations about a lecture or case study points or to provide participants with a means to understand their colleagues' viewpoints on topics. As discussed here, small group methods—discussions, games and simulations, and role plays—can provide strong vehicles for learning.

FIGURE 7-1
A TYPOLOGY OF QUESTIONS

Open-ended questions:
What was your first reaction to the situation? What key points do you recall?

Diagnostic questions:
Who were the key players in the case? Who had the most to win or lose from the proposed operational changes? What was at the root of the problem?

Information-seeking questions:
What are the organization's procedures and rules for backing up data? What part of the copyright law addresses how application software can be archived?

Challenge (testing) questions:
What are your reasons for saying that? What led you to this conclusion? What could your opposition say?

Action questions:
What steps should be taken? What procedures should be followed?

Questions on priority and sequence:
Given the organization's goals and resources, what should we do first? Second? Third?

Prediction questions:
If we implement this policy, what might be the outcomes? If nothing is done, which department would be impacted the most? The least?

Hypothetical questions:
What would have been the results if X had not occurred? What would have happened if the Y had been outsourced?

Questions of extension:
What implications can you draw from the results of this case? What would be the impact of this occurrence happening in our organization here and now?

Questions of generalization:
Based on your study of video conferencing, what do you consider to be the major forces that support the use of this technology?

SMALL GROUP DISCUSSIONS AND REPORTS

Perhaps the most common small group activity is a *group discussion* on a topic, followed by the group reporting what it discussed and what it concluded. Reporting is often accomplished by asking each small group to sum up its discussion on a flip chart and nominate a teammate or two to present the chart to the entire class. Other options for small group reporting depend on time and resources and what will work with the participants and their culture. The options range all across the presentation spectrum:

- All members of the small group, rather than just a single spokesperson, are part of the team presentation.
- Discussion teams are supplied with video equipment and are asked to display their presentations on videotape.
- The small groups express their findings in a creative way: a playlet, a song, a drawing, etc.

Such small group strategies not only provide variety, but are also excellent ways to tap into the creative, playful dimensions of the program participants. Providing a team of adults with crayons or felt-tip markers and asking them to draw a colorful picture of the desired future state of their organization breaks through the formality and discipline with which professionals normally operate. While such techniques offer powerful potential, it is extremely important that they not embarrass the participants in any way, and that they be fundamentally acceptable in the culture of the organization. As always, situational fit is a crucial element of successful training.

GAMES AND SIMULATIONS

Games are icebreakers or exercises, illustrations, or activities that support learning. Newstrom and Scannell, coauthors of *Games Trainers Play* (a series of books described in Endnote #9), explain that games are typically brief, inexpensive, participative, require the use of props, are low-risk, adaptable, and single-focus.[6] *Simulations*, on the other hand, allow students to engage in activities that are akin to realistic situations. While more conventional methods are best used to achieve cognitive objectives, games and simulations can favorably impact learner motivation and participation.[7]

For example, Figure 7-2 can be used as an icebreaker or to make an interesting opener for a training program on creativity. More content-related games such as popular TV shows like Jeopardy, Wheel of Fortune, or Who Wants to be a Millionaire, can be used as models to create learning activities. Other models are well-known board games like Trivial Pursuit or Monopoly. The trainer uses the formats of these popular games, and fits the content of the training program into the game's content. In addition, simulations have been designed specifically for training purposes, such as "The Prisoner's Dilemma," where participants are arrested and charged with a serious crime. This particular simulation introduces learners to plea bargaining and the workings of the criminal justice system.[8] Thick reference binders of ice breakers, games, and exercises are readily available[9] and offer materials suitable for use or adaptation for a wide variety of program designs.

Using Games and Simulations Effectively

Games tend to have a competitive aspect where one or more teams compete for points, placement, or prizes. Balancing teams may require considering the personalities, skills, and experiences of team members. Simulations, while possibly in a game format, more often tend to be designed to place students in a real-world environment and may or may not contain a competitive aspect. Games and simulations can be expensive to develop, and typically take several hours or more to run. Essential to their effectiveness is building in time for group discussion about key learning points.

FIGURE 7-2
CREATIVITY EXERCISES*

1. By adding one line, turn the following into a 6.

   IX

2. What is the ordering in the following numbers?

   8, 5, 4, 9, 1, 6, 3, 2

3. What is the next letter in the following sequence?

   OTTFFS

4. What is the pattern that differentiates the following two groups?

   Group 1: A E F H I

   Group 2: B C D G J

* Bostrom, Robert. Presentation in a workshop, University of Baltimore, 1990. Any number of answers are correct. One set of correct solutions is: (1) place an "S" before the IX; (2) alphabetic; (3) "S" for Seven; (4) Group 1 is made of straight-line letters; Group 2 is curved letters.

ROLE PLAYS

We know that skills are not developed by listening to lectures. When the learning objectives are behavioral, it is imperative that learners have the chance to practice, to try the prescribed methods, and get feedback on how well they did. The acquisition of skills, whether they are keyboarding skills or interpersonal communications skills, requires practice, practice, practice—the chance to make mistakes in a safe, penalty-free, environment. The amount of practice required will vary from topic to topic and from individual to individual, but practice is always necessary.

Role plays are excellent ways to have trainees practice skills they are learning in a program. *Role-playing* typically takes the form of two or more program participants enacting various roles while the instructor and/or other program participants observe and offer feedback when the role play concludes. In fact, role plays are sometimes referred to as skill practices. For example, supervisory personnel who need to learn how to conduct staff performance appraisals might use role playing to practice exactly what they will be doing later. In exercises where one learner plays the supervisor and another the staff person, role plays provide an opportunity to see what might happen when the skill is actually put to use. In this example, the point of the role play would be to see how the learner—the supervisor—handles situations where he or she is expected to work with a staff member to settle on mutually agreeable goals or provide coaching for skill improvement. Other role plays might entail practicing techniques that help supervisors describe what they have observed in behavioral, nonjudgmental terms, which are calculated not to stir up defensive reactions.

Using Role Plays Effectively

Good, useful feedback concerning role plays is important, and learners themselves can be an excellent source of it. Note that *all* participants in the small group sessions are learners, not just the individuals who are performing. Trainees often claim they learn more as observers than as players. However, it is usually necessary to guide participants in how to give feedback. This instruction, and a template to guide them in capturing their observations, help structure the role play for maximum results. The key is to get observers to focus on specifics rather than on generalities, and this often requires participant coaching.

To understand the importance of coaching in peer feedback situations, consider the following responses given by participants about a colleague's performance in a role play:

1. Megan did well as supervisor.
2. Megan set the objectives well with Jonathan.
3. Megan made sure Jonathan understood what he was going to have to do by asking him to repeat the objectives in his own words.

The third example provides Megan with the most specific information on what she did well, the tactics she used, and how she involved her performance partner. The first example is of no use at all, other than to make Megan feel good. Likewise, while the second response is better, it is still too general to be very helpful. Megan—and her observers—will learn only if the feedback is specific.

Role plays and other skill practices can be made more intense and more powerful by videotaping them. Videotaping a skill practice allows learners to see their behaviors for themselves. Videotaping is very influential for most people, as learners can view their actions in private and can be encouraged to redo their performance until they are pleased with the outcome. Learners are often their own worst critics in such situations. Note, of course, that videotaping adds a significant dimension of complexity to a program in terms of time, equipment, and physical facilities.

Other approaches to using role plays include doing the role play in a "fishbowl" style. Here, role players perform in front of classmates who form a circle around them, as in a fishbowl. The group then discusses how well the target skills were practiced and, in so doing, provides feedback to the players. When time permits, inviting different participants to perform the role over again is useful. A fishbowl design is not terribly complex, but it does run the risk of adding the element of "face" to the role play, putting pressure on participants to perform for the crowd. It can even put the focus on competitiveness, on performing better than the last set of players. These nuances can easily interfere with the role play's primary learning value.

INFORMAL LEARNING

While most of this book defines and discusses training as learning initiatives with fairly concrete outcomes, learning happens in a wide variety of ways within organizations, and training departments often are responsible for providing scaffolding—rather than direct interventions—to support the way people learn. Scaffolding here means that the training department may not actually provide direct learning experiences, but works with managers in supporting initiatives whereby individuals in the organization share their experiences and expertise with each other. The term *communities of practice*, coined by Etienne Wenger and Jean Lave (in *Situated Learning*, Cambridge University Press, 1991), has at its basis the idea that individuals with common goals and passion for their work learn in informal, unplanned ways. This discussion includes a description of ways in which we learn from each other—self-directed learning teams, coaching, and mentoring—and concludes with suggestions for how a training department may be able to aid in their development.

Self-Directed Learning Teams

Self-directed learning teams tend to be naturally occurring groups of people who have a short-lived, common goal. Much learning takes place at the water cooler and in office corridors. Learning takes place just at the time one needs it, and instances exist where the training department does not have a ready answer. A good example was the Y2K problem that affected organizations' information systems operations on January 1, 2000. No one really knew just what havoc computers programmed in Cobol and with codes for dates that included only two digits would do when the clock moved into the year 2000. To solve the problem, teams of computer technologists—self-directed work groups—worked together to determine the scope of the problem, to research ways others were suggesting to combat the issue, and to determine how best to solve the problem in their own organization. Other examples of self-directed work teams are groups assigned tasks, such as opening a new manufacturing plant or creating new applications that could be supported by e-commerce.

Coaching

Coaching is undoubtedly the way we all would prefer to learn how to do almost anything! A good coach provides help just at the time that learning is needed, and is continually encouraging its team member(s) to do their best. Coaching is one of the best means of transferring not only learning, but also transferring the corporate culture: "This is how we do this in this organization." Instruction and positive reinforcement, given at just the right time, well supports learning to do a job or task.

Mentoring

Like coaching, mentoring is yet another means to pass on an organization's culture. Mentoring is defined here as a process whereby an experienced member of an organization provides problem-solving strategies and career advice to new members of the organization. In an organization with a "learning" culture, informal mentoring occurs among its employees continually. Increasingly, organizations have found benefits from establishing more formal mentoring programs, with new hires assigned to more senior members of the company, rather than assuming that such relationships will evolve on their own.

Supporting Informal Learning

These three examples of ways in which informal learning occurs in organizations—self-directed work teams, coaching, and mentoring—can be facilitated by a training department. The first step would be to identify the overall goals of such programs and then provide the scaffolding—or support—for them to occur. In some cases, such as self-directed learning communities, learning specialists may best serve as a means of helping learners locate information from databases and libraries regarding the issue. Supporting coaching might be done via a workshop for managers and supervisors as to how to help new hires learn and provide positive reinforcement. Formal mentoring programs can be assisted by actually helping managers establish a formal mentoring program and then monitoring the success of matches, making changes when needed. Supporting the sharing of tacit knowledge and experiences is an important responsibility of today's training department.

Distance Learning

Distance learning is a form of instruction used when (1) learners are geographically or organizationally dispersed; and/or (2) few qualified instructors are available to reach a large target audience; and (3) technology is available to support communications between/among learners who are not in the same place.

Distance learning can be synchronous, with an instructor in real time leading a class session. The term *synchronous* comes from two Greek words (syn + chronos) meaning, respectively, "together," and "time." When instruction is asynchronous, meaning a live instructor is not necessarily present at the time a learner is using course materials, it is considered a form of mediated learning, and is discussed later in Chapter 8. The discussion in this chapter centers on the use of a wide range of communication/conferencing tools that enable instructor(s) and learners to meet in real time. These technologies include audio conferencing, videoconferencing, and computer conferencing (the use of groupware tools), and business television.

Audio Conferencing

Audio conferencing is voice-only interaction using the telephone system between/among individuals at two or more physically separated sites at the same time. In its simplest form, audio conferencing is direct interaction via telephone or speakerphone. Audio conferencing can be used in many different types of learning situations where people need to hear information and have direct communication with the information-giver and each other. Examples of its application include informational announcements about new products or markets, or new operational policies and procedures.

The only hardware needed for an audio conference is an ordinary telephone; however, a speakerphone, which frees the listener's hands, is useful. When multiple sites are involved, meet-me bridges are needed to tie the communications links together. In such cases, participants either call into a central service, or the central service calls and connects each site at a given time. Audio conferences are also often supported by technologies such as facsimile machines or electronic whiteboards that are used to send graphs, charts, or pictures between/among sites.

Videoconferencing

Initially, videoconferencing was heralded as a way to lower instructor and trainee travel costs. Today, however, the videoconference's biggest selling point is the timeliness and convenience it offers: quick communication with little disruption in normal work patterns.

Videoconferencing allows for facial expressions and body language, which are lost in text-based, audio-only, or chat conferencing. Videoconferencing can be one-way video/two-way audio; or two-way video. One-way videoconferencing systems allow the instructor to be both heard and seen at remote sites connected to each other and the instructor. Usually, a voice connection is also established from the participants back to the instructor, allowing for two-way audio. Two-way videoconferencing systems, on the other hand, allow all participants to see and hear each other. Either form of conferencing has the potential to closely emulate a traditional classroom because it allows for learner-learner as well as learner-instructor interaction. Marketing departments, for example, find videoconferencing a fast, effective way to disseminate new product information to a diverse sales force. Videoconferencing has also been effectively used in training programs at manufacturing sites where topics such as quality control can be offered without pulling employees off the job for any length of time.

In some organizations, specially equipped rooms have been created to support videoconferencing. Such dedicated facilities are designed to account for acoustics, lighting, seating, and technology placement. Increasingly, however, videoconferencing is moving to the desktop computer, a result of compressed digital transmission technology and increasing bandwidth in transmission lines.

Small, high-quality desktop systems allow communication directly to and from the user's individual workstation. While room-sized video systems may be expensive and complex, desktop videoconferencing systems are incredibly inexpensive and simple. Figure 7-3 lists several current vendors. The only technology required is a small camera that sits on top of the user's microcomputer, a microphone, and software to compress the audio and video files. The software allows the user to send and receive information that is stored on the computer. Because the user is in his or her office rather than a conference room, training sessions can be set up quickly and conferees have instant access to everything on their computers.

Because the features of desktop videoconferencing systems are similar, video quality depends on the bandwidth of the network at both ends of the connection. The quality of images when POTS (plain old telephone services) lines are used can be shaky, and because the audio and video are often not synchronized, an annoying one-second delay is often the result. However, addressing bandwidth issues are Digital Subscriber Lines (DSL) that can push data more quickly over POTS lines and direct-broadcast satellite. Also addressing these issues is Internet II, a development effort funded by the U.S. government, that would be a separate network offering data transfer rates 100 to 1,000 times faster than the Internet. It is anticipated that once desktop systems are Internet-based, multimedia communications will be more standard.

FIGURE 7-3
DESKTOP VIDEOCONFERENCING PRODUCTS

CU-SeeMe (CUseeMe Networks)	cuseeme.com
NetMeeting (Microsoft)	microsoft.com
MeetingPoint (CuseeMe Networks)	cuseeme.com
PictureTel (PictureTel)	picturetel.com
PictureTalk (Pixion, Inc.)	pixion.com

COMPUTER CONFERENCING

Increasingly, computer conferencing software that supports synchronous Internet or Intranet communication, including instant messaging, chat rooms, and/or other groupware tools, is used in training situations.

Instant messaging allows users to see who else is on-line. A user can send a message that instantly pops up on the addressee's screen, and two or more users can have an interactive discussion. Chat sessions allow (usually) larger groups to communicate either publicly or privately by typing to each other. However, some products in this category are blurring distinctions between instant messaging and chat sessions to include audio and video. For example, the instant meeting technology in Lotus' Sametime© product builds on the product's existing real-time chat technology. Sametime lets users know when others in their group are on-line and instantly convenes an interactive data conference, complete with documents, spreadsheets, interactive presentations, and other applications. Vendors are also creating audio and video add-on products to their instant messaging and chat tools.[10]

Additionally, group support systems (GSS) can add additional facilitation tools to same-time/same place or same-time/different place group communications. In GSS-supported sessions, participants can share information, brainstorm ideas, develop plans, make decisions, and negotiate. GSS's value to training applications is just beginning to be appreciated and understood. Most GSS systems, such as groupsystems.com's (formerly Ventana Corporation) GroupSystems, feature participant anonymity and simultaneous input. Thus, the use of GSS supports those training situations in which the trainer acts as a facilitator—helping a group of managers, for example, share their cases and problems with others in the firm, asking for and sharing help and support.

Business Television

Business Television is a medium often used to broadcast informational sessions within an organization. Such presentations may be closed-captioned or dubbed in various languages as needed. Direct satellite broadcast most frequently involves one-way video and two-way audio. Such sessions are designed to be highly interactive and provide opportunities for participants to communicate with both the instructor and other participants.

Using Distance Learning Tools Effectively

Synchronous distance learning has become a very real and viable teaching method. Success stories abound in corporate training situations, as well as in traditional academic institutions. Based on these experiences, the next section has suggestions for using distance learning tools effectively with regard to both selecting and presenting the content, as well as for instructor training.

Selecting and Presenting the Content

Distance learning experiences whereby an instructor merely delivers a lecture by conferencing often meet with resistance on the part of the learners. In fact, straight lectures transmitted by videoconferencing technologies are known as "talking heads" because, in such situations, the sending camera typically zooms in on the lecturer who talks or reads from a prepared script. While many such talking heads existed in the early applications of distance learning technologies, these situations are relatively uncommon today. Lecturers know how important it is to give audiences ample opportunity for interaction.

When conferencing technologies are applied to delivering learning experiences, two key areas require attention. The first is technical quality. Support technicians usually ensure that visual aids are clear and easy for those at the remote site to read. Technicians will also ensure that the audio transmission is satisfactory, which is an absolutely crucial requirement. Low audio quality, even more than poor video quality, greatly reduces comprehension. The instructor him or herself can quickly learn operation skills such as operating the camera, the facsimile, the computer, while staying within the physical limits of the camera and microphones. Such skills come by hands-on experience with the tools, and practice, practice, practice!

The second key component of conferencing is the adaptation of traditional stand-up-and-deliver techniques to the medium being used. Instructors must be sure to employ a full range of adult-oriented, learner-centered activities such as small group activities and role plays. To keep remote learners interested and motivated, the instructor should encourage learner participation by directing questions to individuals at remote sites by name and pausing frequently for participant comments or questions. Like learning any technical skills, adapting teaching skills to distance learning applications comes with practice.

An interesting observation by those who have evaluated instructors' use of distance learning technologies is that technology itself does not make a poor instructor good; it will only allow him or her to reach more people. However, technology *can* make a good instructor even better. All good instructors know their target audience and stick to the learning objectives in any environment. Using distance learning technology effectively requires additional planning in these areas. Such preplanning on the part of the instructor makes for a good learning experience.

Figure 7-4 lists situations where a variety of live instructional approaches are used, along with their advantages and disadvantages. Selecting the "right" instructional technique requires that the trainer determine how learners can learn in the most effective and efficient way, given the content to be delivered, the audience, and the time frame available.

Figure 7-4

Advantages and Disadvantages of Selected Live Instructional Techniques

Approach	Commonly Used in Situations Where	Advantages	Disadvantages
Lecture	the learning goal is informational	instructor can reach large numbers of participants at once	speaker is active; learners are passive; to be effective, must be coupled with other learning strategies, e.g., small group discussions, games
Lecturette	program activities must be explained or content provided though other means, e.g., a video or small group exercise needs to be expanded upon	provides an opportunity for the instructor to set up learning experiences or expand on the content of exercises	speaker is active and participants are passive, unless questions are encouraged
The Socratic Method	learners have a reasonable amount of knowledge about the topic already	requires high involvement on the part of learners	requires much planning on the part of the instructor and great confidence to handle things when the Q&A does not go as planned
Case studies	the learning goal is to teach skills of problem identification and diagnosis	draws on the knowledge and experience of learners	relevant cases are difficult to create; instructor must be flexible and able to take risks
Informational treasure hunts	the goal is to teach people how to find, use, and apply existing information	learners learn how to find information on their own	time consuming and learner motivation is key to successful implementation
Small group discussions	the learning activity is to encourage discussion of topics or problem solving	offers learners a chance to interact with each other	can be taken over by powerful personalities; reluctant participants may still not contribute
Games and simulations	the instructional goal is to establish interest in a topic, or serve as an icebreaker	games make learning fun; simulations provide real-life experiences without personal risk	instructions must be carefully considered; may be too time consuming for desired outcomes
Role plays	learners need an opportunity for hands-on practice and immediate feedback	learners are put into a specific role and learn appropriate behaviors	can be misused; must be taken seriously; a role play is an act unless its purpose is clear and immediate feedback is given
Distance learning	learners and instructors are geographically dispersed; adequate technology exists to support interaction	learners can access instruction without travel; instructors can reach large numbers of learners	telecommunication technology can be costly; traditional instructional methods must be adapted
Informal learning strategies	learners' goals are broad and not easily quantified	learners learn at the time they need to learn; corporate culture is shared	challenges exist in designing and implementing formal programs

INSTRUCTIONAL AIDS

Instructional aids, sometimes referred to as *audiovisual aids or materials*, are those items that an instructor uses within the class session to help learners understand key points. Pictures, charts, graphics, animation, video—the list goes on and on—can be used to provide structure and add variety in learning situations. Instructional aids needed to deliver a program are typically created at the program design phase of the training cycle (See Figure 1-10). They are tested in the pilot program(s) and then made available for instructor use as part of the program rollout. Their development should be governed by the following three principles:

- Professional quality—In these days of desktop publishing, powerful PCs, presentation software, and sophisticated copiers, there is no excuse for anything less than high-quality, perfectly legible materials (18 point type—or the equivalent—on visuals, 4-inch letters on flip charts, a maximum of half a dozen lines on any one visual). While crisp, clean, readable black-and-white visuals are a perfectly adequate minimum, artistic design and color can add interest to the presentation. The "6 x 6" rule, no more than six words on a line and six lines on a page, also helps ensure readability and aids comprehension.
- Timeliness—If the organization's quarterly financial report is part of the program, it should be the most recent financial report, not a copy of the one used when the program was piloted two years ago. If a videotape of senior executives discussing ethical issues is part of the program, both the executives and the issues must be reasonably current in the organization. If this means frequent updating of the tape, that may be a signal that video is not the right choice of medium. A slide show with voice-over or printed materials might be more appropriate.
- Simplicity—The less complicated your materials are, the less likely there are to be problems with them. This is particularly applicable to those situations in which instructional materials are created in one place, by one trainer or training department, and then used elsewhere by other trainers or departments.

In addition to preplanned instructional material, instructors often create real-time materials in the classroom, inspired by the need or opportunity of the moment. Examples of spur-of-the-moment materials include flip chart sheets to sum up a particularly incisive case discussion, a blackboard filled with the product of the afternoon's brainstorming session, or an overhead transparency with a scribbled formula that captures an idea not previously considered. These are the results of learning in action and are not at all to be restricted by the criteria set for preplanned materials.

Six kinds of preplanned instructional aids, as used by an instructor engaged in live instruction, will be discussed here. The four most common are overhead transparencies, handouts, flip charts, and films. A fifth classroom aid, which is very powerful and is a commonly available tool, is presentation software. The final instructional aid, in a class all by itself, is the *Leader's Guide*.

Overhead Transparencies and Projector

Simple to create, highly portable, readily adaptable to changes, inexpensive, and easily turned into handouts, *overhead transparencies* are a staple of live instruction. Transparencies, also called foils, can be mounted on frames or have a cloth strip along one side, either surface capable of bearing penciled speaking notes for the instructor using them. Transparencies can come in colors. They can be masked, and the mask removed one step at a time for a reveal technique or the gradual build-up of a concept. Given the right kind of wall, overheads do not need a screen, nor do they require dimmed lights. Transparencies can be created by word processing or presentation software or by hand with a grease pencil or marking pen.

The transparency itself is placed on the projector, where a light source is focused through the transparency, and bounced back 90 degrees to a wall, screen, or other flat surface. The projected, enlarged result allows the presenter to face the audience and maintain eye contact as the audience attends to the image. Using two overhead projectors at once permits an instructor to put an overview up as one visual, then explode the components of the overview in a second image, one component at a time. Skilled use of an overhead projector keeps an audience focused on key points and helps maintain interest.

Tips for Using the Overhead Projector

The use of an overhead projector is an important training skill to develop, and the projector itself deserves attention, as well as the transparencies. Many projectors are equipped with a second bulb, so if the first bulb goes out in mid-presentation, the show can go on with the flip of a lever. Simple as it is, the overhead projector nonetheless exemplifies the first law of audiovisual equipment: Take nothing for granted, and always kick the tires—check, check again, and then recheck. Be sure equipment is operable and that whatever backup is provided is also in working order. Make sure that an extra bulb is available and that you know how to install it. Aim the projector so that the visuals are properly focused and visible from every seat in the room before the session begins. Also, be sure that the projector's electrical cord is taped down so no one will trip over it.

Perhaps the most important thing to keep in mind when using overheads (the term *overhead* is used by trainers to refer both to the transparencies and the projector) is to face the audience and point at the image on the projector's glass rather than directly at the image on the screen. It is very easy to forget this simple rule and get caught up in looking at the wall/screen along with the audience, gesturing and talking to it rather than to the audience. Also remember to turn the projector off when you remove one transparency and do not immediately replace it with another. A projector with no visual on it throws a blindingly brilliant light that can easily be a major distraction.

Slides

Slides are generally 35 mm color negatives and are much less common in day-to-day training situations than are overheads, though they are often used for large-scale informational sessions, as they can provide stunningly colorful images. Unlike overheads, slides are not very flexible: Once they are loaded into a projector's tray or carousel, they are not easily changed or re-sequenced. They cannot be written on, are relatively expensive to make, and require a darkened room for full effect. The impact of slides, however, is very effective when a planned, formal presentation is required.

Slide projectors are somewhat more complicated than an overhead and thus require even more careful checking and backup. If you are going to use a slide projector, be sure to test it thoroughly beforehand (both its mechanics and its projection). Insist on a remote control device to change the slides so you are not tied to a podium. Use slides primarily for informational sessions and prepared speeches.

Handouts

The most basic form of instructional aid is the *handout,* papers or materials distributed in a class session that capture or summarize the information being conveyed by the instructor. Handouts provide the learners with memory assistance, space for note-taking during instruction, and reference material for using the instructional content later. While the handout may be basic, it is an extremely useful tool for learners. Instructors frequently provide program participants with a copy of the visuals used in the instruction as a handout, often condensing a dozen illustrations on a single page. This tactic gives the learners perfect material on which to take notes and jot down questions. An alternative is a summary outline of the instructional content, which provides the same information as the visuals without the necessity of duplicating them. Presentation software, discussed later in this section, makes creating handouts with exact, high-quality miniatures of the visuals quite easy. Handouts ensure that the participants have the information in a useful form that is helpful to them. It is, of course, critical that the handout material be of first-class quality.

Flip Charts

Flip charts are pads of approximately 22-by-42-inch paper fastened together at the top and (usually) mounted on an easel or a wall unit. Flip charts are another common instructional aid. They can be used for both presenting and recording ideas, are inexpensive, travel fairly easily when rolled up in a tube, can include color and graphics, and offer great flexibility in use. Flip charts created in advance ("flips," working trainers call them) carry information such as the agenda(s) for the modules or days of the program, summaries of program content, logistics, directions for program activities, and the like. Note that it is not necessary to prepare a flip chart *pad* in advance, just the individual pages. These pages can then be organized and taped onto a pad wherever and whenever needed.

Flip chart pages can be produced by specialized copying equipment. The original visual is drawn or desktop-published on an ordinary sheet of 8 1/2-by-11-inch paper, which is then fed into a special copier to produce a flip chart-sized version. It is also possible to lightly laminate flip chart sheets so they will wear longer and can be written or drawn on, erased, and then reused. In addition to these pre-written charts, flip charts are also often created in the classroom in real time, either by plan or spontaneously drawn by the instructor as an aid to expressing certain points in the program, displaying content, or capturing ideas from participants. Similarly, program participants often use flip charts for the same kinds of purposes. Figure 7-5 includes guidelines for their effective use.

FIGURE 7-5
TIPS FOR EFFECTIVE FLIP CHART USE

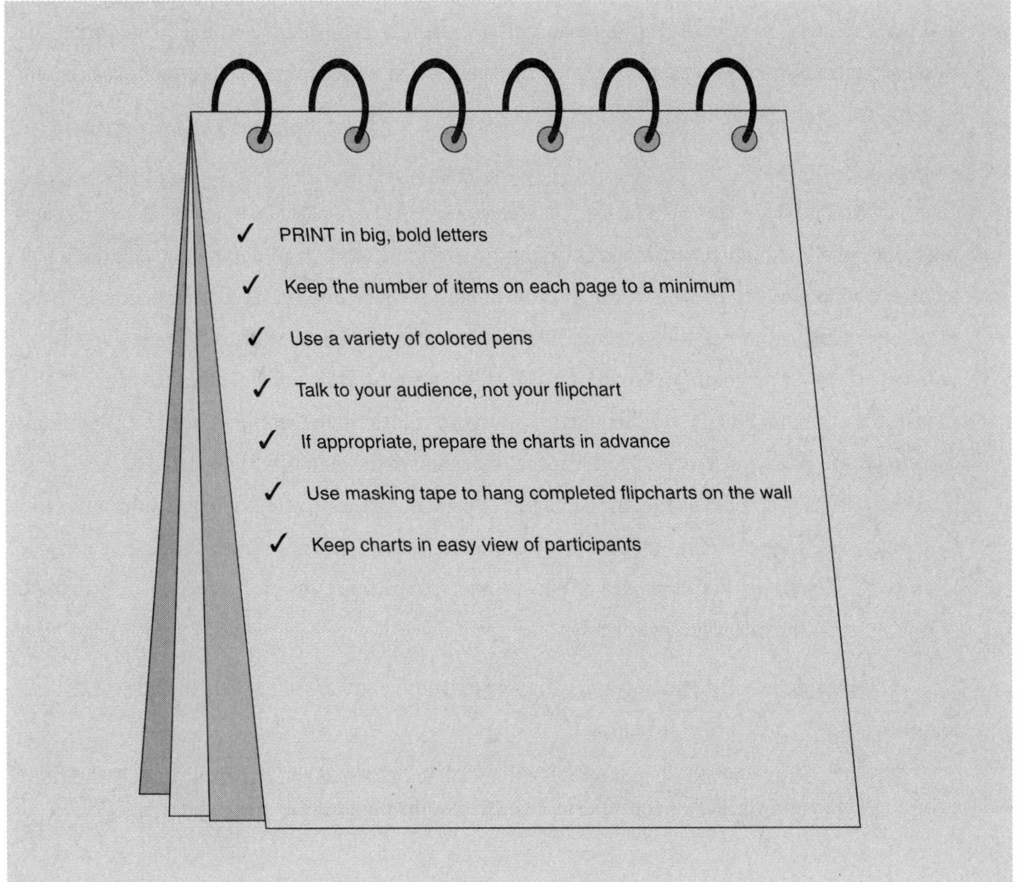

VIDEOTAPES

The training film is an idea that has been around a long time, but the availability of videotape, the camcorder, and the videocassette recorder/player (VCR) have revitalized the use of film in training contexts. Whether shown on television sets via a VCR, or shown via large-screen projectors, video is a powerful way to present information. A tape of a senior executive talking about a new policy gives a certain panache to the material that the trainer cannot usually equal. A professionally produced video of the features and benefits of a new product is a high-quality way to introduce this information, again with a gloss and graphic excellence that a trainer's live presentation usually cannot match.

In addition to its use for the presentation of information, another important use of video is to model behavior. A demonstration of the proper way to communicate or interact with staff or to give a speech, especially when followed by skills practice, has a marked impact on the learning of target skills. "Show me" has always been the cry of learners faced with a need to learn a specific skill. Video has raised the level of showing-by-pictures to a whole new dimension of possibility and power. Entire libraries of training material on videotape are available on the open market. Because videotape is also used in mediated instructional situations, a more thorough discussion of using videotapes is offered in Chapter 8.

PRESENTATION SOFTWARE

Presentation software can be used to create overhead transparency masters, as well as computer presentations; moreover, its use is becoming commonplace. Presentation software gives the lecturer a set of tools to use that result in professional, easy-to-modify instructional aids. Software products, such as Microsoft's PowerPoint, allow the user to add pictures, animation, sound, and video to otherwise stagnant presentations. Direct links can be established so that by a click of the mouse, the presenter can go to a Web page. PowerPoint slides can be stored in html on Web pages, allowing users—both instructors and learners—access whenever a link is available to the Internet. Because you plan ahead, the structure of presentation software also has a side bonus of helping to keep your presentation on track. Additional features, including speaker notes pages, allow you to remember key examples or illustrations that make your point. Handouts consisting of miniature slides, are easily produced.

Some guidelines for creating and using presentation software effectively include the following:

- Choose an appropriate font for your slide; what looks good on paper may not translate well to an overhead. Keep your font consistent throughout the presentation.

- Choose backgrounds and colors that are conducive to getting your point across. Test your presentation on the equipment you'll be using for the presentation; colors tend to fade or show up differently given a particular projection device.
- Keep their attention where you want it. Use bullet "builds" to keep your audience with you. This reveals bullets one at a time, so viewers aren't racing ahead of you to the next point, then dims them once you're ready to move on.
- Limit the number of transition and animation effects. Use them only for interest or humor.
- Limit the length and number of audio and video clips; they can become tiring.
- Avoid long, complex quotes.
- Don't "read" your screens; use bullets and text as discussion starters, not as text.

The Leader's Guide

The main resource for the instructor in preparing and teaching a program is the *Leader's Guide* (See the discussion in Chapter 6). The Leader's Guide lays out the entire program, module by module, so an instructor knows what to say and what to do throughout. Formats vary, but a good Leader's Guide provides an overview of the program as a whole, explains its overall objectives with its components and modules, and states clearly how they all fit together. The Leader's Guide will include the following:

- The objectives and learning points of each component, so the instructor knows why the component is part of the program and what its results are to be.
- The "talking points" for everything the instructor is to say—something less than a script but more than a mere content outline. The Leader's Guide is a teaching outline that tells the instructor what needs to be said or done about each learning point—and sometimes even how to say it—at every major juncture of the program. It is not a script to be memorized, but it does make each and every point the organization and the training designers want made in the program.
- A copy of all participant materials.
- An explanation of each activity in the program at the point where it is to be used—what the purpose of each is and how it is to be done, together with copies of all materials necessary for the exercise: flip charts, other visuals, game or discussion materials, handouts, role play directions, feedback forms, and the like.
- A copy of all visuals to be used in the program—overhead transparencies, PowerPoint slides, flip chart pages, wall charts, etc.—all in the Leader's Guide binder, sized for ease of packaging and transport.
- A suggested time schedule for each component of the program—approximately 15-minute segments and aggregation of the components into larger units as useful.
- A transition into/from the next/previous component(s) of the program.

The Leader's Guide is typically a three-ring binder with tabs for each component or day of the program, and tabs for the handouts, flip charts, overhead transparencies, and any other program material the instructor should have. The purpose of the Leader's Guide is to provide the instructor with everything needed to deliver the program in a quality fashion with the required degree of consistency. Most instructors will make some form of teaching notes for themselves—file cards they can tuck into their shirt pockets, post-it notes gummed to the pages of the Leader's Guide or Participant's Manual, pieces of paper with summary notes, etc. These all begin with the Leader's Guide itself. Another way to sum up the role and scope of a Leader's Guide is this:

> Observing an offering of the program with the Leader's Guide available for note-taking should provide all that an experienced instructor needs in order to teach the program, given adequate time for personal preparation.

The Leader's Guide should not be viewed as a straitjacket, but as a help. It tells the instructor what the program sponsors/designers want said and done, and states how to achieve what the program is to deliver. It should therefore be followed. At the same time, the Leader's Guide is a tool with a purpose, not an end in itself. If some part of it no longer works, the instructor on his or her feet in front of a class will discover this and should feed the information back to the Leader's Guide's developer for possible modification. Deviating from the Leader's Guide should be neither common nor capricious, but it should not be considered impossible. A great deal is typically left to the instructor's discretion. Nevertheless, an instructor must also remember that he or she is the deliverer of the program, not its designer or its redesigner.

Figure 7-6 shows two pages from the Leader's Guide of an actual management development program at Chase Manhattan Bank, *Managing at Chase.*

FIGURE 7-6
SAMPLE LEADER'S GUIDE PAGES

The following two pages are taken from the Leader's Guide for Managing at Chase, a one-day orientation to management responsibility at Chase Manhattan Bank. The two pages guide an instructor in setting up a team activity in the program. The pages do not follow each other in the actual Leader's Guide, and the contents have been shortened a bit for the sake of practicality.

Segment 4.2 Instructor Presentation: Managerial Tools and Resources

Purpose:

- To introduce a variety of tools and resources available to the Chase manager in managing human-resources-related issues.
- To give participants the opportunity to become familiar with the Chase Human Resources Guide and the Chase Code of Ethical Standards.

Figure 7-6 (Continued)

Time:	9:15-9:40
Method/Media:	Lecturette, Class discussion
INTRODUCE	Introduce team discussion with ideas such as the following: As managers, we are often called upon to deal with HR situations. Some of these are messy or complicated. How often have you wished you had a guide or specific tools to help you figure out what to do. We want to introduce you to several such tools in this exercise.
ELICIT	Ask: what are some examples of messy or complicated HR situations you have faced?
CAPTURE	Use blank flip to capture key words of examples participants provide. Use alternating colors for ease of reading. (Typical responses: poor performance, excessive lateness/absenteeism complicated by a diversity issue, low motivation, unrealistic expectations, unethical behavior, not living our behavioral values and/or dept standards)
HR GUIDE	Point out that there are a variety of resources available to managers to help with situations such as the ones we've listed on our flipchart here. Among those resources is the Chase HR Guide, the so-called "red book." Ask how many participants have a copy of the Guide. Mention that you will tell them in a minute how to order a Guide if they don't have one.
DISTRIBUTE	Pass out copies of the Guide to all. Mention that the copies being used in the classroom today must be returned.
PRESENT	Using Flip 4.2.2, make following points re Guide: We have a written HR policy guide chiefly for consistency — becoming familiar with the Guide and its contents is an important managerial responsibility • Employees need to know what they may expect in the way of HR policies • Managers need a common policy framework to help ensure fairness and reasonable consistency Ask participants to look at the Guide's table of contents. Review categories of policies: Employment, Time Off, Compensation, Staff Development, Employee Services, etc. Tell participants to look in the back pocket of the Guide. There they will find a form they can use to order a copy for themselves if they need it. Tell participants we will do an exercise in a few minutes in which they will have to use the Guide to find the solution to a typical HR problem.

(Continued)

Figure 7-6 (Continued)

The instructor introduces three additional policy documents, making much the same points about them as are made above concerning the HR Guide and teeing these documents up for use in a team activity as above. The three documents are the Chase Code of Ethical Standards, the Chase Performance Management Policy, and the Chase Vision and Values. Once the class has all 4 policy documents, the instructor leads the program participants through an exercise designed to get them to use the documents to gain familiarity with them.

Segment 4.3 **Team Activity — Case Analysis**

Purpose: To give program participants the opportunity to analyze an HR situation from the perspective of the policy documents provided them.

Time: 9:40-10:30

Method: Team discussion and presentation, policy book search

INTRODUCE You will now have a chance to use the policy documents we've been discussing.

- Take out the cases handed out for reading last night.
- You will work in teams, each team on one case that I'll assign you.
- You individually will analyze the case from the perspective of one of our four policy documents.
- You will then analyze the case as a team, each team member bringing to the discussion the policy perspective assigned — so that each team sees the case from all 4 policy points of view.
- Each team will then present its case and educate the rest of us on the case, the policies that apply to it, and why you recommend the course of action you've decided on.

ACTIVITY analysis and presentation by each team

A final note regarding the instructional aids discussed here concerns the purchase of a packaged training program for use in live instruction. Such a purchase should include a complete set of appropriate aids. It is certainly not essential that every program include video, powerful as the medium may be. However, visuals, flip charts, and handouts—or a master copy of them to be used for their production—should be an expected part of any program package designed for live delivery. Most important of all, the package should include a detailed Leader's Guide. Because the development of a Leader's Guide is a complex, demanding, and detail-intensive task, it is often the case that the seller of a packaged program offers considerably less than a full-scale Leader's Guide. The purchase of the program may, of course, still be made, but the purchaser should be aware of what is *not* included in the package. The omission of a Leader's Guide may well have an impact on price, or on selection itself if one is choosing among two or more competing packages. Happily, the trainer is often faced with the situation in which a vendor not only provides a

Leader's Guide, but also offers reasonable train-the-trainer support to certify instructors for the program under consideration.

THE MANAGEMENT OF TEACHING

The selection of people for teaching responsibility is a key step in ensuring that live instruction is properly done. It is truly crucial to select teachers for their ability to communicate. The selection may be for a permanent position in a training department as an instructor. It may also be for a contract instructor, a consultant to be hired to teach on a per diem basis. It may be for a line person to teach on a visiting basis, either in a particular program or for a period of time (this is called the "line on loan" approach[11]). In all these cases, the focus of selection is on the candidate's instructional skills, which are essentially twofold:

- *Platform skills*—the ability to organize and present material, hold a class's attention, read and react to audience messages, use the customary teaching aids, facilitate group process (including discovery methods), and ground instruction in the principles of adult learning.
- *The communications mindset*—the perspective that communication (and therefore teaching) has not been successful unless and until the listener has received and internalized the message. This is the mindset that understands it is not enough to present information, not sufficient just to facilitate, not enough to follow a Leader's Guide in a planned, systematic way. It is the mindset that understands that all these things are important—even necessary—but not enough. It is the mindset that takes as fundamental that the learner's acquisition of skill or knowledge is essential and the single most important measure of instructional success.

Platform and communications skills are not always easy to identify. Standard interviewing techniques, particularly in multiple interviews, can provide a great deal of information. A history of successful teaching says much about the possession of platform skills. A candidate's familiarity with the literature on adult learning and its principles can be successfully probed. One can pick up on just how well a candidate listens in interviews, which is at least some indication of the ability to listen in a classroom. It is possible and certainly within the bounds of careful selection to ask a candidate to audition. Requiring a candidate to teach a carefully chosen module of a program, in either a real or artificial setting, is usually a revealing demonstration of both platform skills and the individual's communications mindset. Note that platform skills are far easier to acquire than the communications mindset. While individuals can be trained in presentation and group facilitation skills, the communications mindset is typically the product of a long seasoning process and can seldom be acquired in a brief five-day train-the-trainer program.

Once selected, instructors should be managed like other professionals, with respect for their dedication and intelligence and with ample opportunity for growth and creativity. A particular teaching risk is burnout, as organizational training tends to be a world of short workshops offered repeatedly. No instructor should be asked to teach the same workshop too often in too short a time. "Too often" and "too short" are relative terms, but asking an instructor to teach the same class over and over with little respite or change is a surefire recipe for instructor burnout.

Preparation time is another relative matter, but a rule of thumb is 3-1, or three hours of preparation time for one hour of teaching time, given a reasonable level of experience on the part of the instructor. Most instructors find the chance to observe someone else teaching a program an enormous help in preparing to teach it themselves. If this opportunity can be furnished, it usually pays off handsomely. The 3-1 rule will obviously vary according to the individual, and will, in any case, change as familiarity with a program grows through experience with it. Unrushed, uninterrupted preparation time, however, is a reasonable expectation on the part of an instructor, as well as a solid principle of good instructor management. To avoid ringing phones and other distractions, preparation can best be done away from the office—in a library, in a borrowed office or conference room, or at home.

The manager of a group of instructors should observe them in the classroom from time to time. Observational data can provide the information needed for coaching the instructors, as well as for rewards and recognition. Performance plans for instructors often specify the number and variety of programs to be taught. Such activity measures, however, should not be equated with instructional success. Good instruction results in learning outcomes, which is a far more complex measure, as discussed in Chapter 3.

As a way of getting at these real instructional outcomes, teachers and managers may agree on an average rating from participant questionnaires at the end of a class. A more productive approach is to manage these ratings by exception. After all, good end-of-class ratings are to be expected and are the norm, but do not really provide much useful information about how good a job a teacher is doing because an experienced instructor *can* and *should* get good ratings. On the other hand, managing participant feedback by exception means scanning the end-of-class comments and ratings for anything that deviates from the norm. This approach takes favorable ratings for granted, assumes the instructor should and will get them, pays attention only to those that are exceptions, and *puts the teacher's performance focus on the learner*. If this management-by-exception approach is used, performance goals for teachers will reflect agreed upon limits for the number of exceptions noted, with the limits obviously a function of factors such as program and audience type, instructor experience, environmental conditions, and the like.

Finally, the manager of teachers must exercise care to avoid the so-called "shoemaker's children" problem: trainers and development specialists not receiving sufficient training and development themselves. Just as each member of the training department has a performance plan, so also should each member have a development plan. The focus of this plan should be a mix of preparation for immediate job responsibilities and longer term career thinking as appropriate. Line-on-loan instructors will obviously have job and career needs different from training professionals. The crucial point here is to make sure that reasonable levels of professional development for its own people are as much a part of the training department's plans as are its implementation schedules.

SUMMARY

The teacher with students in a classroom is a time-honored image in our society. Today's professional trainer will work to enhance that picture and will also work to ensure that the instruction supplied in such a setting is learner-focused and well-considered for the learning need at hand. Two categories of live instruction were presented in this chapter: whole group methods (the lecture and discovery techniques); and small group methods (such as group discussion, games, and role plays).

The lecture method was described as an efficient means of providing information to a large group. When coupled with question-and-answer periods, this method allows learners to hear, see, and ask questions about the topics presented. However, long periods of lecturing are usually not motivating. Thus, the competent lecturer breaks up long discourses with other activities that require more active participation on the part of participants, such as making lists or small group activities. The lecturette, a brief lecture, is a staple in most training situations.

Discovery methods challenge training participants to learn for themselves. Actively engaging learners to discover concepts for themselves requires careful preplanning on the part of the instructor. The Socratic Method, case studies, and informational treasure hunts are situations where learners are not given solutions to problems, but must discover appropriate responses/behaviors that are based on their own experiences and the materials available.

Small group methods are important strategies in most training situations. Trainees in small groups learn from each other and are active participants in learning activities. Small groups may be asked to review materials and come to their own conclusions, which are later shared with others in the class. Small groups can be motivated to learn—and learning can be fun—through games and role plays. The role of the instructor in small group methods is to plan the activities carefully and to ensure that participants not only get feedback from the instructor, but also learn to give—and get—feedback to and from each other.

Informal learning stratagies including self-directed work groups, coaching, and mentoring, are nonstructured approaches to supporting tacit learning in organizations. Trainers can support self-directed work groups by facilitating group meetings or helping learners find information about their needed knowledge or skill. One-on-one coaching provides learners with the right learning at just the right time. Trainers can support coaching by ensuring that supervisors and managers are skilled in providing positive feedback. Mentoring, whereby a senior member of the organization is paired with a new hire, allows individuals with organizational experience to share what they know and provide job and career advice to those entering the organization. Training departments are often in a position to provide structure and monitoring to formal mentoring programs.

In the global or on-the-move organization, distance learning is increasingly being used. In this category, the instructor and trainees are not in the same location, but are supported by a form of conferencing technology. Audio conferencing is voice-only communication; videoconferencing is audio plus video; and computer conferencing is the use of special communications software that facilitates group communication in both synchronous and asynchronous modes. The implementation of distance learning requires that the instructor be able to use the technology well, and adjust his or her traditional teaching methods. Adapted methods include less talk on the part of the instructor, small group work to ensure more active participation from participants, and directed questions to ensure that all participants feel that they are part of the group.

Instructional aids—overheads, handouts, flip charts, presentation software, and video—can be brought to the classroom and be used by the live instructor to enhance learning. Behind the scenes as an instructional aid is the single most important one: the Leader's Guide, which details the objectives, content, methods, and major points of the program. Ensuring that instruction is delivered according to the Leader's Guide is one way to sum up the responsibilities of teacher management. These responsibilities also include an emphasis on careful teacher selection, on approaches to teacher performance management that require a learner focus, and on appropriate development for teaching personnel.

THINK IT THROUGH

1. Has there been a teacher in your life who has "made a difference"? Describe the teacher and the circumstance in which he or she made a difference. What was the impact of this teacher? What was the result of that impact? From your experience with this teacher, what would you like to bring to your students?
2. "Lecture only if you must." Do you agree or disagree with this statement? Support your response.
3. Identify three of the many alternatives for delivering training programs face-to-face. Give an appropriate training problem/opportunity for each.
4. What are communities of practice? How can a training professional use self-directed learning teams, coaching programs, or mentoring programs to support learning in the organization?
5. Describe some characteristics of effective overhead transparencies and PowerPoint slides. Why is it so important that such visuals be of professional quality?
6. List several pointers to follow when using flip charts.
7. Define distance learning. What alternatives do organizations have for delivering instruction from afar? Give an appropriate training situation for each alternative.
8. The Leader's Guide has been described as a teaching resource, not a teaching script. When is it acceptable for a trainer to deviate from the Leader's Guide?
9. Imagine you are a junior training professional just hired at the XYZ Company as an instructor. Plan an initial personal development discussion with your manager. What sort of development would you consider appropriate for yourself for your first year? Why?

IDEAS IN ACTION

1. Break into pairs. Tell each other about a teacher-led learning experience that you thought was very effective. What was it about the experience that contributed to its success? Next, tell each other about a teacher-led learning experience that was not successful. What caused the experience to be problematic?
2. Attend a computer trade show and try (or observe) demonstrations of a variety of presentation graphics packages. Obtain literature from vendors. List key features and compare them across packages. Which seems most appropriate for a trainer?
3. Create a T-Chart. On the left-hand side of the "T" write "good ways to handle student questions." On the right side, write "bad ways to handle questions." Complete the chart based on your own experience.

4. Contact a local training manager and ask about the issue of instructor burnout. What has been the manager's experience with it? How/why does it happen? Has the manager developed any telltale signs of its approach? Any methods for handling it? Any ways of preventing it?

ADDITIONAL RESOURCES

RECOMMENDED READINGS

Eitington, Julius E., *The Winning Trainer.* 3rd ed., Houston: Gulf Publishing, 1996, 625 pp.

A comprehensive reference book for training professionals. Includes an appendix of valuable resources—forms, checklists, and other practical job aids.

Mager, Robert F., *Making Instruction Work: or Skillbloomers.* Belmont, CA: Lake Publishing Company, 1988. 200 pp.

One of Mager's best in his bookshelf of superb work. The book is about what he calls the "craft of instruction," and he is at the top of his form in providing guidance to ensure instruction is properly chosen as a solution and well done in its implementation. Written with a practitioner's wealth of experience and Mager's usual dosages of puckish humor.

McKeachie, Wilbert J., *Teaching Tips: Strategies, Research, and Theories for College and University Teachers.* 10th ed., Lexington, MA: Houghton Mifflin, 1999, 379 pp.

This very well written and organized paperback is crammed with helpful information intended for instructors at all adult teaching levels and in a wide range of teaching environments. If you can not find instructional help here, it probably does not exist anywhere.

Powers, Bob, *Instructor Excellence: Mastering the Delivery of Training.* San Francisco: Jossey-Bass Publishers, 1992, 246 pp.

A fine discussion of the issues involved in stand-up teaching. Note the book title's implicit equation of instruction with training delivery. The book itself is smarter than that. Particularly useful in evaluating and managing teaching.

Stamps, David, "Communities of Practice: Learning is social. Training is irrelevant?" *Training,* February 1997, pp. 34-44.

Stamps provides an overview of community of practice in terms that are very useful for the training professional, including an excerpt from the Wenger book, described in this section.

Wenger, Etienne, *Communities of Practice: Learning, Meaning, and Identity.* Boston: Cambridge University Press, 1999, 318 pp.

The publisher of this book says that *Communities of Practice* presents a theory of learning that starts with the assumption that engagement in social practice is the fundamental process by which we learn and so become who we are. The theory explores in a systematic way the intersection of issues of community, social practice, meaning, and identity. The result is a broad conceptual framework for thinking about learning as a process of social participation.

WEB SITES

http://www.cttbobpike.com

Visit the Web site of noted consultant Bob Pike for a variety of resources ranging from articles and research to case studies on effective teaching.

http://pages.nyu.edu/~lbq0313/geststart.htm

Lynn Bacon's PowerPoint Page provides step-by-step instruction for the novice PowerPoint user.

http://www.presentations.com

Provides speaking tips and links to a variety of resources. While you are visiting the site, see if you are eligible for a free subscription to Bill Communications' *Presentations* magazine.

ENDNOTES

1. Eitington, Julius, *The Winning Trainer.* Houston: Gulf Publishing, 1984, p. 232.
2. Davis, Barbara Gross. *Tools for Teaching*. San Francisco: Jossey-Bass, 1991, pp. 88-89.
3. Duncan, O. Carm., Quentin, in speech class held at Whitefriars Hall, Washington, D.C., circa 1958.
4. Christensen, C. Roland, David A. Garvin, and Ann Sweet. *Education for Judgment: The Artistry of Discussion Leadership.* Boston, Mass.: Harvard Business School Press, 1991, p. 11.
5. Ibid. pp. 159-160.
6. Newstrom, John. W., and Edward E. Scannell, *Games Trainers Play.* New York: McGraw-Hill, 1980, pp. xii-xiv.
7. Davis, op. cit., pp. 137-138.
8. Davis, Ibid., p. 137.
9. See three sources:

    Pfeiffer, J. William (ed.) *The 1994 Annual: Developing HR.* San Diego: Pfeiffer and Company, 8517 Production Avenue, San Diego, CA 92121, (619) 578-5900/ Fax: (619) 578-2042. A three-ring binder published annually with sections devoted to games and other experiential learning techniques, inventories of surveys and questionnaires, and resources for presentations/discussions on topics of current interest in the world of human resource development. The binder format makes it easy to use the material provided.

Nilson, Carolyn, (ed.) *The Training and Development Yearbook.* Englewood Cliffs, NJ: Prentice Hall. This annual is rich in training materials, tips, current practices, hot topics, new techniques, and the like. The book comes in standard book binding.

Newstrom, John W., and Edward E. Scannell.

Games Trainers Play. New York: McGraw-Hill, 1980.

More Games Trainers Play. New York: McGraw-Hill, 1983.

Still More Games Trainers Play. New York: McGraw-Hill, 1991.

Games and program exercises gathered from experienced trainers at annual training conferences and other gatherings. A wealth of material in categories such as icebreakers, communications, listening, and perception. Each entry states objectives of use, materials required, how to do the game or exercise, time needed, and suggested debriefing questions. This book comes in standard book binding, but with perforated pages for ease of use in programs.

10. Regan, Elizabeth A., and Bridget N. O'Connor (2001). *End-user Information Systems: Implementing Individual and Work Group Technologies*. Upper Saddle River, NJ: Prentice Hall.

11. *Line-on-loan* is the term used in ASTD's Benchmarking Study for line personnel who are visiting instructors.

CHAPTER 8
Mediated Instruction

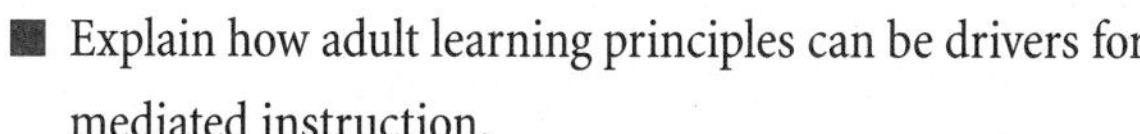

- Explain how adult learning principles can be drivers for mediated instruction.
- Discuss the role of books and journals and manuals in mediated instruction of all types.
- Offer examples of training goals that can be supported by audiotape and/or videotape instruction.
- Summarize the evolution of Computer-based Training (CBT).
- List the functionality of computer-managed instructional systems.
- Discuss the role of CDs in the development of interactive multimedia systems.
- Describe how Help Desks, on-line help, and performance support systems support just-in-time learning needs.
- Appraise the value of expert systems and databases in tracking knowledge and learning.
- List the attributes and benefits of Web-based Training (WBT).
- Appraise the future for WBT to support individual and organizational learning goals.
- Develop strategies for delivering mediated instruction.
- Suggest ways that mediated instruction outcomes can be evaluated.

SETTING THE STAGE FOR MEDIATED LEARNING

New technology does not usually diminish the use of old methods; we use a technology when it serves a particular purpose, when it is effective.[1]

When individuals are asked what they have learned in the workplace, they invariably describe their experiences in formal training programs. They might describe a workshop on communication skills or Microsoft Word. They might describe a three-day course on strategic planning. However, when asked what they learned informally over the years, they describe how they used the wizard in PowerPoint to create their first sales presentation. Or, they describe how they mastered a technical problem using software manuals. They might even describe how they were part of a team that worked together to expand their market into Asia. It is clear that learning is not limited to the classroom.

One of a training department's key responsibilities is to constantly explore new ways to encourage and support learning, not just training. Trainers in organizational settings use every conceivable method to ensure that their workforce can do what is necessary for the organization to survive and prosper. Traditional classroom-based delivery of training is widespread and popular. However, trainers also employ a whole gamut of other delivery methods, attempting to discover the best possible match among organizational expectations, learner needs and abilities, and content for each learning situation.

Mediated instruction is both an alternative and a complement to the live instructional methods discussed in the previous chapter. *Mediated instruction* has been called self-paced learning, individualized instruction, or prescriptive learning, and has been used as a synonym for technology-assisted training ranging from books to the World Wide Web. The term *mediated* describes a situation in which instruction is delivered by some form of media rather than by a live instructor. Training departments use many different mediated approaches to learning. The times demand innovation in providing the quantity and quality of learning experiences that workers need. Moreover, the World Wide Web as a distributor of information has made the sharing of knowledge found in databases, spreadsheets, documents, and the like readily available to an employee just at the time learning needs to happen. The communications capabilities of the Web also support information-sharing between and among employees.

This chapter begins with a brief discussion of selected adult learning principles applied to mediated instruction, and then continues by describing how mediated learning fits into the training cycle and how it differs from traditional live instruction. The bulk of this chapter will describe specific mediated learning methods and how to use them. Mediated instruction includes a wide range, and often a combination of, learning tools—books and tutorials, Computer-based Training (CBT), interactive multimedia systems, and performance support. This chapter includes discussion of Web-based Training (WBT), also known as Web-based Learning (WBL), and Internet-based Training (IBT), or E-learning. WBT, which usually includes live interaction among learners and instructor, is the fastest growing method for delivering mediated training. The chapter concludes with suggestions for implementing and evaluating mediated instruction.

MEDIATED INSTRUCTION AND ADULT LEARNING

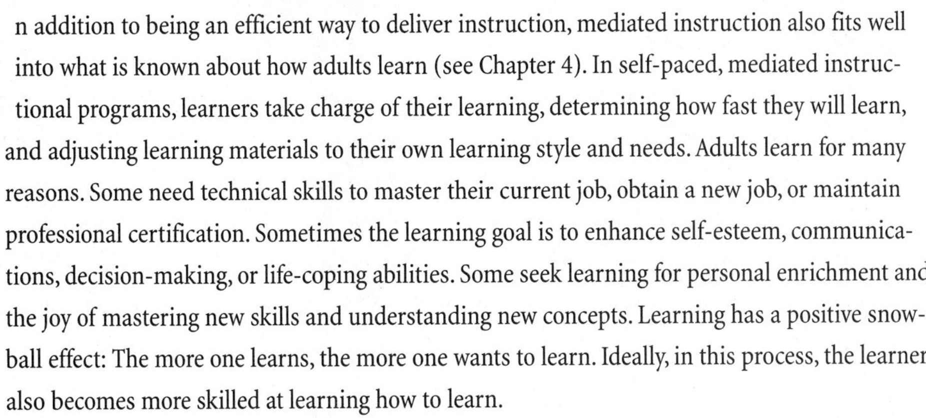

In addition to being an efficient way to deliver instruction, mediated instruction also fits well into what is known about how adults learn (see Chapter 4). In self-paced, mediated instructional programs, learners take charge of their learning, determining how fast they will learn, and adjusting learning materials to their own learning style and needs. Adults learn for many reasons. Some need technical skills to master their current job, obtain a new job, or maintain professional certification. Sometimes the learning goal is to enhance self-esteem, communications, decision-making, or life-coping abilities. Some seek learning for personal enrichment and the joy of mastering new skills and understanding new concepts. Learning has a positive snowball effect: The more one learns, the more one wants to learn. Ideally, in this process, the learner also becomes more skilled at learning how to learn.

With mediated instruction, learners determine when to learn, can progress at their own speed, are able to review lessons any number of times, can self-diagnose progress, and can more easily fit learning into a busy schedule. In mediated instruction, participants are actively involved in their learning experiences. This inherent participation, combined with control over the medium, encourages the learner's ownership of the learning process and ultimately leads to the mastery of the content.

CHOOSING AN INSTRUCTIONAL STRATEGY

Consistent with adult learning principles, it is important that needs assessment be *co-diagnostic*. In any needs assessment (see Chapter 2), members of the target audience (learners) should be deeply involved in the process of identifying their own needed knowledge, skills, and abilities. With such codeveloped needs assessment outcomes in hand, one can then determine if the best way to address the learning needs is through live or mediated instruction. In making this decision, one starts with the objectives of the organization and the learner, as well as the learning content. At this point, too, one takes organizational constraints, such as time and budget considerations, into account.

Mediated instruction is often used when the audience has a wide range of experiences and/or abilities, since its self-paced nature accommodates such a population. Similarly, mediated instruction can also be used effectively when a large audience is spread out geographically. It is also appropriate when a small number of learners needs to learn a specific skill, or when a repeated need for new people to learn the same skills occurs. Increasingly, its match with many learners' preferred learning styles and schedules have put it in the mainstream of delivery options. Mediated instruction may, of course, also be used in conjunction with traditional, live instruction. The two approaches to instructional delivery—live and mediated—can complement rather than replace each other.

Choosing the appropriate mediated method is a process of matching the learning objectives, the learning style of the target audience, the characteristics of the various media, and the media's ability to support appropriate learning activities. Moreover, the expense and time related to developing these learning materials are major considerations. Developing mediated instructional materials in-house can be a very expensive, time-consuming process. It is almost always less expensive to buy off-the-shelf materials, and then, if necessary, adapt them to a particular audience.

A VARIETY OF MEDIA

Following is an overview of selected media, including examples of their use in instruction: books and journals, audiotapes and videotapes, and the many types of Computer-based Training, concluding with a discussion of performance support. While we can discuss these approaches as separate options, in reality, mediated instruction is often a combination of them.

PAPER-BASED MATERIALS

The printed document is an extremely comfortable, familiar, simple, transportable, inexpensive, and easy-to-use learning medium. Much informational training is paper-based. Company newsletters, bulletins, and simple job aids are usually developed internally and are appropriate for a wide variety of learning needs. Entire courses can be developed and distributed via paper. The skilled use of desktop publishing allows training departments to internally develop and produce professional-looking and high-quality learning materials.

BOOKS AND JOURNALS

Books and journals are other paper-based learning resources. Many organizations maintain large libraries, complete with up-to-date subscriptions to relevant business magazines and journals. These libraries often have a wide range of classic and best-selling books on a number of topics of interest to employees. Reference books such as atlases, statistical abstracts, handbooks, manuals, or writing guides such as Strunk and White's *The Elements of Style* (Macmillan, 1987) also line the shelves.

However, simply having print materials available may not be enough to reach the desired learning outcome. While it is valuable to have a library, if a book is to be part of a specific learning strategy, it should be packaged with other learning resources, such as study guides or checklists. Examples of ways to help a reader use print-based materials proactively include the following:

- Well-articulated learning objectives that are tied to performance goals.
- A study guide that includes exercises such as requiring the reader to outline a chapter, respond to discussion questions, and/or complete related application activities.
- An interactive log, whereby the reader is asked to record reactions that are meaningful, and explain why they are meaningful.
- Learning activity sheets, where the learner identifies his or her progress in mastering materials, and then provides these sheets to the training facilitator.

Written Tutorials

Another type of paper-based instruction is a *written tutorial* on how to do something, such as use application software. Such tutorials are often found as part of a software manual, and while they can be useful in initial training efforts, they are often difficult to follow for the first-time user. Tutorials are often developed as a part of application systems, and when they are computer-based, they are considered within the category of computer-assisted instruction, which is discussed later in this chapter.

Audiotapes and Videotapes

Audiotapes and videotapes add communication channels to print-based learning materials. Audio provides an oral, human element to learning, while video provides an added visual dimension. "Books on Tape" is a popular section of many bookstores, and audio and video libraries are commonly found in organizational training departments. Tapes offer content, discussion, demonstrations, and examples that assist the learning process. Typically, audiotapes or videotapes are used in conjunction with print-based materials. Like all mediated instruction, audiotapes and videotapes allow learners to follow at their own pace and convenience, as shown in the three figures that follow: Figure 8-1 describes the use of a prerecorded audiotape used for informational training; Figure 8-2 shows the use of videotapes for participant self-evaluation; and Figure 8-3, which is quite different from the other examples, depicts an advertisement for a commercially available videotape and book that teach customer service techniques.

The medium for the delivery of audio and video material is clearly changing. While the existing stock of analog audiotapes and videotapes is enormous and will be around for a good while, industry experts expect digital media storage, specifically CDs, to replace analog tapes. Moreover, WBT has emerged as a key way to distribute CBT learning materials.

FIGURE 8-1
PRERECORDED AUDIOTAPE (SALES INFORMATION)

The sales representative of ArtWorld pops an audiotape into the sound system of the car and, after a few seconds, a popular song fills the air. The song tapers off and the voice of the marketing manager comes on: "What's new at ArtWorld is an improved method to silk-screen prints ...." Another song follows the information about the new system and, after that, more news about other ArtWorld updates. The audiotape, thus, allows the automobile to serve as a learning environment.

FIGURE 8-2
STUDENT-PREPARED VIDEOTAPES (SELF-EVALUATION)

As part of a sales training program in a large insurance company, trainees learn sales presentation principles through videotaped examples and print materials. They are required to prepare a series of tapes depicting their own sales presentations for different types of clients and for selling different types of insurance. The trainees outline their presentations, practice them, and then schedule an appointment with the media group to be recorded on videotape. In one scenario, for example, they are asked to role-play making a presentation on disability insurance to the board of directors of a large corporation. After the videotaped presentation, they review the recording and evaluate their performance using a checklist provided in the learning materials. If they are not satisfied with their performance, they can redo the tape. Since no instructor is present, the inexperienced salesperson is not embarrassed by mistakes. Later, at a time chosen by the trainee, an instructor will listen to and critique the tape with individual trainees. The final step in the training program is a "live" presentation, with another trainee playing the client's role.

FIGURE 8-3
THE LILY TOMLIN CUSTOMER TRAINING SERIES (CUSTOMER SERVICE TRAINING)

This all-new series from Mentor Media comes with the best possible pedigree: It features well-known comic actress Lily Tomlin playing an incredible repertoire of characters, and it's based on Ron Zemke's and Kristin Anderson's highly regarded book, *Delivering Knock Your Socks Off Service.* Each program is accompanied by a Facilitator's Manual and a Participant Workbook developed by Ron Zemke and Kristin Anderson of Performance Research Associates.
Here is what you will see and learn:

- **The Seven Deadly Sins of Customer Service**

  Lily Tomlin stars as Bobbi Jeanine, cocktail organist in Dante's Lounge, who reveals the Seven Deadly Sins of Customer Service in a fiery show that is the last stop before descending into Customer Service Purgatory. This film will help everyone avoid the costly sins of offending and losing customers.
  21 minutes.

(Continued)

- **Dealing with Disappointed Customers**

  Lily Tomlin as Shirley Wright shows viewers how to handle disappointed customers when no one is at fault. Learn how to redeem any difficult situation by learning to listen, probe, and solve. 20 minutes.

- **One Ringy Dingy: You Are the Company**

  Everyone who answers the phone should see this one! Caught in the act as she commits every receptionist's error in the book, Ernestine—the rudely real telephone operator extraordinaire—learns five secrets of perfect telephone technique and five ways to improve vocal quality. 18 minutes.

- **What Customers Want**

  Set in "Krabbie's," a restaurant of Krab-cakes and Krab-apple pie, Lily's characters learn that customers expect responsiveness, assurance, tangibles, empathy, and reliability. 19 minutes.

Computer-Based Training

Computer-based Training (CBT) is an umbrella term used here to refer to a variety of ways in which the computer is used for learning. In fact, a 1998 *InformationWeek* reported results from a survey that found that the second most popular computer training method was the learner's own PC. (The most popular method remained the hands-on workshop.) While the least-used training at that time was Web-based Training (WBT), WBT is also the newest and fastest growing instructional method.[2]

Mediated learning strategies, particularly those that incorporate technology, are changing the way learning takes place in organizations almost overnight. Tightly coupled with the concept of Knowledge Management, technology has been instrumental in providing platforms that tie learning to job performance, putting learners in control of what and how and when they learn. Knowledge Management systems capture, store, and distribute databases, communications, protocols, and learning experiences. What differentiates Computer-based Training from classroom-based training is that the goal is to complete a task just at the time learning is needed.

This section will overview a number of CBT options, with the caveat that learning should be the driving force for choosing an instructional medium. Technology for its own sake should be avoided.

Under the umbrella of Computer-based Training is an alphabet soup of acronyms and specialized terms that refer to a variety of learning options that involve the learner's use of a computer. Beginning in the early 1950s with Programmed Instruction (PI), an early version of CAI, and cumulating today with WBT, the use of technology to deliver instruction has been revolutionary.[3] This discussion of CBT includes the following:

- CAI: computer-assisted instruction
- CMI: computer-managed instruction
- Interactive multimedia systems
- CSLR: computer-supported learning resources
- PSS: performance support systems
- WBT: Web-based Training

By design, CBT requires that learners be *participants* in their learning experience. Users must frequently keyboard answers, touch the screen, use a mouse, draw a graphic, and/or seek and find information. Active learners learn more and retain more than do passive learners. Research has shown that the use of CBT materials fosters individual activity and ownership on the part of learners and thus results in learning that is not only quick and efficient, but also is retained for longer periods of time. Following is an overview describing each of these tools, along with examples of how they are used. This discussion is somewhat historical in nature, and includes WBT as a delivery option. A vast array of communications capabilities including E-mail, chat rooms, and audio and videoconferencing are available. The discussion concludes with a discussion of performance support.

Computer-Assisted Instruction (CAI)

Initially, *computer-assisted instruction (CAI)* programs consisted of mainframe-based versions of linear programmed instruction. This Programmed Instruction quickly evolved into random-access, multi-branching learning modules that could be accessed on a variety of computer platforms. CAI supports self-directed and personalized learning, since the user can navigate among the learning modules, selecting topics of interest in whatever order is deemed logical and that fits the user's problem-solving style. Applications of CAI include tutorials, drill and practice, instructional games, modeling, simulations, and problem-solving. Moreover, CAI systems are not limited to text-based applications, since multimedia instructional systems (discussed later in this chapter) include text, graphics, animation, sound, and video.

Computer-Managed Instruction

Computer-managed instruction (CMI) refers to the use of a computer system to keep training administration information. CMI can be used with any instructional delivery approach since CMI is used for registration, assessment, maintaining student records, prescribing and controlling individualized lessons, as well as assessment and actual instruction. CMI systems can store data such as learner profiles and transcripts, class rosters, and class schedules. They can also generate, administer, and score tests, and many have built-in pre-and post-tests. This means that learners have a reinforcement and feedback source available that allows them to control the point at which they self-determine that they have mastered a given learning module and are ready to demonstrate that mastery. Figure 8-4 offers sample reports from Pathlore's Registrar© system.

FIGURE 8-4 A&B
SAMPLE REGISTRAR© REPORTS

Compliments of Pathlore (www.pathlore.com)

FIGURE 8-4A
SAMPLE REGISTRAR© INDIVIDUAL PROFILE REPORT — OPTIONS TO ONLY SHOW "UNMET" CLASSES OR ONLY SHOW "MET" CLASSES

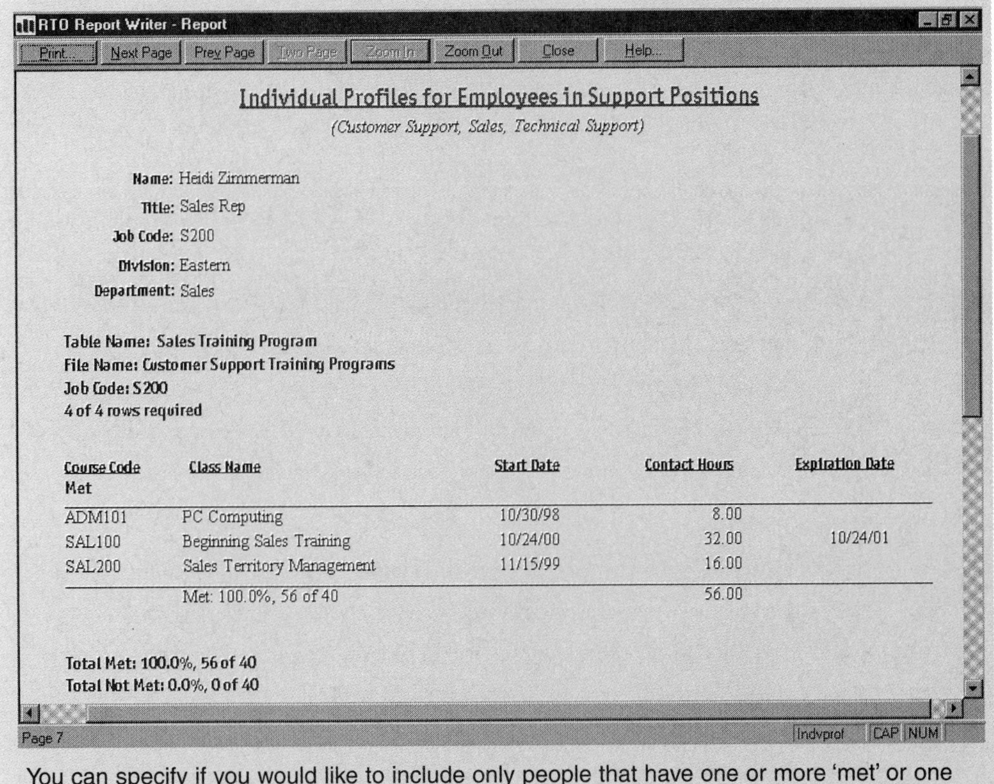

Individual Profiles for Employees in Support Positions

(Customer Support, Sales, Technical Support)

Name: Heidi Zimmerman
Title: Sales Rep
Job Code: S200
Division: Eastern
Department: Sales

Table Name: Sales Training Program
File Name: Customer Support Training Programs
Job Code: S200
4 of 4 rows required

Course Code Met	Class Name	Start Date	Contact Hours	Expiration Date
ADM101	PC Computing	10/30/98	8.00	
SAL100	Beginning Sales Training	10/24/00	32.00	10/24/01
SAL200	Sales Territory Management	11/15/99	16.00	
	Met: 100.0%, 56 of 40		56.00	

Total Met: 100.0%, 56 of 40
Total Not Met: 0.0%, 0 of 40

You can specify if you would like to include only people that have one or more 'met' or one or more 'unmet' requirements.

Figure 8-4B
New Course Delivery Folder in Registrar

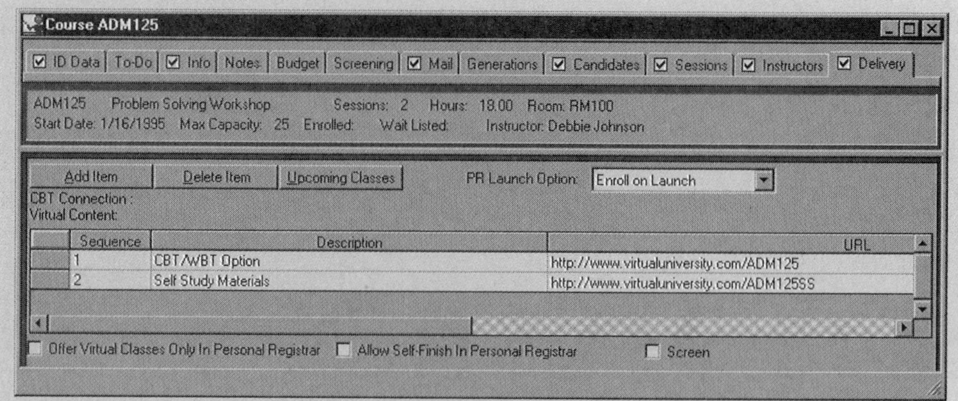

New folder in Registrar allows you to specify Virtual Courses. A Virtual Course may be a CBT/WBT course that may or may not be set up in CBT Connection. A Virtual Course can also be a course comprised of virtual content such as PowerPoint presentations, tests, and so forth. Content listed in Registrar's Delivery Folder is accessible on-line using PersonalRegistrar.

The organization's management may also be interested in collecting training administration information in order to manage issues such as training efficiency and effectiveness. Test scores provide some insight into whether people are learning as planned. Usage statistics—frequency, repetitiveness, and length of access—help assess effectiveness: Are the right people doing the learning? Do all or some have to repeat lessons? Does the learning take longer than planned? While such questions are certainly legitimate issues for management, care must be exercised to ensure that such data are gathered only with the full knowledge and concurrence of the learners.

Interactive Multimedia Systems

Multimedia-based, interactive learning systems combine the capabilities of many media and initially came in four formats: interactive videotape; laser disk; compact disk read-only memory (CD-ROM); and compact-disk interactive (CD-I). The interactive computer feature of these media enables self-paced and self-directed instruction. Because of the sensory input of graphics, animation, sound, and video, multimedia systems match many learners' preferred learning style. The interactive videotape and laser disk technologies are discussed here solely to provide an historical understanding of how the technology of mediated instruction has evolved, since they are no longer mainstream learning tools.

Interactive videotape format. To use the interactive videotape, the user responds to instructions that appear on a video monitor. An interface device links the computer with the video player, allowing the user to match the video presentation with specific lessons. This process is relatively slow because the videotape, which is linear in nature, does not allow for random access. While videotape is the least expensive interactive multimedia format, its use has faded because of limitations related to ease of use, the need for specialized equipment, and the increasing availability of alternative media, especially CD-ROM and Web-based Training.

Laser disk format. The laser disk, which is about the size and shape of an LP record, offers much higher resolution than videotape. Its major advantage is that it can hold huge volumes of digital information in a variety of formats that can be randomly accessed. However, large, single-purpose laser disk players are required. For this reason, laser disk technology has largely been replaced by CD-ROM technology.

Compact Disk Read-Only Memory (CD-ROM) format. CD-ROM is a technology in which data are permanently stamped in the aluminum reflecting area of small, 4 1/2-inch disks. CD-ROMs usually contain a woven stream of digital image, audio, video, and text data, as opposed to compact discs, which contain only audio data.[4] CD-ROM can be used to archive large amounts of data. Thus, CD-ROM technology allows a collection of teaching/learning materials to consist of any number of different media organized around a single topic.

CD-ROM is a driving force for multimedia applications, as its storage capabilities are enormous and it overcomes the access limitations of videotape. CD-ROM also overcomes the added expense of specialized equipment required for laser disks, as CD drives are standard equipment on most computer systems today. Almost all software vendors offer their software and documentation on CD-ROM instead of on disks or on paper. The advantages CDs have over Web-based Training is that of easy access and file transfer speed. A learner using his or her own computer CD drive does not have the problems of accessing remote sites and what can be slow data transfer rates.

CD-Recorders (CD-R) are machines that allow users to create compact discs themselves. Philips Electronics, an international consumer electronics corporation, offers the following three advantages for CD-Rs:[5]

- It is cheaper—you make the initial "one-off," or gold master, which then goes to a duplication house. The discs are then reproduced in volume, usually ending up costing less than $1 each.
- You can make limited editions—if you are using the discs for archiving purposes, or only making a small number of duplicates, a CD-R is ideal.
- Privacy—again, only if you're making a small number, and the information on the disc is sensitive.

Moreover, this storage and retrieval technology is evolving rapidly. Compact Disk-Rewritable (CD-RW) allows the user to write to the disk since it has a recording layer. The user can also rewrite or change information previously stored. At the time of this writing, however, CD-RW discs cannot be played on the current computer CD-ROM drives. However, a new generation of CD-ROM players will be able to read these discs.

CD-I interactive format. Philips Electronics developed a multimedia delivery standard known as compact disk-interactive (CD-I) in 1987. Their newer stand-alone CD players feature full-motion video and audio decompression technology, which connects to a television. Initially considered an option for delivering CBT, today most are used for 3D video games.[6]

Web-based Training and Support

Web-based Training (WBT) and support involves learners using the World Wide Web to access learning materials, connect to a wide range of supplementary resources, and have direct communication with their fellow learners, as well as the instructor. WBT is increasingly the distance learning medium of choice. In fact, WBT vendors such as SmartForce predict that in the near future, 80 percent of all corporate education will be delivered via the Internet. While this prediction is lofty, WBT has a distinct advantage over CD-based learning, as instructional and informational programs can be easily updated and even more easily distributed. When materials are Web-based, the learner can access them whenever he or she has access to the Internet. Moreover, WBT tools are designed to support self-paced instruction, as well as live interaction with an instructor and other learners.

WBT products, which are typically instructor-facilitated, can support registration, discussion boards, chat rooms, multi-point audio and video, whiteboards, class assignments, interactive quizzes, and even course development. Internet streaming—both audio and video—allows learners to replay educational lectures on demand. A total distance learning solution can integrate other products that support data and/or video transmissions. Software components can include an instructor client, a student client, and a server.[7] Figure 8-5 lists several popular products, along with their vendors.

Figure 8-5
A Sample of Web-Based Training Vendors

Product	Vendor	Web Site
Course Online	Course Technology	course.com
Learning Space	Lotus Development Corp.	lotus.com
ClassPoint	CUSeeMe Networks (formerly White Pine)	cuseeme.com
Blackboard	Blackboard	blackboard.com

Additionally, training vendors are packaging content along with Internet delivery tools. A corporate training department might choose, for example, to purchase an entire learning solution related to core competencies, such as supervisory skills or communications skills, from any number of vendors, including SmartForce (www.smartforce.com), click2learn (http://click2learn.com), and Cyberstate University (cyberstateuniversity.com), which even has an electronic student union. Moreover, entire WBT learning solutions are available from many traditional universities, including New York University, Columbia University, and Stanford University, which have created for-profit entities that sell complete learning solutions to corporations and educational institutions alike. Most WBT content vendors also provide products via CD-ROM, as well as through the Internet. Figure 8-6 lists the attributes and benefits of WBT.

FIGURE 8-6.
ATTRIBUTES AND BENEFITS OF WEB-BASED TRAINING

ATTRIBUTES	BENEFITS
Dynamic	Continually updated content repository ensures up-to-date information. Access to experts and learning community supports continually evolving knowledge base.
Current	Web links to other resources—libraries, software applications, the press, etc.—keep us in touch with rapid changes in the environment. Performance support tools expedite on-the-job learning process to improve individual productivity and organizational responsiveness.
Systematic	Enables continuous learning to prevent employee obsolescence. Systems approach supports job transfer and incorporates new experiences back into the organization's knowledge base.
Collaborative	Virtual learning communities within the system encourage peer relationships and learning teamwork. Access to on-line mentors encourages use of experts when problem-solving and making decisions.
Personal	Personalization engines and assessments create tailored learning experiences that evolve in response to increased learner competency. Personalized access creates individualized programs designed to accomplish specific tasks.
Comprehensive	Curriculum paths enable learners to manage their own career development. Access to internal and external courseware creates comprehensive and complete curricula.
Empowering	Encourages us to take responsibility of our learning journey by giving us control over our learning experiences. Enables a networked organization by supporting frontline employees with instant access to information and knowledge resources.

Source: Lawrence, Janice. "President." Web page (accessed March 30, 2000). Available at http://www.smartforce.com/corp/marketing/articles/frames_elearn.html Reproduced with permission.

Performance Support

Performance support is defined as an application of technology that directly links training and support to performance. The most effective learning happens when training is imbedded in the work that needs to be done. Noted consultant Gloria Gery (See "Voices from the Field" at the end of Part 4) pioneered this area by emphasizing what CBT *could* do, rather than what was being done with it. Gery's classic books in the field, *Making CBT Happen* (1987) and *Electronic Performance Support Systems* (1991), both from Weingarten Publications in Boston, have gone through six editions. Performance support tools include CBT-based course modules, as well as on-line help and reference, hypertext, computer-based training, multimedia, databases, and expert systems. Performance support can also encompass printed materials, video, classroom training, or other more traditional materials. Like Knowledge Management, which describes efforts to capture an organization's collective experience and make it accessible to everyone, performance support's objective is to provide information or assistance at the time the user needs it, rather than to teach some broader set of skills and knowledge for future use. Sometimes one needs information, not learning. See Figure 8-7 for examples of performance support in action.

Figure 8-7
Performance Support Examples

Eli Lily's Scientific Performance Improvement Network (SPIN) is based on Lotus Notes and includes threaded discussions, a directory of subject-matter experts who can be contacted, links to databases, and entire, on-line courses. SPIN is an example of performance support that is designed to impart existing knowledge, as well as create new knowledge through human interaction.

J. C. Penny's performance support system of help, reference, and just-in-time training is integrated with their network of transaction processing systems that support their retail stores. Each of Penny's 1,200 plus stores formerly relied on more than 100 reference manuals that had to be updated regularly. On-line help and reference was built into existing systems and all new applications include help and training capabilities built right into the design. At J. C. Penny, hard-copy documentation is disappearing.

Organizations often find that performance support is an efficient and effective way to deliver learning resources to its workers, putting the resources of the organization at the fingertips of the learner. Such *just-in-time learning (JITL)* is considered the most effective type of learning, as it is purposeful, and the user applies it immediately, thus reinforcing the learning.

This discussion breaks down performance support into four distinct modes that serve as just-in-time learning and reference materials: Help Desks and on-line help, expert systems, databases, and hypermedia. Performance support is used much as a library—but with the added computer capabilities that ease communication, retrieval, examination, and manipulation of data.[8]

Help Desks and On-line Help. One thing we know about systems is that they sometimes don't work exactly as expected: System glitches and operator errors are commonplace. And one thing we know about formal training is that its designers can not anticipate every application or every problem a user may have. So it is ongoing support—or just-in-time learning—and troubleshooting that is the focus here, which for the most part (but not always), concerns computer training.

Help Desks and on-line help facilities are distance alternatives to face-to-face coaching. Most *Help Desks* (also called hotlines) offer centralized tutoring from a person at the other end of the telephone line. *On-line help* is assistance from the computer program itself at the touch of a key or click of a mouse. Both services are highly interactive, and both offer support at the time when the support is needed.

Help Desks can be located anywhere—within the organization, at the software vendor's site, or elsewhere over an 800-number. Help Desk agents, trained in troubleshooting and with strong interpersonal skills, can offer the learner immediate help via the telephone. The objective of the Help Desk is to increase user satisfaction and morale through personalized coaching, as well as troubleshooting hardware and software glitches. Highly trained Help Desk agents work to help the perplexed user solve specific, real problems. Because 800-numbers can reach anywhere, vendors have a great deal of flexibility in assigning their help facilities. Digital Equipment Corporation's Help Desk, for example, is in Ireland, the site of a competent and inexpensive workforce.

A technology-based aid to Help Desks is desktop conferencing, or *screen-sharing* software. Desktop conferencing or screen-sharing systems can allow the Help Desk agent to:

- see and operate what is on the user's desktop, taking over keyboard and mouse controls;
- type information into dialog boxes;
- install new programs;
- open configuration files;
- transfer or retrieve a file; or
- use the screen to demonstrate new products.[9]

Screen-sharing software can also be built into many classroom network programs. Reminiscent of language-training laboratories, this capability allows an instructor to "tune into" whatever the learner is doing to assess learning progress.

Another option would be for a user to get on-line with an agent via desktop conferencing software such as Microsoft's Net Meeting. In yet another model, the user could initiate an instant messaging or chat session with an agent. When a Help Desk supports these Web-based services, it typically also supports faxes and E-mail messages. In such "blended calls," agents respond to users using the most appropriate tool available. The key here is that users should have a variety of choices to address their learning needs.

On-line help programs, on the other hand, offer computer-based assistance that is built directly into the software application package. When the help function is context-specific, a user having difficulty mastering a word processing package's mail-merge function, for example, presses the help key and is immediately offered text-based instruction on how to use this function. Context-specific help, including embedded wizards such as Microsoft Word's "Office Assistant," which actually guides the user through a function, is an increasingly important marketing feature of nearly all best-selling software packages.

Expert systems. When knowledge is rule-based, rules can be automated. An *expert system* is a computer program that incorporates the knowledge of an expert or group of experts on a particular subject and enables a user to systematically ask questions related to that knowledge. It mimics human reasoning by using facts, rules, and inferences, which respond to nonlinear thinking and problem-solving skills. Expert system development requires a computer programmer, known as a knowledge engineer, to work closely with a subject-matter expert (or domain expert) to ascertain the facts, identify the rules, and then develop an effective user interface. See Figure 8-8 for examples of expert systems in operation.

FIGURE 8-8
EXPERT SYSTEMS CASES

The manager responsible for monitoring the huge soup vats at Campbell Soup Company is planning to retire. Knowledge engineers are "saving" his years of experience and expertise for his successor. Westinghouse uses an expert system to monitor steam turbines, to alert operators when something goes wrong, and to recommend solutions. General Electric uses an expert system for locomotive repair. Morgan Stanley Dean Witter uses an expert system that assesses securities market conditions and provides trading recommendations.

Adapted from: Regan, Elizabeth A., and Bridget N. O'Connor. *Automating the Office: Office Systems and End-user Computing.* New York: Macmillan, 1989.

Databases. While expert systems support structured information, most knowledge is less structured and takes the form of wisdom, experience, and stories rather than rules. Knowledge systems have been developed on groupware products such as Lotus Notes. Hughes Space &

Communications has connected "lessons learned" *databases* so that designers of new satellites, for example, have better and more timely access to technical and regulatory information. [10] Engineers at General Electric Appliances in Louisville, Kentucky, use a knowledge-based system to search stored documents and published articles for answers to specific questions. Described as a concept-based document retrieval method (as opposed to a keyword retrieval method), users get quick responses to their queries. [11] The goal of such databases is not simply to create a warehouse of information, but to keep track of the wide variety of wisdom, experience, and stories that comprise information. A side benefit is that such systems can reduce the need for paper documents and books, which can be hard to search and catalog. [12]

Hypermedia. Hypermedia is a way of accessing text as well as graphics, video, and audio information. The term *hyper* means over or above. One way to describe hypermedia is that it is software that sits over the application software. This provides navigation functionality that is independent of the sequential flow of the text. Employing hypermedia commands allows users to take multiple, alternative routes through information, depending on their particular needs. Hypermedia functionality is part of most CD-ROMs. And hypertext is the tool that allows users to surf the Web. This flexibility provides a wide variety of opportunities to meet the needs of audiences who have varying expertise and diverse strategies for using diverse sources and reference materials. Figure 8-9 describes situations where specific mediated methods may be appropriate, along with their advantages and disadvantages.

Producing Your Own Courseware

Producing original learning materials is an art as well as a science. To do it well takes time, practice, expertise, and money. The development of study sheets for print-based materials or audiotapes and videotapes that already exist may be quick and inexpensive. However, to develop *courseware*, a term often used to describe coordinated mediated instructional materials, requires not only high-level instructional design skills, but often teams of subject-matter experts, artists, technicians, documentation writers, analysts, and programmers. To develop good Computer-based Training of all types from scratch requires considerable skill, time, and effort, and it has been estimated that courseware teams can spend 200 to 300 hours to develop one hour of instructional materials.

Courseware development or selection always begins with the learning objectives. An extensive variety of mediated learning materials already exist, of course, and whenever possible and appropriate they can be purchased for a given learning outcome. Modifying such purchased materials is an option, but modification can be costly and possibly void supplier warranties and support. Printed materials must be of publishable quality and any multimedia materials must

FIGURE 8-9

ADVANTAGES AND DISADVANTAGES OF NINE MEDIATED INSTRUCTIONAL APPROACHES

Approach	Commonly Used in Situations Where	Advantages	Disadvantages
Books and Journals	the content to be learned is reflected in excellent concepts/skill materials that already exist	excellent self-paced instruction; materials are extremely portable; inexpensive; familiar	to be effective, must be coupled with quality learning activities
Written Tutorials	learners have a content base to build on; are highly motivated to learn	no special equipment required	learner may have difficulty keeping attention on materials
Audiotapes and Videotapes	training program is continuous; need to reach dispersed audience	additional sensory input (sound and sight) valuable	to be effective, tapes must be high-quality; time-consuming and costly to develop; hard to maintain
Computer-Assisted Instruction	actual situations need to be simulated; provides opportunity for appropriate practice	provides continuous feedback; learners are active participants	time-consuming and expensive to develop; hard to maintain; multimedia may be required to keep learner interest
Computer-Managed Instruction	recording of learner performance is important	provides learner assessment and record-keeping	effective for learning only to the extent that it is linked to other learning resources
Multimedia	large numbers of dispersed learners exist to offset high development costs	offers sophisticated storage and access of learning resources; highly engaging medium	technology may not be portable; development time long and expensive; quality lessons require significant effort
Performance Support Systems	dispersed users needs just-in-time assistance	quick, easy access to expert assistance at the time learning is needed; reduces the need to memorize procedures	development time can be long; comfortable, logical user interface necessary
Web-Based Learning (groupware tool)	content needs frequent updating; learners are geographically dispersed	easily distributed learning option; communications with instructor and other learners supported	course development time and costs can be high
Web-Based Learning (complete solution)	content to be learned is reflected in excellent materials that already exist; learners are geographically dispersed	easily distributed learning option; role of training department usually is in evaluating options, not design or delivery of instruction	can be expensive; may be hard to customize to learner population

have quality graphics, animation, video, and/or sound. Thus, development can be an expensive and time-consuming process. Such quality materials are essential, however, if learners are to get the full benefit of the content being described. Learners have little patience with poorly designed and executed materials.

But instruction is more than professional-looking materials. Enhancement of presentation and the effectiveness of the learning experience are two different things. In selecting a delivery option, one should keep in mind that excellent media can never compensate for bad writing, poor design, trivial information delivery, or mundane feedback.

Once we become enamored by the delivery system, and perhaps even dazzled by our own magnificence at mastering its use, we are in grave danger of losing sight of our original goal, which should be to deliver information that is useful to the learner.[13]

DELIVERING MEDIATED INSTRUCTION

Mediated instruction can be centralized, occurring in a learning center, where learners go to a specific location for learning resources and use them there. This is often the case when technical resources such as VCRs are required. The learning center may be housed at a company site or at a vendor's location (See "CBT at PHH Vehicle Management Services" later in this chapter). However, the ideal—increasingly achievable through computer networks—is that mediated instruction be distributed, meaning that the location of learning is anywhere appropriate and convenient for the learner.

The trainer's delivery role in mediated instruction is to create an implementation plan for the learner, and then guide or coach him or her in the effective use of the learning resources. Getting the mediated materials in the hands of the learners is only the first step, and an easy step with WBT. The ongoing role of the training professional is to ensure that instructional materials are useful and that users of performance support systems are skilled in using the tools. This means that careful planning is required. Especially when the learning effort is extensive and affects a large number of learners, it is extremely important that the mediated materials be pilot-tested and opportunities for learner feedback be worked out.

Pilot Test

A *pilot test* is a planned and managed test drive, or trial, of the training program. Trial results are analyzed and fed back to program designers and developers who then ready the learning materials for the larger population (multiple locations or the entire organization). The pilot test is an opportunity to:

- determine that use of the mediated materials can result in the desired learning outcomes;
- determine the ease of use and usefulness of support materials;
- determine how long it takes learners to master the content;
- determine types and levels of live support needed;
- develop and test strategies for offering feedback;
- obtain the general reaction of users to the usefulness of the materials and their ease of use;
- modify materials based on trial results; and
- collect data on all of the above to use to sell the package to learners and the organization.

Distribution Strategy

With traditional live instruction, the learner comes to a classroom and is led through a series of planned learning exercises. When mediated instruction is involved, implementation means developing a strategy to get materials to learners, maintaining the materials, and in some cases, distributing changes or updates. Implementation also means supporting the learning process itself by answering questions, clarifying instructions, and dealing with any glitches that may exist in the learning materials. This aspect of implementation is often overlooked in planning. The trainer cannot simply give the materials to the learner and then assume that the training job is over. Especially when mediated instruction is being used for the first time, the trainer needs to be sure trainees *and their managers* understand that quiet time needs to be set aside for learning even though learners may not be going to a classroom. Figure 8-10 illustrates how one organization solved the quiet time problem. "CBT at PHH Vehicle Management Services," on the next page, illustrates a variety of issues related to implementing other types of mediated instruction.

Figure 8-10
Crime Scene? No, Learning Scene!

At the 1999 Organizational Systems Research Association's annual conference, SmartForce's Brenda A. Benedet told the story of how one of her clients uses crime scene tape to ensure that computer-based training sessions occur without interruptions. Yellow crime scene tape is used to seal learners' work pods, easily and effectively letting others know that learning is in progress, so please do not disturb. The resultant "learning scene" has become a respected, useful way to ensure quiet time for learners.

CBT at PHH Vehicle Management Services

The introduction of mediated methods in an organization is a complex issue. Risks can be high and costs can be great. Training professionals must have a vision and a tolerance for risk if they intend to encourage innovational approaches to learning. Management must also have effective delivery strategies that not only support learning, but also support the organizational culture.

PHH Vehicle Management Services (PHH VMS), Hunt Valley, Maryland, specializes in fleet leasing and vehicle support services. The 900+ employees of PHH VMS obtained their computer skills training through a local vendor who provides full-day courses on the basic use of the computer, MS Word, Excel, PowerPoint, and Windows. Course delivery was coordinated through the PHH VMS small training department. Courses were popular. However, as a service business, employees were concerned that they needed to be close to their customers, and often could not devote a full day to learning.

Marc Sokol, Director of Human Resource Development, was asked to examine CBT as a possible alternative to, or as an additional strategy for, delivery of computer skills training. He asked himself if a small training department could support CBT, even if it were an appropriate alternative. Would the organization need to develop CBT internally? If not, who were the major CBT vendors? How could the applicability of CBT to his organization be examined? To help him answer these questions, a study team (consisting of Sokol, one trainer, one human resource information specialist, and two people from PHH VMS' information technology unit) started by visiting three very different types of organizations that were heavily involved in developing and using CBT.

First, they visited United Parcel Services (UPS), a large information-intensive organization, in New Jersey. At the time of system development, UPS' CBT development group creates training modules that are shipped when the new software is shipped. UPS has a large number of specialized CBT developers; their CBT outcomes are sophisticated, tailored, intensive, and expensive. Of course, because they support a large number of users worldwide, the investment is extremely cost-effective.

Next, they visited a smaller company, an insurance company, GEICO (*Go*vernment *E*mployees' *I*nsurance *Co*mpany), located in Washington, D.C. While not nearly as extensive as UPS' CBT group, GEICO had a subgroup of four training professionals, reporting to the Human Resources and Training Department, that were directly involved in CBT development. GEICO's CBT products were labor-intensive and expensive but considered extremely effective for their distributed users' learning needs.

The last site visited was a small leasing company, O-E Midlantic, a value-added reseller that specialized in the CBT equipment, software, and learning facilitation. Hardware, including state-of-the-art computers, laser disks, CD-ROMs, and sophisticated computer software, was set up in O-E Midlantic's learning center. Visiting the learning center at any time between 8 a.m. and 5 p.m., clients—who came from many diverse organizations in the metropolitan region—could pop in a program, and a video within the system would guide the learner on one of three levels: beginner, intermediate, or advanced. The learner would choose an appropriate level, and by using a toggle, could switch between the instruction and the actual software application.

The study team was intrigued with the third organization, as its approach was not as staff-intensive as the other approaches; the individual learner had control, and, like the teacher-led instruction, it was an outsourced solution. PHH VMS' culture to date had been high-tech/high-touch, and the company employees were used to, and expected, live instruction. Therefore, the study team determined they would examine the learning tools in a manner that would also support the change in the learning delivery itself (remember this as you read Chapter 11). So, they developed a three-month, three-stage test.

For the first month, everyone in a single department—the Human Resources Department—was signed up for two courses. Sokol encouraged employees in his unit to go to the O-E Midlantic site for two, half-day courses. At the end of the month, department members discussed their experiences. Experiences were generally positive, but the team still wasn't sure that CBT was for "everyone." Specifically, the group felt that this might not be the best solution for someone with absolutely no prior computer experience or for someone who wanted the feeling of comfort that comes with an instructor-led class.

During the second month, the study team identified 15 people from throughout the organization who had previously used the instructor-led computer training, and invited them to participate in the training free of charge. This time, individuals could go to O-E Midlantic when they had time—anytime within the 8 a.m. to 5 p.m. learning center hours. These more experienced users could work at a level appropriate to their learning needs, and were very enthusiastic about their experiences. However, they reported that the 8 a.m. to 5 p.m. time frame was too restrictive and the learning center itself was noisier than they would like.

During the third month and the final phase, the study team leased two complete learning systems, set them up in a small room, offered headphones, advertised that the equipment was available on a sign-up basis, and brought in the vendor to demonstrate the equipment in the firm's cafeteria and in the lobby. Advertised as "free training for a month," individuals were urged to sign up for a trial use of the system. To the team's astonishment, more than 100 people signed up and, by the middle of the month, the room was booked from 7 a.m. to 7 p.m. during the week *and* frequently on weekends. Users' feedback was that the system was easy to use, more effective than the live instruction, and fit more easily within their busy schedules.

As the third month wound down, the question changed from "should we use the system" to "should we lease or buy it?" Given the pace of technological change, did it make sense to buy the system outright—or lease it? Sokol explained that this is a standard issue faced by the computer industry, as well as training departments. "It's a paradox," he said. "You can't afford to wait, and yet there's an inherent risk in buying equipment outright." Moreover, Sokol explained that CBT wasn't for all learners. Users with little computer experience, for example, needed more direct support. Scheduling the classroom site and the requisite facilitator support were complex administrative issues. Other questions

the team examined related to evaluation–how to determine if learning actually took place. For example, are on-line computer-generated evaluation tests useful?

For the future, Sokol intends to address the issue of portability–the use of the system at the desktop or at home. "We've come a long way from early programmed instruction which was simply a series of branching screens of text," said Sokol. "We moved on to graphics and colors to display information, then interactive software, and now multimedia applications. The challenge is to move from computer-based training to computer-based support."

Interview with Marc Sokol, then Director, Human Resources Development for PHH Fleet America.

EVALUATING MEDIATED INSTRUCTION

The use of mediated instruction in no way lessens the necessity of appropriate evaluation. Mediated training programs are planned learning experiences, and everyone involved in the learning will want feedback on the program. Evaluation of learning that results from mediated instruction differs little from traditional instruction. To expand the evaluation framework provided in Chapter 3—process, learning, reaction, job behavior, and organizational results—simply requires rethinking some of the questions.

For example, the training department might want to ask trainees process questions that could include their satisfaction with their role in the determination of learning objectives and the adequacy of the implementation plan. Reaction questions would gauge the learner's evaluation of the preparation and organization of materials, the study guide, and the expected pace of learning. Learning outcomes could be reviewed by any method appropriate to traditional methods, such as tests, simulations, or role plays.

In fact, if the purpose of evaluation is feedback to the learner, mediated instruction materials can afford the user instantaneous information regarding subject mastery. Like evaluating live training efforts, evaluating mediated training means matching course objectives with measures of actual outcomes. This means choosing evaluation methods that will result in information that is useful to training professionals, trainees, line managers, and organizational decision-makers.

SUMMARY

Mediated instruction is a learning experience where instruction is offered through print, audio, video, or computer-based materials, rather than via a live instructor. Mediated instruction fits well with what we know about how adults learn, and can be an effective instructional strategy. Mediated instruction is often used when the learning audience has a wide range of experiences and/or abilities; when it is spread out geographically; when only a small number of individuals need training; or when repetitive, ongoing learning needs to take place.

This chapter took a developmental approach to describing mediated methods, starting with paper-based books and tutorials, moving on to audiotapes and videotapes, and concluding with computer-supported learning resources and performance support systems. These methods build on each other and are often used in combination.

Audiotapes and videotapes are mediated instruction tools when they are supported with additional learning resources, such as study guides, books, programmed instruction, tutorials, and manuals. Computer-based Training (CBT) is an umbrella term for computer-assisted instruction (CAI); computer-managed instruction (CMI); interactive multimedia systems; Web-based Training (WBT), and performance support. All of these tools require that learners be active participants in their learning experiences. CAI includes tutorials, drill and practice, instructional games, modeling, simulations, and problem-solving exercises. CMI systems also include capabilities of registration, assessment, record-keeping, and testing—the administrative side of training. Interactive multimedia systems combine CAI with text, graphics, animation, sound, and video, and exist in a wide range of formats. Because of its huge storage capability, CD-ROM is an integrating medium for multimedia systems.

Web-based Training (WBT) involves learners accessing learning materials—readings, assignments, interactive quizzes, and the like—and using a variety of communication tools, including discussion boards, chat rooms, and whiteboards, to communicate with fellow learners and an instructor. WBT supports self-paced instruction as well as live interaction. Software vendors offer learning solutions that are software shells, where the instructor creates, manages, and distributes the learning, or complete learning solutions, whereby the vendor also offers the content. Because it can be easily updated and accessed independent of geography, and particularly because of its universal availability, WBT is a powerful option for supporting learning needs.

Performance support encompasses computer capabilities that support the communication, retrieval, examination, and manipulation of data. These are resources that can be accessed at the time support is needed. Performance support includes Help Desks and on-line help; expert systems, hypermedia, and databases. Help Desks offer centralized tutoring from a person at the other end of a telephone, and on-line help is built directly into a software applications package, available to the user at the click of a mouse. An expert system is a computer program that is developed by a subject matter expert and a knowledge engineer, and includes a user interface that allows the user to systematically ask questions of that knowledge. Sophisticated databases are compilations of unstructured information that can be easily searched. Groupware tools, such as Lotus Notes, are expanding the capabilities of database searching, allowing concept searches of documents, manuals, and shared experiences to assist users at the time they need help. *Hypermedia* is a term that describes searching capabilities that are independent of the sequential flow of text. Hypermedia systems allow the user more control over "what's next." Performance support systems can include the entire gamut of instructional media discussed in this chapter, and provide just-in-time learning, often reducing the need for learning.

Producing mediated materials from scratch is a sophisticated, costly, and time-consuming activity. To develop mediated materials can require teams of subject matter experts, artists, technicians, writers, and programmers.

Delivering mediated instruction requires planning on the part of the training staff. Determining the location of training, planning for the delivery and maintenance of needed learning materials, and creating mechanisms for support and feedback are important considerations. Evaluation of outcomes is conducted much the same way as for live instruction. The instructor, of course, must also redefine his or her role from that of a live deliverer of instruction to a coach, one who stands behind the scenes assisting the learner as a manager of instruction rather than as a live teacher. The focus of instruction—whether mediated or live—is always on learning.

THINK IT THROUGH

1. With the training cycle as a framework, summarize the major differences between live and mediated instruction.
2. Paper-based mediated instruction methods remain popular despite the widespread availability of computer-based instruction. Why?

3. Reread Figure 8-2, Student-Prepared Videotapes. What principles of adult learning are inherent in this case?

4. Given the following knowledge/skill sets to learn, which mediated method best fits your own learning style? Why? Are there some instances in which a variety of media (as well as live instruction) would be useful to you?

   a. The newest version of Word.

   b. How to write a training proposal.

   c. How to speak Japanese.

   d. Basic supervisory management skills.

5. Discuss the implications of the following statement: Performance support systems actually decrease the need for learning.

6. How does Web-based Training compare with other types of CBT? What is its outlook for the future?

7. List learning and support strategies commonly used to ensure a successful mediated instruction implementation.

IDEAS IN ACTION

1. Identify a book of interest from the *New York Times' Nonfiction Best Seller List* (www.nytimes/books/) that would be appropriate reading for an executive development program.

   a. Develop a study guide for the book—exercises that would help a reader retain and learn the content.

   OR

   b. Summarize the key points of the book on an audiotape. Listen to your tape; what did you learn about the book; what did you learn about creating an audiotape?

2. Refer to your responses to Question 4 above or identify a learning goal of your own. Search the Web to find appropriate media to support your goal. You could browse on-line bookstores and the Web sites of vendors, as well as universities. If possible, determine the total costs of your learning plan.

3. Interview someone at your institution or school who has taught a course over the Web. Ask him or her to describe the content of the course developed. Also ask how the course was implemented and what evaluation data are available. Are there time and cost estimates? Report your findings back to your classmates.

4. Interview individuals at your institution who have taken a course over the Web. Ask them to describe the content of the course. What were their reactions to the course? Were their learning goals achieved? Ask them to compare the course to one they might have taken in a traditional classroom environment. Report your findings back to your classmates.

5. Use a tutorial software program for a computer applications package that you have never used before (most popular programs include one). How helpful was the package? Summarize any advice you would offer the tutorial developer.

6. Using data from the PHH VMS case, write a memo to employees describing the new system and why they should sign up for courses.

7. Check out the Web sites of at least three Web-based Training vendors that provide software for instructors to support Internet-based learning, and three Web sites of vendors that support a total learning solution. Make a list of the services each site offers. Take advantage of any offer to "test drive" their products. Write a brief report summarizing what you found and how you perceive the relative value of their sites.

8. Peruse a recent issue of *Technology Training.* In addition to reading articles related to technology and training, check out their "Product News" section and their "Advertiser Index," which includes links to advertisers' home pages. Compile your own list of the "Top Ten" products of the month. And while you're there, see if you qualify for a free subscription to the journal.

ADDITIONAL RESOURCES

RECOMMENDED READINGS

Czegel, Barbara *Running an Effective Help Desk* 2nd ed. New York: John Wiley & Sons, Inc.,1998, 434 pp.

This book guides readers step-by-step through every phase of setting up traditional and Web-based Help Desks.

Ellis, Alan L., Ellen D. Wagner, and Warren R. Longmire. *Managing Web-Based Training: How to Keep Your Program on Track and Make It Successful.* Alexandria, VA: American Society For Training & Development, 1999, 180 pp.

This book is advertised as a "primer" for training and HRD professionals charged with managing Web-based Training. It provides a grounding in the basic language of Web-based Training and offers advice on everything from the cultural challenges of Web-based Training to constructing a successful Web site.

Schank, Roger. *Virtual Learning: A Revolutionary Approach to Building a Highly Skilled Workforce.* New York: McGraw-Hill, 1997, 185 pp.

Schank offers case histories and examples of organizations, including Andersen Consulting, that have used computer simulations and role-playing scenarios in virtual learning environments. Schank's argument is that virtual learning results in better, more effective learning outcomes. This book is a must-read for all training professionals.

WEB SITES

www.influentrx.com

Influent Technology Group's Information Resource Exchange is being compared to *Consumer Reports*. It allows participants to rate the value of technology-based courses, authoring tools, software, and the like.

www.phillips.com

For an up-to-date primer on compact disk technology, check out the Philips Electronics Web page.

http://www.masie.com

TechLearn Trends—Technology & Learning Updates. The Masie Center, Elliott Masie, Editor. Visit the Masie Center for links to numerous learning resources. While you're there, learn how to sign up for their on-line newsletter.

ENDNOTES

1. Lipson, Joseph. "Learning by Distance: How Effective?" Presentation delivered to the Regional Forum on Distance Learning, Austin, TX, April 5, 1984.
2. McGee, Marianne Kolsabuk. "Save on Training." *InformationWeek,* No. 688, June 22, 1998, pp. 141-146.
3. Regan, E. A. and B. N. O'Connor. *End-User Information Systems: Implementing Individual and Work Group Technologies*. Upper Saddle River, NJ: Prentice Hall, 2001.
4. Philips Electronics. "CD-ROM an introduction." Web page, (accessed March 30, 2000). Available at http://www.os.philips.com/cd/cd-rom/geninfo/index.html.
5. Ibid.
6. Ibid.
7. Ibid.
8. Reynolds, Angus, and Ronald H. Anderson. *Selecting and Developing Media for Instruction*. New York: Von Nostrand Reinhold, 1992.
9. Regan, E. A., loc. cit.
10. Stewart, Thomas A. *Intellectual Capital: The New Wealth of Organizations*. New York: DoubleDay and Co., 1998, 320 pp.
11. Thilmany, Jean. "Tapping into Know-How." *Mechanical Engineering,* 122, No. 4, 2000, pp. 46-48.
12. Ibid.
13. Quinn, Herb. "The Trouble with Glitz." *DataTraining*, April, 1991, p. 25.

from the FIELD

VOICES

Gloria Gery on Training Delivery

Gloria Gery is an internationally known training consultant. Her consulting firm, Gery Associates, Consultants in Business Learning and Performance Support, is located in Tolland, Massachusetts. She specializes in performance-centered software design and in implementing interactive training and performance support systems. She is the 1998 inductee into the HRD Hall of Fame sponsored by *Training* magazine.

BRIDGET O'CONNOR: Gloria, your name has been described as synonymous with performance support. Can you describe the types of services you provide organizations as a consultant?

GLORIA GERY: Basically, I work with an organization to consider strategies, tactics, and software tools to serve as an alternative to traditional training as the primary means of performance development. Training is working less and less and is "falling of its own weight" in many organizations due to the volume, complexity, and change in content and task/process requirements. I help my clients understand how they can integrate support for task or work processing with knowledge, data, tools, and communications so they can generate immediate performance by people who do not know how to do the work. I also show them how they can integrate resources to permit learning that is collateral with doing (rather than as a precondition).

This work involves making people unhappy with the status quo, demonstrating and describing alternatives, educating people on what it takes to do these new things, and sometimes actually working with them in the design and development of such systems.

BRIDGET O'CONNOR: What business benefits have you seen derived from performance support?

GLORIA GERY: Lots. Mostly, it enables people to reduce, or even eliminate, training on work process and factual/conceptual content, reduces coaching and supervisory requirements, allows work to be assigned to different people–even directly to customers. Because comprehensive performance support systems build best practice and strategic goals within them, the goals can include such high-level outcomes as finally enabling the implementation of strategy.

The idea here is to consider efficiency, effectiveness, value-added and strategy outcomes, and see how achieving all of them can be built into the support system. Because performance support is an integrating viewpoint, it typically requires collaboration with those in the line of business and information systems to achieve the above.

BRIDGET O'CONNOR: What trouble have you seen people get themselves into in trying to implement technology to support learning?

There are many pitfalls, but to me, the biggest one is not exploiting the power of the technology. People start and often stop with "automating the past." They apply technology to old mental models for design and old methods for development. They don't consider, for example, how learning and the need to learn changes when information is ubiquitous and available to all. They continue to "teach" at people rather than present problems or goals and enable people to meet them. They fail to employ collaboration technologies and stick to the model that the "student is a vessel to be filled." I am a Constructivist at heart and believe we can now implement that approach to learning. Getting stuck in the past and failing to adapt point of view, goals, methods, and techniques to the new realities is a shame. But it happens more than not.

Misuse of media is another pitfall. People integrate gratuitous animations, sound, video, etc., because they can. Designers must control and constrain and use only value-added representations of knowledge. The Law of Diminishing Astonishment operates overtime here. The things that seduce don't sustain. Learners quickly tire of cute and trivial elements. They are hungry for relevant and filtered content–not a lot of glitz. This is not to say that quality production values should not be achieved, but a little media goes a long way. And the criteria should be "value-added." That is, does the representation improve time to understanding or performance. That's the measure.

BRIDGET O'CONNOR: So what do you see as major trends concerning mediated instruction of all types?

GLORIA GERY: My response depends on who/what I am thinking of. Of course, everyone's rushing to the Web or the Intranet. This is good in a small way: universal access. But because the Web is based on a "page" metaphor, because the development tools are so limited, and because there's no local memory/storage/processing assumed in Web design, it reduces the potential to designing for the lowest technology denominator–the dumb terminal. I find it frightening that we must regress to the early days of CBT in a dumb terminal environment, but the regression is a trend.

One of the best things I see is the effort to integrate learning and knowledge resources into the work context. Good designers consider how they can anticipate needs for knowledge, understand the best representation of that knowledge, and provide on-demand, just-in-time, just-enough, best-represented content. The moment of need is the teachable moment. We must be there. It is more or less difficult to achieve this integration. But even when it's difficult, it is our responsibility as those responsible for enabling learning. If we don't achieve integration, then chance operates and the learner/performer may or may not be motivated or able to search out knowledge, evaluate it, filter it, integrate it, and use it.

BRIDGET O'CONNOR: What impact do you think improved bandwidth and computer capacity will have on Web-based Training?

GLORIA GERY: High bandwidth and fast, cheap, large machines connected in powerful networks are the necessary, but not sufficient, condition for achieving good, rich, sufficient learning environments. Design of good learning resources and performance support systems by knowledgeable people is as important. Power without appropriate content is an empty vessel. We shouldn't underestimate the technology's significance–or depend on it entirely.

BRIDGET O'CONNOR: How do you know when WBT has taken place successfully?

GLORIA GERY: How do you know when any learning occurs? When people can do things. Performance is the measure. Teaching people the threads (i.e., subjects, systems, etc.) is inadequate. We must help them weave the threads into desired performance.

BRIDGET O'CONNOR: Gloria, what books or other resources related to performance support would you recommend?

GLORIA GERY: My books: *Electronic Performance Support Systems* (1991) and *Making CBT Happen* (1986)

- My Web site: http://www.epssinfosite.com
- Donald Norman's books:
    - *Invisible Computer: Why Good Products Can Fail, the Personal Computer Is So Complex and Information Appliances Are the Solution* (October 1999)
    - *The Design of Everyday Things* (March 1990)
    - *The Psychology of Everyday Things* (May 1988)
- Online Learning Conference, BillCom, Minneapolis MN (www.onlinelearning.com)
- *About Face: The Essentials of User Interface Design,* by Alan Cooper, IDG Books Worldwide, 1995.
- *E-Learning: Strategies for Delivering Knowledge in the Digital Age,* by Marc Rosenberg. New York: McGraw-Hill Professional Publishing, October 2000. It's on e-learning strategy and has cases.
- ProCarta software for conducting task analysis and integrating/mapping related knowledge (http://www.domainknowledge.com).
- "The Attack on ISD," by Jack Gordon in *Training* (37)4; April 2000, pp. 42-54.

BRIDGET O'CONNOR: Gloria, what roles do you see trainers playing over the next few years or so? How do you see the training role changing within organizations?

GLORIA GERY: I see people shifting from developing events to designing learning environments. That means integrating more with others who create knowledge in various forms (e.g., those in documentation and training, Help Desks, product engineers, and those in Knowledge Management). I see a shift from learning to performance ... and performance consulting will be a part of it.

BRIDGET O'CONNOR: What would you say are important tasks training professionals must do for their organizations?

GLORIA GERY: Focus on outcomes, not on activities or events. Play a significant role in designing software interfaces and linking knowledge to the task context supported by new computer systems. This is in direct contrast to using training to compensate for badly designed or data-driven software. Shift design of learning experiences from information-transfer events to problem-solving or simulation-based learning events involving collaboration with others (through technology).

BRIDGET O'CONNOR: What specific advice can you offer training professionals to help them make training an organizational investment rather than an overhead expense, and help them persuade others to see it as an investment rather than an expense?

GLORIA GERY:

- Make it work-oriented, not content-focused.
- Integrate the threads of decomposed knowledge that are in most training courses to help learners synthesize.
- Make learning practical and applied.
- Stop being focused on our design needs and focus on the business and performer's needs; think of participants as performers, rather than students.

BRIDGET O'CONNOR: Gloria, thank you for sharing your considerable insights and expertise in this area. You've given us much to think about.

GLORIA GERY: You're very welcome.

PART 5
Additional Professional Competencies

PROLOGUE TO PART 5

Orville and Wilbur Wright were successful because they were systems thinkers. They alone identified three *interconnected* facts of flight demonstrated by birds without motors. Before you could hang wings on a bicycle and ride it through the sky, you had to figure out how to:

1. Get it into the air.
2. Keep it in the air.
3. Make it go where you want.[1]

Part 5 is all about creating an environment in which training efforts can fly. Even the best learning solution will flounder if it is not described in such a way that decision-makers have enough information on which to determine its worth (get it into the air). Even the best learning solution will fail if it is not administered appropriately—for example, learning materials must arrive on time and participants should be able to hear a presenter (keep it in the air). Even the best learning solution will be useless if its outcomes are not consistent with the "way we work around here" and, therefore, resisted by learners or their superiors (make it go where you want). This systems approach forces you to consider that there are many things inside and outside the learning solution itself that must be considered.

Systems thinking also includes the concept of *equifinality*, which is another way of saying there is more than one way to do anything. The chapters that follow are not foolproof templates for problem-solving. Rather, they can be considered a toolkit of ideas and suggestions that may fit some circumstances perfectly; others partially; some not at all. Part 5 is all about the effective use of a communications and leadership tool kit: writing, speaking, delegating, organizing, and facilitating. How a training professional gets the learning program into the air, keeps it there, and ensures it does what it is supposed to do depends on many factors that are related to the individual, the current circumstances, and the organization that is being served.

Therefore, in addition to being a purveyor of sound learning practices, the training professional needs further skills to work within the organizational system and communicate how training solutions address a business need, manage the process by which solutions are implemented, and understand how he or she can participate as a full functioning member of the organizational management team.

The training *proposal* is a comprehensive planning document. It includes an analysis of the needs assessment data and shows how the training solution it offers fills a performance gap or organizational need. Chapter 9, "The Training Proposal," suggests structural outlines, writing strategies, and cost/benefit analysis techniques that are frequently used in successful proposals. The training proposal itself must offer decision-makers the information they need to make the "go or no-go" decision regarding whether or not the training program is feasible.

Chapter 10, "Training Administration," provides a menu of suggestions for operating a training department and administering the logistics of training delivery. Good administrative support includes ensuring that program descriptions are available, that participant registration is easy and efficient, that learning materials arrive on time, that the physical facility is set up properly, and that any equipment used is in good working order. This chapter includes checklists that can be adapted to many situations. This chapter also includes a sample program costing work sheet that can help establish budgets.

Part 5 concludes by taking you back to Chapter 1, where training was described as all about learning, and learning as all about changes in knowledge, skills, or attitudes. Change, and therefore learning, is a constant in all organizations. Chapter 11, "The Trainer as Change Agent," begins with a simple change model—innovation, infusion, assimilation—and shows how the training professional contributes expertise to a problem-solving process. To provide a framework for understanding the concept of change, the chapter includes excerpts from the work of Everett Rogers and Kurt Lewin, and current perspectives from Peter Senge. The chapter includes a sampling of techniques for facilitating group processes and emphasizes the increasingly important role of the trainer as a business partner.

To maintain control, the Wright brothers invented their own wing, elevator, rudder, engine, and propeller.[2] They had to think how each part of the system affected the plane's ability to fly. They had to go beyond solving isolated sets of problems. The training professional, likewise, must understand how important it is that the right (no pun intended) things are trained for in the right way, for the right people, at the right time, and in the right priority order. Leadership for the training function requires an understanding that organizational need is the push for training interventions and that organizations are complex entities. Ensuring that training solutions are understood, administered appropriately, and are useful interventions requires teamwork and an understanding that training is a business function, which requires an understanding of the entire organizational system, not simply or solely the training enterprise.

ENDNOTES

1. Weisbord, Marvin R. *Productive Workplaces.* San Francisco: Jossey-Bass, 1988, p. 162.

2. Ibid., p. 163.

CHAPTER

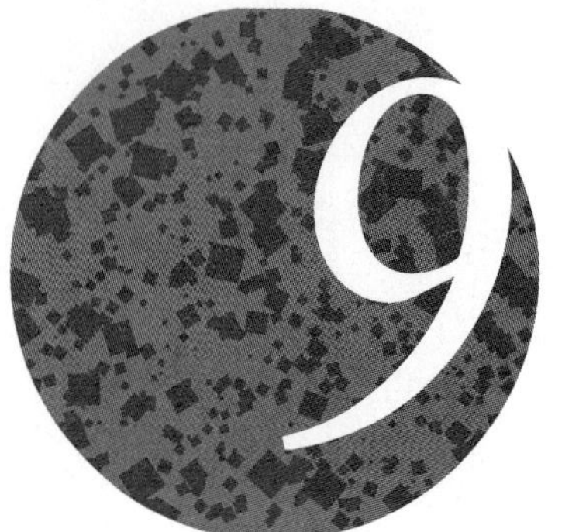

The Training Proposal

- List the key components of training proposals.
- Suggest training proposal design and structure.
- Identify variables on which to evaluate training proposals.
- Determine training costs and benefits, including return-on-investment figures.
- Recommend strategies to ensure a winning proposal presentation.

WHAT IS A TRAINING PROPOSAL?

Training providers, whether internal or external to the organization, must communicate their training plans to decision makers. The document that describes the work to be done is the *proposal.* A proposal is a request for action. Its purpose is to persuade decision makers that a need exists for action, and that the action described in the document is the best response to that need. Preparing a proposal requires skill in writing thoroughly and convincingly. It will also benefit from the use of sharp, creative desktop publishing skills. Occasionally, the proposal writer may be asked to present the proposal in person to a decision-making group; in this case, effective oral presentation skills are critical.

The training proposal will most likely compete with other proposals. External competition includes other vendors and consultants; internal competition may include competing with other proposals for scarce resources and funds. Either way, the task is to convince organizational decision makers that the need that has surfaced deserves priority in their decision-making, and that the proposal's solution provides the best solution to the need. The proposal must communicate ideas and plans with such eloquence that it will rise to the top of possible solutions.

COMMUNICATING TRAINING PLANS

The first prerequisite in planning a proposal is to have a very clear idea of the organization's training needs, which were discussed in detail in Chapter 2. The second prerequisite is to have a very clear idea of the individual(s) who will be reading the proposal, which was discussed in Chapter 3. Sometimes written proposals must adhere to strict corporate guidelines. Federal agencies, for example, often provide a boilerplate format that makes it easy for decision makers to compare proposals. Other times, proposal writers use a format that is appropriate to the problem at hand and indicates the individuality of the writer and/or the training provider's organization. Determining an approach to proposal writing is, therefore, dependent upon the organization to be served and the problem to be addressed. Writing the first proposal will be much more difficult than the 100th one; writing is a skill that is honed with practice and feedback. One learns as much from proposals that work as well as from those that are not accepted.

Following is a list of the components of most proposals. Examples of a full proposal and an abbreviated proposal appear in an appendix at the end of this book. Note that the list follows the four phases of the training cycle—assessment, design, implementation, and evaluation. Not every training proposal will have all of these components, and they may not be in this sequence. Many winning proposals are brief—only three to five pages long. One rule of thumb is that senior executives usually want a summary view with few details. Middle managers will need much more information. Another rule of thumb is that the larger the scope of the project and the more expensive the solution, the more detailed the proposal needs to be. Therefore, the best rule is to know your audience, your purpose, your project… and write accordingly. Following is a discussion of proposal components. The list suggests both content and sequence.

- Title Page
- Table of Contents
- Executive Summary
- Background of the Problem*
- Analysis of the Problem*
- Target Population*
- Rationale and Goals of the Proposed Training
- Learning Objectives and Topics*
- Evaluation Strategies
- Overview of the Training Solution
- Program Outline*
- Training Resources Required
- Capabilities of the Training Providers
- Development Schedule
- Delivery Schedule

- Costs
- Projected Benefits
- Appendix

*These elements may be combined or merged under the subhead indicated if a shorter proposal is desired.

Title Page

The title page should include, of course, a descriptive title of the training proposal. Avoid giving training programs names that could well depict the titles of college courses, since such course titles tend to be very general in nature. A proposal for a business writing course designed to help managers prepare performance reports, for example, could be called "Writing Techniques for Preparing Performance Reports," but should not be entitled "Fundamentals of Business Writing." The title page should also include the name of the proposal writer and a means to contact him or her: address, telephone number, facsimile number, and the like.

Table of Contents

A table of contents is generally provided for lengthy and/or detailed proposals, but may be omitted for shorter ones. A complete and accurate table of contents is important for lengthy proposals to give the reader a quick overview of what is to come, and also serves as an easy reference to the various sections.

Executive Summary

Time is critical to everyone; therefore, a tightly written *executive summary* should be considered for all proposals. A sample of an executive summary follows:

> Newly hired inspection employees at the Xanadu Corporation have a much higher product rejection rate than established employees. The high rejection rate costs this corporation a considerable amount of money as the products rejected are often well within the acceptability range.
>
> A needs analysis, consisting of employee interviews and observations of both groups, indicates that new hires are employing different acceptance standards from their experienced counterparts. A training program, consisting of product information lecturettes, role plays, and small group discussions, is recommended to make sure new hires learn the correct standards.

Background of the Problem

The background of the problem should show how the proposal was initiated, who performed the needs assessment, and what procedures were involved in the process. This section serves to put the proposal into the context of the business problem to be solved. One way to make this connection is to list the names of stakeholders who initially raised the issues or who participated in the needs assessment process. An example of this section follows:

> The trademark of this business is quality. New hires are rejecting too many acceptable products. They seem to be overly cautious in their goal to maintain the highest quality control standards. Thus, excessive numbers of acceptable machine tools are rejected. New hires' judgment calls err on the side of caution rather than on the side of acceptability.

Analysis of the Problem

What is the problem to be addressed? In the analysis section, describe why the training program is needed—how the training solution bridges the gap between an identified problem and the learning required. Show how the training solution solves a specific business problem. If the needs assessment is complete, data from the results will show an understanding of the organization, the individuals to be trained, and the training task(s). If the needs assessment has not yet been conducted, this section could outline how the problem was discovered, by whom, and when. In *very brief* terms, the writer should describe the needs assessment process—the instruments that were developed, the people who were interviewed or surveyed, and data that were collected. Providing the results of these assessment processes shows how a training solution matches a learning need. Thus, an analysis describes the impact of the identified performance gap on the business. Perhaps customers need to be served more efficiently and effectively by sales staff. Managers may need to manage more flexibly as the organization flattens. Insurance agents may need a new, more efficient way to track prospects. Support staff may need better customer relations skills. The number of accidents in a certain area is related to an increasing number of reported back problems.

In other words, in this section the problem that will be solved by the proposed training is addressed. Oftentimes, the training proposal writer (or his or her group) conducted the needs analysis and is proposing a solution. However, sometimes providers may be using needs analysis data from a *request for proposal* (RFP), which had outlined the identified problem and solicited the proposal. Either way, describing the problem is what this section is all about. The length and comprehensiveness of the analysis component is situation-specific. An excerpt of a narrative of this section follows:

> Interviews were conducted with three (3) first-line supervisors in the Quality Control Department (here their names and/or titles would be added), to explore the perceived gap between the quality of machine parts produced and rejection rates from newly hired employees. Observations were conducted of both new and long-time employees over a two-day period, and our observation checklists support the perception that the newly hired are being excessively cautious. A

higher percentage of rejections came from the new hires than from the established group, which suggests that different standards are being applied by these two groups.

Target Population

Referring back to the needs assessment bull's-eye (See Figure 2-2), the target population reflects those individuals in the center of the target who are to be served by training: those who will directly benefit from participation in the training program. Examples of target populations might include newly promoted supervisors in a specific department, all local-area network managers, all production managers, or even everyone in the organization. The target population section should describe as accurately as possible the number of potential trainees and their functions. A sample narrative follows:

> The target population to be addressed in this proposed training activity includes all supervisors in the Quality Control Department. All should receive training at the same time to make best use of their experiences.

Rationale and Goals of the Proposed Training

Rationale and goals are the heart of the training proposal. This section should be tied back to the analysis of the problem and the impact of the problem on the organization. Here, the writer shows why the training is needed, the goals for the proposed training, and its anticipated outcomes. This section should answer the question: "What is the purpose of the proposed training and what are the anticipated benefits to be derived from it?" This section presents the scope of the proposed training *content*. An illustration might include an overview of the course goals and objectives, target blocks for specific training, and assumed qualifications of the participants to undertake the proposed training. A sample narrative follows:

> The needs assessment conducted (date/location), indicated that additional training is needed for new hires (less than three months). These new hires have been responsible for excessive recalls. The proposed training will focus on establishing the best way to install and check to ensure complete compliance with the firm's existing standards. Since a number of new hires are Spanish-speaking, training staff will be proficient in both English and Spanish.
>
> Course goals and objectives include a review of the overall wiring installation procedures used for the product, as well as specific and newly developed methods for update modifications. New manuals will be developed, color-coded, and pilot-tested for this audience. Anticipated outcomes will include workers meeting acceptable standards.

Learning Objectives and Topics

In describing the training program, it is useful to match learning objectives with training program topics. These learning objectives can be stated either in broad, general terms, or they may be described in performance terms. As described in Chapter 5, for cognitive and skill-oriented outcomes, performance items are preferred; for attitude change or the affective domain, more general terms are acceptable. Examples of components of a training solution to address computer skill development follow:

Skill Block 1 - Document Management

Upon completion of Skill Block 1, participants will be able to complete the following tasks with 100 percent accuracy:

- Create directories.
- Move and copy files from different directories.
- Save files on the network.
- Transfer files to distant locations.

Skill Block 2 - Advanced Functions and What-If Analysis

Upon completion of Skill Block 2, participants will be able to complete the following tasks with 100 percent accuracy:

- Use the IF and VLOOKUP functions.
- Use various financial functions, including PMT, IRR, NVP, and FV.
- Use data tables.
- Use the scenario manager.
- Use goal seek.
- Create pivot tables.

Skill Block 3 - Graphing Work Sheet Data

Upon completion of Skill Block 3, participants will be able to complete the following tasks with 100 percent accuracy:

- Chart continuous and noncontinuous work sheet data.
- Create a chart using the ChartPrep function.
- Create a chart in a separate document.
- Change the chart type.
- Change formatting options.
- Add text to a chart.

With the framework provided by these learning objectives, the list of specific topics to be covered can be presented. Learning objectives always drive the topics; it is not the other way around.

Evaluation Strategies

Evaluation strategies outline how the organization will know that the training has achieved its designed outcomes. Training professionals, as business partners, are accountable for results, and in this section the writer should describe how the planned learning objectives and consequent business results are to be measured. The entire gamut of evaluation options described in Chapter 3 are available—participant reactions, tests, attitude questionnaires, observations, performance reports, and the like. This section should also indicate the follow-up activities that will be used to determine if the training met the goals that learning set out to achieve. By presenting the goals *and* the evaluation strategies sequentially, management can see both the starting and ending points for the proposed training intervention. In some instances, evaluation at the end of the training program may be appropriate; however, for others, evaluation may be continued over a period of weeks or even months. An example of this might show the following:

Goals: To introduce new product line X to the sales staff—specifically ensuring that learners leave with information that:

- Describes the product line.
- Shows how the line will mesh with existing products currently in use.
- Identifies strengths and weaknesses of line and individual units.
- Enforces selling points and objection responses.
- Details implementation strategies and methods.

Evaluation of Training: Effectiveness of training will be measured by:

- Trainers' use of checklists to assess performance in role plays with members of sales staff and supervisors/managers at the completion of the training program.
- Trainees' self-evaluations of three videotaped sales demonstrations during the training.
- Trainers' review of trainees' performance reports three and six months after training.

Overview of the Training Solution

The overview broadly describes the training solution to the identified problem. This description should include the types of learning activities proposed, where they will take place, and who will be involved. Describing the nature and type of training that will occur over a designated period of time provides the decision maker(s) with a picture of the training experience. Examples of this might include the following:

> The two-day sales presentation skills workshop will include group presentations and role plays, and culminate with trainees developing videotaped sales presentations.

or

> The hands-on safety training program will include the operation and safety features of the new equipment, Model 43, by use of a series of simulations and models. The program will take approximately two hours.
>
> or
>
> Two half-day sessions will include the extensive use of role play in conflict resolution scenarios. Scenarios will depict common stress points between peers, as well as between staff members and supervisors.

Program Outline

The program outline simply consists of the topics—in a logical order—that detail the content, organization, and sequence of the proposed training program. The outline also provides the basis for a *Leader's Guide* (See Chapter 7). The program outline must be as complete as possible. An example of a program outline to train new air-conditioning installers might include the following:

1. *Description* of air-conditioning unit with full and cutaway views.
2. *Identification* of major components and functions.
3. *Overview* of installation process.
4. *Presentation* of installation procedures—sequential elements and steps from "make-ready" to clean up.
5. *Description* of safety considerations.
6. *Illustration* of checkout operation.
7. *Examples* of adjustment and tuning activities.
8. *Description* of customer materials and service options.
9. *Post-installation* self-evaluation.

Training Resources Required

With the training actions described, identifying the materials needed is the next step. These resources will include instructional materials, hardware and software, and personnel. Any prework to be completed by participants before the training event also should be described here, as well as a list of handouts and other related materials needed.

- Instructional materials—prework, binders, Leader's Guides, training manuals, handouts, models, transparencies, flip charts, white boards, reference guides
- Hardware and software—computers, application packages, video cameras, multimedia setups
- Personnel—personnel required for the assessment, design, implementation, and evaluation stages

Capabilities of the Training Providers

While describing oneself may be unnecessary if the writer is an internal training consultant, this section is an essential component when the proposal is in competition for a training contract. This section describes an individual trainer's or an organization's capacity to produce an effective training solution and to deliver it in a timely manner. It includes individual qualifications and perhaps references of other similar projects completed, as well as a list of satisfied clients. For example, if a videotape will need to be developed as part of the training solution, what evidence exists that the writer can do this? How many staff members can be dedicated to this project? Does the provider have access to special facilities or equipment (e.g., computers, video systems, special software)? Key to describing the capacity to deliver is matching capabilities with the needs identified earlier. A brief description may be all that is necessary for a short proposal. However, for a more complex, expensive, or strategic training effort, training consultant résumés should be appended. A sample qualification narrative follows:

> The proposed training will be developed and delivered by an organization with more than 30 years of extensive experience in production and quality control areas. With headquarters in Chicago and offices in 11 major metropolitan areas throughout the U.S., Canada, and Mexico, our 220 trainers and support staff speak multiple languages. All trainers are required to hold a minimum of a four-year business degree, and most hold graduate degrees in their specialty. All trainers are fully certified through our rigorous development process. Satisfied clients include General Electric, IBM, and PepsiCo.

Development Schedule

The development schedule outlines the sequence of planning events in a step-by-step process covering blocks of time, which describe what needs to be done, when it will be done, how long it will take, and in what sequence. The development schedule takes the form of a Gantt Chart, such as the one shown in Figure 9-1.

The development schedule outlines the stages necessary to complete specific and separate phases of the needs assessment and design of the training project, and provides an overview of the specific tasks to be done. It shows which tasks will be done sequentially and which may be done at the same time as another activity. Figure 9-1 numbers the major tasks in a sample schedule and plots them according to when they should begin and end. The development schedule charts the most expeditious plan—the critical path—to design the training program. Task 1, for example, is the needs assessment analysis; Task 2, the client review, is a detailed discussion with decision-makers or the target audience. Note the overlap with other tasks. The task list continues, culminating with the final project ready for pilot-testing.

FIGURE 9-1
TRAINING DEVELOPMENT SCHEDULE

Development Schedule (January through March)

Task	Period 1	Period 2	Period 3	Period 4
1. Needs Assessment, Interviews, and Observations				
2.		Client Review		
3.			Validation of Needs Assessment (and Possible Extension)	
4.			Program Development	
5.			Leader's Guide Draft	
6.			Instructor Preparation for Pilots	

DELIVERY SCHEDULE

A second schedule to be developed is for testing the materials and procedures designed earlier. *Delivery* outlines when the pilot(s) will occur, when any needed revisions will be done, and when the product should be available for rollout for the entire organization.

Figure 9-2 is a sample delivery schedule. The schedule may cover a period as short as a few days or it may cover a year or more, depending on the nature and strategic importance of the project. The delivery schedule, thus, provides a time line of when major tests and revisions will be done and when the project is ready for full implementation. Note that if a Leader's Guide was not developed earlier, it can be done as part of delivery. Watching a skilled trainer in pilot-test situations can be an excellent way to ensure that a Leader's Guide provides useful teaching strategies and suggestions for easy transition from topic to topic.

FIGURE 9-2
DELIVERY SCHEDULE

Delivery Schedule

	Quarter 1 Jan-March	Quarter 2 Apr-June	Quarter 3 July-Sept	Quarter 4 Oct-Dec	Available January 1
Program Title	**TFX Training**				
	Materials Development Period	Pilot 1 Revised	Pilot 2 Revised	Pilot 3 Revised	Rollout
			Leader's Guide Developed/Revised		

Costs

The cost section of the training proposal details the expenses involved in doing what is proposed. Because proposals are written to sell decision-makers on a proposed solution to an identified problem, it is extremely important that costs be fully explained and well-documented. Training proposals compete for the organization's scarce resources. They must provide sound estimates of costs.

The two sample proposals included as Appendix A and B provide very different approaches to providing cost figures. The longer proposal (A) provides a detailed description of cost categories, while the shorter proposal (B) gives broad categories of costs.

Projected Benefits

A training program is designed to close a learning gap, performance gap, or a lack of knowledge. Rather than leave expected gains to speculation, the benefits accruing to the organization should be identified. While many productivity benefits may be easily documented and can help to cost justify the expenses of the training program, there are a number of "soft" benefits that are not as easy to identify. Soft benefits include measures of enhanced morale and greater team spirit. Typically, however, benefits fall into one of the following three categories:

- Productivity improvements: Individuals can do more.
- Quality improvements: Individuals do what they do better, and products or services will be enhanced.
- Workplace improvements: The workplace environment supports individuals and their work better, thus enhancing the overall quality of work life (QWL).

While difficult to do, it is useful to place hard dollar figures on all the soft benefits identified. Doing so allows the proposal writer to create a *return on investment* (ROI) figure that will be very important to the individual charged with making the go/no-go decision regarding the proposal.

ROI is a ratio that represents the anticipated value the training program is expected to offer. The formula used for ROI is the projected lifetime benefits minus the projected lifetime costs divided by the projected lifetime costs. The formula can be used to cost justify one training solution, or to compare various solutions.

$$ROI = \frac{\text{Projected Lifetime Benefits - Projected Lifetime Costs}}{\text{Projected Lifetime Costs}}$$

An example of this follows:

$$\frac{\text{Projected Lifetime Benefits - Cost of Delivery}}{\text{Projected Lifetime Cost of Delivery}} \qquad \frac{\$300,000 - \$100,000}{\$100,000}$$

Results equal a 2:1 ratio or, if multiplied by 100, equals a 200 percent return on the training investment.

Appendix

An appendix may include statistical data, or sample data collection instrument(s), trainer résumés, reference lists, and/or any other supporting materials that may aid management in making an informed (and favorable!) decision on your behalf.

Other Proposal Designs

Keep in mind that the foregoing list—and its sequencing—is only one model. For example, in certain circumstances it may be more logical to describe the capabilities of training providers at the end, allowing the proposal itself to support the provider's qualifications. When it is desirable to get the reader's attention quickly, the projected benefits may be the first item discussed.

PROPOSAL PRESENTATION

The most carefully crafted proposal in the world will never gain approval unless its presentation is professional-looking. This means, first of all, that the proposed training fits the identified problem. However, it is also very important that the document itself be mechanically perfect, grammatically correct, and attractive. Layout and design features must be carefully considered and any graphics involved must be skillfully used. Knowing the reader and presenting a quality document contributes to a positive reaction.

Knowing Your Audience

Depending on the magnitude of the proposal, readers will probably consist of middle managers for operational proposals and more senior management for informational or strategic training proposals. This, of course, may differ depending on the importance and timeliness of the proposed training. What is true, however, is that middle managers will probably dwell on the specifics, while higher levels will concentrate on larger issues of policy and strategy.

Presenting the Proposal Live

In most cases, the written proposal will probably be evaluated on the basis of the document itself. In other cases, the writer may have an opportunity to present the proposal live. In this situation, the trainer should practice so that the presentation will fit within the time allotted for it, with time for questions and interruptions. Some presentations may be allotted 30-45 minutes with about 15 minutes for questions, while others may be given only 5-10 minutes. Most everything takes longer than one thinks it will, so careful planning is essential. Being prompt, outlining and developing the major issues, and highlighting key elements in the proposal will focus attention on the primary points of the meeting. As mentioned earlier, some presentations will be more formal than others, and this will likely depend on the experience the decision-makers and the proposal writers have had with each other. In some cases, a training manager may even ask for the presentation of a unit of instruction to demonstrate an ability to deliver instruction, or a videotape that can be viewed at the convenience of the decision-making panel members. In all cases, the proposal presenter should be well-prepared, efficient, and precise.

SUMMARY

This chapter has described the training proposal—its function, content, and organization. The proposal should communicate your plans and match the organization's business objectives and other related training activities. The proposal should stem from the analysis of the needs assessment activities, include a rationale and description of the training program to be developed, and outline the training program goals within the context of the organization. It should clearly address the skills and knowledge gaps identified and how the proposal will fill these gaps.

Training proposals should identify the scope of the project to be undertaken and describe the training audience to be involved. Specific learning objectives and major topics should be included to meet these objectives. Proposals should also describe the resources that will be needed to provide the training. Proposed time frames for both development and delivery are useful and should include their sequencing and time required.

Training costs and benefits are very critical components. Not only are these financial numbers carefully scrutinized by organizational decision-makers, but how they are determined will also be questioned. Putting dollar figures on benefits is difficult, but when benefit figures and cost figures are used to measure return on investment, the results provide an extremely powerful argument for saying "yes" to the proposed training solution.

The physical document—the proposal itself—should be clear, concise, and attractive. Knowing what readers expect dictates the length and format of the document. On occasion, a proposal developer may do a live presentation of the proposal, and the skill set for effective oral presentations must be followed. Materials that are well-presented—in writing and/or in an oral presentation—have a competitive edge.

THINK IT THROUGH

1. Of the many elements of a training proposal, which do you consider to be the three *most* critical ones? Why?
2. Writing effective training proposals is both an art and a science. What are some rules of thumb to consider when beginning the writing process?
3. Two timetables were described in this chapter: a Delivery Schedule and a Training Development Schedule. What tools exist to help the proposal writer present these figures?
4. What is meant by return on investment (ROI)? Why are ROI figures difficult to develop?
5. What advice do you have for the individual who is to present a proposal live to a decision team? Offer specific suggestions for an effective presentation.

IDEAS IN ACTION

1. Draft a sample proposal for delivering training on the following topic, with members of your class as the learners: Developing and writing a training proposal. Assume your instructor will be the management decision-maker. Limit your written proposal to three (3) pages.
2. Make a brief, five-minute oral presentation to a small group of classmates on the proposal identified above. If possible, have someone in your group videotape the presentation. By yourself, critique the presentation. Make a list of "what I did well" and "what I need to improve."

ADDITIONAL RESOURCES

RECOMMENDED READINGS

Nilson, C. *Training Program Workbook and Kit.* Englewood Cliffs, NJ: Prentice Hall, 1989, 430 pp.

A major volume of work sheets, hints, checklists, and guides for the training professional at every level—designer, instructor, manager. This how-to workbook provides guidance for everyone in training and is a reference for every training library.

Phillips, Jack J. *Return on Investment in Training and Performance Improvement Programs: A Step-by-Step Manual for Calculating the Financial Return on Investment.* Houston: Gulf Publishing Company, 1999, 320 pp.

For creative ways to develop ROI figures, check out this guide. It includes methods and work sheets for developing both hard and soft dollar figures for ROI calculations. Includes a case study where you are taken step-by-step through the process.

Zemke, R., L. Standke, and P. Jones, eds. *Designing and Delivering Cost-Effective Training—and Measuring the Results.* Minneapolis, MN: Training Books, 1981, 1983, 415 pp.

This 11-chapter reference book contains the best articles from 250 issues of *Training* magazine since 1964, featuring the best "… ideas on the design, development, and evaluation of cost-effective training." While this book has been around awhile, its contents are as current today as they were in 1983.

WEB SITES

http://www.astd.org/virtual_community/research/What_Works

This site is a resource offered by ASTD. Every quarter, What Works Online takes the latest and best research on a particular topic, identifies the most important challenges, and distills proven solutions to those challenges.

The second-quarter 2000 issue is devoted to developing ROI figures for E-learning; the third-quarter issue is devoted to developing ROI in general.

http://www.m-w.com/

This site is Merriam-Webster Online. Available free through this site is the Merriam-Webster dictionary and thesaurus. Use these tools as you develop your training proposals! The site also includes word games and puzzles.

CHAPTER 10
Training Administration

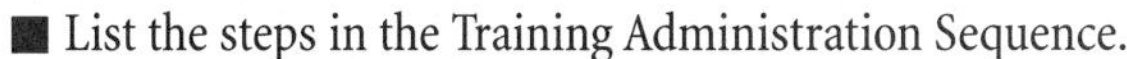

- List the steps in the Training Administration Sequence.
- Discuss training administration's contributions to training effectiveness.
- Offer pros and cons of developing and distributing course catalogs.
- Discuss ways in which training administration software and the Internet/Intranet support training administration tasks.
- Offer examples of prework activities that must be implemented and monitored by training administrators.
- Develop checklists to support the successful rollout of training programs.
- Configure a classroom and its equipment to support a particular training program.
- Compare and contrast centralized vs. decentralized approaches to developing training budgets.
- Develop a training costing work sheet.
- Identify training reports useful to the organization.

THE IMPORTANCE OF TRAINING ADMINISTRATION

The administrative support of training is a key training responsibility. While not the most glamorous of tasks, it is nevertheless crucial to training success. If program administration[1] is not done properly, the most elegant design and most compelling delivery will, at best, struggle to be successful and will more than likely be simply wasted.

Good administrative support for training provides for learner needs such as the following:

- Informative and easy-to-access program descriptions
- Customer-focused registration procedures
- Well-organized and appealingly presented participant materials

- High-quality visuals and copies
- Properly prepared physical facilities
- All required equipment in good working order

These kinds of logistical details are the foundation on which program implementation rests. They provide a sort of training infrastructure, a necessary condition that enables trainees to attend to program content and allows instruction to focus on smooth, crisp delivery of that content as planned.

THE TRAINING ADMINISTRATION SEQUENCE

The administration of training, whether in support of instructor-led or mediated programs, includes a number of tasks, reduced here to seven steps. Organizations may modify the sequence, tailor the steps, combine or add some, or outline them differently. The steps can be restructured to meet the specific needs of a particular training initiative. No matter how they are defined or structured, however, the following administrative support issues—called here the "Training Administration Sequence"—must be properly handled to provide training successfully. Note that some of these administrative tasks can be done concurrently rather than in linear sequence. Indeed, efficient, effective, and responsive program administration often requires multitasking. The Training Administration Sequence includes the following:

1. Informing interested parties of program availability.
2. Registering participants.
3. Distributing and processing prework.
4. Preparing instructional materials.
5. Preparing the physical facilities—site and equipment.
6. Supporting the actual delivery of instruction.
7. Supporting evaluation.

These administrative responsibilities are typically met by support staff working in the training department. In a small department, the support staff may consist of an administrative assistant or two, perhaps even part-time workers. A larger training department often includes an operations or support team with its own division of labor. Typically one person, ideally with a backup, serves as Registrar, handling all the processes involved in registering people for programs.

Other support requirements are dealt with in two basic ways. One way is to assign an individual support person to a specific program with responsibility for taking care of all the logistical needs of that program. The second approach is to have logistical services supplied by a central support group that handles requirements on a team basis, rotating responsibilities and assigning them as needed. These two approaches offer the classic trade-offs of individualized, in-depth knowledge of product and programs vs. the efficiencies of leveraging expertise centrally. There is clearly no hard and fast rule to follow in how to choose between these basic options for organizing and managing support resources for training. In fact, support work can be deliberately alternated between the two approaches over time, just for the sake of variety.

No matter how support work is organized, however, three key principles flow from experience:

- Repetitive administrative tasks can easily become routine, even boring, and thus susceptible to error. Care must be taken to build in reasonable variety for those carrying out such tasks.
- It is critical to seize the routine nature of logistical work and turn it into a strength. Support must be provided and controlled in a highly disciplined, systematic way, checked and double-checked by procedures as routine as the content of the work itself. It is the kind of responsibility that must be managed by checklists, buddy systems, and any other means of verifying accuracy in routine, repetitive work.
- In a department made up of training professionals and clerical support staff, a hierarchy of roles/status almost invariably emerges. Predictable and legitimate as this may be, given the nature and purpose of the department, it is also important for both groups in this situation to keep in mind the contribution *each* makes to the implementation and success of training. It is particularly important for the trainers to recognize the critical role played by support services and to not let them become taken-for-granted resources.

With these three principles in mind, each of the seven steps in the Training Administration Sequence will be explained in this section. Tools typically used in training administration will be treated at appropriate points in the sequence. A discussion of training finances will conclude the chapter.

Step 1: Informing Interested Parties of Program Availability

Potential participants, their managers, the organization's Human Resource professionals—indeed, the organization as a whole—need to know of the training programs that are available. Potentially interested parties need a description of each program with enough detail to enable them to understand its learning objectives, its target audience, its fit within a larger curriculum if appropriate, its prerequisites and prework if any, its length, and its costs. Also of importance is information on how to access the program: where and when it will be offered, the requirements and methods of registering for it, and its cancellation policy.

Some of these items—for instance, registration methods and cancellation policy—need be explained only once for multiple programs; they need not be repeated as part of each program's description. Some items must be explained on a program-by-program basis, even sometimes offering by offering.

Catalogs and Schedules

Often training departments issue a *catalog of programs* that contains solely *descriptive information* on the content of programs in some sort of logical order: alphabetic, grouped by subject matter, by location, or by offering department. A catalog's length can range from a few to many pages, depending on the size of the organization and the number of its training programs. The production of a catalog of significant size—particularly one shared by more than one training department—is a major task and is thus, typically done on an annual or other relatively infrequent basis.

A catalog describing program content must be complemented by a *schedule of offerings,* a much simpler document to produce, containing merely the *administrative information* necessary to register for the programs: dates, locations, and times. The purpose of the *catalog* is to enable people to *select the right program*. The purpose of the *schedule* is to enable them to *access programs* once selected. The schedule may, of course, be for the organization as a whole, or may be for a single training department, a particular site, or any organizational component of the organization that makes sense.

The two documents—catalog and schedule—are often combined into a single document that contains both descriptive and administrative information. The decision as to whether to provide the two kinds of information separately or in combined form is at least partially a function of size. A single catalog combining both kinds of information requires more frequent updating. It must be updated every time the schedule runs out. This may be acceptable if the catalog is small and updating it is not too onerous. Splitting the catalog and the schedule, on the other hand, has the advantage of keeping the program descriptions fixed while the scheduling data changes as needed over time or by location. In either case, commercially available software is available to help a training group organize and publish its catalog/schedule. Figures 10-1a and 10-1b show sample pages from actual catalogs published in a business organization.

Putting the catalog and schedule on the Internet, or on an internal company network, simplifies the whole matter of catalogs and schedules. In fact, the training department can get out of the distribution business altogether. Once on the Internet or Intranet, the catalog and schedule can be accessed by anyone with authorization. This single network location becomes the only place where training information needs to be updated, and the updating usually takes place in relatively easy fashion. Using a network for this kind of information publishing is but one example of today's technology very favorably impacting the administrative side of training.

FIGURE 10-1
PROGRAM DESCRIPTIONS FROM ACTUAL TRAINING CATALOG USED IN BUSINESS:

Figure 10-1A Sample Page From Chase Manhattan Bank Training Catalog Describing "Business Writing Skills" Program.

PROGRAM NAME

Business Writing Skills

OBJECTIVES

To help participants write memos, letters, and reports that are clear, direct, and easy to read.

DESCRIPTION

Using case studies and exercises, this program focuses on guidelines for making business writing more persuasive and dynamic. Participants have opportunities to practice and critique business correspondence. Topics include the following:

- How to make your writing easier for others to read, understand, and act upon
- How to organize your ideas
- How to select appropriate language and tone
- How to edit and proofread

FORMAT

Instructor-led

LENGTH

Two days

TARGET AUDIENCE

Officers and Professionals

PREREQUISITES

Participants should be proficient in English vocabulary, grammar, and syntax.

OFFERING DATES

March	3-4
April	28-29
June	16-17
September	19-20
October	24-25
December	8-9

CONTACT PERSON

Registrar, Corporate Education

Figure 10-1B Sample Page from Chase Manhattan Bank Training Catalog Describing "Performance Management at Chase" Program

PROGRAM NAME

Performance Management at Chase

OBJECTIVES

To develop skills in managing the performance of staff to achieve business goals consistent with the Chase Vision.

DESCRIPTION

With a focus on business results and the Chase Values, participants learn and use communication skills in the areas of performance planning, coaching, performance appraisals, development planning, and career coaching. Methods include management practices feedback from staff, manager, and self, extensive skill practice using own situations, small group activities, and videotaping. The program is conducted in three parts offered over time. In order to stay with the same group of people, participants should pick a cluster of dates for Parts One, Two, and Three from the schedule below. If scheduling conflicts arise, other dates may be substituted. Participants should pick their preferred cluster and register for all three Parts upon initial registration. Part One must be completed before attending Part Two and/or Three. Content of the three Parts follows:

Part One: Overview, Communication Skills, Performance Planning/Objective Setting

Part Two: Development Planning, Coaching, Career Discussions

Part Three: Performance Appraisal, Recognition and Rewards

In addition, there will be two, four-day offerings of the program in its entirety.

FORMAT

Instructor-led, feedback instrument

LENGTH

Parts One and Two, one and one-half days each; Part Three, one day, if taken in cluster format; program is four days if taken in its entirety.

TARGET AUDIENCE

Those who have direct performance management responsibilities for others.

PREREQUISITES

Must complete Part One before attending Parts Two and/or Three. Must have directly managed at least one person for at least six months prior to attending Part One.

(Continued)

Figure 10-1B (Continued)

OFFERING DATES

Cluster	*Part One*	*Part Two*	*Part Three*	*Entire Program*
A	February 24-25	April 21-22	June 10	April 19-22
B	March 10-11	April 21-22	June 10	November 1-4
C	April 7-8	May 23-24	July 11	
D	May 5-6	June 13-14	September 30	
E	June 2-3	July 14-15	October 27	
F	June 27-28	September 12-13	November 4	
G	July 11-12	September 22-23	November 17	
H	September 8-9	October 24-25	December 8	
I	October 20-21	November 14-15		
J	November 1-2			

CONTACT PERSON

Registrar, Corporate Education

A Risk Involved in Catalogs

Training professionals must be vigilant not to allow a catalog or schedule to substitute for needs analysis. There will be many people in an organization who, when they come to the conclusion that they or their staffs need training, will automatically reach (or click) for the training catalog to see what program to go to or send people to. This is not entirely unreasonable, since the catalog presumably contains programs known to be needed and good, programs approved by the organization. The professional trainer nonetheless should regard this sequence of events as *the wrong response*. It is, in fact, one of the dangers of publishing a catalog. It is all too easy for people to unthinkingly confine their consideration to the published program offerings if a catalog is available. The trainer must be always alert to help clients think through what the problem really is. Will *learning* actually fix the problem? Or is it a performance need that learning will not address? Only if learning will actually solve the problem at hand should the trainer help the client consider training programs as potential solutions, and even these programs may not be among those already scheduled and in the catalog. The downside risk of a training catalog is that it will be a lens through which training decisions are incorrectly made if care is not taken to ensure otherwise.

Other Ways of Publishing Training Information

While catalogs and schedules can be provided in either paper or electronic form, or both, astute training leaders will see to it that programs and times/locations are provided in other ways that make good sense in the organization's culture. Part of the task is simply advertising and marketing. Internal flyers and desk drops are often used for these purposes, as are articles or interviews published in the organization's internal newspaper. Bulletin boards, both physical and electronic, are another means of letting clients know about program offerings, as well as when/where they are offered and how to register. A cautionary note: Bulletin boards must be kept up to date, with events that have occurred in the past removed systematically and replaced with new material. Failure to do so makes more than the bulletin board look tacky!

Sign-on news flashes, often a feature of electronic networks, are another method of furnishing training information. Live presentations at the staff meetings of client departments or other employee gatherings provide the opportunity to discuss programs in depth, handle questions, even surface issues and learning requirements that need to be addressed. Sometimes the training department can take part in other employee events—benefits or development fairs, for example. Still another possibility might be a booth or desk periodically set up at the entrance to the employee cafeteria or lounge or in a building's main lobby. Finally, if the organization uses business television to keep employees informed, news about training programs and schedules can be broadcast via this medium.

The ways of providing people with training information are many. The point is to use the ways that make sense, to do so in a systematic way, and to be certain to use them in a manner that supports training's mission: helping the *right* people learn the *right* things. The primary emphasis should be on enabling both employees and the organization to achieve legitimate business goals. Getting people into training programs is a worthy and even necessary administrative task, but it is not an end in itself. In fact, doing so can be an activity trap if it is not kept in proper perspective. If a training department often finds itself in the position of having to drum up participation in its programs or cancel them for lack of it, there is something more fundamentally wrong than faulty internal advertising and information processes. Having to beat the bushes for participants is usually a sign that the program offered is not the right program, is not correctly targeted, or is not properly positioned within the organization. Doing a better job of advertising program availability will not deal with these larger, more important issues.

Finally, the members of the training department, particularly the support staff, must be trained to handle information inquiries properly—telephone calls, faxes, E-mail, and even lunchroom or watercooler encounters. These, after all, are often the department's front line of contact with its internal customers. It is important that those who answer inquiries be familiar with the programs the department offers, knowledgeable in its policies and procedures (especially registration), and thus able to directly help callers with the information they seek or refer them to the proper source.

Step 2: Registering Participants

Once people know what programs they wish to take and how to register for them, the next step is registration itself. Registration typically involves the following:

- Registering or wait-listing participants for the programs they desire.
- Producing confirmation letters notifying people of their status on an ongoing basis.
- Producing reminder/prework letters as tickler dates arrive.
- Handling cancellations.
- Producing class rosters.
- Producing a variety of management reports both before and after actual offerings.
- Maintaining an historical database of training accomplished and/or providing links to the organization's employee database.

Software Registration Systems

Information technology provides powerful assistance in registering program participants. Training departments have the three classic choices faced by any organization that wishes to automate part of its work: design the system in-house, purchase a system available in the marketplace, or purchase a system and modify it. Designing a registration program from scratch can be time-consuming and expensive. However, if it is designed correctly, the result can be a perfect fit with organizational needs, and there may well be situations where this approach is necessary. On the other hand, a plethora of off-the-shelf registration systems (see box on page 282) are readily available for purchase at a relatively modest cost. These systems quite successfully handle the standard needs of registering people as listed above, so much so that the notion of developing an in-house, custom-built system should be subjected to extremely rigorous review.

Purchased software typically comes with vendor support, including some form of training in the system's use. Purchased systems can, of course, also be modified to fit particular needs, with the vendor selling the source code and the organization's own systems professionals making the changes necessary to modify the package for internal use. Such modifications are often done with the collaboration of the software vendor, sometimes even on a shared-cost basis. Anyone considering the modification of a purchased system should pay particularly careful attention to the issue of post-modification support.

The following training registration packages were advertised in a single issue (May 2000) of *Training and Development*, ASTD's magazine. The packages are listed here as a representative sample of the registration software available on the open market. They definitely do not exhaust the possibilities (Pathlore's Registrar System, for example–not on the list below—is referenced later in this chapter). Ads are listed in the order of their appearance in the magazine:

1. Pathways, General Dynamics Corp. (508) 880-4209. www.pathways-dl.com
2. SmartForce E-Learning. (888) 395-0014. www.smartforce.com
3. KnowledgePlanet. www.knowledgeplanet.com
4. Training Server. (800) 869-9461. www.trainingserver.com
5. Total Knowledge Mgt System, Generation 21. (888) 601-1300, x1073
6. E-learnframe. (888) 738-9800. www.elearnframe.com
7. Spectrum HR Systems. (800) 477-3287. www.spectrumhr.com
8. TrainingNet. (888) 931-9339. www.trainingnet.com

Registration systems, whether purchased off the shelf or custom written, easily support all the registration steps, from participant sign-up to confirmation and wait-list letters, from program rosters to room assignments and participant transcripts. Figure 10-2 offers samples of typical administrative reports: first a class roster, and second a "person note," which allows comments for a particular participant, such as "needs a vegetarian meal" or "arranged to hand in his prework late."

The Registration Form

A registration form of some sort is typically the trigger for the start of the registration process. Figure 10-3 is a sample showing the kind of data usually captured to register someone for a training program. The form is often on paper, but increasingly the registration process is entirely electronic.

As was mentioned earlier, one administrative person in the department is typically designated as the individual responsible for registration and its associated tasks. This is particularly true if registrations are handled by means of a software package. While these packages are straightforward to operate, there is nonetheless a learning curve involved that needs to be managed. The department's registrar should certainly have a cross-trained backup, but one designated person should take the lead role with regard to registrations. In addition to operating the registration software, this lead person is also usually the one to deal with inquiries concerning registrations, wait lists, cancellations, and registrant status. Such inquiries are usually rather frequent, and the department must make sure that the registrar has the information and

FIGURE 10-2
SAMPLE REPORTS

SAMPLE CLASS ROSTER REPORT

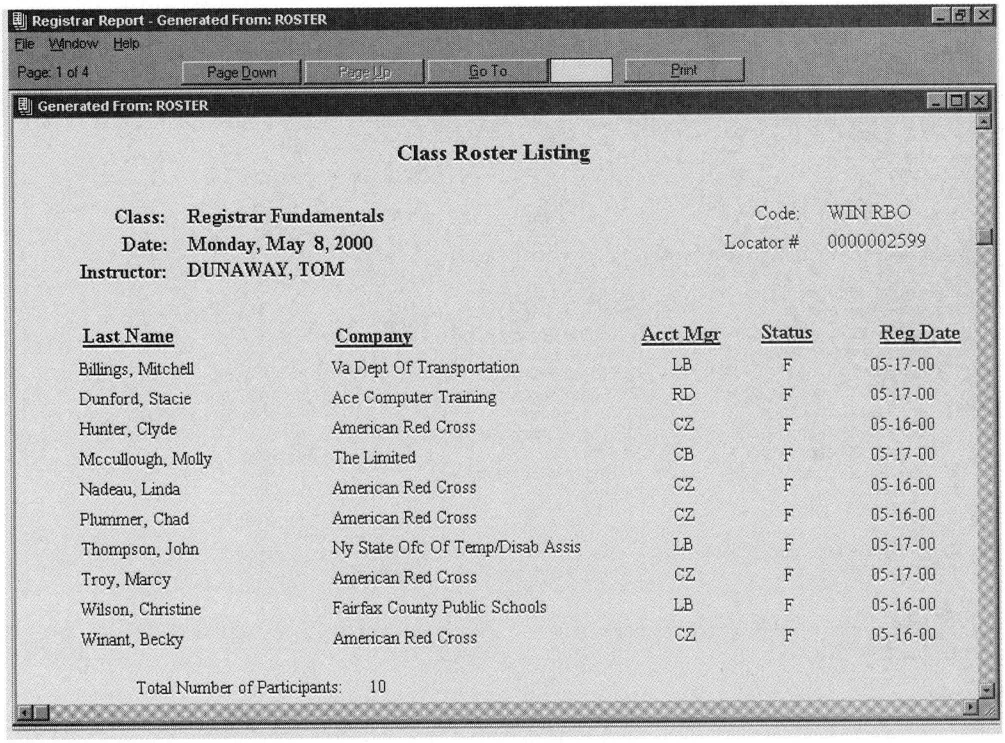

Registrar Report - Generated From: ROSTER

File Window Help

Page: 1 of 4 | Page Down | Page Up | Go To | Print

Generated From: ROSTER

Class Roster Listing

Class: Registrar Fundamentals   Code: WIN RBO
Date: Monday, May 8, 2000   Locator # 0000002599
Instructor: DUNAWAY, TOM

Last Name	Company	Acct Mgr	Status	Reg Date
Billings, Mitchell	Va Dept Of Transportation	LB	F	05-17-00
Dunford, Stacie	Ace Computer Training	RD	F	05-17-00
Hunter, Clyde	American Red Cross	CZ	F	05-16-00
Mccullough, Molly	The Limited	CB	F	05-17-00
Nadeau, Linda	American Red Cross	CZ	F	05-16-00
Plummer, Chad	American Red Cross	CZ	F	05-16-00
Thompson, John	Ny State Ofc Of Temp/Disab Assis	LB	F	05-17-00
Troy, Marcy	American Red Cross	CZ	F	05-17-00
Wilson, Christine	Fairfax County Public Schools	LB	F	05-16-00
Winant, Becky	American Red Cross	CZ	F	05-16-00

Total Number of Participants: 10

SAMPLE PERSON NOTE REPORT

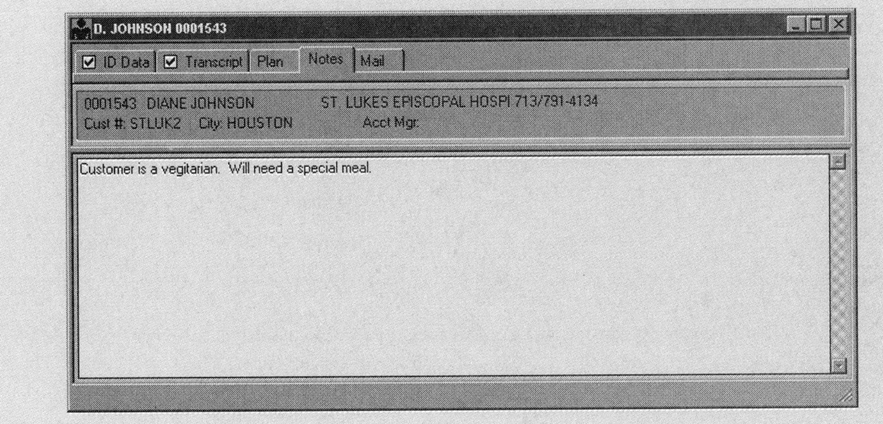

Figure 10-3
Training Registration Form

Course Title: | Course Date/Reference#: (Ref. # for Self-Guided Learning Resources)

Registrant Last Name: | Corporate Title:

Registrant First Name: MI: | Job Function:

Social Security #: | Public Phone #:

Department: | Chase Phone #: CN

Expense Code: Location: FI: Fax #:

Circle the number next to the business or function in which you work:

1. Business Development
2. Capital Markets
3. Case InfoServ International
4. Chief Financial Officer
5. Consumer Financial Services
6. Corporate Communications
7. Corporate Compliance
8. Corporate Human Resources
9. Corporate O and S
10. Economics
11. Customer Planning and Development Office
12. Global Asia/Pacific
13. Global Corporate Finance
14. Global Europe, Middle and Africa
15. Global Latin America
16. Global Private Banking
17. Global Risk Management
18. Global Whole
19. Global United States
20. Legal
21. Regional Banking
22. Other

Ethnic Code*
1 Black
2 American Indian
3 Asian
4 Hispanic
5 White
6 Other
*For Corp. HR Affirmative

Sex Code
F Female
M Male

Do you have a development plan?
Yes ____ No ____

If yes, is this course on that plan?
Yes _____ No _____

Do you require any special service or accommodation?
Yes ____ No ____

If yes, nature of service or accommodation?
Yes _____ No _____

In order to process your registration form, you must obtain signatures from both your manager/supervisor and HR representative. (Not required for Self-Guided Learning Resources.) Then send your registration form to the appropriate sponsor.

Employee Signature

SIGNATURE: | DATE:

Required Approvals:

MANAGER/SUPERVISOR
Print Name:
Signature:
Date: Phone:
Location:

HR REPRESENTATIVE
Print Name:
Signature:
Date: Phone:
Location:

Note: You are *not* confirmed for a program until you receive a Confirmation Letter.

procedures to deal with them. It is also important that others in the department know how to handle such inquiries, either providing the information or referring the caller to the registrar.

Wait Lists and Cancellations

A key registration responsibility, differing from program to program and varying in complexity, is how to deal with a participant who wishes to withdraw from a program. Responding to this kind of request involves issues like wait lists and substitutions, the timing of the cancellation (what if it's too late to get a substitute?), program costs and charges, prework returns and/or costs, and minimums established for the number of participants necessary to run the course. The question of whether or not the program is mandatory in nature can enter the picture as well. It may be one thing for an employee to cancel out of a business-writing class, but quite another to opt out of an orientation to management for newly promoted supervisory personnel. The latter transaction may, for instance, involve the registrar in keeping track of who has attended the mandatory program and who has not. It may also involve reporting the status of registrations and cancellations for a mandatory program.

Step 3. Distributing and Processing Prework

Many training programs require participants to do some work in advance. These requirements range from the simple to the complex. An example of a simple *prework* assignment is that a participant in a writing class is expected to write a memo on some topic (sometimes supplied, sometimes self-selected) and bring it to the program to be used in an exercise. Similarly, participants are often asked to read an article, a case study, or an organizational policy in preparation for a program. Sometimes this involves having participants answer a set of questions concerning the material they have read. In these situations, the support responsibility is simply to make sure the participant is informed of the prework expectation and supplied with anything necessary to do it—a copy of the required reading material and any associated study questions. It is typically part of administrative support to ensure that copyright laws are respected and copy permissions are obtained where necessary.

Advance Submission of Prework

A more complex prework requirement involves the participant not only doing something in preparation for a program, but also submitting it before the program begins (e.g., writing a sample memo on some topic and sending it to the training department in advance so the instructor can read and edit it). The requirement that prework be submitted ahead of time increases the support task significantly. Given the requirement of advance submissions, participants must be informed of what they need to do and provided with the wherewithal for doing it.

A participant's compliance with requirements must also be tracked. The support responsibility now includes establishing deadlines for the prework submissions, keeping track of who has submitted the prework and who hasn't, and reminding the delinquents once or twice. The support responsibility also involves ensuring that the prework submitted in advance is processed for use in the training program. This processing depends, of course, on what the prework is. It involves, at a minimum, giving the prework submissions to the instructor (e.g., the writing sample mentioned earlier). Sometimes the processing means aggregating or summarizing participant submissions, or it may involve getting the prework submissions to a vendor on time for processing (e.g., a negotiations style survey).

Feedback on Participants as Prework

An increasingly common form of prework involves program participants' obtaining feedback from others, feedback on issues that the organization deems important. Examples of such issues are managerial style, teamwork, and career aspirations. Feedback can be gathered for use in training programs on project or performance management, on other general or specialized management topics, on career development, on communications or sales skills, and on many other topics. All sorts of programs include components built around participants' obtaining feedback from others on how or how well they carry out certain tasks or meet certain responsibilities.

The sources of feedback typically include one or more of the following: boss, peers, staff, customers (internal or external), colleagues in other departments whose work depends on the participant, colleagues on whom the participant depends for his or her own work, HR professionals who work in support of the participants' departments, or even individuals from the participants' personal lives. Potential feedback sources include anyone whose input on particular issues would be of value to the participant, anyone who can provide useful insight from a useful perspective. Feedback from *all* points of the participant's compass—called 360-degree feedback precisely because it is from all points— is increasingly frequent, particularly in management development programs.

In all these cases, whatever the purpose or the source, having participants get feedback adds significant demands to program support responsibilities, such as the following:

- Program participants must be supplied with the instructions and the materials needed to ask others to supply the feedback the program requires. This entails paper feedback forms, disks, or Web site addresses, together with the instructions on how those giving the feedbacks are to submit it.
- The training support staff must be prepared to handle questions about these data-gathering processes and deal with glitches in them ("I can't download this form.").

- The staff must also be prepared to deal with submission deadlines, late or lost data, participant additions to, or changes in, feedback sources, and what to do if a participant cancels out of a feedback-based course at the last minute.

These kinds of complexities are well beyond simply sending out a case study for program participants to read in advance. It is crucial that support staff work closely with the department's trainers (usually one trainer who is designated as the "Program Manager") to establish that the support documentation and processes for feedback-based programs are accurate, complete, and up-to-date.

The actual processing of feedback—entering the data if necessary, crunching the numbers, producing the feedback reports that will be used in the program—is a significant task all by itself. The job is often outsourced for reasons of confidentiality. In this latter case, the internal support responsibility is to link with the outsourced processor of the feedback to establish that all is going smoothly. All the required input must be received by the due date, and feedback reports for the program must be received on time.

The Confidentiality of Feedback Data

No matter where the feedback data are processed, in-house or out, the importance of confidentiality would be difficult to overemphasize. Feedback cannot be left lying around on desks or worktables. It should never be discussed over coffee or remarked on in any way. It can be shared only with those identified by careful procedures, usually *only* with the recipient. Care, to the point of obsessiveness, about the confidentiality of feedback data should be regarded as a mark of true professionalism. Once trust about the confidentiality of feedback is lost inside an organization, it would be extremely difficult to win it back. This would, in turn, make future efforts at the use of feedback virtually impossible.

A Sample Prework Checklist

By way of summary of this section on prework, Figure 10-4 shows an actual checklist used for the complex prework necessary for a management development program designed for relatively senior managers and involving 360 degree feedback on participants. The list is offered here as a sample of the level of detail necessary for competent administrative support of a training program. Note that the list is incomplete, dealing as it does only with the prework aspects of the program.

FIGURE 10-4
EXPERIENCED MANAGER PROGRAM (EMP)

Prework Administration Checklist

Three Phases for EMP Prework:

Phase I. Confirmation Memo

Send a confirmation memo to each participant by name ten weeks prior to program date for U.S. delivery, twelve weeks prior for international delivery. (Sample memo in master file.) Reiterate program dates and times. Include a list of participants and a copy of our cancellation policy. Send a copy of the memo to each participant's manager.

Phase II. Prework Package

Send the following to each participant eight weeks prior to program date. Follow directions provided with items:

A. Blue program folder with two pockets, "Prework Memo" clipped to outside of folder. (Sample memo in master file.)
   1. In the left pocket, place the "Participant Instructions Memo." (Sample memo in master file.)
   2. In the right pocket, place the pre-program workbook.
   3. Three-hole punch and include copies of the following in right pocket:
      a. "The New Manager"
      b. "Dealing with Turbulence"

B. Prepare a 3-1/2" disk mailer, with send and return labels. Prepare a label saying, "Reminder: Questions on this disk refer to your manager." Put the label on a 3-1/2" "DIRECT REPORT DISK" (provided by vendor) and place the disk in the mailer. Place six of these prepared mailers in a gray 9 x 12 inch envelope with the memo, "Feedback Gathering Instructions," (sample on file) stapled to the outside of the envelope. Prepare one of these gray envelopes for each participant.

C. Prepare a 3-1/2" disk mailer with return label. Create a label saying, "Self Questionnaire," and put the label on a "SELF DISK" (provided by vendor). Clip it to the memo, "Self Questionnaire" (sample on file).

D. Put one Item B (gray 9 x 12 inch envelope) and one Item C (Self Questionnaire disk mailer) into white 11 x 14 inch envelope, one white envelope per participant. Obtain mailing labels for all participants from the Registrar, put a mailing label for each participant on a white envelope, and put the envelopes in the interoffice mail.

E. Send out "Pre-Program Discussion Memo" to participants' managers. (Sample on file—note two versions, one for men, one for women: to get the pronouns right.) The memo tells managers of the program requirement of a discussion with participants on their staffs. Call the manager to confirm receipt of the memo. Advise that the participant will schedule the meeting, and explain the purpose of the discussion. (Read pre-program workbook for information, and be prepared to discuss the program's feedback features.)

(Continued)

Figure 10-4 (Continued)

Phase III. Feedback Tracking

As disks return from participants and their feedback sources:

A. Scan each disk for viruses, using standard department virus protection software. If virus found, report to Program Manager. Batch clean disks and forward to vendor for feedback report generation.

B. Verify each participant receives feedback from at least four people. Call those who are lacking requisite number on due date. Make clear the necessity: Participants may not attend class if insufficient feedback is received; cancellation charges will apply. Starting three weeks before program, inform Program Manager of status of report generation every other day.

C. Be prepared to talk with participants and their feedback sources concerning questions and problems with disks and/or feedback process. **Read feedback instruction sheets so you can be helpful**. Consider doing a feedback disk for practice so you have that experience to draw on.

D. Two days before program: Verify final participant list with Registrar based upon feedback on hand, obtain class roster, give copy to Program Manager and instructor(s), and inform Program Manager of participants who have not received sufficient feedback to join program.

Step 4: Preparing Instructional Materials

The support job relative to instructional materials is to make sure they are prepared in advance, ready for use when the program begins. "Instructional materials" includes all the items that will be used in the program, whether for instruction or as materials to be given to program participants. Getting these items ready in advance means different things, depending on whether or not the materials in question are purchased or have been created internally. Preparing commercially published workbooks or reference books (often the case in both live and mediated instruction, especially the latter) means making sure a sufficient stock is on hand. Items that have been developed in-house, on the other hand, must be created. If a program of live instruction calls for PowerPoint visuals, overhead transparencies, or pre-done flip charts, they must be created and arranged in the proper sequence as specified in the program's Leader's Guide. Handouts must be photocopied, participant binders stuffed, instructions for role plays and simulation exercises readied in sufficient number, and so on.

The Use of Checklists

The preparation of all these materials is a prime example of work that again is best managed by checklists. Figure 10-5 shows a sample checklist for the preparation of material for a live instruction course, the "Packing and Materials Checklist" for "The Experienced Manager Program," the same program described in Figure 10-4. The purpose of such checklists is to make sure that all the items needed for the program are taken care of. Checklists are often used in a partnered way: One person will use a list to prepare the materials, and a colleague administrator will use the same list to double-check the full and accurate completion of all items. A typical practice is to prepare a "Program Box," literally a cardboard file box designed to hold hanging file folders. One hanging folder is placed in the box for each item the course needs and filed in the correct sequence, day by day, over the program's entire length. The box is then delivered to the classroom as part of the program setup.

FIGURE 10-5
"THE EXPERIENCED MANAGER PROGRAM" ADMINISTRATION

Packing and Materials Checklist
PROGRAM PACKING

- ( ) Binders – One per participant, plus 4
  (See Binder Assembly List, if necessary)
- ( ) ACUMEN Feedback Envelopes (4 per person, sorted into alphabetical sets)
  - ( ) Self
  - ( ) Individual vs. Group
  - ( ) Feedback on Practices A—F
  - ( ) Feedback on Practices G—N
- ( ) Handouts—Day 1—NOTE: All handouts are three-hole punched.
  - ( ) Extra Prework Articles
  - ( ) Extra Pre-Program Workbook (5)
  - ( ) Participant's List (from Ops Coordinator – 30)
  - ( ) Maximizing Profitability Exercise Sheets
    - ( ) 4-Member Team (30)
    - ( ) 5-Member Team (30)
    - ( ) 6-Member Team (30)
  - ( ) Blank ACUMEN Target (30)
- ( ) Handouts—Day 2—NOTE: All handouts are three-hole punched.
  - ( ) Managing Individual Performance Role Play Instructions for:
    - ( ) R.I. (2p, 2-sided) (6)
    - ( ) P.F. (3p, 2-sided, stapled) (6)
    - ( ) T.T. (2p, 2-sided) (6)
    - ( ) S.P. (2p, 2-sided) (6)
    - ( ) N.O. (2p, 2-sided) (6)

    NOTE: Initials represent role-play characters.
  - ( ) Managing Individual Performance Observer Forms (30)

(Continued)

Figure 10-5 (Continued)

( ) Managing Individual Performance Feedback Forms (5 per person—130)

( ) Managing Business Performance Case (1 of 2 needed)

( ) For NY and Domestic, "Big Shoulders" (39p booklet—30) OR

( ) For London/HK/TKO, "Star Wars" (20p booklet—30)

( ) Handouts—Day 3—NOTE: All handouts are three-hole punched.

( ) Managing Business Performance Team Assignments (1p—30)

( ) Managing Business Performance Team Rating Sheets (1p—30)

( ) Handouts—Day 4—NOTE: All handouts are three-hole punched.

( ) Managing Across the Organization Individual Assessment Forms (2p, 2-sided; 6 per person—150)

( ) Program Evaluation Forms (2p, 2-sided; Change Dates and Instructors—150)

( ) Materials

( ) Chase History Slides (14, in carousel)

( ) S-Curve Overheads (set of 11 in labeled Tyvek)

( ) ACUMEN Overheads (set of 10 in labeled Tyvek)

( ) Flip Charts, 1 Pad

( ) Day 1 #'s 1.1—1.16

NOTE: Instructors make other flips during class.

( ) Video—

Tapes Include

—ACUMENT Illustrations

—Nine to Five

—Broadcast News

—Managing Individual Performance

—King (I Have a Dream)

—L.A. Law

—It's a Wonderful Life

( ) Name Tags for Role Plays (sets of 5—R.I., P.F., T.T., S.P., and N.O.)

( ) 6 Wood Slabs (1" x 12" x 12", *Clear* pine)

( ) Safety Glasses (3)

( ) Prizes for Winning Team (Gotham T-Shirts; 6L and 6XL)

( ) Name Tags for Day 3 Cocktail Party (Real Names, Typed Tags—CDC)

( ) Parting Gift (In NY, deliver on Day 4; other locations, ship with program supplies)

(Continued)

Figure 10-5 (Continued)

- ( ) Large Tyvek Envelopes with Mailing Labels (to mail participant's binders, etc., if needed—20)
- ( ) 1/2" Blank Videotape, one per team (4)

( ) Instructor's Kit

- ( ) 5 Rolls 1" Masking Tape
- ( ) 6 Sets of 5 Magic Markers (red, blue, purple, green, black)
- ( ) Pens/Pencils (sharpened)
- ( ) Post-it-Notes—5 tiny (1" x 1") and 5 small (2" x 3")
- ( ) Stapler
- ( ) Scissors
- ( ) Extra Peel-Off Name Tags

EQUIPMENT

( ) Slide Projector (Day 1)
( ) Overhead Projector (Days 1 and 3)
( ) Video Monitor
( ) 1/2" VCRs
( ) Video Camera and Playback (one per team) in each breakout room (Day 3)
( ) Flip Chart Stands and Pads (4 in main classroom, 1 in each breakout room)

BINDER ASSEMBLY

( ) Planning Guide (40p booklet, saddle-stitch, three-hole punched—Inside front cover)
( ) Cover Sheet
( ) Day 1 Tab

- ( ) Program Agenda (1p)
- ( ) S-Curve Growth Model (11p, 2-sided, stapled upper left)
- ( ) Article: "Bringing Spirit Back to the Workplace," W. Matthew Jeuchter (5p, 2-sided, stapled)
- ( ) Acumen Clockstyle Descriptors (1p)
- ( ) Handbook for Using ACUMEN (57p booklet, saddle-stitch)
- ( ) Ideal Manager Profile (Blank ACUMEN target)
- ( ) Managing Individual Performance Team Role Play
  - ( ) Team Instructions (6p, 2-sided, stapled)
  - ( ) Instructions for B. Smith, Observer (7p, 2-sided, stapled)

( ) Day 2 Tab

- ( ) Managing Individual Performance Improvement Model (1p)
- ( ) Managing Individual Performance Reference Guide (7p booklet, saddle-stitch)
- ( ) Management Practices "Placemat" (2p, 2-sided, card stock, 4-color)
- ( ) Performance Analysis Form (2p, 2-sided)

(Continued)

Figure 10-5 (Continued)

( ) Day 3 Tab
- ( ) Managing Business Performance Model (1p)
- ( ) Managing Business Performance Tools and Techniques (19p booklet, saddle-stitch, three-hole punched)
- ( ) Managing Business Performance Team Exercise (1p)
- ( ) Managing Across the Organization Case: "A Rock and a Hard Place" (13p booklet, saddle-stitch)

( ) Day 4 Tab
- ( ) Managing Across the Organization Team Exercise (2p, one-sided, stapled)
- ( ) Bibliography (13p, two-sided, stapled)

One important side benefit of a checklist is to make possible the training program's portability: The list is a perfect vehicle for communicating to another department what is administratively necessary to run this particular program. A good checklist thus clearly identifies the items on it and is further backed up by safely archived master copies of its contents.

Backups and Archives

Providing adequate backup for program materials is an important administrative responsibility. The administrator supporting a training program should be working from not only a checklist, but also from master copies of all the items that appear on the list. These working masters are part of the program's documentation. They are used to make the copies of material each time a program is run, but they are never themselves used in a program. The working masters should themselves be duplicates of a set of materials kept in an archive as ultimate backup copies of all materials. Both the working and archive masters should consist of clean, complete copies of all items on the program checklist, whether they are in-house creations or commercially purchased. Electronic copies of in-house material should, of course, also be backed up and archived. This is sometimes even possible with commercially purchased material, an issue to be negotiated with the vendor of the material.

The purpose behind the care concerning master copies is twofold. First, it serves as a base for the production of high-quality program materials—clean, crisp copies, fully legible, appealingly packaged, and pleasing to the eye. This is a message of respect for participants and their learning efforts, a recognition of the importance of both. Consider the effect of smudged, skewed pages in a participant binder or the impact of sloppy visuals, and the point is crystal clear. The second reason for care concerning masters and backups is the classic one: providing for disastrous contingencies. Good program administration takes measures to make sure it can always recover from the loss of materials in the mail or due to ordinary human error or because of disasters such as a fire or a flood. (A runaway sprinkler system in a building can wreak havoc on a supply room!)

Once program materials are ready, a major aspect of logistical responsibility is making sure the materials get to the physical location of the program and are returned at its end. The materials must then be checked and restored to inventory, if possible, or reordered/remade as needed. A sound practice is to replenish supplies when materials are returned at program-end rather than waiting until the start date of a program approaches. This is not essential, but it prevents supplies from being part of the last-minute crunch at program-start.

Preparing Program Materials

Materials vary enormously from program to program. The administrative responsibility for them is to supply them as called for by the Leader's Guide, on time and with a high-quality appearance. Initially creating the materials, the master copies, is a task done as part of program design and development, not of administration. Chapters 7 and 8 dealt with program materials from an instructor's point of view. Here we will discuss a few of the most commonly used materials from the perspective of the administrator who must prepare them.

- Visuals of one kind or another: These are contained in the Leader's Guide and are now typically created using output from a presentation software package such as PowerPoint, sometimes from desktop publishing software. The visuals may be used in the program as overhead transparencies or as projections directly from a computer. Transparencies are made on clear or colored transparency sheets using standard photocopying equipment, most of which can produce color. The transparencies may include overlays, may require colored patches, and may or may not be mounted on cardboard frames. Frames give the visual a finished look when displayed, make them a bit easier to handle, and provide a convenient space for speaking notes. Unframed overheads, on the other hand, are much easier to pack for travel—they can be three-hole punched for placing in a binder or can be slipped into clear plastic sleeves which are prepunched for a binder's rings. Electronic visuals, such as those produced by PowerPoint, are even easier to transport: They can be carried in a laptop's hard drive or on a 3 1/2-inch floppy in a shirt pocket. Typically, visuals are not consumed in a program, and thus do not require remaking unless the content changes.
- Flip charts: Visuals planned as flip charts are to be found usually as 8 1/2 x 11 inch masters contained in the Leader's Guide. These masters must be turned into actual flip chart pages. They can be lettered/drawn by hand directly on a flip chart pad, or they can be produced mechanically by special copiers. The copier output is then taped into a flip chart pad one at a time, skipping a couple of pages between each chart to prevent see-through. Flip chart pages also serve sometimes as wall posters in a program. They can be lightly laminated to enable writing and erasure on their surface.
- The participant binder: A staple of most programs, this binder contains the material the program calls for its participants to receive. It is typically divided by tabs for each day or section of the program. Custom binders can of course be printed; more commonly used

are generic binders with clear slipcovers on the front and the spine, allowing for customization with a simple sheet of paper. Very often a training department will want to give all its programs—or a particular curriculum within its offerings—a special "look" for identification and marketing purposes. The availability of desktop publishing and presentation software provides powerful and exciting visual opportunities for logos and print design and other visual initiatives. Note that the participant binder often includes the program evaluation form, given a place of prominence in the binder so participants can find it and use it *during* the program rather than simply have it as a handout at the end. Many training programs include all participant materials in the participant binder, reducing handouts to a bare minimum or eliminating them altogether, a tactic which simplifies both program support and instruction.

- Training programs often include what the trade calls a "giveaway," some memento of the program that ideally reinforces and supports the skills/knowledge it delivered. An example is a handy pocket calculator, perhaps with an appropriate slogan or logo, for a program on budget procedures. A clear plastic paperweight with a computer chip embedded in it might remind people of a technology program. Canvas carrying bags, writing pad folders, photographs or certificates, pens—the possibilities are limited only by the imagination and creativity of the program's designers and the funds at their disposal. If there is such a giveaway, program administrators must make certain that they are available in sufficient quantity and present in the classroom when needed.
- Consumable supplies: Paper, pads, pens and pencils, erasers, colored markers, paper clips, rubber bands, Post-it Notes, and anything similar that the program requires. Some of these items will be called for by specific exercises or games within the program, and some are just general supplies potentially needed by people in a learning situation. Making sure enough of such supplies are on hand for a program should always be an item on an administrative checklist.

One final note about program supplies. They offer the opportunity for volume purchasing, which can provide significant savings for an organization. Every effort should be made to aggregate generically needed materials for purchase so as to obtain the best price possible. And every effort should be exerted in program design to use materials and tools that are generically available.

Step 5: Preparing the Physical Facilities—Site and Equipment

Appropriate, comfortable physical facilities and working equipment are all important support considerations. People learn best in settings that are conducive to the task. Learners should be able to concentrate on program content rather than on a lack of ventilation, missing chairs, or malfunctioning projectors. Learning activities such as lectures, role plays, or small group work dictate appropriate room arrangements and seating. Careful attention to these sorts of details results in comfortable facilities and equipment that performs as expected. The administrative task here is to ensure that the physical facilities are set up as called for in the Leader's Guide, which typically includes a facilities layout plan and an equipment list as part of its program documentation.

Kicking the Tires

We have already seen a checklist for equipment (see Figure 10-5). The program administrator should not only see to it that the equipment is provided as called for, but also that it is in good working order. On the program's first day, the administrator will test the projectors and the computers, check that the right pads are on the flip chart easels, and make sure the magic markers actually write. He or she will verify that the correct handouts, visuals, and films are in the room and that the proper binders are at the participants' places. He or she will also check the name tags and table tent cards, if supplied, and check the ventilation and the lighting. All of these steps—the training version of kicking the tires on a used car—are something the experienced instructor will want to do as well. It may well be that the administrator can leave them entirely to the instructor. The point is that the checking has to be done, on the spot and in detail, so that participants can learn as effortlessly as possible and so that the instructor can instruct as planned.

Principles and Issues

For reference purposes, facilities plans are offered here for the most common program formats and delivery approaches. Decisions about facilities are part of program design and development, and a layout similar to one of the following is to be expected in the Leader's Guide. In reviewing the facility choices listed below, consider the following principles and issues:

- The role of tables. A table is useful for reading or writing. However, it may be a barrier between the instructor and training participants and/or among the participants themselves. Consider how you feel in a group where tables (or desks) are available—and when they are not.
- The position of the program facilitator. Should the trainer sit or stand? Is a lectern needed? Should the trainer be in front of the group or behind it? Is the trainer *part* of the group or its leader? Can everyone see the trainer? Can everyone see the audiovisual materials?
- How to provide for break-out groups. Large groups often need to separate into small discussion or task groups. Depending upon the size of the main facility, these small groups can meet in specified corners of it or move as a group to another nearby room to perform a task.
- How many chairs are needed? The answer to this question is to have *exactly* enough chairs for everyone—no more, no less—so there is room for all, but no obviously missing persons. Most facilities will ensure that extra chairs are available—but out of sight—to add as needed.
- The desirability of seating instructions. Most programs establish that participants know they are welcome—and expected—by providing name tags and/or tent cards as nameplates. This I.D. material can be preprinted or left blank for participants to fill in with markers. Name tags and tent cards are particularly valuable when participants do not know each other, and are usually a great help to the program facilitator. They ease introductions, help break the ice, and make it easier to mingle. Tent cards can be provided for

participants who then pick their own seats, or they can be pre-placed at specified seats to manage who sits where and with whom.

Room Arrangements for Lectures

By definition, learners in a lecture setting have low involvement with each other. Contact with the lecturer is often limited to a question-and-answer period. It is important that learners be able to see and hear the trainer. Any support equipment—flip charts, overhead projectors, VCRs, and the like—should likewise be easily accessed. Any number of different seating arrangements may be appropriate. Figure 10-6a shows sample seating arrangements for lectures for different size groups and various support technologies. Figure 10-6b shows a sample seating arrangement for panel discussions.

FIGURE 10-6 A&B
ROOM ARRANGEMENTS FOR LECTURES AND PANELS
FIGURE 10-6A SEATING CONFIGURATIONS FOR LECTURE GROUPS

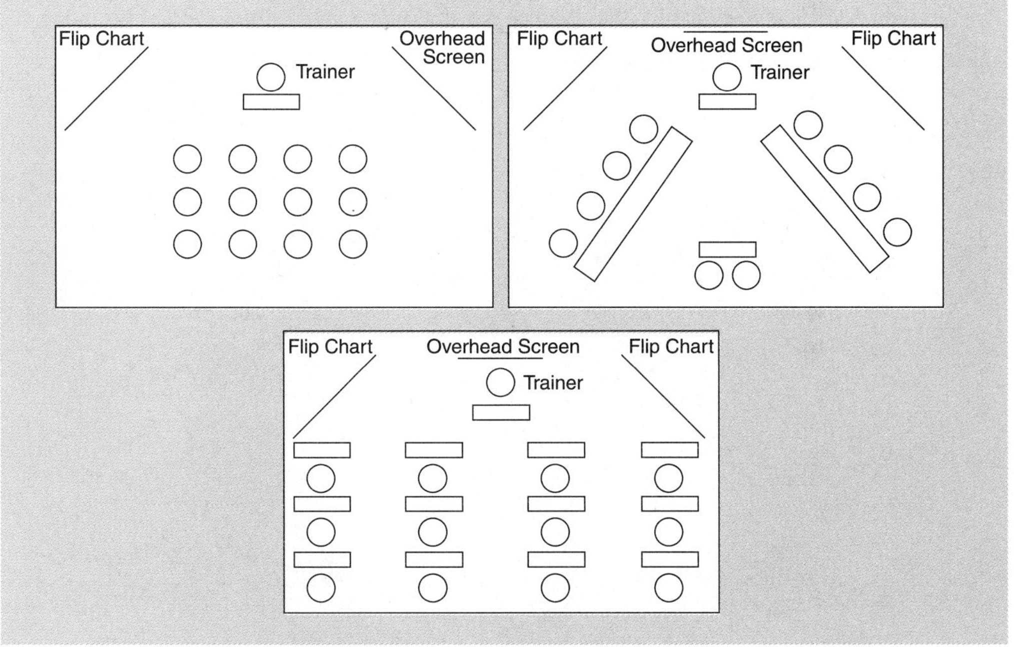

Figure 10-6b Seating Configurations for Panel Discussions

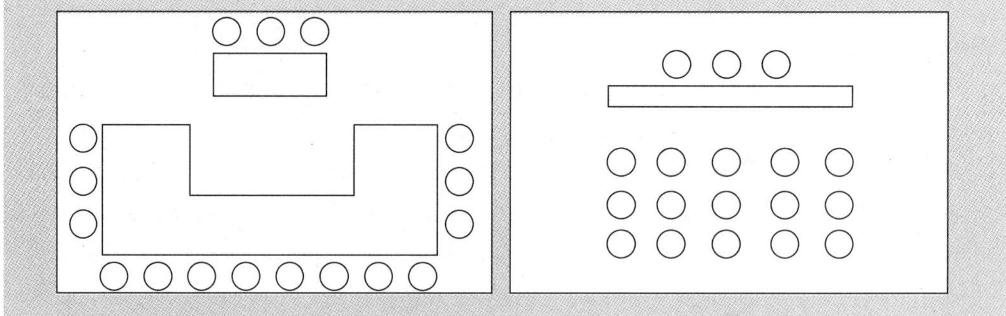

Room Arrangements for Small-Group Work

Small-group work can be used as a lecture break or as the primary instructional method. In small groups, trainer contact varies, depending upon the task at hand. As Figure 10-7 shows, in some instances a trainer takes a strong leadership role, and in such cases the trainer and his or her support tools must be easily seen. In other instances, the trainer becomes part of the group, and line of sight is not an important issue.

Figure 10-7
Seating Configurations for Small-Group Work

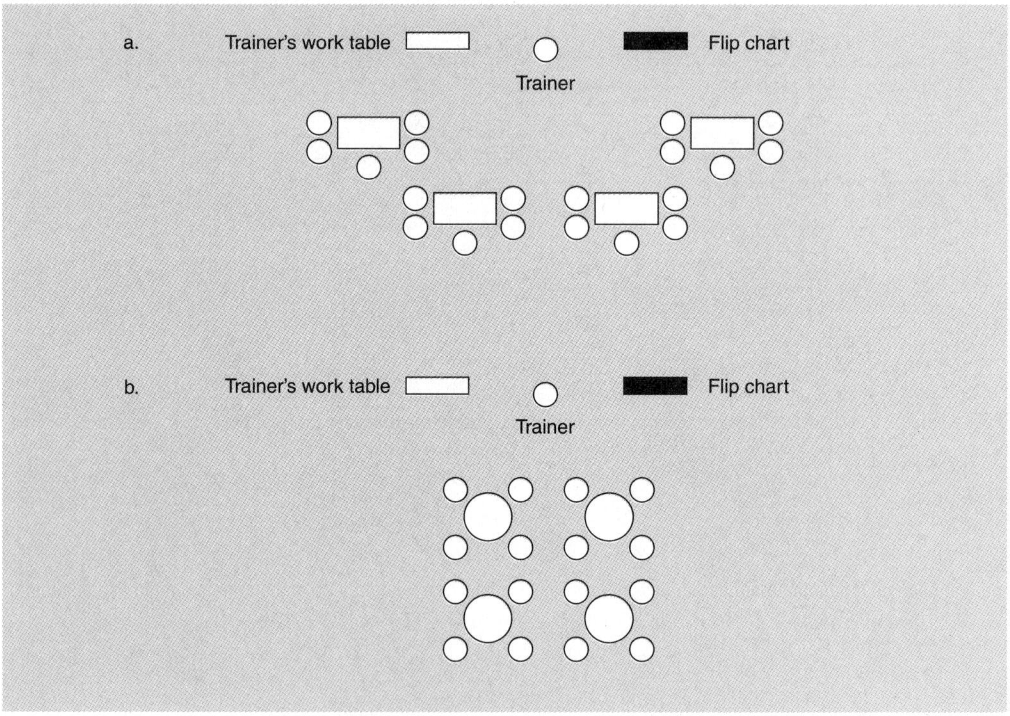

a. Trainer's work table Trainer Flip chart

b. Trainer's work table Trainer Flip chart

Room Arrangements for Problem-Solving Sessions

Problem-solving sessions require high involvement on the part of participants. Whether or not the trainer is a team member or a group facilitator is an important variable that dictates the location of tables and chairs. Figure 10-8 shows seating arrangements illustrating these points.

FIGURE 10-8
SEATING CONFIGURATIONS FOR PROBLEM-SOLVING SESSIONS

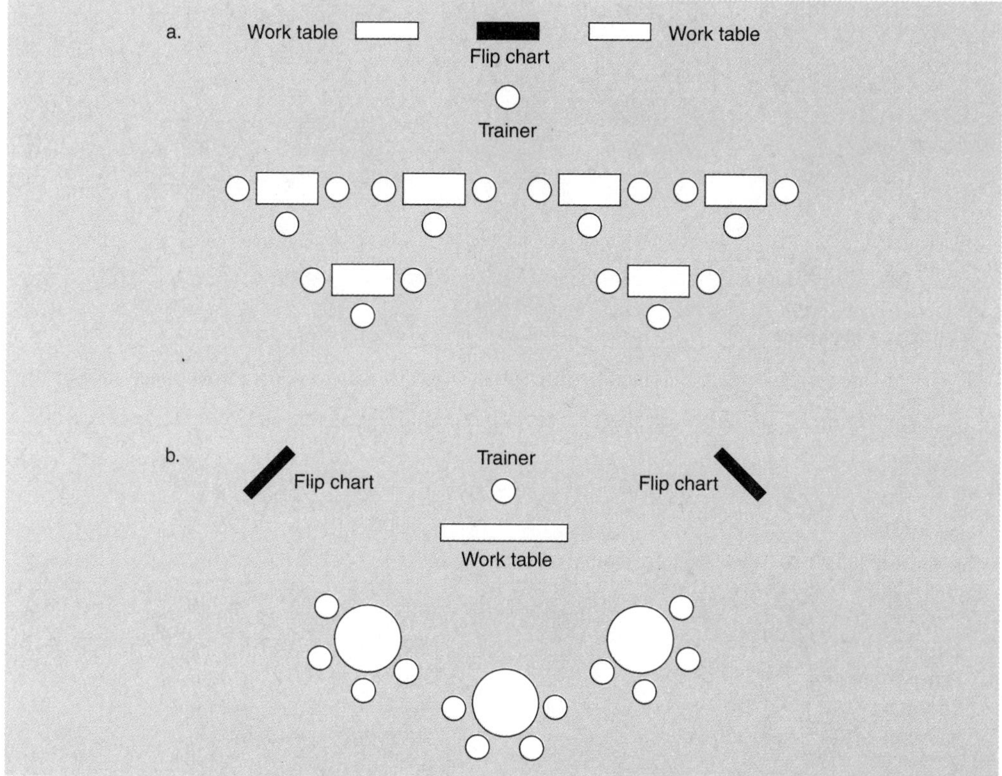

Room Arrangements When Computers Are Used

In addition to these traditional arrangements, when participants each use a computer—either as the basis for what they are learning or as the basis for group processes—additional care must be taken to provide space for the equipment. Figure 10-9 is an example of such an arrangement. Another consideration in designing computer training rooms is whether or not the trainer needs to—or should—see the participant's computer screen. If the session were a course on desktop publishing, the trainer would want full view. However, if the group were using group support systems, a trainer's view of screens could affect participant anonymity.

FIGURE 10-9
SEATING ARRANGEMENTS WHEN COMPUTERS ARE BEING USED

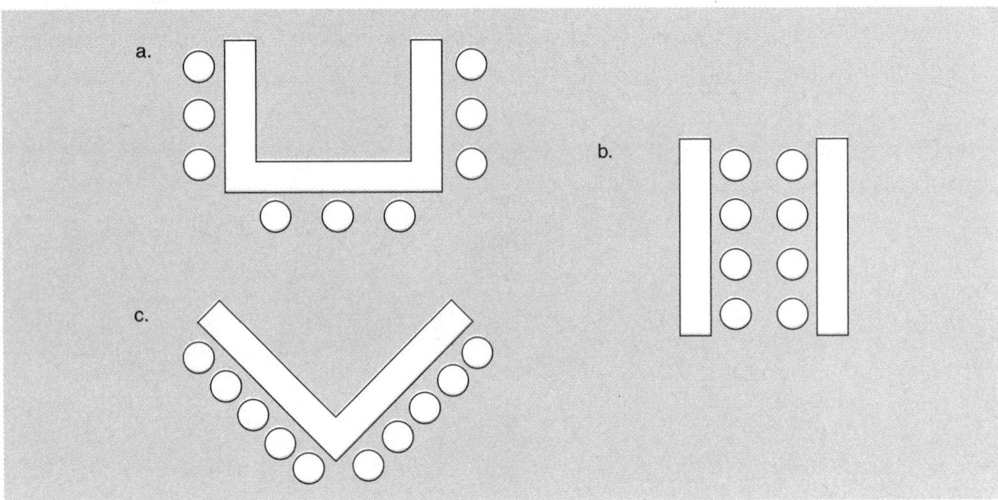

A Facilities Checklist

One way to be sure that facilities are set up correctly is to develop a work sheet, such as the one in Figure 10-10. This work sheet serves as a reminder list as well as a completion check-off sheet.

FIGURE 10-10
A SAMPLE CHECKLIST TO ASSIST FACILITY ADMINISTRATION

ADMINISTRATION GUIDE

Client: Contact:
Program Name: Date:
Location:
Number of Participants: Number of Instructors:

Facilities Checklist

____ Main Conference Room (MCR)
____ Lounge(s)
____ Break-out room(s) (BR 1…2…3) to accommodate___ teams of____ people.
____ Instructor office
____ Telephone in instructor office
____ Wall clock in main conference room

Equipment Checklist

	MCR	BR1	BR2	BR3
____ Flip chart easel	____	____	____	____
____ Flip chart paper				
blank	____	____	____	____
grided	____	____	____	____

(Continued)

Figure 10-10 (Continued)

____	VCR (3/4")/monitor	____	____	____	____
____	VCR (1/2")/monitor	____	____	____	____
____	Camera	____	____	____	____
____	Microphone				
	table/floor	____	____	____	____
	lavalier	____	____	____	____
____	Blank videotape cassette (90 minutes)	____	____	____	____
____	Audiotape recorder	____	____	____	____
____	Blank audiotapes (90 minutes)	____	____	____	____
____	35 mm slide projector and screen	____	____	____	____
____	Remote control	____	____	____	____
____	Overhead projector and screen	____	____	____	____
____	Blank transparencies	____	____	____	____
____	Transparancy markers	____	____	____	____
____	Computer	____	____	____	____
____	Data projection device	____	____	____	____
____	Printer	____	____	____	____

Standard Materials		Number
____	Pens /Pencils	____
____	Writing pads	____
____	Participant binders	____
____	Participant registration forms	____
____	Felt tip markers	____
____	Masking tape	____
____	Pencil sharpener	____
____	Stapler/staples	____
____	Post-it note pads	____
____	Thumb tacks	____
____	Paper clips	____
____	Scissors	____
____	Rubber cement	____
____	Ruler	____

Special Materials

____ Prepared flip charts
____ Timer
____ Instructional game files
____ Shoelaces (#   )
____ Popsicle sticks, bunches (#   )
____ Videotape(s) Name: ______________________________
____

____ Case(s) Name: ______________________________
____
____

Room set-up diagram (provide separate sheet)

Step 6: Supporting the Actual Delivery of Instruction

Logistical responsibilities are usually completed for the most part once a program gets underway. There are times, however, when delivery requires a certain amount of ongoing support. The requirements here are generally rather light, not very demanding, and not of the same order of magnitude as the pre-program support.

A program of mediated instruction, for example, will require the administrator to make sure the needed self-study materials are available according to schedule: the next videotape is on hand, or the next workbook, or the next reading assignment. Indeed it is often an administrator who actually schedules self-study facilities, equipment, and materials. Programs of live instruction sometimes also require an administrator's assistance—to tally some data, to operate a handheld video, to set up a movie, or to provide certain materials just at the right time.

One particular in-program requirement deserves a bit of attention. Live program administration often entails taking care of food and drink. This is usually not a requirement for mediated instructional programs, but most live programs offer participants refreshments at breaks, often lunch of some sort, maybe a continental breakfast, and even perhaps a cocktail hour or formal dinner on an evening or two. This component of training support will vary from program to program, and from one organization to another. Whatever the specifics are, however, the task here is quite straightforward, and many organizations have a cafeteria or food service of some kind where an administrator can turn to provide whatever is necessary. Once again, the administrative necessity is making sure adequate planning is done and that what has been planned is implemented efficiently.

Step 7: Supporting Evaluation

Chapters 3 and 4 detail a wide variety of tools and techniques for conducting evaluations of training and ensuring that those who can benefit from evaluation data have access to it. There is an administrative role in a training department's evaluation efforts.

The most common form of evaluation is asking program participants for their reactions to a program they have just completed. Obviously, it is an administrative responsibility to include the appropriate evaluation form in the program's materials. The form itself, if it is program-specific, will have been created by the design team as part of its generation of program materials. Sometimes a training department will want the evaluation forms completed by program participants to be summarized in a report. The same can be said of follow-up evaluations collected from program graduates after they have returned to their jobs and had some time to use the knowledge or skills acquired in training. Figure 10-11 shows a summary of evaluations collected at the end of a program. The example demonstrates how ratings are averaged, as well as how participant comments are captured verbatim.

Figure 10-11
Evaluation Summary

1. ***Please rate each of the following items to indicate your reaction to the session. If rank is less than average, please comment on the back of the form.***

	Poor	Adequate	Average	Good	Excellent
Program Content (Concepts, facts, skills, procedures, knowledge, etc.):				7	5
Applicability to your job, responsibilities and needs:				10	2
Sufficiency of examples and chances to practice in order that you be able to apply new skills or knowledge back at work:			2	9	1
Use of activities and materials in order that learning be easy and enjoyable:			1	9	2
Opportunity for discussion with other participants to exchange experience and ideas:			3	5	4
Length of the program relative to its objectives and the needs of the group:		1	3	7	1
Appropriateness of pre-session information, materials, directions. Did you know what to expect?:			9	3	

2. ***Which part of the program was of most value to you? Why?***

(7) **The Acumen feedback-**
- The Acumen feedback gave insight of what I do and what my subordinates expect
- Lots of interesting comments and solutions were thrown out
- Hear what staff expect and find areas to improve
- Able to start to refocus and address relevant issues
- Understand my perceived weakness by myself and the subordinates so that I can identify area for improvement
- The Acumen data discussion is useful to analyze our skill
- Since it gives me a chance to look into myself, and how my people think about me

(5) **Role Play**
- The role play cases helped better understanding to the organizational issues
- Stimulate interaction and prompt new practice
- The various role plays which are interesting, provocative and relevant

(Continued)

Figure 10-11 (Continued)

- Case study and role play are valuable to me to understand better
- Give a chance to see how others use different approaches

(I) **Managing Upwards** - my role requires substantial involvement in key issues for the trade business in a changing market
(I) **The references materials** which are comprehensive.
(I) **Group discussion** about each individual's observation on each other because can listen with really open mind
(I) **Group discussions** -all the behaviors of the teammates are clearly exhibited because of the assignment

3. ***Which part of the program was of the least value to you? Why?***

(I) **Case Studies** - Gotham/Star War
- Too hypothetical, comments from participants are easier said than done.

(I) **Managing Individual Performance** - too little time
(I) **Skill Model/Visioning** - not clear objective/instruction
(I) **Managing Business Performance -** although I found it very interesting, I'm on the Ops & Sys side and don't really manage a business for revenue generation. On the other hand, I do manage a unit within expense targets and productivity levels
(I) **Growth Model** by different phases - a simplistic way at putting complicated comparison and dynamics
(I) **Team exercise** to act out solutions for Chapman case - don't see the value in it.
(I) The part where we had to discuss our **history and goals**. The time was too short (understandable) and it was difficult to put across your thoughts, visions, ideas with a person whom you met just 3 days back.
(I) **Managing co-workers** - we were a well-known team with the same goals/customer focus.

4a. Please use the following scale to comment on each instructor's ability to lead the program, where:

1=Needs Improvement *2=Adequate* *3=Good* *4=Excellent*

Instructor #1

Item	1	2	3	4	*Avg.*
(A) Organization/preparation of subject matter		2	2	8	3.50
(B) Presentation of subject matter	1	1	2	8	3.42
(C) Clarity of instructions	1		5	6	3.33
(D) Ability to control time			4	8	3.67
(E) Ability to link content to your business	1		9	2	3.00
(F) Ability to stimulate productive discussion			7	5	3.42
(G) Ability to create a productive learning environment	1	2	5	6	3.42

(Continued)

Figure 10-11 (Continued)

Instructor #2					
Item	1	2	3	4	Avg.
(A) Organization/preparation of subject matter			3	9	3.75
(B) Presentation of subject matter			3	9	3.75
(C) Clarity of instructions			4	8	3.67
(D) Ability to control time			3	10	3.77
(E) Ability to link content to your business			9	3	3.25
(F) Ability to stimulate productive discussion			6	6	3.50
(G) Ability to create a productive learning environment			5	7	3.58

4b. Please add your comments on the instructor's ability to lead the program.

(I) I was skeptical coming in and enlightened going out! Both instructors did well in helping me overcome my skepticism
(I) Generally both are very experienced
(I) Both the instructors led the program well and as a team
(I) They are really professional on managing this seminar. Really thanks for the things I've learned during this seminar
(I) I learned a lot for the good way to facilitate/lead a meeting/class from the two instructors
(I) Both instructors are excellent facilitators
(6)No comment

	1	2	3	4	Avg.
5. How would you rate the overall reaction to the program?			8	4	3.33
6. How would you rate your level of skill or knowledge?					
a. Before the program		10	2		2.17
b. After the program			10	2	3.17

7. ***Other Comments:***

(I) Very good learning experience, esp. productive for the group discussion
(I) It was an excellent experience. A great and rewarding experience
(I) Each countries/LOBs have different cultures and objectives. due to the limited time, I think these differences on managing people/business are not well instructed
(I) Somewhat insufficient time period for the class
(2)Can the program be shortened to 3 days? It lasts too long, 4 days is too long
(I) Need to modify to cope with Chase Vision
(I) Unfortunately I am very tied up by my office work and have not much time to prepare for the case studies. Prefer to attend the course out of town and that with more participants from my LOB to share more relevant experience
(5)No comment

Summaries of participant reactions should not be overvalued, nor should they be dismissed as useless. They should not be viewed as hard, statistical data as they are not scientifically valid. The ratings summarized, after all, simply reflect participant reactions and are only as objectively valid as those reactions. On the other hand, such summaries are a good way to highlight any consistently negative findings among participants with regard to either program design or delivery. A pattern of such negative findings may well indicate areas where training management needs to make some changes. Such a pattern may also trigger a memo to participants thanking them for their feedback and explaining changes made on the basis of it.

The other forms of training evaluation discussed in Chapter 3 deal with the training outcomes of learning, job behavior, organizational results, training department process. Undertaking any of these approaches to evaluation means mounting a formal project to do so. The administrative staff in a training department should certainly expect to play a role in such projects. A typical administrative support role would include contacting people, mailing materials, taking notes, capturing data, tracking project progress, etc.

THE TRAINING BUDGET

Creating and controlling a budget for training is a major administrative responsibility for the training manager. The budget covers all the phases of the training cycle (See Figure 1-7), with funds requested to carry out the cycle in a particular budget year. The actual budget—the funds granted in response to this request—reflects the organization's appetite for training, how much of its resources it is prepared to devote to training as the means for its people to learn what they need. It is thus crucially important that training management work hard and continuously to position training in the minds of its internal customers as support for learning, not merely as the source of classroom programs; not just as the department where teaching is done, but as the management resource that helps employees learn what the organization needs them to learn and helps that learning occur faster, cheaper, easier, and better.

When budget cutbacks occur, the received, cynical wisdom among trainers is that training money is the first thing to get cut. This is often true. It is also often only half the story. Cuts to the training budget are frequently followed by another phenomenon. Later on, after the cutbacks are over, if the organization needs people to learn something—if there is a clear need for training—the dollars for it will somehow be found. They may come out of the supplies budget, they may be drawn from contingency money, they may come from a manager's discretionary fund, *but the dollars will be found!* The unmistakable lesson in this is that when learning is clearly seen to be needed, it will be funded. Needless to say, the time for training management to argue that its function is to enable and maximize learning is *not* when budget cuts are announced. The point should be made constantly, on a noncrisis basis, and above all should be backed up by a track record that makes the argument more strongly than any words can.

Centralized and Decentralized Approaches

Organizations allocate funds to training in basically two different ways. Sometimes all the dollars for training are placed in a central budget, to be dispersed in the most efficient way possible by training management for the organization as a whole. Sometimes an organization decentralizes its training funds. The training department is allocated enough money to run itself—to pay its people and its overhead, and buy supplies, services, and space. The money necessary to pay for actual programs, on the other hand, is put in the budgets of line departments, which then pay for training as needed. In this latter scenario, the training department typically charges internally for its services, a process usually called a *chargeback*. The chargeback can be simply a proportionate per-participant share of the cost of running a particular program, or it can be a fixed cost the training department establishes as a kind of tuition.

The centralized approach to the training budget is generally more efficient in terms of program planning, rollout, and resource planning/usage, and is certainly the approach to be used when the training department is organized as a teaching faculty. The focus of the decentralized approach is effectiveness rather than efficiency. It has the advantage of putting the money where the learning need is. This helps ensure that what the training does is what the line departments, see as needed. They, after all, have the money! In the decentralized approach, the training department tends to be organized as internal training consultants, training analysts, and brokers.

Strategic Funding

In either case, especially in the decentralized approach where a short-term focus can all too easily prevail, training management should set aside money for *strategic training* (See Chapter 1 for a full discussion of strategic training). There are things people need to learn that offer no immediate, short-term payback. These include entry-level training to feed the talent pipeline, orientation to the organization's culture, awareness of other departments and projects, and the learning necessary for infrastructural programs that lay the groundwork for future organizational growth—e.g., new buildings, new technologies, or new products. This kind of learning is most effectively funded by a training budget under the control of management at a senior enough level to appreciate the need for, and value of, strategic initiatives. The learning demanded by these kinds of organizational requirements will be supported by a *strategic* perspective, not the short-term, business results-oriented focus of operational line management. Thus, budget authority for strategic training should be lodged with strategic management.

Budget Categories

There are no hard and fast rules concerning the proper *budget categories* for training, sometimes referred to as *budget accounts* or the *chart of accounts*. Organizations define and set up categories in a wide variety of ways. The following list of budget categories are those used in a recent calendar year for the annual budget of a typical training department. Every organization has its own terminology for budgeted items and its own way of categorizing items, and the categories themselves can change over time. However, the list that follows is a representative sample of the types of expenses a manager of training needs to provide for in a training department's budget. Each budget category is briefly discussed to clarify its meaning. No attempt will be made to offer guidance as to sample dollar figures for these categories, since appropriate amounts are a function of time, place, and circumstance.

Sample Training Budget Categories

1. **Salaries:** The annual salaries paid to members of the training department. This budget category is often subdivided into clerical support staff as distinct from trainers. Sometimes managers are split out from the whole. Sometimes full-time workers are handled distinct from part-timers. Funds for temporary workers can be included here, or may be put in the consultant category.
2. **Benefits:** The cost of benefits—e.g., paid vacation, health and life insurance—provided to its employees. This is, typically a percentage of salary determined by the organization's financial controllers or its benefits staff.
3. **Staff Development:** The cost of professional development for the members of the training department. This is partially an aggregate of the individual development plans of department members. Money is also often added for development deemed necessary by management for needs which are not a function of individual development interests. An example of this is funding for the training necessary to put new desktop software into all the department's workstations, a step that necessitates retraining everyone from old software to new. This category also includes memberships in professional associations, subscriptions to professional journals, and attendance at conferences.
4. **Recruiting:** Agency fees and any other costs associated with hiring new people. Other costs included here are travel for candidates or recruiters, as well as recruiting brochures and other marketing material.
5. **Consultants:** Fees paid to consultants for work in the department, plus applicable travel expenses. These costs are often put in subcategories that reflect the purpose for which consultants are hired: design, delivery, evaluation, a specific project or program, etc.

6. **Furniture and Equipment:** The cost of adding, replacing, repairing, or renting furniture or equipment for use in the training department or its programs. Note that an organization typically has rules and procedures to determine if a piece of equipment or furniture is a capital expense or not. If an item is treated as capital (e.g., a large-scale, sophisticated copier), then the annual depreciation for it is included here. Computers are included here; software is sometimes here, sometimes in a separate category. (Hardware and software are sometimes treated as capital expenditures.)
7. **Occupancy:** The cost of the building space occupied by the training department. Very often included here are heat, light, and ventilation. This is usually a nondiscretionary item, the amount supplied by internal accounting or the building department.
8. **Marketing:** Money the training department spends to advertise itself and its programs. An example is a brochure used for a desk drop or given out as part of new-hire orientation.
9. **Communications:** The cost of telephones—equipment, repair, calls—as well as fax equipment and supplies, E-mail, memberships in public networks or news wires, and all usage charges.
10. **Supplies:** The pad, pencils, and other sundry items the department needs for members to function. Supplies for programs and supplies for staff are often divided into separate subcategories.
11. **Postage:** The cost of the department's outgoing mail, with special attention to express courier costs and the shipping of program materials.
12. **Travel:** Travel expenses incurred by department members in the conduct of business.
13. **Entertainment:** The costs involved in providing food and refreshment for training programs, hosting guests of the department, or perhaps interviewing job candidates or potential consultants.

Once budgeted funds are allocated to the appropriate categories, the training department uses these same categories to track spending across the year. A spreadsheet report is typically generated each month that lists the categories, shows the annual budget amount for each, the spending in the category done in the current month, plus the year-to-date aggregate and the balance left for the remainder of the year. Final columns in the spreadsheet are often a calculation of whether the year-to-date figures are over or under what they should be, plus a forecast of what the final spending in the category will be. All organizations have policies, methods, formats, and forms established for tracking and reporting financial data, and a training manager should simply follow the organization's lead in these areas. Reported financial information is a tool for the customary management decisions: slow down spending or speed it up, reallocate funds from one category to another, analyze the reasons for the spending level in a category of particular interest. Most organizations, for example, keep a very watchful eye on consultant costs.

Estimating Costs

One final budget issue is that of estimating the cost of particular programs. Figure 10-12 shows a blank program cost estimation spreadsheet.

Note that the categories of program expense provided here form a generic template. Not all costs are necessarily used for every program. Note also how the estimation sheet aggregates expenses in the larger categories of variable, fixed, and total costs, and provides an estimate of cost per offering ("open session," on the work sheet.) Actual dollar figures must be plugged into this work sheet. The figures will be a function of time, location, and economic conditions.

The data that go into the costing spreadsheet will also vary depending on program type. The idea is to use the line items in the costing sheet that reflect the actual factors involved in the program being costed. There will be money needed for an instructor in live programs, but not in purchased Web-based programs. There will be no vendor package in a self-study guide developed completely in-house.

Note finally that this cost estimation template does not include trainee salaries as part of the cost of a program. Some organizations add trainee salaries to program costs, arguing that including their salaries gives a true and complete picture of what training actually costs. Other organizations ignore trainee salaries on the grounds that the trainees would be paid anyway, whether they are in training or not, and thus their pay should not be viewed as a true training cost. The important thing is that a cost estimation work sheet reflect the particular organization's decisions on costing issues. The work sheet then can put structure and consistency into the establishment of costs for budget requests. The cost estimations may well get more accurate with time and experience. They will clearly benefit from the structure of a common cost estimation template.

TRAINING DEPARTMENT REPORTS

On some regular basis, usually monthly, a training department will report its program activity. Programs are listed, perhaps in appropriate categories of training, with totals shown for each category and for the department as a whole. The report typically details the number of programs and participants for each program and category listed. Cancellations and costs are also sometimes included. Figure 10-13 shows a sample of such a training activity report. The report was produced in September of a particular year, and shows activity as of that month ("YTD"—year-to-date) against the year's plan as a whole ("Plans"), including program activity where none was planned. The report also shows the current estimate of program activity by the end of the year— "Current Year Forecast."

Figure 10-12
Program Costing Work Sheet

		ITEM COST	# for yr	Tot Yr Estimated $
1.	Product: skeleton		0	
2.	Lgth (dys)		0	
3.	# sessions		0	
4.	#'p's desired @ session		0	
5.				
6.	total year's expected p's		0	
7.				
8.		ITEM COST	# for yr	Tot Yr Estimated $
9.	**VARIABLE COSTS**			
10.	**Consultant costs**			
11.	Instructor Fee	$0	0	0
12.	T&E Costs	$0	0	0
13.	Video Ass't	$0	0	0
14.	Other	$0	0	0
15.	Tot Consultant Costs			$0
16.				
17.	**Supplies**			
18.	Binder/Repro		0	$0
19.	Giveaways		0	$0
20.	Vendor Package	$0	0	$0
21.	Videotapes		0	$0
22.	Other	$0	0	$0
23.	**Tot Supplies**			
24.				
25.	Post/Ship	$0	0	$0
26.	Followup/reinf	$0	0	$0
27.	Evaluation	$0	0	$0
28.	Other	$0	0	$0
29.	Contingency	$0	0	$0
20.	**TOT VARIABLE COSTS**	$0	0	$0
31.				
32.				
33.	FIXED COSTS			
34.	Video/Film			$0
35.	Software			$0
36.	License			$0
37.	New Binder/Pkg.			$0
38.	Other			$0
39.	**TOT FIXED COSTS**			$0
40.				
31.	***TOT YEAR EST COSTS***			$0
42.				
43.	Tot # P's expected this year			$0
44.				
45.	RAW COST (cost/tot # p's)			
46.				
47.				
48.	ADJUSTMENT +/-			$0
49.				
50.	**OPEN SESSION COST**			$0

Figure 10-13
Training Activity Report

Individual Development Portfolio

Programs	This Years' Plans # pgms	# ptcpts	Year-to-Date 9/30 # pgms	#ptcpts	Current Year Forecast 12/31 # pgms	# ptcpts
1. Presentation Skills	22	176	17	121	23	169
2. Instructional Skills	6	48	8	66	9	80
3. Writing Skills	4	96	5	95	7	131
4. Managing Personal Growth	6	144	4	81	6	114
5. Negotiations Skills	6	108	5	80	7	112
6. Influence Skills	6	96	5	75	8	127
7. Responsible Decision Making	0	0	3	48	3	48
8. Equity at Work	6	100	6	99	6	99
	56	668	53	665	69	880
	Projected Programs and Participants		Actuals Year-to-Date		End-of-Year Forecasts	

The value of this kind of report is that it is a tracking tool for training management. It enables managers to view training efforts against plans and against the expected future. Are programs going as planned, and if not, why not? The report can be used to map activities against priorities and adjust resources accordingly. It permits a manager to calculate ratios like cost-per-program day or participants-per-staff member. These kinds of ratios serve as useful measures of efficiency and productivity, especially when measured consistently against data from previous calendar periods.

It is important to remember that these reports have to do with activities, not results. While activity must be tracked and controlled, the real training issue is always the impact of training results on the organization's functioning: Do training outcomes affect the organization's operation? Do they help people do their jobs and grow their careers? Do they move the organization in planned/desired directions?

One very useful report of results is a training transcript. The training department should be able to produce transcripts of training completed by individual employees, information helpful for career planning and tracking by individuals and their managers. Figure 10-14 shows a sample transcript from Pathlore's *Registrar* registration system.

FIGURE 10-14
SAMPLE TRANSCRIPT

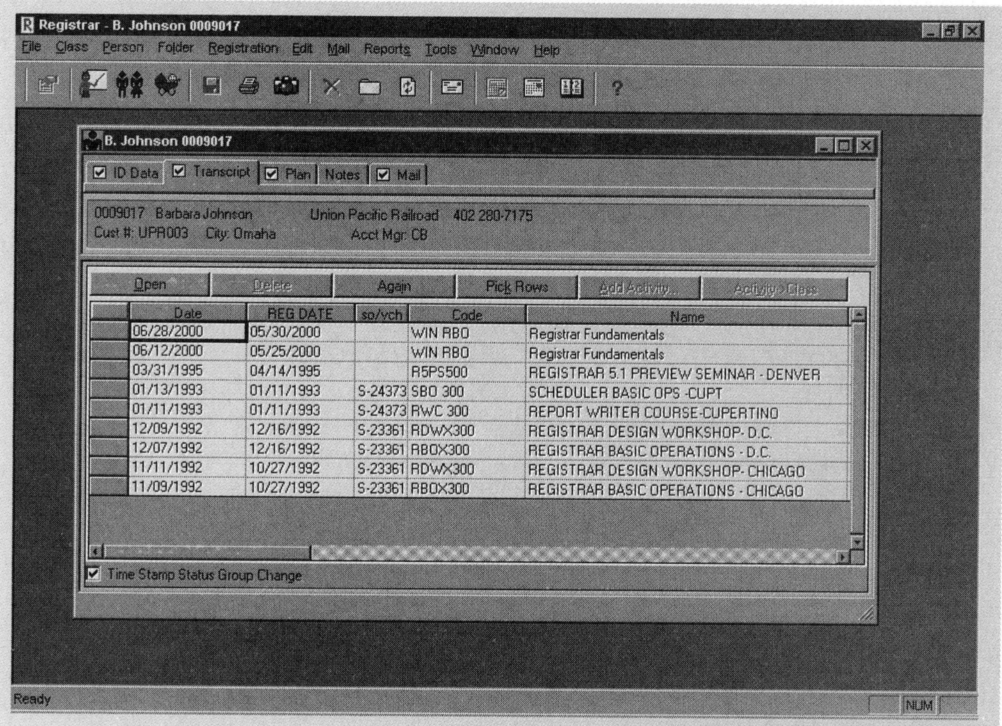

The production of a transcript is a simple matter for the kind of registration systems mentioned previously. These systems also have the capability of providing training records for input to a central employee file. When the organization has more than a single training department, the matter of centralizing training data must be given careful thought. The issue is one of values and priorities—a cultural and organizational decision, not a technical one. Does the organization want training data to be kept centrally? The benefit of doing so is that information about training accomplished by an individual, a particular department, or the organization as a whole is readily available. The growth of Knowledge Management and the Corporate University will highlight the value of capturing data about skills and knowledge all across the organization.

When the answer to the above question is no, training data are left decentralized, making it harder to get an organization-wide picture of training. Some organizations decide that it is simply not worth the collective effort necessary to create and maintain a centralized training database on an ongoing basis.

Another dimension of training reports has to do with business results. Have the sales training programs had an impact on sales? Are sales up? Has the product development cycle moved faster following the introduction of automated design tools and the training in how to use them? Has the number of customer complaints dropped since we introduced the new training program in customer service?

These are ultimately the kinds of questions to which training management will want to respond. The answers depend on making sure that these outcomes are specified up front, at the planning and design stages of training. Looking for these kinds of results must also be done with the awareness that many factors can contribute to an increase in sales or a decrease in defects. While a results-orientation is the ultimate bottom line for training, care must be exercised to ensure claims are realistic. Reports concerning business results based on training are best done by gathering impact data from trainees and their managers a month or two after training completion. These reports are not usually statistical work sheets of numbers in columns. They are the thoughtful gathering and analysis of best judgments from trainees, their managers, and their clients—best judgments concerning training effects. See Chapter 3, Evaluating Organizational Training, for a fuller discussion of follow-up evaluation strategies.

SUMMARY

The administration of training is an important responsibility, essential to training success. This chapter described the Training Administration Sequence, a comprehensive set of steps that can be followed—or adapted—to ensure that the administrative side of training is handled efficiently and effectively. The sequence begins with informing prospective participants of program availability, which can be done in many different ways involving both paper and electronic media. Administration includes registration and all that is involved with it: wait lists, cancellations, participant communications, and the use of registration software systems.

Training program prework, which comes in a wide variety of types and differing levels of complexity, requires intense, detailed attention from those responsible for program support. The program administrator must also prepare instructional materials, prepare the physical facilities, and provide necessary support as instruction is actually delivered. The final step in the administrative sequence requires support for the evaluation of training. The chapter advocates the use of checklists to manage the level of detail necessary for most administrative tasks.

The chapter concludes with a discussion of the training budget, followed by a discussion of training reports. The training budget is an important administrative issue. Its creation is typically the responsibility of the training manager. Its tracking and reporting are tasks taken on by support personnel. Different budgeting philosophies—centralized vs. decentralized—are explained, as are the issues of cost chargebacks and strategic funding. Representative budget categories are discussed, and a sample work sheet for estimating the cost of a particular program is included. Training reports are also explained in terms of activities and results. The value and limitations of both kinds of reports are discussed, and samples of each are provided.

THINK IT THROUGH

1. What experiences have you had where physical surroundings played a major part in the success or failure of the experience itself? (a party? a job? a restaurant dinner? a class? other?) How did the physical facilities impact the outcome?
2. What benefits to the learner (training's customer) does good program administration provide?
3. Describe how the logistical needs of mediated instruction vary from live instruction. Which is generally more complex? Why?
4. Why do you think people involved in training program design and development should give thought to training administration? What sort of implications for design are there in the logistical support that will realistically be available once a program begins to roll out?
5. Give some thought to a centralized training budget vs. decentralized. What do you see as the major difference between the two approaches? Which appeals to you? Why?

IDEAS IN ACTION

1. Identify a training administrator at a local organization and invite this individual to come talk to your class concerning the work that goes into the logistical support of training. Ask to see reports the administrator is responsible for preparing, and discuss how these reports are used.

2. Consider the impact the following have on your classes in school: janitorial or cleaning services, food service, security, housing. Talk with a teacher of your choice, and ask that teacher to tell you of any experience he or she has had in which administrative service has had an impact on teaching, for good or ill. Prepare a report on your discussion for class. Draw an analogy with the support services discussed in this chapter as typically available to a training department.
3. Research current training literature to identify the computer software available to automate registration. Contact a sample of the vendors of this software to obtain demonstration packages and show them in class.
4. Identify in the training literature any other administrative software that appears interesting and prepare a report on its benefits to be discussed in class. (Do *not* include authoring or presentation software—confine your focus to software that a training administrator would use.)

ADDITIONAL RESOURCES

RECOMMENDED READINGS

Greer, Michael. *The Manager's Pocket Guide to Project Management.* Amherst, MA: HRD Press, 2000.

This inexpensive paperback book includes a set of useful work sheets, guidelines, and checklists in support of project management tasks.

Nilson, Carolyn. *Training Workbook and Kit.* Englewood Cliffs, NJ: Prentice Hall, 1989.

An excellent source of generic training forms and checklists, with intelligent discussion of the procedures that go with them. A bit dated, but a first-rate source book.

WEB SITES

www.my.placeware.com

This is a Web site that offers free conferencing services for trainers, including administrative support personnel working in training. You can basically gather a professional group to discuss professional issues around specific training topics, administrative or otherwise.

www.officeclick.com

This is a portal for administrative professionals. While it is not focused specifically on work in training departments, it deals with issues that arise there, issues that arise in administrative support work anywhere.

ENDNOTE

1. The term *administration* in this chapter refers to the routine back-office work done in support of training, as distinguished from front-end delivery, the actual instruction. As used here, administration does not mean—as it often does in academic circles—the leadership or executive management of an institution.

CHAPTER

The Trainer as Change Agent

- Explain the role of training professionals as change agents in planned organizational change efforts.
- List major factors that impact the rate of change in organizations.
- Apply force-field analysis to identify pressures and resistance to change.
- Appraise techniques that are helpful in facilitating group processes.
- Summarize the importance of the training professional operating as a full business partner.

INTRODUCTION: UNDERSTANDING THE ROLE OF A CHANGE AGENT

Organizations are in a continual state of change. Competitive organizations initiate new strategies or reorganize frequently. Pushing for change are critical issues including mergers and acquisitions, global competition, new information and communications technologies, the changing demographics of the workforce, and shifting value systems. These issues give new meaning and urgency to the need for continuous learning in organizations. Michael Hammer took the need for learning one step further in explaining that "Radical change in how work is done inevitably leads to the definition of new jobs with new skill requirements, which in turn demands new kinds of people."[1] In fact, Peter Senge says that in the long run, the only sustainable source of competitive advantage is your organization's ability to learn faster than its competition.[2]

Senge goes on: "How [organizational] development people respond to such issues will depend upon their ability to understand the business, to understand and help manage change, and to master educational and learning processes."[3] The field of organizational development (OD) is all about helping an organization get where it wants to go, and trainers are often called upon to play a role in OD efforts. Any number of strategies are available, including temporary structures and strategies to improve communication processes. OD specialists call planned changes *interventions*; the person who wants the results, the *sponsor*; and the individual or team responsible for designing and implementing interventions, the *change agent*.

A *change agent* is either an individual or a team responsible for designing and implementing an innovation, such as a new technology or a new managerial process. A change agent must help translate the vision of how new ideas, new skills, and new techniques can be translated into step-by-step plans to achieve desired goals.[4] As a change agent, the training professional is an important resource when needed changes deal with modifying the skills, knowledge, and abilities of the workforce. To adapt to these changes, for example, the organization's leaders must be willing and able to put aside management approaches used in the past and learn new techniques that are appropriate for a diverse, global workplace and marketplace. It is likewise important that individuals who are expected to use new information and communications technologies be skilled in their use. In this regard, the training professional works with organizational sponsors and OD specialists and helps ensure that the right people learn the right things in the right way, at the right time, and in the right priority order.

In Chapter 1, the terms *strategic*, *informational*, and *operational* were used as a means to describe the linkages of training strategies to organizational goals. The focus of this chapter is to describe how and when the training professional uses a tool kit of instructional strategies to ensure the learning needed for targeted changes takes place. To plan for organizational learning requires a keen understanding of the content matter to be learned, the individual learners, and the organization. Not surprisingly, training professionals are usually more adept at training program development and delivery, for this is what they are specifically trained to do, than the special managerial skills needed to guide new learning into use by the organization. Even the best of training programs, expertly taught, will not succeed if organizational and environmental factors are not considered and understood.

This chapter serves as a reminder that training is all about *learning*, and that training professionals have an organizational role that goes far beyond that of simply providing instruction. To help understand this role, we describe some important thinking related to understanding the need for systematic planned change efforts and strategies for forming collaborative relationships within the organization. The premise is that training is a business function, and training professionals need to consider themselves key organizational players as well as adult learning and instructional design specialists.

UNDERSTANDING PLANNED ORGANIZATIONAL CHANGE

Learning alters the behavior or job tasks of individuals, groups, or the entire organization. Learning is the goal of training programs, and the application of learning goes beyond the training program itself. Research shows that individuals and organizations typically progress through a number of phases in integrating new ideas (knowledge, skills, or abilities) into their work. A model captures these phases, organizes them, and serves as a reminder of the need for systematic change. Various models have been developed to describe the change process, and most are variations on the basic innovation model:

innovation (the new idea)
↓
infusion (delivery strategies)
↓
assimilation (integration/use of the new innovation)

Progression through the stages of the innovation model is not automatic. Therefore, we offer some useful ways to think about the major issues related to assimilating new learning: the innovation itself, the individuals who are asked to use it, and the organizational culture. Understanding these components helps explain why some change efforts are more complex than others. This section uses Everett Rogers' characteristics of innovations and adopters, as well as N. Dean Meyer's categories of organizational culture that help explain the environment and the rate at which change occurs.

CHARACTERISTICS OF AN INNOVATION

Everett Rogers, in *Diffusion of Innovation* (The Free Press, 1983), explained that characteristics of both the innovation itself and the adopter (user) influence the infusion of an innovation. Rogers argues that the rate of adoption differs depending on the five characteristics of the innovation itself:

relative advantage:	the degree to which the innovation is perceived as better than the idea it supersedes
compatibility:	the degree to which the innovation is perceived as being consistent with existing values and past experiences
complexity:	the degree to which the innovation is considered easy to use and understand
trialability:	the degree to which an innovation may be experimented with
observability:	the degree to which the results of an innovation are visible to others[5]

The higher any innovation can score on these five characteristics, the faster learning will be assimilated into the organization. Likewise, the lower any innovation scores on these characteristics, the more difficult assimilation will be.

Rogers compared two innovations, blue jeans (quick adoption) and the metric system (slow adoption). Describing these innovations by their characteristics, it is easy to see why nearly everyone wears blue jeans but few people in the United States have completely adopted the metric system. Blue jeans offer *relative advantage,* in that they are more comfortable and rugged than other pants. Blue jeans can be worn with almost anything, so they are *compatible* with the way we dress. Because blue jeans are simple to care for, they are not *complex*. Blue jeans are *trialable* as they are inexpensive—at least until designer jeans came along—and they are *observable* since nearly everyone wears them.

The metric system, on the other hand, replaces a system that is still functional, so the system offers little *relative advantage* and is not necessarily *compatible* with the way we have always measured weights and volume. Learning the metric system is *complex*, and its use requires study and practice. The metric system is also difficult to experiment with (*trialability)*, as it requires a major conversion effort. Finally, the metric system does not physically change objects, only the way they are measured, so its benefits are not easily *observable.*

Using these characteristics to describe organizational innovations, it is easy to see why learning how to search the World Wide Web is more readily assimilated than learning how to manage people and processes. While there was a time when only "innovators" or "early adopters" (see the next section) used the Web, today because outcomes of its use are so readily *observable*, nearly everyone uses the Web as a research and learning tool. Accessing the Web holds a *relative advantage* over going through reams of documents or physically visiting a library. Using the Web does not change the need for search skills (skills are *compatible*). Because it is not a *complex* skill, most learners can begin using basic Web searching skills immediately. Often, learners browse the Web for enjoyment, effectively *trying out* the tool before they move to using it for work purposes.

On the other hand, outcomes of training programs designed to alter management skills are not necessarily perceived as better than the old way (little *relative advantage*). Moreover, new managerial skills may not be *compatible* way managers believe people are or should be managed, or compatible with the organizational culture. Management skills are *complex.* To *try out* new skills may be very risky, and managerial skills are often difficult to *observe*. Delegating once closely held duties, for example, can be a risk if the duties are not performed as expected, and this delegation may not be observable to the rest of the management team.

Characteristics of the Adopters

Rogers also suggested that planners should take into consideration the characteristics of individuals who will be using the innovation. The following description of the overall population[6] explains why training programs themselves may be well-received, but their outcomes never achieve their intended productivity benefits. Also, understanding differences among adopters can help training professionals target individuals for pilot programs.

Innovators:	Risk takers. They want to learn everything. They are the first to try something new. They make up 2.5 percent of the population.
Early Adopters:	Hedgers. They wait until the innovators have proven the learning useful, but once its usefulness is shown, they are quick to implement it. They make up 13.5 percent of the population.
Early Majority:	Waiters. They wait until 16 percent of their peers exhibit the new behavior. They make up 34 percent of the population.
Late Majority:	Skeptics. They change their behavior only when it is well accepted by others. They make up 34 percent of the population.
Laggards:	Slowpokes. They change their behavior only when their resistance gets them nowhere. They are set in their ways, and will change only under duress. They make up 16 percent of the population.

You can use these categorical terms to describe yourself and people you know with regard to how quickly software programs are upgraded, Web-based Training is used, or current fashion is followed. For example, consider how long it took bank customers to use automatic teller machines (ATMs). When ATMs were first introduced, few people would use them. It took banks years to gain widespread acceptance for ATMs among their customers. Even today there are people (laggards) who will stand in line to talk to a teller rather than use an ATM, which would almost always allow them to do their banking faster.

Characteristics of the Organization

The rate at which change is assimilated into an organization has also been described in relationship to characteristics of the organization itself. How an innovation is adopted into an organization reflects the organization's culture, which defines jobs, lines of authority, responsibility, accountability, and controls the flow of information. N. Dean Meyer and Associates has researched the impact of corporate culture on change strategies. Following are Meyer's definitions and findings:[7]

Traditional culture. Vertical organizational structure (top-down decision making); large organizational groupings (usually departments) structured around functions. Communications are up and down. The central staff is powerful. Decisions are made high up in the organization. Such organizations are often reluctant to recognize the need for change. Changes are made slowly. There is active resistance to change. The military offers a good example of a traditional culture.

Consensus-driven culture. Wide rather than vertical organizational structure. Decisions are made by a consensus of middle managers. Staff groups are large but do not carry as much authority as line management. A matrix organization is common. Innovations are assigned to task forces or committees. New ideas can get lost in the bureaucracy. Risk taking is limited to senior management and committees. High-tech aerospace industries such as Boeing exemplify a consensus-driven culture.

Profit-center culture. Cluster structure—small, autonomous modules with clearly stated goals. Small central staff. If the innovation is not related to business goals, they reject it, even if the return on investment is good. Overall, favorable toward innovations—payoffs of success are high. Payoffs could include profits and/or promotions. Consumer goods manufacturers, such as Procter and Gamble, illustrate a profit-center culture.

Futurist culture. Small, flat, fluid structure. Characterized by a charismatic executive and organized around a mission or new idea. Decision making occurs at the lowest possible level. Positive toward innovations, but few are implemented successfully; each person has his or her own pet project. These are small, leading-edge, creative organizations. Organizations that are entrepreneurial, such as Apple Computer in its early years, fit into this classification.

Understanding the impact that culture has on acceptance or resistance to innovation can help the trainer plan learning strategies that better ensure infusion. For example, a highly traditional organization may have work rules or policies that actually work against new management practices. To simply provide learning experiences without taking steps to ensure that individuals will be able to use the new skills back on the job would be a fruitless activity. Therefore, regardless of the type of change and culture of the organization, working closely with all stakeholders in a discovery process regarding the need for change and how to achieve it will significantly increase the rate of the change's acceptance and the likelihood of its long-term success. Moreover, stakeholders play a key role in the process by reinforcing and even modeling the desired new behaviors.

BRINGING CHANGE TO THE WORKPLACE

Legendary social scientist Kurt Lewin, who died in 1947, provided conceptual tools to bring change to the workplace. His action research model—assessment, design, implementation, and evaluation—is the basis for the training cycle, which was described in Chapter 1. Action research has at its heart the notion that we learn from our experiences, and that problems are best solved by those who are impacted by the problem. Lewin also explained that organizations represent a sea of forces in motion that continually push for and resist change. Therefore, understanding the organization's learning needs can be understood by having stakeholders identify those relevant forces—both negative and positive—that are at constant odds with each other. The approach Lewin developed for identifying those elements is *force-field analysis.* The *three phases of change* describe how change actually takes place.

Force-Field Analysis

Through force-field analysis, an understanding of the organization and its learners at a given point in time is developed. First, the driving and restraining forces related to changing behavior are identified, as shown in Figure 11-1. Then, those things from the list that cannot be controlled are put aside. For example, the changing nature of the workforce or overall economic forces cannot be controlled. While the natural tendency is to increase pressures—the left side of Figure 11-2—the change agent is instead advised to reduce resisting forces.

Consider, for example, the concept of business process redesign (BPR), the process of redesigning work processes to take better advantage of new tools and skills. This innovation is difficult to assimilate, and attempts to help (primarily through training efforts) can be interpreted as attempts to interfere. Simply proclaiming the value of BPR is not a useful strategy. Explaining that employees need to change the way they work because of resource limitations is not enough. What is recommended are strategies that would lessen the resisting forces. For example, assurances that while job tasks may change, individual jobs will remain intact. The most effective way to ensure organizational change is to identify possible forces of resistance and reduce or eliminate as many as possible.

Identifying the drivers and resisters of change is the first step to any planned change effort. Of course, once the forces are identified, they are apt to change as new drivers and resisters emerge. Because of this flux, the concept of a workplace in equilibrium is at best a very temporary phenomenon. Force-field analysis provides only a snapshot of an organization at one given point in time.

Figure 11-1.
Forces Driving and Resisting Changes In Organizations

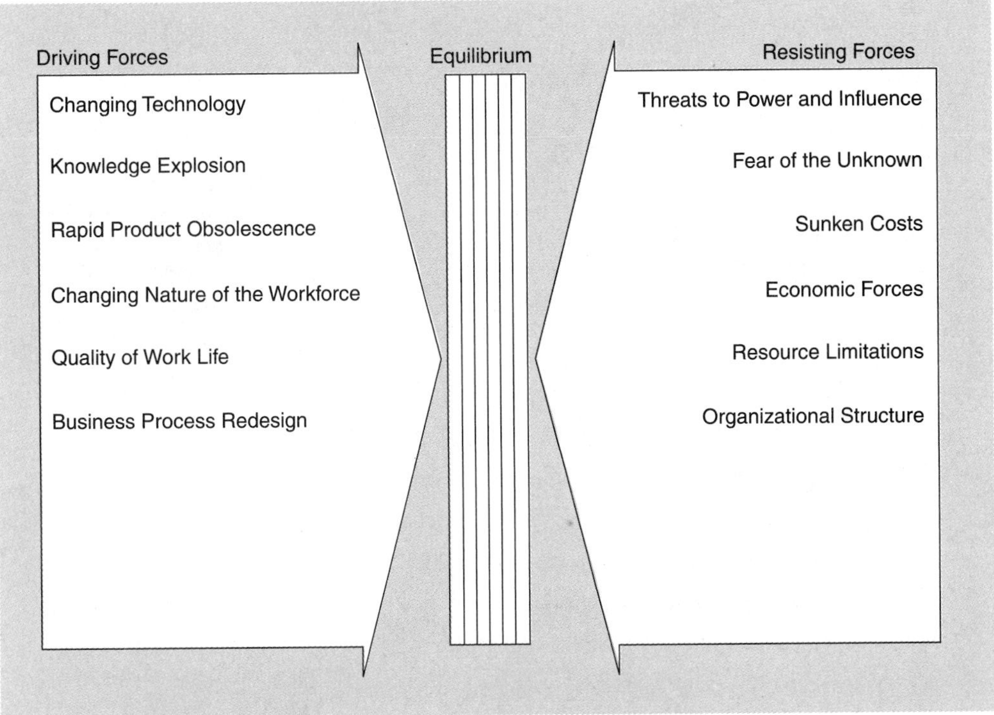

Thus, identifying the pressures for change is important, but we change our behavior only when we are ready to change.[8] We must feel a need to change. We modify our behavior when we feel it is important that we do so. One way to develop that felt need is to draw the needs assessment bull's-eye (see Chapter 1) with the target audience in the center, and have everyone who will be impacted *participate* in the needs analysis as well as the development, implementation, and evaluation of the proposed solution. Therefore, the role of participation is an underlying notion in describing the phases of change.

The Three Phases of Change

Force-field analysis is a tool to help identify the forces at work in situations, determining what to do (the idea/innovation). The next step is to determine specific strategies and when to implement them (delivery/infusion). Successful infusion requires an understanding of *how* individuals change. Lewin suggested that planned change efforts are made up of three phases: unfreezing, changing (or moving), and refreezing. As Figure 11-2 shows, *unfreezing* is the phase where a readiness for learning is created. *Changing* is the period where new skills are actually acquired, and *refreezing* is the time when new skills are assimilated into the way work is done.

Planned change efforts are all about getting people to change their behavior. The three phases of change are a useful framework for matching learning strategies to an appropriate time in the assimilation process.

FIGURE 11-2
LEWIN'S THREE PHASES OF CHANGE

Phase I: Unfreezing →	Phase II: Changing →	Phase III: Refreezing
Creating a felt need for change; minimizing resistance to change	Changing people (individuals and groups); tasks; structure; technology	Reinforcing outcomes; evaluating results; making constructive modifications

Figure 11-3 shows training delivery strategies that are suitable for use at the unfreezing, changing, and refreezing phases. Depending upon the situation, the strategies listed may serve double-or triple-duty; a book, for example, may provide an incentive to learn, the learning itself, or reinforce learning that has already occurred. While instructional strategies (the change phase) may have definite start and stop dates, ensuring that learning is assimilated into the organization requires ongoing learning support strategies. It is difficult to determine in some learning situations where the unfreezing stops and the change begins or when the change phase stops and refreezing begins.

FIGURE 11-3
TRAINING AS PART OF AN IMPLEMENTATION AND LEARNING SUPPORT SYSTEM[9]

Phase	Change Strategies
Unfreezing	Promotional pieces Books, brochures, and journals Demonstrations
Changing	Instructional strategies; e.g.: Print-based materials Audio/video/multimedia tools Computer-based Instruction Web-based Training Classroom-based activities: lectures, role plays, and the like On-line help Help Desks and coaching Manuals and job aids
Refreezing	Seminars, conferences Books and journals User groups Employee councils

Unfreezing Strategies

At the unfreezing phase, the change agent establishes and defines the problem and assesses the client's needs, ability, and readiness to change. Attempts are made to change attitudes and mindsets by reducing the negative forces with new information. The need for the change may come from within the organization itself or be caused by environmental forces. The learner must *see* the need for change. Unfreezing strategies get people ready—and willing—to learn before actual instruction (changing) takes place. At this stage, the change agent provides information that explains why the status quo needs to be reconsidered or describes new opportunities to improve work, such as new technologies.

Many different strategies for disseminating information exist. Information can be presented in a wide variety of forms, ranging from newsletter items or descriptive brochures to corporate television spots. When innovations are completely new, providing demonstrations in nonthreatening ways can be useful. The goal of disseminating information is to give people an opportunity to begin considering that a better way to do something may exist.

Again, in any change effort, stakeholder participation in the needs assessment and design stages actually serves as a means to ensure acceptance of the program at a later date. This is because people who were consulted, or were even just kept aware of the development of a training/change effort, tend to be receptive to its implementation. Moreover, awareness and participation can help promote the change, and organizational support is critical for true assimilation.

Changing Strategies

As used in this book, changing strategies are the learning approaches that ensure that learners can actually use an innovation to carry out existing work more efficiently or effectively. Note from Figure 11-3 that changing strategies include but go beyond instruction. To learn new skills or knowledge fully, learners often need access to ongoing support such as job aids, coaching, and performance support tools. Throughout this phase, the learner actually learns how to change his or her behavior. Therefore, it is the trainer's role to design, develop, and implement the instructional strategy—live or mediated (see Chapters 7 and 8)—as well as develop ways to ensure that support is available at the time it is needed.

In developing learning plans, the needs assessment data and data from ongoing evaluations are used (see Chapters 2 and 3). Plans are shared with all interested parties along the way. Therefore, training strategies that specify exactly what is to be done, when, and by whom, are not a surprise. Participation in planning also means that scheduling has been discussed openly and the training itself is introduced at an appropriate time.

An important consideration during the changing phase is that with new learning, individual learners' job performance may initially *decrease* until the learner is able to take full advantage of the new way of working. Behavior changes are seldom easy. As discussed in Chapter 3, success in the classroom does not always translate into the assimilation of new skills on the job. However, trainers can work with line managers and take joint responsibility for the assimilation of learning beyond the learning environment and the scheduled training activities. Such partnering (discussed later) helps ensure desired outcomes.

Refreezing Strategies

Refreezing strategies allow learners to take better advantage of new skills and develop new functions and activities. At this point, the new learnings are assimilated into the organization, and stabilized as "the" way to work. Learners often leave training programs with enthusiasm and excitement. However, because no good idea succeeds simply on its own merit, care has to be taken to reinforce what was learned, and ensure that learners have an opportunity to practice and develop new skills.

Assume, for example, that an innovation to be considered is a 360-degree performance appraisal system. A 360-degree performance appraisal system is a means of providing feedback to employees based on the evaluation of their supervisor, their peers, their subordinates, and in some instances, their customers or suppliers. To prepare people for this new concept/practice, books and journal articles describing the system and its use in other institutions should be distributed (unfreezing, changing) prior to classroom learning experiences. Once the system actually begins to be used, invite employees to attend special seminars, sharing experiences and offering suggestions—"here's what I've done!"—to others who are going to use the system. In addition, special discussion groups can be organized—computer conferences, listservs, and bag lunches—to discuss the application of the performance review process. Applying what was learned in the organizational context oftentimes is a learning experience itself. And what better teachers are there than the individuals who are actually already using the innovation?

The refreezing stage lasts only as long as it takes to realize that change is needed again. Referring to the training cycle, evaluation asks if the innovation did what we expected it to do. One way to determine the success of an innovation is to compare productivity measures such as costs, profits, quality, and quantity before and after the changing stage. Then the training cycle starts all over: The solution just implemented becomes the target of the next inquiry as to whether or not we are doing the right things. Ideally, another outcome of the cycle is that the trainer not only provided a solution to a specific organizational need, but he or she also learned from mistakes as well as successes at all stages and will be better prepared to address future problems.

FORMING COLLABORATIVE RELATIONSHIPS

The training professional's relationship with the target audience varies depending upon the philosophy of the training department, the needs of the organization, and his or her own individual preferences. The trainer's organizational role has traditionally been that of a live instructor. This role has subsequently evolved to that of an internal *consultant* who is a learning specialist with skills in problem assessment, training design, implementation, and evaluation.

As a consultant, the training professional provides professional advice or services and is the conveyer of best practices. To consult means to advise. Consultants are expected to bring "new ideas" or best strategies to the problem-solving table. It is the consultant's responsibility to keep up to date on the organization, specific content areas, and problem-solving approaches. A consultant needs to know up front what clients expect, and be very specific about the anticipated results.

Therefore, in addition to being a learning specialist, a trainer must often be a *group processes facilitator*, helping groups throughout the organization define problems and develop learning solutions. The trainer's organizational role is, furthermore, evolving to that of a full *business partner* who is credible, knowledgeable, adds value to the organization, and is results-focused. The skills related to being a learning specialist have been discussed in previous chapters; this section discusses skills related to performing in these latter two roles.

THE TRAINING PROFESSIONAL AS GROUP PROCESS FACILITATOR

Increasingly, today's training professional realizes that only in understanding the organization's needs can solutions be developed and effectively implemented. This means that the training professional works with the most informed people—often policy managers, line managers, organizational development specialists, and the target population itself—to define needs in terms that everyone understands and to work to facilitate change. Sometimes the need is best identified and solved by one-on-one interviews, questionnaires, and the like. However, because the trainer may not always be the content specialist and because people must feel a need for change (unfreeze) before they will learn new ways to work, there is much value in the trainer learning how to facilitate group communications and decision-making.

All business relationships require process facilitation, whether the relationship involves interpersonal relations, long-term teamwork, or organization-wide change efforts. While the techniques vary, process facilitation involves clarifying purposes and goals while ensuring trust. As a facilitator, the role of the training professional is to lead a group in a problem-solving process. Process facilitation is an art as well as a science. Wise problem solvers spend more time pinpointing the problem than in implementing ad hoc solutions. After all, why develop a training program (a solution) to improve the selling skills of insurance salespeople, for example, if the problem is really related to ensuring that they have up-to-date information on rates and benefits?

A group's ability to solve problems is considerable. "Two heads are better than one," and "many hands make light work" are maxims that illustrate the value of group problem solving. VanGundy (See "Recommended Readings" at the end of this chapter) identified and classified more than 100 different structured problem-solving techniques. Structured problem-solving techniques can be used to ensure that all possible solutions are on the table and that "groupthink," the tendency for some groups to agree just to agree, do not come into play. Structured problem-solving techniques can assist the facilitator at all stages of problem solving. Some techniques help groups orient themselves to the problem at hand, while others help the group define a problem so that all agree on what the problem is. Still other techniques are used to help a group develop alternative solutions and assess the viability of options generated. In this discussion, a sampling of frequently used techniques that support problem analysis and definition, decision making, and evaluation are described.

Analyzing and Defining Problems

Organizational problems and opportunities are identified in many ways. A line manager may identify workforce performance problems. Workers may identify new software application skills they believe could help them with their individual or group productivity. The organization may be planning to reengineer the way inquiries or shortages are handled. The Information Systems manager may be planning to implement interactive video teleconferencing systems in the branch offices. Any number of individuals and operating units may want the attention of the training department at any one given time. Chapter 1 emphasized that successful training professionals focus heavily on ongoing needs analysis to ensure that the right people learn the right things at the right time and in the right priority order. Unsuccessful training professionals jump to training solutions before determining that the real problem is being addressed.

The physical tools of the trade for structured problem solving in teams are flip charts, white boards, and increasingly, computer-based group process tool kits such as GroupSystems.com's (formerly Ventana Corporation) *GroupSystems*, which is discussed later in this chapter. As a facilitator, the first objective is to establish and manage the meeting process. This does not mean ignoring the content of a meeting. An understanding of the issue/problem is needed as key tasks are to ensure that an agenda is developed, that relevant information is available, and that priority items are given the most consideration. Structured techniques can help ensure that everyone has an opportunity to participate, and that appropriate levels of consensus exist. A well-articulated organizational need or problem definition, agreed upon by those concerned, is the first step in ensuring that a useful solution is developed. An overview of four techniques that can support problem analysis and definition follows.

Brainstorming

Brainstorming is a method of idea generation where everyone is encouraged to contribute ideas (usually orally) without regard to criticism. The concept is to produce as many ideas, one stemming from another, in a no-holds-barred environment. In some instances, a facilitator records ideas on flip charts. In other instances, brainstorming sessions are audio recorded and later transcribed to ensure that no ideas are lost. Large Post-it Notes are also often used, one idea per note, to capture ideas. The advantage here is the ease of grouping the ideas once captured.

Storybook Technique

Using the *storybook technique*, a leader presents a problem, and participants verbally generate solution categories. The leader asks idea-prompting questions about each category, and participants write their responses down on cards. With the agreed-upon categories as headings pinned to a corkboard, the leader then uses thumbtacks to pin the cards up under an appropriate category. After an appropriate number of "rounds," the group ranks ideas under each of the categories. Again, Post-it Notes offer an alternative tool to the corkboard.

Nominal Group Technique

The *nominal group technique* involves the silent generation of ideas in writing. Then, in a round-robin fashion (one-at-a-time, everyone gets a turn), each participant offers one idea, until all ideas are recorded. Then, the ideas are discussed, clarified, and voted upon.

Charting

Any number of techniques exist for graphically depicting processes. *Flow charts*, for example, which break down processes into discrete steps, can be useful in identifying bottlenecks or locations for productivity improvement that would not be apparent otherwise. *Histograms*, or bar charts, can show how often something happens. A picture is worth a thousand words. Charting data graphically can help a group focus on the problem at hand.

Computer Support for Group Processes

Figure 11-4 shows how one software vendor, GroupSystems.com (formerly Ventana Corporation), added the power of computers and networks to support group processes. Of special interest is such systems' ability to support dispersed groups. Increasingly, group work involves working with people who are in the same place at the same time. The next chapter, which is a glimpse of the future, shows how a trainer may work within such groups.

Figure 11-4
Sampling of Computer-Based Tools from GroupSystems.com that Augment Group Processes

Electronic Brainstorming	This tool is designed to gather ideas and comments in an unstructured manner. Participants contribute simultaneously and anonymously to a discussion that can later be used as is or sorted by keywords. Comments can be imported into other tools where they can be categorized and evaluated.
Vote	Vote supports consensus development through group evaluation of issues. Participants can be polled in seven quantifiable ways: rank order, multiple choice, agree/disagree, yes/no, true/false, a ten-point scale, and allocation. Results are tabulated electronically and can be displayed graphically or in text.
Topic Commenter	Topic commenter supports structured idea generation. Participants use multiple windows that resemble file folders. They open each window, write relevant comments privately, and then submit them to the group for review.
Policy Formation	The policy formation tool enables groups to develop and edit a statement through an iterative process of review and revision.
Questionnaire	The questionnaire tool allows a prepared survey to be distributed to participant workstations. Collected data can be compiled into a single report.

Selecting the Best Solution

The best solution is one agreed upon by all those who will be impacted by it. The ideal is to involve as many stakeholders as possible. Many procedures are available to ensure that the pros and cons of potential solutions are fully understood by all concerned. Especially important is that procedures should be used to help ensure that minority opinions are heard and that the power or influence of one individual does not dominate. The same techniques for idea generation, such as brainstorming and the nominal group technique, can be used. Other systems of voting and analysis, including determining how far apart group members are or specific aspects of solutions they like/dislike, can be very useful. It is not always advisable to rush for closure. When groups cannot agree, it is usually advisable to postpone making decisions or obtain more data that would help the group decide. When decisions are reached, it should be made clear that each group member is equally responsible for the decision.

Evaluating Results

Decision-making groups should not exist for the purpose of making a decision and then simply disband. The life of a decision-making group continues into the evaluation phase as well. Evaluation means looking back at the original problem and determining if the solution solved the problem as measured by the agreed-upon criteria for success. When decision-making groups continue working together through the evaluation stage, with shared responsibility for outcomes, the training professional can be considered a business partner.

THE TRAINING PROFESSIONAL AS BUSINESS PARTNER

A trainer is a *business partner* when he or she works *with* clients rather than *for* clients to improve workplace performance. As a partner, the training professional brings a human resources skill set to the table—knowledge of issues such as workplace demographics, organizational culture, assessment and evaluation, and teaching/learning techniques. As partners, the training professional, the line manager, and the OD specialists are accountable together for the introduction of new learning into the organization. This role differs from that of being a learning specialist or process facilitator. Its emphasis is on being part of a management team, helping make decisions that positively impact the organization.

Some organizations are promoting the idea of a Chief Learning Officer (CLO) or Chief Knowledge Officer (CKO), the learning and development equivalent of an executive in finance or marketing. In fact, Knowledge Management has been referred to as training's "new umbrella."[9] There's a wealth of information in organizations that needs to be harnessed—knowledge scattered all across the firm. "Knowledge doesn't happen in a vacuum. It's all about relationships and trust—people's willingness to share what they know for the greater good of a group."[10] Often, developing such trust requires planned change efforts, as organizations must develop an environment that supports and rewards those who share what they know.

SUMMARY

The trainer as change agent is a mix of learning specialist, process facilitator, and business partner. The change agent learns what works and what does not work through trial and error. Training professionals of today are moving away from simply solving problems to helping create the future. By involving as many stakeholders as possible in creating the future, the trainer helps everyone learn.

To ensure organizational learning, change agents think carefully about how innovations fit into organizational goals, and once a decision is made, work with key decision makers to ensure that needed resources are available to ensure the innovation's full implementation. They know that major innovations are usually best managed as an incremental, goal-oriented, interactive learning process, depending upon the characteristics of the innovation, adopters, and the organization itself.

Successful change agents attack a problem from several angles simultaneously. An innovative training professional supports multiple learning strategies to address learning needs at each phase of the planned change effort. Moreover, as the organization learns to use and assimilate the innovation, the successful change agent is able to take advantage of organizational learning.

The need for group or team participation in problem identification, solution development, and implementation cannot be too strongly reinforced. Moreover, when changes are large-scale, time needs to be built in for line managers to get involved with their employees' learning, so that new skills are not a threat and the manager learns—along with the training audience—how best to assimilate the skills into work. It may also be useful to develop additional training for managers if employee training changes *their* roles.

Previous chapters described specific job skills related to designing and implementing training efforts in organizations. This chapter goes full circle back to Chapter 1, reminding you that training is all about *learning*, and that training professionals today have an organizational role that goes far beyond that of provider of instruction. Ensuring that learning takes place—that new skills are assimilated into an organization—requires skills beyond that of program development and delivery. This chapter suggests that the training professional play a role as a change agent, working with others in the organization to help ensure that new learning is assimilated into the organization.

A change agent needs to understand the innovation itself, individuals who are expected to assimilate the innovation, and the organization. Rogers described characteristics of innovations, explaining that the higher an innovation scored on each of the characteristics, the more readily it will be adopted. The characteristics are its relative advantage, compatibility, complexity, trialability, and observability. He also described adopters as on a continuum from most receptive (innovators) to least acceptive (laggards). As the ultimate goal of learning is assimilation into the workplace, the training professional needs to understand that the entire organization does not change at the same rate. In addition, organizational culture is a determinant of the rate of change. Whether an organization is traditional, consensus-driven, profit-centered, or futuristic helps the change agent determine appropriate change strategies.

Kurt Lewin explained that an organization is a sea of forces in motion. Force-field analysis provides a means to identify those forces. Lewin also suggested that planned change efforts go through three phases: unfreezing, changing, and refreezing. At the unfreezing phase, specific learning strategies attempt to create a felt need for change. Specific strategies include brochures, informational pieces, and demonstrations. At the changing phase, learners learn new ways to work. In this phase, instruction takes place. At the refreezing phase, the trainer works to reinforce outcomes, ensuring that new learning is assimilated into the way work is done. Training strategies that support refreezing include coaching and hotlines, books and journals, seminars, and user groups or management councils.

As a change agent, the training professional must form collaborative relationships within the organization. The training professional can be viewed as a learning specialist, known for instructional design expertise. The training professional can be viewed as a facilitator, with skills related to helping groups solve problems. Solving problems means coming to agreement on the definition of the problem, generating ideas for problem solving, selecting the best solution, and (eventually) evaluating results. A sampling of facilitation tools—brainstorming, the storybook technique, the nominal group technique, and charting—were described. The most visible role of the trainer as change agent is when the trainer is viewed as a fully functioning member of a management team, with shared responsibilities for learning outcomes—a business partner.

This chapter concluded with some guidelines for the training professional to consider in changing from a provider of learning services to a fully functioning member of the management team, including the top role of Chief Learning Officer (CLO) or Chief Knowledge Officer (CKO). Increasingly, the trainer's organizational role is evolving away from being an instructional specialist to being a change agent who can help the organization create its future and help everyone learn. To quote Peter Senge one last time: "If any one idea about leadership has inspired organizations for thousands of years, it's the capacity to hold a shared picture of the future we seek to create."[11]

THINK IT THROUGH

1. Why must the training professional also be a change agent?
2. Using Rogers' characteristics of innovators, categorize yourself. Offer specific examples of times where you have shown your selected characteristics.
3. Recall an occasion when someone tried to force some help on you. How did you feel? How did you react? What did you learn from this exercise that is applicable to delivering training programs?
4. Assume your university is implementing an Internet-based course registration system. Using Lewin's force-field analysis approach, identify pressures and resisters for the system. Will there be resistance on your campus? If so, what learning strategies would you recommend to minimize resistance?
5. Think about the last time a group you were in made a decision. Did everyone have a chance to share their ideas or did one or two individuals dominate the group? What did you learn from your experience?
6. Why is the trainer a mix of learning specialist, group process facilitator, and business partner? Do you have the competencies required for each role? If not, which skills do you need to develop?

IDEAS IN ACTION

1. Reread the PHH Vehicle Management Services case found in Chapter 8. First, using force-field analysis, identify the drivers and resisters to changing the way training was done at that organization. Then, identify the change strategies employed, and categorize them as unfreezing, changing, or refreezing. What did you learn from this exercise?
2. Interview a training director for examples of two successful and two unsuccessful training implementation strategies. Using characteristics of the innovation, the adopters, the organization itself, and/or the three phases of planned change, analyze why the strategy worked or did not work.
3. As a group project, search the World Wide Web for information regarding the contributions of Kurt Lewin to the field of modern social psychology. One link to get you started on your search is http://www.pathmaker.com/resources/leaders/lewin.htm Write a brief report on his contributions and share it with others in your learning group.

ADDITIONAL RESOURCES

RECOMMENDED READINGS

Galagan, Patricia A. and Jennifer J. Salopek. "Training's New Guard," *Training and Development*, Vol. 54, No. 5, May 2000, pp. 34-56.

Authors discuss new roles for trainees, presented as a series of short profiles of business professionals at work in a wide variety of settings that demand and support learning. A common thread is a focus on business results. The article ends with a self-assessment template: "How do you stand up next to training's new guard?"

O'Hara-Devereaux, Mary, and Robert Johansen. *Global Work: Bridging Distance, Culture, and Time.* San Francisco: Jossey-Bass, 1994, 439 pp.

Identifies key competencies that managers need to succeed in a global workplace. Of particular interest to trainers is a model of team-building for face-to-face as well as electronic meetings. A must for anyone interested in the global workplace and communications technologies.

Stewart, Jim. *Managing Change through Training and Development.* Herndon, VA: Stylus Publishing LLC, 1996.

This paperback book demonstrates how training interventions can be used to manage change. Stewart looks at change on three levels: the organization, the team, and the individual. The book includes self-analysis instruments and cases studies.

VanGundy, Arthur B. Jr. *Techniques of Structured Problem Solving,* 2nd ed. New York: Van Nostrand Reinhold, 1988, 386 pp.

VanGundy explains, demonstrates, and evaluates 105 tested problem-solving techniques (including those in Figures 11-4 and 11-5). Flow charts and guidelines help you understand which one is best for addressing a particular problem. This book is a classic reference book for any group process facilitator.

WEB SITES

http://www.GroupSystems.com

The Web site of GroupSystems.com includes a "knowledge library" that provides links to research and books related to using electronic tools for group processes.

http://www.amanet.org/research

The Web site of the American Management Association includes access to the many research reports produced by AMA on topics of interest to general management, as well as human resource management and Knowledge Management.

ENDNOTES

1. Hammer, Michael. "Reengineering: The Mistakes and Misunderstandings." *World Link.* Davos, Switzerland: World Economic Forum, January-February 1994. Cited in Senge, Peter. *The Fifth Discipline.* New York: Currency Doubleday, paperback edition, 1994, p. xv.
2. Senge, Peter. *The Fifth Discipline*. New York: Currency Doubleday, paperback edition, 1994, p. 6.
3. Ibid., p. 585.
4. Regan, Elizabeth A., and Bridget N. O'Connor. *End-User Information Systems: Perspectives for Managers and Information Systems Professionals*. New York: Macmillan, 1994, p. 394.
5. Rogers, Everett. *Diffusion of Innovations,* 3rd ed. New York: Free Press, 1983, p. 11.
6. Ibid., pp. 248-251
7. N. Dean Meyer and Associates. *GamePlan,* microcomputer-based simulation and guidebook. Ridgefield, CT: N. Dean Meyer and Associates, 1992.
8. Rogers, op. cit., p.233
9. Masie, Elliott. "Knowledge Management: Training's New Umbrella," http://www.masie.com/articles/knowl.htm Spring 2000.
10. Quinn, James Brian. "Managing Innovation: Controlled Chaos." *Harvard Business Review*. May-June. 1985, pp. 73-84.
11. Senge, op. cit., p. 9.

VOICES from the FIELD

Ron Zemke on Additional Professional Competencies

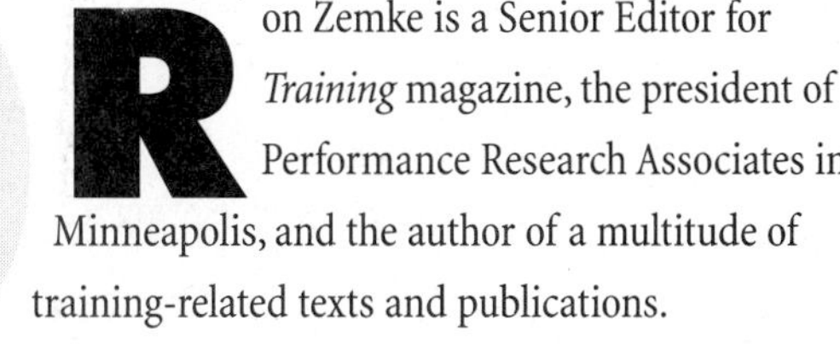

Ron Zemke is a Senior Editor for *Training* magazine, the president of Performance Research Associates in Minneapolis, and the author of a multitude of training-related texts and publications. He is a frequent speaker at national and international conferences and is a highly sought after expert in the training and development arena.

MICHAEL BRONNER: Ron, thanks for agreeing to this interview and sharing your experiences with us. First, what experience have you had in creating, evaluating, and administering training proposals?

RON ZEMKE: Early on in my career, I ran a training department and we did all that. Now, as a consultant, I write proposals all the time—and we administer them when we are successful bidders. Proposal development is just a step in the business process.

A good proposal should be 20 percent about you, 30 percent about the client's problem / request / need /opportunity, and 50 percent about what will be done, how it will be done, what the responsibilities are on both sides of the table, and a specification of deliverables.

MICHAEL BRONNER: What business benefits have you seen when a training professional works as an organizational change agent?

RON ZEMKE: I see training as one change strategy – or a tactical part of a change strategy. Trainer's themselves as "change agents" is a bit of a non-sequitor. It is the information and skills delivered and acted on, that brings about change. The trainer as an agent of that process, is fulfilling an important and critical function. His or her job is to create enthusiasm for and understanding of what must take place for the organization to be successful in the days, weeks, and months ahead, as well as deliver information and train people in new skills.

MICHAEL BRONNER: What troubles have you seen people get themselves into in trying to actually conduct training?

RON ZEMKE: The list is a long one. Lecturing rather than facilitating, being too domineering or too passive, not being prepared to deal with trainees' day-to-day issues, not knowing the information or not having personal mastery of the skills involved. Using training as a platform for one's own ego or the practice of rhetoric rather than the passing along of knowledge or skill. Not understanding the difference between problem-oriented instruction and a survey course. I'm continually amazed at the creativity people bring to "getting it wrong."

MICHAEL BRONNER: So, to help us 'get it right,' what do you see happening?

RON ZEMKE: There is great unrest around the role of Internet and Computer-based Instruction among those who see the value of instructor-led learning. Enthusiastic advocates of the former tout these "new"—though they are not really that new—"media" and make it seem that the classroom instructor is a dinosaur headed for extinction. It is a fear that has surfaced regularly and periodically since the invention of the first teaching machines in the 1930s. In fact, the advent of radio and later television were both forecast as media that would end classroom instruction. Yet classroom instruction, this very simple and humble way of transferring information and skills between people, endures.

MICHAEL BRONNER: What sort of impact do you think training will have on future corporate outcomes?

RON ZEMKE: In periods of rapid change, and massive relocation of competence, formal organized training is a reasonable and appropriate way of equipping a large number of people to master new skills and come to grips with new processes and ideas quickly and with fidelity. Training is a "for want of a nail" role; training doesn't drive an organization's success, but without it, success is much harder to achieve.

MICHAEL BRONNER: Ah, success. How do you know when effective training has taken place?

RON ZEMKE: It is the sponsor's role—facilitated by the trainer or training executives or evaluator—to decide what constitutes success. It is never the trainer's job to decide this independently or unilaterally. For instance, if the job is to change an attitude or transmit a new organizational direction, it is the trainer's job to lead the client through a discussion that will end with agreement on what constitutes a measurable outcome that can be independently verified and agreed upon.

MICHAEL BRONNER: Nicely said, Ron. By obtaining agreement, you support our premise that a trainer should be a business partner, not an independent agent. Partners work together to set acceptable outcomes.

RON ZEMKE: Yes, agreement on what constitutes proof is critical since achieving a state that will generate that proof drives much of the design of effective training.

MICHAEL BRONNER: What books or other resources would you recommend concerning the development of training proposals and for effective instruction?

RON ZEMKE: I have several suggestions, starting with my own book:

> ***Figuring Things Out,*** by Ron Zemke and Thomas Kramlinger, Addison-Wesley, Boston, MA. 1980.
>
> ***The Best of Training: Designing and Delivering Cost-Effective Training***, Lakewood Publications, Minneapolis, MN 1997.
>
> ***Training Needs Assessment***, by Allison Rossett, Education Technology Publications, 1987.

MICHAEL BRONNER: Who would you consider to be the leaders in today's training enterprise(s)? Who stands out as exemplar?

RON ZEMKE: This is a tricky and difficult question. There are any number of organizations—companies, universities, government agencies, not-for profits—who appear to be doing great work. They have impressive facilities, big staffs and up to the minute technology dedicated to training. But those implied criteria of "excellence" belie the only thing that matters—results. And those, we are never privy to. My cynical and suspicious nature—developed from my years of playing journalist as well as trainer—suggest that the higher the public visibility of an organization's training team, the less likely that unit is to be delivering a strategic impact.

MICHAEL BRONNER: Perhaps, then, many unsung training organizations are reaping big dividends from their training efforts! What sorts of roles do you see trainers playing over the next few years or so? How do you see the training role changing within organizations?

RON ZEMKE: Training people need to associate themselves more with line operations and less with corporate human resources in for-profit organizations. Credibility today comes from effecting local results, not from being associated with massive organization-wide endeavors.
In addition, trainers will increasingly be split in two camps; in-house gatekeepers and purchasers of service, and external vendors of products and production. Yes, internal people will do some training, but a better use of their time, training and local knowledge will be in needs assessment and results evaluation, and managing external resources.

MICHAEL BRONNER: What would you say are the three most important tasks training professionals must do for their organizations?

RON ZEMKE:

- Assess needs and evaluate results.
- Separate training amenable from non-training tactical problems and issues.
- Say "no" to management when a problem isn't most effectively addressed by training.

MICHAEL BRONNER: What would you say are the key skills needed to carry out these tasks?

RON ZEMKE: Assessment and evaluation are different sides of the same coin. Training as an evaluator or problem analyst covers both glories. A good understanding of the tools of both qualitative and quantitative research are essential.

General business skills from accounting and finance through sales and marketing, and operations are important. Too many trainers become isolated—or worse, pariahs in the organization—because they don't know the business of the business and have no general business skills.

MICHAEL BRONNER: Good point. So, what specific advice can you offer training professionals to help them make training and organizational investment rather than an overhead expense? And help them persuade others to see it as an investment rather than an expense?

RON ZEMKE: Stay away from corporate functions where training programs have a tendency to be over-generic and personnel or HR related. Diversity, employee orientation, et al. may be—are important—but they are seen by line managers as legal imperatives and adherence driven, not production enhancing. Attach your efforts where the organization's main profit thrust is focused. If the organization is sales and marketing driven—that's where to cast your allegiance. That's also where the best score keepers are and where you can collect data that relate outcome to efforts. It's also where the organization is most likely to be willing to invest in measurement and spend money to get it right.

MICHAEL BRONNER: What is the most successful training effort you have ever seen in an organization? What did it accomplish? What was the key to its success?

RON ZEMKE: I've seen many successful training efforts. One comes easily to mind. A company was spending six weeks training repair technicians to fix a certain piece of office equipment. But even the best techs were experiencing high service recall rates after leaving the training program. A careful analysis revealed that (a) most of the recalls (80-90%) came from a body of fewer than 20 faults and (B) sixty percent of the training was focused on theory and operations that never generated a repair call. The training was revised to focus primarily on the common faults and extensive job aids were developed to handle the most frequent exotic repair problems. The course was reduced to two weeks in length and repeat repairs dropped by 90 percent.

MICHAEL BRONNER: What is the worst, most unproductive training effort you have ever seen? Why was it a disaster? What lessons can be learned from it?

RON ZEMKE: A different office machine manufacturer, in a vain effort to improve sales, brought hundreds of reps from the field to a big conference. There they exchanged sales ideas and were given extensive new product and sales technique training. Sales did indeed improve for a quarter—then slowly drifted back to former levels. An extensive observational assessment found that the most successful sales people made five more contacts a week and asked for the order three times as frequently. Hundreds of thousands of dollars had been spent on boosting morale and doing training that didn't address the real problems and opportunities. Morale building is fine—even necessary in sales and marketing—but having a clear understanding of the dynamics of the problems of performers in the organization is much more important and a more productive use of scarce resources.

MICHAEL BRONNER: What have been your experiences with professional associations and publications in the field? Are there any you specifically recommend? (*Training* magazine, of course!)

RON ZEMKE: Professional associations and publications are good for idea starting and staying in touch with your field. However, most success stories fall short of truly informing you, and you never hear or read those all-important cases of complete failure.

For associations, I recommend the American Society of Training and Development (ASTD) and the International Society for Performance and Instruction (ISPI). Additionally, many industries have their own specific training association. For example CHART – Council of Hotel and Restaurant Trainers; PACT—Professional Association of Computer Trainers.

I'd recommend *Training, T & D Journal, HRD Quarterly, and Performance and Instruction* as excellent publications.

MICHAEL BRONNER: How about outside the field of training? Are there groups trainers should join or network with? Are there outside publications trainers should read based on your experience?

RON ZEMKE: Always join trade groups and associations of your core industry. If you are a trainer in foodservice, join food service groups first, training groups second. Ideally, there will be training groups within your "home" industry like the Council of Hotel and Restaurant Trainers (CHART) in hospitality that give you an opportunity to network and share industry specific ideas.

MICHAEL BRONNER: Anything else? Anything you would like to say to college and graduate students preparing for a career in training? And anything for experienced, mid-career training professionals?

RON ZEMKE: Training is a fun and easily seductive craft to be taken up. It can seem to be second cousin to a performing art and often tugs individuals in that direction. That is favoring process over outcome. It is critical to always be concerned with outcomes over processes. To *not* do so places you at risk of becoming an entertaining irrelevancy in your organization.

MICHAEL BRONNER: Ron, many thanks for your insights, thoughtful comments and suggestions.

PART 6

Trends for the Future

EPILOGUE

Chapters in this book have described current practices, issues, and trends related to understanding training for organizations. The training cycle—training needs assessment, design, implementation (delivery), and evaluation—was discussed in detail, with how-to's offered for each step of the cycle. In addition, the book overviewed specific training job skills, such as writing proposals, providing administrative support for training programs, and facilitating change efforts. Armed with this understanding, you are now in a position to sit back and think about your future as a training professional and how the training field will evolve as you grow in your career.

Trends impacting the workplace include the flattening of the organizational structure, evolving demographics, and the globalization of business and society. Moreover, despite all that has happened in the world of information technology, we have only begun to see its possibilities and implications. Computer experts repeatedly tell us that we are in the midst of a computer revolution. They tell us this so often it has become almost a cliche. It behooves us to remember that cliches get that way precisely because they are so true!

We have indeed gone through a revolution in information technology, with computing power roughly doubling approximately every two years over the past decade and a half. Computer chips have in truth become smaller, vastly more powerful, and above all so much cheaper that they can be used anywhere and in increasing numbers. The better, faster chips have been coupled with new chip materials, new manufacturing methods, and whole new computer architectures. The net result has been ever faster, less expensive, more functional, and more portable computers. Indeed, the net result has been not just more and better computers, but more prevalent and accessible comput*ing*, from a wide variety of "information appliances."[1] These advancements, combined with new input/output technologies—voice, image, and video—absolutely guarantee more of the same: continued hardware and software development, faster and cheaper computing, and more personal and functional systems.

There is, however, something more. Information technology is undergoing a transformational change because of a second revolution, this one in networks, the technologies that connect all those revolutionized computers. The linkages between computers have progressed from massive copper cables to combinations of fiber optics and video cables and wireless connections. These enormously more powerful and speedier connections have spawned the Internet, the World Wide Web—a virtual sea of information and contacts available "24/7," as the phrase has it now: 24 hours a day, 7 days a week. And it's all available from any location from which an information device—mainframe, PC, Palm Pilot, cell phone—can access the Net.

The bottom-line result of all this is not just more of the same, but a true transformation of both information technology itself and of how work is done through the technology. This change will not simply put a more potent PC on your desk. In fact, your desktop workstation will very likely not be merely a self-contained computer at all. It will, rather, be a device that provides you with the entree to a massively powerful, worldwide, integrated network of computing and information facilities, all tailored to you and the kind of work you do.

The purpose of this chapter is to paint a picture of what's coming and how all these changes will impact training. In this chapter, the traditional trainer in the workplace is transformed into the learning specialist of the 21st century. Throughout this book, you have learned that while the trainer's organizational role may change, the trainer's overall goal of guiding and supporting learning in the organization remains constant. The future-oriented scenario you are about to read is designed to get you thinking creatively beyond what *is* to what *can* and *may be.* As you read the scenario, reflect upon the important societal and workplace trends we all face. Consider the changes that have been discussed here and in other sources as well. Think of trends such as the outsourcing of staff functions, the emphasis on wellness and controlling health costs, and the aging and shrinking of our workforce. Cluster them together with the expected information technology transformation. Consider the resultant impact on knowledge workers. Finally, consider how the combination of computer, societal, and workplace trends will affect the world of organizational training.

ENDNOTE

1. Piller, Charles "The Cutting Edge: Focus on Technology," *Los Angeles Times*, April 3, 2000.

CHAPTER 12

The Trainer of the 21st Century

- Articulate a vision of an evolving future for the training function.
- Describe scenes of a likely informational and communications infrastructure.
- Discuss useful perspectives on the importance of just-in-time learning.
- Identify instances of how a trainer of the future juggles work and family.
- Offer advice to the prospective trainer—what to do now!

A TRAINER AT WORK IN THE YEAR 2000[1]

Meet Casey Callahan Melendez, a training professional at her workstation in the year 2008. Numbers in the picture of Casey at her desk (see Figure 12-1) match the numbered sections in this chapter. Each section explains a component of the picture. Taken all together, they add up to a prediction of work and the workplace in the future, with special emphasis on knowledge work and training.

1. Figure at Desk

Casey Melendez is a freelance learning specialist working on a contract basis for the Human Development Corporation (HDC). HDC has a major, multiyear contract with The Zeta Group to implement Zeta's human resource development policies. Casey reports to Charlee Jones, HDC's account manager for Zeta. Charlee's contact at Zeta is Rabindranath Somashekara (known as Sam to his colleagues). At Zeta, Sam is a senior officer, holds a seat on the organization's Management Committee, and is the firm's CLO—Chief Learning Officer.

Under contract with Zeta, HDC provides a full range of human resource development services: staff planning, succession and job mobility systems, career models, learning needs identification, individual learning plans, learning program design, learning and group process facilitation, and instructional delivery. As a matter of deliberate choice, Sam has the evaluation of

Figure 12-1
A Trainer at Work in the 21st Century

learning outcomes performed by Zeta's own internal auditors, and purchases recruiting services from an HDC competitor.

2. The Desk As a Whole

Casey's desk, with all its devices, is wired into an information and communications infrastructure that is as widespread as its predecessor, the telephone system. The infrastructure is built and maintained jointly by a government-regulated consortium of United States telecommunications firms and linked to similar networks in other countries. Zeta, HDC, and Casey all subscribe to the network, and both Zeta and HDC have linked their private company networks to this public one, with access to each network controlled by stringent security measures. Casey's subscription to the public net gets her a personal database on it, in addition to its usual messaging services, and her choice of several information services (e.g., the ASTD Electronic Research Facility). Her memberships in ZetaNet and HDC's InfoMail are provided by the companies as tools for her work. Whenever Casey activates her workstation at the office or at home, she enters her personal identification code and password. The network sees the code and password as keys that unlock the electronic doors to all the data and software that Casey owns or for which she is authorized.

3. The Desktop Device

This integrated device is the heart of Casey's workstation and is commonplace on knowledge worker desks all across the world. The device combines artificial intelligence, a telephone, a computer, a single gateway to various telecommunications networks, a fax, a copier, a printer, a path to all the data and software to which Casey is entitled, and graphics/image technology up to and including full-motion video for both stored film imagery and interactive, real-time, desktop videoconferencing. In addition to its messaging, E-mail, and personal productivity features, the device serves as a vehicle for a significant amount of workplace training.

The workstation is the major delivery platform for *Just-In-Time-Learning (JITL)*— the training approach that makes context-sensitive learning material available on-line, in short omni-media modules, to be called up in real time, precisely when a worker needs to learn a specific something. The workstation is an automated job aid/Help Desk/performance support system/on-line reference tool all rolled into one. A lot of training work goes into the design, creation, and maintenance of this just-in-time material. JITL has in fact become so much a part of the workplace that the acronym has entered the language: JITL materials are "JITLware" or "jittleware," and using them is "jittling."

Casey's sign-on this morning brought her a video announcement from the president of Zeta to all employees and associates concerning Zeta's acquisition of the Estes Park Ranch Resort in Loveland, Colorado. The announcement triggered an E-mail message to Casey (return receipt requested) from Charlee, copy to Sam, to contact the Estes training department to begin the process of involving HDC in its internal and customer work. Casey's desk sent Charlee the return receipt as soon as Casey read the message and, at the same time, set up a tickler for Casey to check completion. (Casey, of course, defines the priority levels for her desk's tickler function.) Charlee selected Casey for this assignment because another specialty that Casey has been developing is the use of video-based groupware as a survey and discussion tool, a process she seems to have a knack for designing and doing in nonintrusive ways.

4. Arm of Chair with Knobs/Dials

The electronic devices at Casey's desk are integrated into this control pad: volume knobs for voice devices, brightness and focus controls for screens, toggles for activating/switching between devices, and the like.

5. Wall Screen with Bar Chart on It

Casey has given HDC's InfoMail a template of topics to watch for in certain publications. InfoMail's scanning software has spotted a report on the morning newswire concerning training for retirees interested in part-time work in bed-and-breakfast inns, child care, and family budget counseling. When Casey activated her desk this morning, the desk informed her that one of her research interests had a hit, and she has pulled the report summary up onto this wall screen to see if she wants to access and/or print the entire report. Casey has made a specialty out of retiree retraining, and it is important for her to stay current with developments in this niche.

Also at this morning's sign-on, Casey's usual baker's dozen E-mail messages included one from Dwight Feeley, an HDC employee. Feeley informed Casey that he has just completed a publicly available training program in air conditioning mechanics. This was a program of his own choice that he took on his own time via Internet links to his home TV and computer, all at his own expense, and with no real connection to his HDC job as a customer service representative. Feeley asks Casey to certify that he has learned air conditioning well enough to enable him to be considered for posted air conditioning jobs at the HDC headquarters complex. (One of Casey's internal HDC assignments is responsibility for technical learning of all sorts.) The second half of Feeley's E-mail asks Casey to assist him in evaluating advanced air conditioning training for his future use.

Casey has seen clear growth in this sort of client request—the certification of learning achieved and the evaluation/selection of training desired. More often than not, such requests pertain to situations where the learning specialist has played no part in the design or delivery of the training in question. This type of client need has grown dramatically as learning programs of all sorts have proliferated in the virtually bottomless ocean of material that has become available through the growth of the Internet.

6. Wall Screen with Writing on It

Casey is currently using this wall screen for two different purposes: a Focus Group on performance management, and a Scrub Team in HDC's Knowledge Management Initiative.

The Focus Group began as part of HDC's continuous learning needs analysis within Zeta. Casey created an electronic Focus Group to discuss the issues around performance management.

The members of the group are seven mid-level Zeta managers who had reported problems in their units concerning this issue. The eight people on-line in this morning's session are physically located in four different cities, three in the U.S. and one in Switzerland. K.K. Cheung, Zeta's operations manager in Shanghai, is also part of the Focus Group, but is not on-line now because of the 13-hour time-zone difference between himself and most of the group. K.K. will see and hear the entire Focus Group session at his desk when he logs on to the network tomorrow, and will be able to add his thoughts at that time.

The group has agreed at this point that the problems they have identified relative to performance management are not because of a skill deficiency on the part of their supervisory staffs. Thus, training will not solve anything. Rather, the problems are due to a weakness in Zeta's standards for performance feedback. They have each accessed Zeta's *Management Practices Manual,* part of the electronic library of manuals maintained on-line at corporate headquarters, and have printed the manual's three relevant pages at their desks. The group has faxed back and forth several scribbled marginal notes on the standard and has reached consensus on a change they think should be made. They are now discussing how best to get this modification made to Zeta's corporate standard, and how in the meanwhile to manage a more productive performance management process in their own units.

The second purpose to which Casey puts this screen is for what she calls her Scrub Team in HDC's Knowledge Management (KM) Initiative. The name, Scrub Team, comes from its purpose: to "scrub" information from knowledgeable professionals, to capture the rich depths of experience that HDC associates have, and somehow make that experience accessible to others in useful form. "We would like everybody to make *new* mistakes as they work," is the way Sam Somashekara has put it. In fact, "*New* Mistakes" has become the slogan of the entire KM initiative, which is a company-wide effort with sponsorship right from the Management Committee. Casey is just one of numerous learning specialists who have been assigned a target population to "scrub." Her group of professionals,13 of them, are all HDC Financial Managers working in 11 different locations around the world. They represent collectively 203 years of experience in handling HDC finances, and the goal of the KM Initiative is to mine the lode of specialized, irreplaceable knowledge that they represent. When Casey has all members of the group on-line at once, her screen filled with 13 little windows of talking heads, it takes all her facilitation and organizational skills to keep the discussion on track and productive. Difficult as it is, though, she is excited about the kind of information the group is surfacing and capturing. She has told colleagues that KM is going to be a major learning initiative for some time to come and that she wants to get more deeply involved in it.

7. Casey's Sweat Suit and Towel

Casey's HDC contract contains a bonus clause for fitness maintenance. She is working assiduously to earn that bonus. If both she and her husband, Cruz—the Assistant Chief Administrator at a local municipal hospital—earn their incentive bonuses, they will have the money for a summer rental on a nearby lake.

8. Doorway into Next Room

Casey rents her desk by the hour at the Bartlett Workcare Center, a small office complex located in a campus setting about 15 minutes from her home. The Center is a private business that provides (a) day care for children and elderly relatives, and (b) work facilities for knowledge professionals like Casey. Many of the elderly relatives serve as staff (some paid, some unpaid), helping with child care and office chores of various kinds. The Center's office facilities include the electronic workstation at which Casey is sitting, as well as meeting rooms, classrooms, group videoconferencing facilities, full-scale graphics/printing capabilities, a gym, and a cafeteria. Casey, like most of her peers, works two or three days a week at home, where her personal workstation is a powerful but somewhat less fully equipped one than the Center's, and two or three days a week at the Bartlett Center or others like it. At a center she can also meet as needed with colleagues or clients from HDC, Zeta, or other companies with which she has contracts. The center's full-scale videoconference room, for example, has proved very helpful in Casey's KM assignment. It is only on relatively rare occasions—usually when she is delivering instruction—that she is physically present at HDC or client offices.

9. Wastebasket with "FEA" Brochure

Casey's HDC contract provides a Family Education Account (F.E.A.), a fund into which Casey contributes money tax-free and which HDC matches. The money in this account remains tax-free as long as it is used for educational purposes by Casey or the members of her family. Casey and Cruz are planning to use the money for their daughter's college education, less the funds used for Casey's mandatory annual program of 12 days of training. (Casey and her supervisor jointly select the content of that training.) Casey and Cruz each get a menu of possible employee benefits from their employers, some of them government-mandated, and are able to select the mix from the two sources that best suits their family situation and lifestyle.

10. Electronic Clipboard

Last week, Casey traveled to HDC headquarters in South Bend, Indiana, for the company's annual Learning Conference, an event that is part education, part recognition, part personal networking, part politics, and mandatory for all HDC Learning Specialists Level XII and above. To handle the logistics of her trip, Casey called on a feature of her desk's artificial intelligence, a *software agent* or *knowbot*. She gave the knowbot her trip parameters (destination, departure and return dates), and the knowbot then accessed HDC's preferred on-line vendors and made all the arrangements: flights, hotel, car rental—all with Casey's dietary, seating, airport, and frequent-flyer preferences taken into consideration. Today, with the trip over and done with, the knowbot has retrieved the proper travel and entertainment expense form from HDC's on-line library and brought it up on Casey's electronic clipboard. A light pen will allow Casey to fill in items by hand, with the clipboard doing the necessary calculations and verifying her signature. The completed form will be routed electronically to Charlee for her approval signature and will then travel by InfoMail from Charlee to HDC Accounting. Funds to reimburse Casey for her out-of-pocket expenses will be electronically deposited in the bank account Casey has specified, and the system will send her an E-mail note to let her know that the deposit has been made.

AN ENTERPRISE-WIDE LEARNING INFRASTRUCTURE

We are not yet in the work environment in which Casey finds herself, and we will not get there overnight, but we are definitely moving in its direction. Certain overall trends and issues are apparent in the scenario pictured here. Chapter 1 of this book described training efforts as strategic, informational, and operational. No matter what type of training is needed in the networked organization, everyone will be able to share a wide variety of learning resources and will be expected to be a learning resource to others. Communications technologies will allow change agents to respond to evolving forces and continually provide learning experiences that can help the enterprise grow. Powerful, versatile technology will provide an information infrastructure in support of the organization's constant need to manage change and learn. It will also offer a wide range of options as to where employees physically work and how they manage their personal and work lives.

VERSATILE INFORMATION SYSTEMS

Because of the increased power of microminiature computer chips and growth in the capacity to transport huge amounts of information, technology will continue to integrate into vast global networks with access for hundreds of thousands of people.[2] Information will be increasingly available in varied and mixed formats: data, text, voice, image, and video. Users of the computing resources of tomorrow will have networked, interactive, multifunction workstations through which they function as processors, consumers, and transmitters of information. They will also have a wide variety of "information appliances"—notebook computers that slip easily into a purse and personal digital assistants (PDAs) that fit in a shirt pocket—with which to access information and processing power. What all these systems have in common is their ability to connect to the Internet, making ubiquitous computing a real and intensely individualized possibility.

In the scenario pictured in this chapter, Casey's desktop device furnishes an entry into computing systems, telecommunications networks, databases, the Internet, and the private, secure Intranets operated by her client companies. Her workstation provides any number of means to input and output information. It is tailored to her work and personal needs, ranging from knowing which databases are useful to her, to providing her a means to communicate with her clients, to enabling her to deliver training services to them.

The Increased Flexibility of the Workplace

Just as technology is becoming more adaptive to personal needs, so is the workplace. The trainer of the future will be working in organizations that increasingly support the particular needs of individuals. Telecommuting, satellite work centers, and outsourcing will be commonplace. Such flexibility will dramatically impact not only who does work, but also how and when it is done. These trends are important to the training professional on several levels. First, the trainer him or herself will be impacted by them personally, working in new ways, under new rules, with new options. Second, providing training services to a dispersed workforce will offer new challenges for remote learning support—needs assessment, solution design, implementation/delivery, and the evaluation of outcomes. Third, people will need to learn new skills to work effectively in a dispersed, distributed workplace—a need particularly urgent for those who manage others in this environment.

Telecommuting is the idea that a person works at home, using a terminal connected to the company network (Intranet) via a communications line—often a normal telephone line, increasingly a DSL line or cable modem. No one knows exactly how many telecommuters are in the workforce today, but the numbers are significant. Estimates range from 20 million (Cyber Dialogue) to 30 million (Gartner Group).[3] Telecommuting is seen as a potential means of employing/retaining valuable skills by helping workers balance work and home demands, as well as reduce commuting costs and time.

In the picture painted by this chapter, Casey Melendez worked part of the time as a telecommuter, from her home, part of the time at a *satellite work center*, and part of the time at a company facility. A satellite work center (private or company-owned) is a compromise between telecommuting and traditional, full-fledged commuting to the office. Satellite centers are usually fully equipped technical facilities. Note that Casey's Work Center serviced multiple companies and a variety of knowledge professionals. It also offered child and elder care, as well as a wide range of other social and health-related services.

Outsourcing is the practice of contracting out responsibility for part of an enterprise's operation. In our scenario in this chapter, the Zeta Group outsourced its training and development activities to the Human Development Corporation (HDC). Casey was a freelance (independent) training consultant hired on a contract basis by HDC. Note, too, that the Zeta Group deliberately outsourced its recruiting services to a different subcontractor, an HDC competitor. Enterprises are finding that outside contractors can often do the job faster, better, or less expensively than full-time, in-house staff. More importantly, outsourcing selected responsibilities allows an organization to concentrate fully and exclusively on its core business/professional concerns. The practice of outsourcing is increasingly common in the world of the flattened, networked organization.

Putting Trends and Issues into Perspective

To sum up the trends described in this chapter and the likely future to which they are leading us:

- Your desktop workstation will be an intelligent device tailored specifically to your job and your interests, both professional and personal. The ergonomically designed workstation will support text and numeric data, printing, image and communications technologies, graphics, full-motion video, and two-way sound. You can expect multiple information appliances—PDAs, notebook computers, palmtops, cell phones—that provide information and processing power when and where you need it.[4] These appliances will all be fully compatible with your desktop workstation.
- The workstation and other information appliances will be your entree to a rich matrix of information and computing facilities. The network will know you and the data and software for which you are authorized. Knowbots, research templates, on-line libraries, and warehouses of forms and manuals will be routinely and readily available. The desktop will be a major delivery vehicle for electronically based learning material.
- Electronic mail, electronic bulletin boards, and groupware will enable you to contact and work with friends, colleagues, customers, subordinates, and bosses across the boundaries of organization, time, and geography. A general description for this network of knowledge work tools is "any to any." That is, on an any-to-any network, *any* one can use *any* workstation in *any* location to get at *any* data or *any* software or *any* application for which he or she is authorized.
- The workplace itself will be flexible and supportive of a very diverse workforce with a wide variety of needs in terms of how and where work gets done. Wellness will be explicitly encouraged in an effort to not only keep health expenses down, but also to keep productivity up.

A Myriad of Driving Forces for High-Quality Learning Support

Significant forces in our world, including changing demographics, the globalization of work, and new technologies, have resulted in the requirement that all employees have learning opportunities to acquire or enhance the skills needed to maintain the company's and our society's competitiveness. Unions, as well as the federal government, are increasingly involved in ensuring continuing education options. The United Auto Workers, for example, won a $20 million retraining fund as Ford Motor Company revised its Human Resource Management policies. The union agreement was later expanded to include managerial personnel.[5] Similarly, the federal government has considered legislation that would require all business organizations to invest a minimum percentage of total payroll in employee training.

Today, as well as in the near future, employees have any number of options available to them for continuing education. In the Casey Melendez scenario, Dwight Feeley had completed a training program completely outside the purview of his company's training resources. Casey's department did not deliver—or even know of—Dwight's training program. Nor did HDC! Casey was nevertheless expected to furnish competence measurement to certify that Dwight had indeed mastered specific skills to levels of proficiency required for certain jobs. Moreover, workers are increasingly less likely to be tethered to an organization for life. Individuals will therefore be taking fuller charge of their own learning needs, designing and managing their own careers. To do this, they will choose from a plentiful supply of learning options including, but not limited to, training furnished by their organizations. Other learning resources, such as programs on the Internet or on CDs, will be increasingly available. Also, courses at community colleges, universities, and private training companies—accessible either physically or through distance learning—will be available. Organizational training departments will continue to design and develop traditional training programs, but they will also work with individuals, unions, schools, and universities to become clearinghouses of learning opportunities.

WHAT SHOULD I DO?

Given this new world aborning, what does today's trainer need to do? The one thing you really cannot do is think that you can ignore the massive and continuing changes taking place in the world of work and the world in general. Consider the following as you prepare yourself for the training field of the 21st century:

- For starters, you will want to be computer literate. Georges Clemenceau, a French government official at the end of World War I, remarked that war had become too important to leave to the generals. Similarly, technology has become too important to leave it to the technicians, and computer literacy is a genuine must for the trainer of today and the future. On the other hand, this does not mean you need to become a computer scientist. Computer literacy should mean what literacy has always meant—an appropriate degree of fluency in a particular medium. Consider the level of literacy you have concerning home appliances. Most of us simply know how to use them. We do not design or repair them, and know little or anything about what makes them work. The same thing holds for computers and networks. The degree of literacy necessary, of course, will be dictated by your work: Some settings will require more of it than others. However, we can all expect work to be significantly more information technology-centered than it is today.

- In *The Changemasters* (See Recommended Readings), Rosabeth Moss Kanter explains that you must become a master of change. Change is indeed a constant, another cliche that cannot be ignored. Furthermore, its frequency curve continues to climb and its impact continues to widen. Technology is but one cause, and may not even be the most important. None of us can escape the inevitability of having to deal with change, and the trainer can further expect to be called on to help others do so. Thus, change should be seen as one more medium in which fluency is required for the trainer, to the point of mastery.
- ASTD—The American Society for Training and Development—is perhaps the most focused source of information on trends and best practices in training. It has a national office and numerous local chapters. Participation in the society (it offers special student memberships), particularly for those learning the field, is a productive way to network with others and tap into trends. The Society's magazine, *Training and Development*, publishes from time to time articles that cover the past, present, and future of learning in the workplace, usually including predictions from noted experts on the future of training. ASTD's magazine and Web sites are filled with ideas and suggestions that trainers can use to measure their own work, plan their own development, and keep themselves up to date, well-positioned for the future. ASTDs national office (and all its research) is located at 1600 King St., Alexandria, Virginia, 21313. The phone number is (703) 683-8100. Its Web site is www.astd.org.
- *Training and Development* and its counterpart publication, *Training* (Lakewood Publications, Minneapolis, MN), both go through extensive data-gathering to present annual "State of the Training Industry" reports. Usually published in the latter part of each year, these surveys provide trainers with a detailed picture of how things are changing in the field. The survey data provide a firm base on which to stand in planning organizational directions or career moves.
- Above all, the skill that is key to success in the Information Age requires adding a fourth "R" to the traditional three. Literacy is no longer just *R*eadin', '*R*itin', and '*R*ithmetic. We must now add the fourth R: *Relearning*. Relearning means the ability to unlearn the old and learn the new, as often as needed. As a training professional, you will be expected to develop your own relearning strategies and at the same time facilitate learning, unlearning, and relearning throughout the organizations you serve.

SUMMARY

This chapter offered a glimpse of a training specialist at work in the 21st century. Its premise is that in step with all the projected societal trends and new technologies, the job of the learning specialist will continue to be to support learning throughout his or her organization. Sophisticated information technologies will put required knowledge at our fingertips precisely when needed and help us deal efficiently with matters of administration. Computer literacy will thus be an essential tool of the workplace, and this literacy will be just a beginning. As has always been the case, the knowledge worker of the future, learning specialist or otherwise, will need to have an inquiring mind, will have to be a person ready to learn continually and adapt constantly to new knowledge and new ways of doing things. While specific skills and tools will be important, knowing *what* to do and *why* will, as always, be far more important than knowing how.

In the face of all the changes of our times, the old saying still holds true: The more things change, the more they stay the same. Thus, the job of the learning specialist in the 21st century will be done with new tools, in new contexts, and under new assumptions. It will nevertheless continue to be that of ensuring that the right people learn the right things at the right time and in the right priority order—this is, and will remain, what effective training for organizations is all about.

THINK IT THROUGH

1. Assume you are a technical trainer at a large insurance company and a member of the American Society for Training and Development (ASTD). An upcoming evening program at your local ASTD chapter involves a roundtable discussion of trends in the information technology of the future. Because of your expertise, you have been asked to lead this discussion on technological trends.
   a. What are the major trends expected?
   b. What issues may trainers face as organizations implement the technologies?
   c. Which of the technology trends do *you* believe will have the largest impact on the trainer of the future?
2. What benefits do work-at-home and work centers offer employees and employers? What are the pros and cons? Do you believe that the number of organizations offering such flexible workplaces will grow? Why? Why not?
3. Discuss the concept of just-in-time learning (JITL). What forces are pushing for increased JITL?

IDEAS IN ACTION

1. Prepare a two-page report on current developments in videoconferencing. Conclude your report with a short essay on how these developments may impact how training is offered in the future.
2. Draw pictures of you sitting at your work desk today and in the year 2020. Share and compare your pictures with your classmates in small groups. What technologies did individuals in your group develop that went beyond the scope of this chapter?
3. Search for trends by searching the last 12 issues of either *Training* or *Training and Development* for articles related to trends in workplace learning. Summarize the information your research uncovers, and bring it to class for discussion, with special attention as to how trainers should prepare for the future.
4. Search the Internet for current sources on Knowledge Management. Prepare a report for your class on the results of this research. If possible, approach one of the sources for an interview (live or on-line) about what they are doing with KM. Contact this organization's training department to explore their involvement in KM work. Prepare a report for class.

ADDITIONAL RESOURCES

RECOMMENDED READINGS

Kanter, Rosabeth Moss. *The Changemasters: Innovation for Productivity in American Corporations.* New York: Simon and Schuster, 1983. 432 pp.

Kanter argues compellingly and at length that the single most important skill organizations need to master for our time is that of managing change. Otherwise, she insists, the productivity gains necessary to be effective and competitive in the global marketplace will not be attainable, certainly not sustainable.

Newsweek Extra: "2000. The Power of Invention." New York: *Newsweek* Magazine, Winter 1998.

This special issue of the weekly news magazine is devoted to a discussion of how a vast array of inventions has changed human life. From zeppelins and paper clips in 1900 to baboon-human liver transplants at the end of the century, the issue explores the impact of inventions on human life in the 20th century. It goes on to a discussion of "What Awaits Us in the 21st." for each major aspect of our world—the way we "work, live, fight, and heal." The banner subtitle for the section on work is a summary of the trends highlighted in this chapter: "Good jobs will require more training than ever, and full-time positions will give way to freelance talent-for-hire."

O'Hara-Devereaux, Mary, and Robert Johansen. *Global Work: Bridging Distance, Culture, and Time.* San Francisco: Jossey-Bass, 1994. 439 pp.

Two researchers from the Institute for the Future describe innovative practices found in global organizations such as American Express, Apple Computer, and AT&T. The authors identified key competencies that managers will need to succeed in a global workplace. Of special interest to trainers is the section on process facilitation of groups in remote locations.

Zielinski, David. "Training Careers in the 21st Century." *Training*, January 2000, pp. 26-38.

Zielinski offers his views on where training careers are headed.

WEB SITES

www.astd.org

ASTD Trends Watch: The Forces that Shape Workplace Performance and Improvement. Alexandria, VA: ASTD (The American Society for Training and Development), ongoing. A series of short, focused reports on trends impacting work, *Trends Watch* intends to keep ASTD members informed of issues that deserve the attention of HRD professionals.

ENDNOTES

1. An earlier version of this chapter originally appeared as an article by Chester Delaney in *Training and Development Journal* (March 1991, pp. 45-49), the magazine published by ASTD. The essay has been modified and updated for use here with ASTD's permission.

2. Regan, Elizabeth A., and Bridget N. O'Connor. *End-User Information Systems: Implementing Individual and Work Group Technologies*. Upper Saddle River, NJ: Prentice-Hall, (2001).

3. Deeprose, Donna. "When Implementing Telecommuting, Leave Nothing to Chance." *HR Focus,* Oct., 1999.

4. Palmer, Jay. "Palmed Off." *Barron's,* February 28, 2000.

5. London, Manuel, and Emily Bassman. "Retraining Midcareer Workers for the Future Workplace." In *Training and Development in Organizations*, edited by Irwin Goldstein and Associates, San Francisco: Jossey-Bass, 1989, p. 357.

from the FIELD

VOICES

John Humphrey on Training's Future

John Humphrey is the Chairman of The FORUM Corporation, one of the premier training companies in the world. He is a past Chairman of ASTD's Board of Directors. He is widely regarded as an industry leader and an insightful thinker on training and its role in organizations. He is much in demand as a speaker on training, particularly on its emerging business and financial aspects.

CHET DELANEY: John, thank you for giving me the time for this interview. My coauthors and I wanted to interview you as someone who can comment on the section of our book that looks to the future of training.

JOHN HUMPREY: Could I begin with some introductory remarks?

CHET DELANEY: Sure thing.

JOHN HUMPREY: A couple of years ago in my State of the Industry presentation at ASTD, I called these years "the good old days" of training. I think ten years from now we will look back to now as years in which we made enormous progress as a community. Progress in focusing on helping people learn in ways that affect business results. The trends that have brought this progress about are clear and obvious.

CHET DELANEY: Would you say something about those trends?

JOHN HUMPREY: I had the experience of leading a task force for ISA (The Instructional Systems Association) on what the learning industry would be like in 2005. We gathered several training executives in a room, and there turned out to be a wonderful consensus on the trends that were shaping the future of training. Everybody had the same view of where we're headed.

Everybody–this was uncanny—had the same five trends. The view was that the trends are there, inevitable. The only variable is the rate of adoption or change.

CHET DELANEY: And those trends are?

JOHN HUMPREY: Let me name all five. Then we'll talk about them. The five are:

- Disruptive technology.
- Changing customer expectations.
- Investment.
- Competition.
- Globalization.

CHET DELANEY: Would you explain "disruptive technology," please?

JOHN HUMPREY: It's a technology that changes the way consumers use a product. Mini steel mills, for example, were a disruptive technology to large, traditional, vertically integrated steel mills. Today, for the world of training, e-learning is the disruptive technology. The view of the ISA task force was that at least 40 percent of learning will happen via technology. There was some discussion about that number, some opinions ranging as high as 60 percent, but 40 percent was the agreed-upon minimum.

CHET DELANEY: We're talking here about how learning content gets delivered?

JOHN HUMPREY: Yes. What everybody was in agreement on is that there will be mixed modes of delivery–some in classroom, some in teams, some individually, with some 40 percent of the total done via the desktop. This last will be more than just a form of CBT. There's going to be a blurring of content, delivery, and work process. There's going to be simultaneity with the work. A huge trend in this respect is ERP–there's going to be a second wave of ERP installations, and that will be a big drag-along for the training industry.

CHET DELANEY: ERP–you're referring to Enterprise Resource Planning systems?

JOHN HUMPREY: Yes, like SAP. The only way you are going to be able to do business is by having your processes automated and integrated across the whole enterprise. A lot has been done here, but there's going to be a second wave of it—focused, I think, on the management of customer relations. This will be a big event for learning.

CHET DELANEY: In what way?

JOHN HUMPREY: People have got to learn how to use these systems. Up to now, the training for ERPs has been poor. The human side of ERP systems was—as so often happens—underestimated. This second time around I think businesses are less likely to make the same mistake. So the training demands will be higher.

This ties neatly with the second trend I listed above — customer expectations. Customers are looking for outsourcing. Right now this is fairly small, perhaps 2 percent of customers. Our task force expected it to grow to 25 percent by 2005, again with remarkable agreement among the task force members.

CHET DELANEY: Would you define outsourcing?

JOHN HUMPREY: It means a supplier takes full responsibility for a segment of training for a customer. The chunk can be defined in lots of different ways, but the supplier takes it over for the customer. Given this trend, customers clearly want fewer suppliers who can do more. Suppliers who are stronger, who can provide a broader array of reliable services, multiple modes of delivery. Suppliers who can stay longer and provide enhanced quality. Suppliers who will be liable for major results, significant business impact. It has happened in other industries. Now it's happening in training.

CHET DELANEY: You're saying the training industry is in for some consolidation? Some shaking out?

JOHN HUMPREY: Yes, and that also brings the notion of investment in the training business into our discussion.

CHET DELANEY: That was the third trend you mentioned above.

JOHN HUMPREY: Yes, and this is *very* big news, because when the money flow changes, everything changes.

CHET DELANEY: So what do you see happening here?

JOHN HUMPREY: Well, Wall Street has been disappointed in the performance of training firms, but there has been quite significant investment in the industry, an estimated $3.6 billion in public offerings over the last 18 months, plus another $1 billion in private capital. I probably get four phone calls a week from people looking to invest in training, from venture capital companies or investment houses. I'm also getting calls from technology companies wanting to explore their investment in training … or training's investment in them!

CHET DELANEY: A lot of interest.

JOHN HUMPREY: Yes. John Chambers of Cisco called training "the killer app" of the Internet. Up until now, training has been undercapitalized—And even this has been done by training customers, not training suppliers. This customer capitalization has almost exclusively taken the form of brick-and-mortar expenditures to build training centers.

CHET DELANEY: You're painting a picture of consolidation in the industry again.

JOHN HUMPREY: That's right. You've got customers on one side saying, "We want stronger suppliers." And you've got Wall Street on the other side saying to suppliers, "Here's the capital to make it happen." That ISA task force made some estimates here. We said that in 2005 there would be two firms in the training industry that would be in the $700 million to $2 billion range, ten companies between $100 and 700 million (there are probably ten of those right now!), 20 to 50 companies between $50 and 100 million, and a whole bunch of small ones. What happens in an industry consolidation is that you incubate small firms while the others move up and consolidate through mergers and acquisitions.

CHET DELANEY: Sort of the same thing that's happening to the dot.coms.

JOHN HUMPREY: Absolutely. So what we're going to see here is a much more capable industry. This will translate into—shame on us if it doesn't!—better service, better work, better results, more reliable processes, better careers.

CHET DELANEY: As you say, shame on us if it doesn't.

JOHN HUMPREY: Several years ago, ISA hired Yankelovitch to do a survey of senior business executives to identify the issues that were uppermost in their minds, their top priorities. We wanted to find out where the development of people ranked—was it #42 just after the parking lot and just before the cafeteria or what? It turned out that people development was #3 on their list. Number 1 was responding to customer needs, #2 was dealing with competitive threats. I think that's a good neighborhood, don't you?

CHET DELANEY: A very good neighborhood.

JOHN HUMPREY: So our data say that executives are sold on learning. They're just not sold on training. They were asked in this same survey about how well training served them, served that #3 priority. Their answer was, "Terrible!" The internal people were of mixed quality and too narrowly focused. The external people were also of mixed quality and didn't take the time to learn their business. This kind of feedback has convinced me that trainers are mistaken when they think that executives are not supportive of training. The actual dynamic is different.

Executives are very supportive of learning, absolutely sold on the need for it. But they are disappointed in what training people give them. The outcomes are too often too uncertain. If you think about it, I don't know of any other investment business makes that is as large as the training budget, but which is as unmanageable and so often has no business outcomes.

CHET DELANEY: The classic training gripe is that when budget cuts occur, training is the first to go. The reality is that after that happens and the budget year rolls on, money comes back. Money is found to train people in the things they need to learn for the business to do its work and meet its goals.

JOHN HUMPREY: The money side of training—and the new investments being made in it—are a huge deal. It sort of quantifies the whole thing, makes tracking results more doable. One thing for sure, Wall Street wants metrics of some sort for tracking purposes.

To shift to a slightly different tack: There are tremendous career implications here. One reason for this is that the economics of learning heavily favor variable costs.

CHET DELANEY: Would you go into that a bit, John?

JOHN HUMPREY: Learning has mostly been event-based. We talk about making it continuous, but it actually has a lumpy pattern to it. Learning isn't constant, all the time. It occurs in events. From a cost perspective, it is better to be able to follow that lumpy pattern. Better to be able to hire someone to take care of a learning need—design a program or teach one, etc. Hire someone to just take care of that need, but not employ that person beyond the need. Not have instructors or designers whom you use only from time to time. What you want to do is be able to pay "by the click"—pay for learning support when you are using it, and not pay for it when you aren't using it. We've had experience, which says this approach can reduce training costs by 30 percent.

CHET DELANEY: That's a significant number.

JOHN HUMPREY: Yes, but the point is that this variable-cost model creates all kinds of careers, free-agent careers in the training industry. "Free Agent Nation," *Fast Company* called our society recently. The largest, most rapidly growing block of employees in the U.S. right now is self-employed. There is a growing differentiation in possible careers. Some people are going to be inside organizations, managing the linkage of learning and business results and business strategy. There will be people who administer this linkage, aided by automation. We're getting analysts and designers and appliers who can ferret out a need and respond to it, people both inside an organization and—increasingly—outside it. Materials creators, instructors, coaches (face-to-face and long distance)—there is a whole range of careers being spawned as the industry changes. Your Casey Callahan Melendez is a good example—she works free lance, she's home some, out with clients some, able to deal with family matters as part of her work life. And there definitely is going to be a very high-valued career for people who can make learning work in an organization, to keep it connected to strategy and results.

CHET DELANEY: John, suppose I could put you in front of a class of students who are studying training, considering it as a career. What would you say to them?

JOHN HUMPREY: I'd say it's a *hot* career, one of the keys to economic value in this country now. It's a career in which you yourself have all the room you want to grow and learn and be curious. And at the same time, a career in which you have the satisfaction of helping other people grow and learn, the satisfaction of playing a part in producing business results.

Let me also emphasize that one of the fascinating things about the field is the impact of information technology. We live in a particularly rich, turbulent era, one in which there will be a dazzling combination of learning and technology. One of the things technology is doing is upping the pace a bit, focusing the pace, infusing the learning industry with some of the characteristics of technology.

CHET DELANEY: Do you think we are prepared to deal with the fact that some people cannot learn very well through technology?

JOHN HUMPREY: That's certainly an issue we have to face. Just because training is on the desktop doesn't mean people are going to use it, and utilization is a key indicator. This puts a premium on making sure training content is relevant, that learners are motivated, that there is a connection to their professional community ....

CHET DELANEY: Would you add learning style to that mix? Learner preferences?

JOHN HUMPREY: Absolutely, absolutely. Lorri Bassey, ASTD's research director, says that we are going to find out that the connection between learning and financial results is *not* dollars spent, but participation, frequency, and completeness of participation. I think she is absolutely right.

CHET DELANEY: If I were to ask you for some reading recommendations, what would you say?

JOHN HUMPREY: I'd recommend *Running Training Like a Business* by David van Adelsberg and Edward Trolley. I admit this is a FORUM book, so I may be prejudiced, but the book really talks about how training should be managed. I'd also say, again, that your picture of Casey was dead on target.

CHET DELANEY: Thank you. Anything else?

JOHN HUMPREY: Here's a little trip down memory lane. I gave a talk at ASTD called "Positioning Yourself For the Future." I said there were five things that trainers should do to get ready, to prepare themselves. Let me repeat those five things:

1. Be intentional about your future. In turbulent times there are a lot of choice points. Don't just get carried along by the flow of things. Make decisions, make choices.
2. Build a skill portfolio. Don't think career ladders. Think toolboxes. The world is not about career ladders any more. It's about skilling yourself up to be able to do things like design and implement performance solutions, reduce learning time and costs, identify and deliver results-based solutions. Focus on building these kinds of skills.
3. Get techno literate. If you are not in the game, you are not in the game. Period. Be able to use technology for solutions.
4. Be adept at being connected. Build and expand your network of colleagues and customers; use technology to stay connected.
5. Work with power in the periphery. Realize that impressive work, often the creative work, gets done on the edges, in the power zones of the periphery of organizations. Don't hesitate to work out there.

To sum up: Develop your craft in a network environment. Shift from teaching individuals to supporting learning in a networked environment.

CHET DELANEY: John, thank you very much for all your insights and the lessons of your experience.

JOHN HUMPREY: You're most welcome.

SECOND-YEAR ANALYST TRAINING PROGRAM

BY

SHANNON LALLY, PROJECT DIRECTOR

Competitive Edge
1515 Minetta Lane
New York, NY 10012
Voice: 212.555-5555
Fax: 212.555-5000
November 2XXX

SECOND-YEAR ANALYST TRAINING PROGRAM

EXECUTIVE SUMMARY

Interviews with current analysts, their supervisors, and a detailed job analysis resulted in an identification of needed training for second-year analysts. The proposed training solution targets specific PC-related skills that analysts need to learn. This proposal overviews specific hands-on training strategies that would improve the productivity of analysts by improving their effectiveness and efficiency in their job tasks and roles.

Any questions?

If you have any questions regarding the content of this document or you need clarification, please contact any of the design specialists at their daytime telephone numbers, indicated below.

Kim Heesuek 555-1234

Shannon Lally .555-5555

Ching-Fen Lee 555-8745

Roger Lord 555-9865

In this document

Background of the Problem

In October, Terry Patrick, the Director of Training at Home Bank, asked the design specialists at Competitive Edge to design a PC training program for the second-year analysts in the Investment Banking Department. In this document, we will describe the findings of our needs assessment and a proposed training program and implementation plan.

Analysis of the Problem

When designing a training program, a needs assessment is the first step. In this section, we will discuss the components and the tools used in the needs assessment. Later, we will discuss the proposed training solution.

The Components of the Needs Assessment

In gathering information about the second-year analysts' training needs, we looked at several components, including:

a. Job tasks required of analysts
b. Second-year analysts' current skills and characteristics

The Tools of the Needs Assessment

To gather information about the second-year analysts' job tasks, current skills, and characteristics, we used the following methods:

c. Interviews with second-year analysts
d. Interviews with Terry Patrick, Director of Training
e. Computer Literacy Pretests

Investment Banking's Function and Structure

To begin the needs assessment, we first looked at the structure and functions of Investment Banking and the analysts' positions in the Department. The Investment Banking Department at Home Bank is comprised of 800 people. Of this number, half are professionals and the other half are support staff. The professionals are divided into four levels, each managing a particular function in the marketing and maintenance of Investment Banking clients.

The typical Investment Banking Professional and their qualifications and function are outlined in the following table, with the targeted audience last.

Title	Function	Qualifications	# of Employees
Managing Director	Building and maintaining client relationships, new business acquisition, and the overseeing of the administrative functions of a functional group.	Seasoned employees who have been at the firm for many years and who have set new standards for performance.	60
Vice President	Developing and marketing financial strategies to current and prospective clients.	Employees who have been at the firm a few years and who have demonstrated outstanding potential.	140
Associates	Developing and writing the marketing materials and financial strategies developed by the Managing Directors and Vice Presidents.	Recent MBA graduates from highly rated universities. Position lasts two-three years before they become a Vice President.	130
Analysts	Producing the financial models used to accompany the marketing materials and financial strategies developed by the Managing Directors and Vice Presidents.	Recent BA and BS graduates from highly rated universities. Position lasts for two years, then most analysts will return to school to acquire an MBA.	70

Second-Year Analysts' Skills and Characteristics

After analyzing the data from the interviews with Terry Patrick and several second-year analysts, we found that the analysts:

a. spend 50 percent of time using a PC, and are computer-literate
b. nearly all are 23-26 years old, bright, enthusiastic, and well-educated

Task Analysis

We identified areas where computer training can improve performance. Specifically, by learning how to apply advanced functions and features of Excel, Windows, and cc:Mail to do their daily tasks, analysts can save a significant amount of time. In addition, reports can be streamlined and presentations can be made more effective.

In the following table, we have outlined the most important PC-related tasks that an analyst performs, as well as the PC skills necessary to accomplish the tasks.

Task	Skill
• create financial projections and industry analysis	use advanced Excel functions
• what-if analysis	use Scenario Manager, Goal Seek, Case Manager, Pivot Tables, and Data Tables in Excel
• graph spreadsheet data	use the charting function in Excel
• format and produce attractive spreadsheets	use the formatting and printing capabilities in Excel
• communicate and send files to Home Bank's locations throughout the globe	use cc:Mail to transfer and receive messages and files
• store, find and retrieve documents saved on a computer	create directories, use find file command, be familiar with saving and archiving procedures
• work with multiple work sheets	create workbooks, work groups, arrange files side-by-side and link cells between work sheets

Rationale and Goals of the Training Solution

Course Goals

The major goals of the program are to:

Utilize existing technologies to enhance analysts' performance

Decrease time spent on computer tasks

Targeted Skill Blocks

From the results of the task analysis that is outlined previously, we found the most important PC-related skills an analyst performs can be broken into five skill blocks:

1. Document management
2. Advanced functions and what-if analysis
3. Graphing work sheet data
4. Formatting and printing work sheets
5. Working with data in multiple work sheets

Training Considerations

When designing a training solution for the target audience, we kept several things in mind, including that the second-year analysts are:

Very bright

Strapped for time

Familiar with many of the functions

Overview of the Training Solution and Its Evaluation

The results of the computer literacy pretest indicated that second-year analysts were of relatively equal skill level. However, each analyst lacks in several, but not all, of the five skill blocks. Therefore, we are recommending a flexible training program that will use the data from the computer literacy pretest to evaluate performance in the five target skill areas, identify their areas of weakness, and train them in their weak areas. After the analysts complete training, we propose to give them a posttest and continue training them in their weak areas until a proficiency level has been achieved.

PROGRAM OUTLINE

In the following diagram, we show how the training process will develop. Later, we outline the objectives for each of the targeted skill blocks.

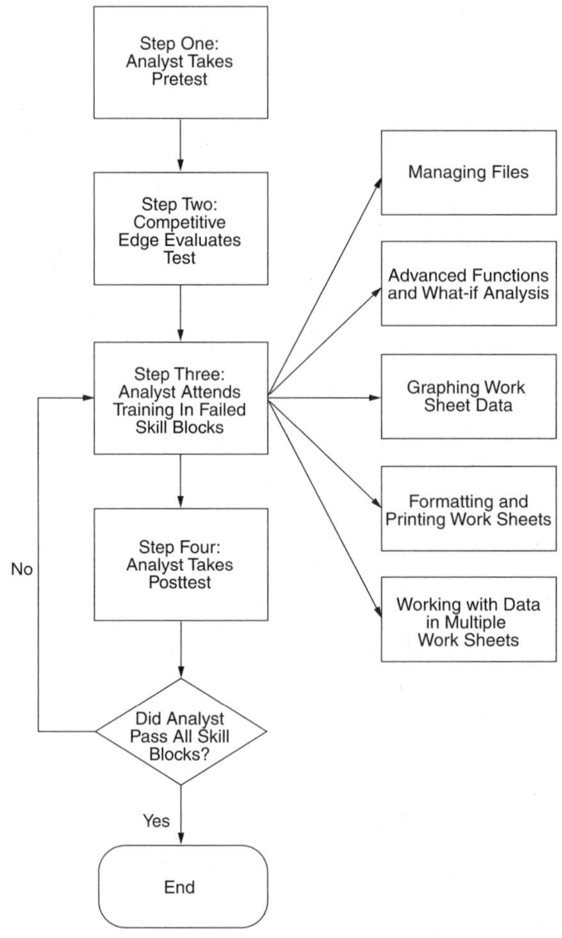

Overview of Training Solution

As described in the previous section, the proposed training will be composed of five skill blocks. Each module will focus on a particular task and will last approximately two hours.

Learning Objectives:

Skill Block One: Document Management

Given a sample set of data, participants should be able to complete the following tasks with 100 percent accuracy:

- Create directories
- Move and copy files from different directories
- Save files on the network
- Transfer files to distant locations

Skill Block Two: Advanced Functions and What-If Analysis

Given a sample scenario, participants should be able to complete the following tasks with 100 percent accuracy:

- Use the IF and VLOOKUP functions
- Use various financial functions, including PMT, IRR, NVP, and FV
- Use data tables
- Use the Scenario Manager
- Use Goal Seek
- Create pivot tables

Skill Block Three: Graphing Work Sheet Data

Given a sample set of data, participants should be able to complete the following tasks with 100 percent accuracy:

- Chart continuous and noncontinuous data
- Create a chart using ChartPrep
- Create a chart in a separate document
- Change the chart type
- Change formatting options
- Add text to a chart

Skill Block Four: Formatting and Printing Work Sheets

Given a problem solving-exercise, participants should be able to complete the following tasks with 100 percent accuracy:

- Format cells using styles
- Display data in outline form

- Create custom number formats
- Add graphic objects to a work sheet
- Create and save a template
- Set and remove print areas, print titles, and page breaks

Skill Block Five: Working with Data in Multiple Work Sheets

Given a sample data set, participants should be able to complete the following tasks with 100 percent accuracy:

- Display multiple work sheets
- Link cells between work sheets
- Link ranges of cells between work sheets
- Group work sheets
- Use workbooks

Training Materials Required

Hardware and Software Required

To effectively deliver the proposed training solution, the following hardware and software are required:

- PC Plate—a computer screen projection device
- A projection screen
- Disks
- Twelve networked computers
- Microsoft Windows
- cc:Mail
- Excel
- Word for Windows

Other Material Required

To effectively deliver the proposed training solution, the following additional materials are required:

- Flip charts
- White board
- Quick reference guides
- Job aids

To effectively deliver the proposed training solution, the following personnel are required in addition to the support staff at Competitive Edge:

- Two lead trainers
- One assistant trainer

A Description of Competitive Edge

Competitive Edge is an Information System consulting firm, which specializes in training for the Financial Services Industry. We are headquartered in New York City, with branches located in six major business centers throughout the country. The organization has a total of 150 trainers, in addition to support staff. Our trainers are highly skilled professionals, who are required to have a business background and a four-year degree in Computer Science or Management Information Systems. Our standards for selecting trainers are high and the training process is rigorous. Hence, our service is of exceptional quality.

Why We Are the Right Choice

Having served the Financial Services community for 25 years, our extensive experiences have enabled us to adapt our programs to industry needs. Our clients can benefit by using our experience and industry insights to take advantage of new technological advancements. We offer training at our state-of-the-art facilities, conveniently located in the Financial District we serve, or on site at the request of our clients.

Available Training Methods

Our company offers a variety of training methods that are designed to be flexible and cost-effective. We work with our clients in designing custom training solutions. We have expertise in developing both live and mediated training programs, which include the following:

- Instructor-led hands-on training
- CD-based tutorials
- Print-based tutorials
- Web-based Training (distance learning)

Development Schedule

Below is the schedule outlining the development time required to ensure a high-quality training program.

	Week 1	Week 2	Week 3	Week 4	Week 5
1.	Interviews				
2.		Client Review			
3.		Validation of Needs Assessment Data			
4.			Program Development		
5.				Leader's Guide Draft	
6.				Instructor Preparation for Pilots	

Delivery Schedule

Training delivery will consist of design efforts, which are pilot-tested and refined prior to rollout.

January	February	March	April	May
Materials Developed Pilot Test 1	Refined	Pilot Test 2	Refined	Rollout →

Development and Delivery Costs

In this section, we discuss the development and implementation costs of the analysts' training program.

Development Costs

The following table outlines the various components of the analyst training program and the cost of each. Please note each development day costs $2,000.

Task	Time	Cost
Needs assessment	5 days	$10,000
Training materials	4 days	8,000
Pretest	2.5 days	5,000
Posttest	2.5 days	5,000
Pilot-testing	2.5 days	5,000
TOTAL DEVELOPMENT COSTS		$33,000

Delivery Costs

In the following table are the implementation costs for delivering the four-week analyst training program. Class size will be ten participants. Seventy analysts will each attend five two-hour sessions. Please note that this last is an extremely conservative assumption. Not all 70 analysts will need all five skill blocks. Thus, the actual cost will be less than the estimates that follow, although at this point we cannot say how much less they will be.

We are offering two options for the delivery of the training:

- Option 1: Program delivery at Home Bank facilities
- Option 2: Program delivery at Competitive Edge

Delivery Cost—Option 1

Lead Instructor	$200/hour x 2 hours = $400/session x 35 sessions	$14,000
Materials	$5/person per class per student	
	$5 x 70 = $350 x 5 classes	1,750
Classroom Prep	$75 x 35 sessions	2,625
TOTAL IMPLEMENTATION COST OPTION 1		$18,375

Delivery Cost—Option 2

Lead Instructor	$200/hour x 2 hours = $400/session x 35 sessions	$14,000
Materials	$5/person per class per student	1,750
Facility Rental	$500 per session x 35 sessions	17,500
TOTAL IMPLEMENTATION COST OPTION 2		$33,250

Total Cost of Program

In the following tables, we have determined the total cost of the analyst training program, both development and delivery.

Total Cost, Option 1

Development Cost	$ 33,000	
Delivery Cost, Option 1	$ 18,375	
Total, Option 1	$ 51,375	
Cost per session:	$51,375 spread over 35 sessions =	$1,468.00
Cost per participant:	$51,375 spread over 70 participants =	$734.00

Total Cost, Option 2

Development Cost	$ 33,000
Delivery Cost, Option 2	$ 33,250
Total, Option 2	$ 66,250
Cost per session:	$66,250 / 35 = $1,893.00
Cost per participant:	$66,250 / 70 = $946.00

Projected Benefits

The purpose of the second-year analyst training program is to increase analyst productivity and the quality of their output. Analysts are paid $40,000 per year and spend half their time on the computer. We estimated they could achieve a 10 percent savings in time, which translates into $2,000. Multiplied by the number of analysts (70), that savings in turn amounts to $140,000 per year, far more than the cost of the training under either delivery option. ROI on Option 1 is 272.5 percent; 211.3 percent on Option 2.

$$\text{ROI: } \frac{\text{Total benefits}}{\text{Total costs}} = \frac{\$140{,}000}{\$51{,}375 \text{ (Option 1)}} = 2.725 \times 100 = 272.5\% \text{ ROI}$$

$$\frac{\$140{,}000}{\$66{,}250 \text{ (Option 2)}} = 2.113 \times 100 = 211.3\% \text{ ROI}$$

PROPOSAL
FOR
MANAGING PERFORMANCE AT OBD, INC.

Philip Elwood and Associates
327 Grey Ghost Avenue
Boise, ID 83704
Voice: (208) 555-5490
Fax: (208) 555-5486
March 12, 2XXX

Background

OBD, Inc., is in the process of communicating to each of its 32,000 employees a newly crafted performance management approach called "OBD Performax."

Education has been identified as a strategic resource in helping OBD employees carry out the tasks required to use Performax. To this end, the Corporate Training Department has formed alliances with Human Resources groups and has created work teams which will identify the shared training and education needs of employees across organizational lines.

Current Need

Performance management skills have emerged as a critical area where there is a need for a consistent approach to training. Corporate Training, with input from Human Resources groups, has spent considerable time designing a performance management program. To date, the following key decisions have been made:

- the target population has been defined;
- the program goals and objectives have been defined;
- program requirements and constraints have been identified;
- an OBD Performax Model has been developed; the components of the Model will drive the design of the performance management program—i.e., a Unit will be designed around each major component of the Model (eight Units in total);
- objectives and learning points for each Unit have been defined;
- content decisions for each Unit have been made; and
- methods and time frames for three Units have been drafted.

Corporate Training is interested in turning this project over to an outside resource to create an Annotated Outline and design program materials which will support and build upon the work that has already been done. This will allow Corporate Training to focus its time and efforts on communicating with HR organizations and defining additional training needs.

Scope of Project

A Performance Management program will be designed as follows:

- The program will be designed in ***three*** phases:

Phase I
Unit I: Introduction/Overview
Unit II: The OBD Performax Approach
Unit III: Establishing Performance Expectations

Phase II
Unit IV: Monitor and Support
Unit V: Performance Appraisals
Unit VI: Recognition and Reward

Phase III
Unit VII: Development Planning
Unit VIII: Career Discussions

- A Design document (Annotated Outline) will be created for each phase.
- Decisions already made regarding program content and flow will guide the design of the program materials.
- Much of the program content exists as parts of other programs; wherever possible existing content will be edited and used.
- Materials in each phase will be consistent in style, depth, and layout.
- Program content and materials will be designed in support of the vision.
- Exercises will draw upon participants' own work experiences and will not be case-driven.
- Materials will be revised, if necessary, after the pilot program for each phase.

Due Dates

The following target dates have been set for each phase of the project:

	Phase I	Phase II	Phase III
Design Meeting	3/ll	April	July
Annotated Outline	3/18	5/30	8/31
Prework	4/1	6/30	9/15
Materials Review	4/8	7/8	9/22
Final Materials	4/15	7/15	9/30
Pilot Program	4/25-26	7/25-26	10/15

*These dates can be modified if it is found necessary to have a complete Annotated Outline earlier.

Fees

A flat fee will be charged for each phase of the project, payable upon acceptance of the final program materials.

Phase I $6,500

Phase II $7,000

Phase III $5,500

Additional Considerations

Consideration should be given to creating a *Leader's Guide* for the program. This is especially important when the program is rolled out by the Regional Learning Centers. You will want to ensure that they have sufficient support to be successful in running the program.

If you wish to proceed with creating a *Leader's Guide,* we can discuss your requirements, time frames, and costs at that time.

APPENDIX C SELECTED TRAINING-RELATED RESOURCES

American Association for Adult and Continuing Education
1101 Connecticut Avenue, Suite 700
Washington, D.C. 20036
(202) 429-5131
www.albany.edu/aaace/

American Society for Training and Development (ASTD)
1640 King St. Box 1443
Alexandria, VA. 22313
(703) 683-8100
(800) 628-2783 (domestic)
(703) 683-1523 (international)
(703) 683-1523 (fax)
www.astd.org
csc4@astd.org

Association for Educational Communications and Technology
1800 N. Stonelake Drive
Suite 2
Bloomington, IN 47404
(812) 335-7675
(812) 335-7678 (fax)
www.aect.org
aect@aect.org

International Federation of Training and Development Organizations
c/o the Manager's Mentors, Inc.
2317 Mastlands Drive, Suite A
Oakland, CA 94611
(510) 531-9453

National Business Education Association
1914 Association Drive
Reston, VA 22091-1596
(703) 860-8300
(703) 620-4483 (fax)
www.nbea.org

International Society for Performance and Instruction
1300 L St., N.W., Suite 1250
Washington, D.C. 20005-4107
(202) 408-7969
(202) 408-7972 (fax)
info@ispi.org

Organizational Systems Research Association
Donna R. Everett, Interim Executive Director
Morehead State University
UPO 868
Morehead, KY 40351-1689
(606) 783-2718
(606) 783-5025 (fax)
d.everet@morehead-st.edu
http://www.osra.org

Society for Applied Learning Technology
50 Culpeper Street
Warrenton, VA 20186
(540) 347-0055
(540) 349-3169 (fax)
www.salt.org
info@lti.org

Society for Human Resource Management
1800 Duke Street
Alexandria, VA 22314
(703) 548-3440
(703) 535-6490)fax)
www.shrm.org
shrm@shrm.org

SELECTED PUBLICATIONS

Please note that those publications marked with an "*" are, at the time of this writing, free to those who meet the occupational criteria of the journal or magazine.

The American Journal of Distance Education
Penn State University
College of Education
403 S. Allen St., Suite 206
University Park, PA 16801-5202
(814) 863-3764
(814) 865-5878 (fax)
www.ed.psu.edu/acsde

Career Development Quarterly
National Career Development Association
5999 Stevenson Ave.
Alexandria, VA 22304
(703) 823-9800

Creative Training Techniques
Lakewood Publications, Inc.
50 South Ninth Street
Lakewood Building
Minneapolis, MN 55402
(616) 333-0471

Education Technology
700 Palisade Avenue
Englewood Cliffs, NJ 07632
(201) 871-4007

Educational Technology Research and Development
Association for Educational Communications and Technology
1800 North Stonelake Drive
Suite 2
Bloomington, IN 47404
(812) 335-7675
(812) 335-7678 (fax)
www.aect.org
aect@aect.org

e-learning
Publishing Office
201 Sandepoint Avenue
Suite 600
Santa Ana, CA 92707
(714) 513-8400
(714) 513-8632 (fax)
www.elearningmag.com

Fast Company
P.O. Box 52760
Boulder, CO 80328-2760
(800) 688-1545
www.fastcompany.com

Human Resource Development Quarterly
Jossey-Bass, Inc.
350 Sansome Street
San Francisco, CA 94104
(415) 433-1767

Human Resource Management
John Wiley & Sons for the
School of Business Administration
The University of Michigan
Publisher, Professional, Reference, and Trade Group
John Wiley and Sons
605 Third Avenue
New York, NY 10158
(212) 850-8832

INFO-LINE
American Society for Training and Development
P.O. Box 1443
Alexandria, VA 22313
(703) 683-8100

Information Technology, Learning and Performance Journal
Organizational Systems Research Association
Donna R. Everett, Interim Executive Director
Morehead State University
UPO 868
Morehead, KY 40351-1689
(606) 783-2718
d.everet@morehead-st.edu
http://www.osra.org

**Inside Technology Training*
50 S. Ninth Street
Minneapolis, MN 55402
(612) 333-0471
(612) 333-6526 (fax)
www.ittrain.com

Journal of Computer-Based Instruction
Association for the Development of Computer-Based Instruction Systems
1601 W. Fifth Avenue, Suite 111
Columbus, OH 43212
(614) 487-1528

The Microcomputer Trainer
Systems Literacy Inc.
P.O. Box 2487
Secaucus, NJ 07096-2487
(201) 330-8923

**Presentations: Technology and Techniques for Better Communications*
Lakewood Publications, Inc.
50 South Ninth Street
Lakewood Building
Minneapolis, MN 55402
(616) 333-0471
(612) 333-6526
www.presentations.com
tsimon@presentations.com

**Technical Horizons in Education Journal*
17501 17th Street, Suite 230
Tustin, CA 92780
(714) 730-4011
www.thejournal.com
subscriptions@thejournal.com

Technical and Skills Training
American Society for Training and Development
P.O. Box 1443
Alexandria, VA 22313
(703) 683-8100

Technology and Learning
P.O. Box 5052
Vandalia, OH 45377
(800) 607-4410
www.techlearning.com

TechTrends for Leaders in Education and Training
Association for Educational Communications and Technology
1800 N. Stonelake Drive
Suite 2
Bloomington, IN 47404
(812) 335-7675
(812) 335-7678 (fax)
www.aect.org
aect@aect.org

Training and Development
American Society for Training and Development
P.O. Box 1443
Alexandria, VA 22313
(703) 683-8100

Training Director's Forum Newsletter
Lakewood Publications, Inc.
50 South Ninth Street
Lakewood Building
Minneapolis, MN 55402
(616) 333-0471

TRAINING Magazine
Lakewood Publications, Inc.
50 South Ninth Street
Lakewood Building
Minneapolis, MN 55402
(616) 333-0471

**Workplace Network News*
Office of Vocational and Adult Education
U.S. Department of Education
Room 4429, Switzer Building
400 Maryland Avenue, S.W.
Washington, D.C. 20202-7240
http://www.hronline.com/forums/training/training.html

ADDITIONAL LISTSERVS AND WEB SITES

TechLearnTrends
Sponsored by the Masie Center
List-Subscribe: mailto:subscribe-techlearn-trends@lister.masie.com

ON-LINE LEARNING NEWS
To receive On-Line Learning News, go to:
http://www.lakewoodconference.com,
click "Free On-Line Newsletter," and complete the form.

TRDEV-L
TRDEV-L operates using the extensive resources and support provided by Penn State's Center for Academic Computing and the Workforce Education & Development Program in Penn State's College of Education. For more information, including how to join, visit the archive site at http://www.hronline.com/forums/training/training.html

ITT CONNECTION
News and dialogue about e-learning products
For information go to
http://insidetech.emailch.com

TRDEV-L, HRNET
Noncommercial training and HR-related Internet resources collected since 1995. Many resources are suggested by veteran on-line HR professionals from TRDEV-L, HRNET http://www.tcm.com/trdev/t2.html and http://www.the-hrnet.com and other on-line communities.

INDEX

C

D

E

J

K

L

M

N

O

P

T

U

V

W

Z